AA
Essential

KT-528-365

explorer
GERMANY

AA Publishing

Essential

Written by John Ardagh, Lindsay Hunt, Michael Ivory, Michael Kallenbach, Stephen Locke, Tim Locke, Colin Speakman

Additional writing and research by Tony Evans, Audrey Horne
Series Adviser: Ingrid Morgan
Series Editor: Nia Williams
Copy Editor: Joan Miller
Designer: Alan Gooch, Design 23

Edited, designed, produced and distributed by AA Publishing, Fanum House, Basingstoke, Hampshire RG21 2EA.
© The Automobile Association 1993.
Maps © The Automobile Association 1993.

All rights reserved. No part of this publication may be reproduced, stored in a retrieval system, or transmitted in any form or by any means – electronic, mechanical, photocopying, recording or otherwise – unless the written permission of the publishers has been given beforehand.

A catalogue record for this book is available from the British Library.
ISBN 0 7495 0564 8

This book was produced using QuarkXPress™, Aldus Freehand™ and Microsoft Word™ on Apple Macintosh™ computers.

Colour origination by L C Repro & Sons Ltd, Aldermaston
Printed and bound in Italy by LEGO SpA, Vicenza

The contents of this publication are believed correct at the time of printing. Nevertheless, the publishers cannot accept responsibility for errors or omissions, or for changes in details given. Assessments of attractions, hotels, restaurants and so forth are based upon the authors' own experience and, therefore, descriptions given in this guide necessarily contain an element of subjective opinion which may not reflect the Publisher's opinion or dictate a reader's own experience on another occasion. The views expressed in this book are not necessarily those of the Publisher. Every effort has been made to ensure accuracy in this guide. However, things do change and we would welcome any information to help keep the book up to date.

Published by AA Publishing.

Elbfähre Coswig/Anhalt
Fährschein 5,00 DM
Nr. 1700

Fahrt. Auf Verlangen vorzeigen!

About this book

This book is divided into three principal sections.

The first part of the book discusses aspects of life today and in the past. Places to visit are then covered region by region, along with Focus on... and Close-up... features, which highlight areas and subjects in more detail. Drives and walks are also suggested in this section of the book. Finally, day-to-day practical information for the visitor is given in the Travel Facts chapter, along with a selected Directory of hotels and restaurants.

Bad Wimpfen, on the River Neckar north of Heilbronn, makes the most of its attractive architecture

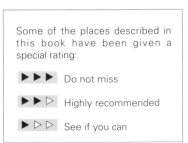

Some of the places described in this book have been given a special rating:

▶ ▶ ▶   Do not miss

▶ ▶ ▷   Highly recommended

▶ ▷ ▷   See if you can

General Contents

CONTENTS

6

CONTENTS

My Germany

**by Professor Werner Niefer, Chairman,
Mercedes-Benz Corporation**

It's an exciting, interesting time in Germany today, as two completely different states – separated for 40 years – grow together again. A great deal is being accomplished as everyone wants Germany to maintain its strong economic role, despite its new size. Germany is one of the most densely populated regions on earth, with more cars per 1,000 inhabitants than anywhere else in Europe – but the image of an over-developed countryside packed with concrete industrial plants and lined with traffic routes is false. Only seven per cent of the country's land area goes to communal and industrial development and only five per cent for transportation, although Germany is certainly the main axis of travel from the European north to the south and, since the opening of eastern Germany, from west to east as well. The rest is countryside and it could hardly be more varied – from flat, sparsely-populated North Friesland with its islands to the picture-book landscapes and high mountains of the Alps. Since the peaceful revolution in the former GDR and the reunification of the two states, our country has grown by about a third. We West Germans marvel at how time has stood still in eastern Germany. We are fascinated with cobblestone streets and endless tree-lined alleys – and have to overlook the bad, hopelessly overtaxed infrastructure, reminiscent of western Germany 40 years ago.

I must admit that for me, my Germany is the southwest – Baden-Württemberg, the heart of Europe where the car was born and where still today the most fascinating cars are manufactured. My Germany is also the rough landscape of the Schwäbischen Alb, the hills and deep valleys of the Black Forest, Lake Constance with its friendly shores and historical cities, the hills and mountains of the Allgäu and the steep peaks of the Allgäu Alps – all unique in their variety and beauty.

Naturally they attract tourists, but for those who live here the variety of landscapes, historic background and cultural richness, the ever-changing views are never dull. May these areas always remain the insiders' holiday gem – not to be missed on any account.

*Bavarian forest
scenery*

My Germany

by Praxedes Leitner

Since unification, Germany has almost doubled in size. Now, we former West Germans have the chance to discover the five *Länder* that comprised East Germany, as unknown to us as to any visitor from another country. For a West Berliner, once living in the 'Island in the Communist sea', going east now is as simple as crossing a bridge.

Well, I'm ready at the wheel of my car to discover the area around Berlin, and what do I find? Everyone else in the city has the same idea – it's bumper to bumper traffic. A little patience, though and soon I'm looking at lush meadows and fields dotted with brown and white cows, rolling hills scattered with wild flowers. There are endless romantic roads – though the East Germans were never known for building good roads, and some are still badly potholed. The houses look outdated, shabby and uninviting. The people seem to be introspective – they're not exactly used to tourists – but, soon, people begin to appear on the pavements, realising that tourists have strong Deutschmarks in their pockets and are willing to spend them. Local residents have erected colourful homemade stalls, offering fruit and vegetables – produce grown on their small plots of land. Feeling hungry, I find an *Imbiss* (snacks) stand taking advantage of the free market economy. The owner is somewhat reserved... should I feel guilty? Am I disturbing his peace and quiet?

It is odd being a tourist in your own country, enjoying the atmosphere and surroundings that haven't changed in 40 years – but soon I've totally overcome any hesitation I had about exploring this part of Germany. I make plans to spend a weekend at the Baltic Sea, rent a kayak in the Spreewald for a couple of days, tour the Elbsandsteingebirge near Dresden and Meissen, to travel through the Saale valley. And I must keep some time for a winter skiing trip to the Erzgebirge.

Why don't you try to find some of the hidden treasures of eastern Germany and then maybe we could swap stories?

GERMANY IS *A Paradox*

■ For centuries, Germany as a country did not exist. The peoples who make up the German nation lived where they live today but the country consisted largely of small, independent units. The differences between the peoples were – and still are – great. Asked to sum up Germany as a country, the simplest reaction of some foreigners is to claim that it just doesn't exist. .....■

First there's the language. Throughout the provinces, a vast variety of words is used to describe the most common objects. More than mere dialect, this reflects the local nature of German thinking. Many youngsters, leaving home to visit another part of Germany, have to abandon the familiar vernacular and use *Hochdeutsch*, the nation's *lingua franca*, to communicate. It can be like a trip abroad.

As with language, so with loyalties. Germans talk lovingly of their *Heimat*, or local area. This emotional attachment is felt by Germans of all ages. The notorious German lust for power just doesn't tally with this world where the small unit is the most important – the club, the choir, the *Stammtisch* (the regulars' table in a pub, labelled as such and respected).

How, then, to explain the determination of the eastern *Länder* to join with the west and form an even bigger national unit? The nation state is a compromise. Easterners have stressed, since unification, that

<< During the national debate in 1991 about whether the united Germany's seat of government should return to Berlin from Bonn, Bavarians often spoke out against this idea, saying that the entire country believed Munich to be the secret capital of Germany. >>

DENMARK

SWEDEN

OSTSEE

Flensburg

Kieler
Bucht

Rügen

Schleswig-

Febmarn

Stralsund

Neumünster

Mecklenburger
Bucht

Usedom

Kiel

Cuxhaven

Holstein

Lübeck

Rostock

Wismar

Schwerin

Neubrandenburg

Bremerhaven

Hamburg

Parchim

Müritz
See

Ludwigslust

Lüneburg

Lüneburger
Heide

Wittenberge

Neuruppin

Oder

Eberswalde

POLAND

Ost-

remen

rsachsen

Celle

Stendal

BERLIN

Frankfurt-
an-der-Oder

Wolfsburg

Brandenburg

Potsdam

Minden

Hannover

Braunschweig

Magdeburg

deutschland

Spree

Cottbus

Hildesheim

ielefeld

Salzgitter

Harz

Dessau

Neisse

Brocken
1142m

Saale

Mulde

Elbe

Paderborn

Göttingen

Lauchhammer

Kassel

Halle

Leipzig

ler

Werra

Fulda

Weimar

Jena

Dresden

Görlitz

Marburg

Eisenach

Erfurt

Gera

Chemnitz

Hessen

Fulda

Rbön

Thüringer Wald

Saale

Plauen

Zwickau

Erzgebirge

ankfurt
Main

Coburg

Hof

Offenbach

Schweinfurt

Main

Bayreuth

CZECH REPUBLIC

armstadt

Würzburg

Bamberg

Odenwald

Fürth

eidelberg

Nürnberg

Böbmerwald

1457m

Neckar

orzheim

Bayern

Regensburg

Heilbronn

Naab

Stuttgart

Ingolstadt

Donau

Baden

Donau

Isar

Passau

Tübingen

Landshut

Schwäbische Alb

Ulm

Augsburg

Freising

Inn

Württemberg

Lech

Amper

München

Ravensburg

Rosenheim

Chiemsee

AUSTRIA

Konstanz

Kempten

Garmisch-
Partenkirchen

2713m

odensee

Zugspitze
2962m

LIECHTENSTEIN

GERMANY

ITALY

0   50   100   150 km

0   50   100 miles

11

The tourist's Germany: an Augsburg café

they feel more attached to their surroundings than to some bureaucracy in Bonn or Berlin. The general attitude is that there has to be a bureaucracy – vital in a truly world-class city – but let it get on with its business and leave individual parts of the alliance that is Germany in peace. That is the measure of the new Germany, which has grown from an understanding of the errors of the old Germany. The emphasis on home, hearth and locality is natural in a nation for whom dogmatic imperialism is a bitter memory.

■ **Sausage, sauerkraut, beer, coffee and enormous cakes come to mind as typical German fare. And yes... sausages come in hundreds of varieties, while cabbage *is* consumed quite frequently, along with large quantities of potatoes. These stereotypical images are, as you might expect, only a small part of the picture. The reality is much more varied and adventurous. .....■**

There are some staple menu items: *Kaffee und Kuchen* – coffee and cake – is a favourite afternoon snack, with rich cakes, usually topped with mounds of whipped cream. Beer is found in a variety of forms, from Pilsner to Berlin's *Weisse*, a beer with a sweet syrup added to it. Local wine can be a welcome addition to a hearty German meal.

Quality and variety Visitors are often surprised at how well prepared German food is – and at the variety. A visit to the food halls in Berlin's giant KaDeWe department store or the elegant Alois Dallmayr store in Munich will bear this out.

<< In KaDeWe's 6th-floor food hall, with its special high-speed lift that stops nowhere else, there are over a thousand varieties of German sausage – overwhelming to the uninitiated sausage buyer! >>

German cooking is reputedly heavy, but the country's restaurant scene has recently been invaded by *neue deutsche Küche – nouvelle cuisine* German style – featuring creative and tasty dishes using traditional German ingredients.

Eating through the day For most Germans, breakfast may include a boiled egg, muesli and yoghurt, but more probably bread with cheese, jam and/or cold meats. Lunch, the main meal of the day, could include a juicy *Schnitzel* (cutlet) – usually pork – roast potatoes and a salad. Dinner

is often a cold and lighter meal of bread, a larger variety of meats and cheeses than at breakfast and, in colder weather, perhaps a soup or small stew. A popular stew is a combination of lentils and sausage. German desserts are almost always fruit or cream-based dishes. The amount of bread consumed by most Germans will astound visitors, and the variety and amount of textured, heavy and dark brown breads in the bakery is amazing. Try them all and decide which pleases you most.

13

Bread is an important ingredient in German cuisine

■ **As the homeland of Bach, Beethoven, Brahms, Wagner and Stockhausen, Germany's reputation for nurturing musicians and composers comes from a tradition that is centuries old and still survives today. Visitors will find a wealth of musical events, ranging from the historic and classical to modern, up-to-the-minute rock. .....■**

Among the joys of a trip to Germany is an evening at the Berlin Philharmonic, the Hamburg Opera or Munich's National Theatre, the home of the Bavarian State Opera, which offer some of the best orchestral sounds and operatic productions to be heard and seen anywhere in the world.

<< The Berlin Philharmonic – the best orchestra in the country and one of the best in the world – had Herbert von Karajan as its chief conductor until his death in 1989. >>

A brief history The German love of music and traditional folksongs can be traced back to pre-Christian tribal times. By the end of the 15th century, with the widespread use of the newly-developed organ in churches, national interest and support for classical music blossomed. In the 16th and 17th centuries, with the Reformation and the flowering of the Lutheran chorale, musical excellence was associated with churches. At this time vocalists, choristers, organists, instrumentalists and their directors worked as professionally paid musicians.

By the 18th century, court patronage was an important source of employment for musicians. German baroque music began to flower in geniuses such as Telemann, Bach and Handel. At the same time, musical theatre was developing in Vienna, and the German *Singspiel* became the rage. At the peak of the *Singspiel*'s popularity, Mozart wrote

Above: Ludwig Van Beethoven
Top: the Munich Oktoberfest

his last opera, *The Magic Flute*, and German opera came of age. Beethoven produced his major romantic symphonies and his only opera, *Fidelio*, soon after this time. Romanticism was in the air in Germany in the 19th century. After Beethoven came Schumann and Mendelssohn, then Brahms, Liszt, and Wagner, who transformed German national folk tales into powerful romantic operas.

German music suffered a setback in the mid-20th century, under Nazism, when all Jewish music was banned. However, since the war the avant-garde – headed by Karlheinz Stockhausen – has pioneered new musical forms.

The music scene today The numerous choirs founded earlier in Germany are still the springboard for much of the country's musical talent.

14

Thanks to the nation's generous tax system, which includes a levy for churches, choirs are found in many small communities. At city, state and national level, huge subsidies for performing arts and symphony orchestras help keep standards extremely high, and the cost of tickets for performances exceptionally low. Thus classical music is enjoyed by a greater segment of society in Germany than almost anywhere else, though this has the drawback that tickets are much more difficult to come by. Visitors are always advised to plan ahead and reserve seats well in advance. However, as in most major cities, the concierge in the bigger hotels invariably has his own excellent contacts and will generally be able to meet your last-minute wishes – encouraged, of course, by a generous tip.

During the 1950s, jazz – totally suppressed by the Third Reich – was effectively a copy of the American scene. By the 1960s foreign jazz musicians had lost their appeal to German youth, and the embryonic rock groups flourishing in Britain, most notably the Beatles, were invited to play in new clubs in Hamburg, Hannover and West Berlin. Their popularity quickly spawned imitators such as the Rattles, who enjoyed great domestic success. Their lack of confidence and rock tradition, however, meant that any songs destined for foreign markets were sung in English. Particularly popular was the heavier, more introspective end of the rock spectrum and artists such as Amon Duul and Tangerine Dream soon released albums – rarely singles – with huge sales, the latter conquering the international market. This 'progressive' music gave rise to the technically sophisticated but rather cold Kraftwerk, a band with a more definable German identity. The varied jazz scene now includes a host of imaginative German musicians, many recording on the adventurous ECM label, a company that promotes contemporary music.

Music in all forms flourishes in Germany. Below: jazz in Hamburg; top: the Berlin Philharmonic Orchestra

■ **Health in Germany is a national obsession. Foreigners living in the country remark at how often they are told by Germans that certain foods, certain activities and many prescribed drugs are 'not good for you'. But the German view of health is not usually negative. Good health is seen as an attainable goal, and Germans tend to take a more positive, active approach to staying healthy. ....■**

16

Even a dentist will try to talk you out of having an injection during a filling because of its poisonous content. Germans, it seems, would rather endure the pain!

With doctors and chemists prescribing homeopathic drugs, and people cycling to work on specially designated pathways during the week or enjoying long hikes in the woods and forests during weekends, it is no wonder that the life expectancy in Germany is one of the highest in Europe.

The spa The best place to study this pursuit of good health is at the *Kurort* or spa town. Spas are dotted all over Germany, from seaside towns to the Bavarian Alps. They all usually have a giant bath house where anyone can take the healing waters.

In most other countries in Europe, spa towns have become relics of the 19th century, but German spas are

Baden-Baden (below and top): a popular spa in the southwest

<< Until recently German medical students were required, as part of their qualifying studies, to take a course in *Balneologie*, the science of taking the waters. >>

kept alive by the nation's long-standing tradition of allowing its citizens six-week vacations, in addition to normal leave entitlement, and employees are expected to rest and recuperate. A generous medical insurance scheme allows doctors to prescribe fully paid spa treatments for a variety of ailments, so people are often able to extend their stays with sick leave. Besides the baths, today's modern spa resorts offer other amenities such as golf, tennis, horse-racing, casinos, boating and skiing – something for every taste. A typical spa treatment might include a mud bath or hydrotherapy, saunas and steam treatments, all followed by a wrap in warm blankets and a compulsory rest. A word of warning: baths in Germany are often not segregated by sex, so visitors who are uncomfortable with nudity should inquire beforehand to find out whether or not the facilities are suitable for them.

A trip to some of the large swimming and bathing centres in spa resorts can be a treat for family members of all ages. The amenities often include wave pools, pools with currents, whirlpools and lap pools. These giant complexes provide enormous fun in all types of weather, since they often have adjoining outdoor bathing sections.

The sporting life Although most visitors will be able to participate in the sports of their choice when visiting Germany, the three national favourites seem currently to be football, skiing and tennis. While many young German children are often allowed to take inexpensive skiing holidays through schools, church groups and other youth organisations, the nation's craze for tennis seems to stem from the recent surge in young and world-famous champions such as Steffi Graf, Boris Becker and Michael Stich.

Lothar Matthaeus in action during the 1990 World Cup

Soccer, as in nearly all European countries, is the national sport and locally sponsored teams are found all over the country. Its popularity surged even more in 1990, the dramatic year in which Germany saw unification – and won the World Cup.

<< The German airline Lufthansa tried to ban smoking on domestic flights, but this caused such an angry response from the tobacco industry that the airline quickly caved in and changed its mind. Given that the longest domestic flight lasts less than two hours, this was rather faint-hearted of Lufthansa. >>

The smoking paradox While so many Germans seem to be interested in good health and fitness, one irony is the number of people who are constantly lighting up. The anti-smoking lobby has hardly taken off in Germany and a campaign to ban smoking in public places has had little effect.

Restaurants are rarely divided into smoking and non-smoking sections in Germany, while cinemas depend heavily on cigarette advertising. Even more peculiar are German sports and fitness clubs, where it is not uncommon to see people participating in heavy aerobic activities, only to light up minutes afterwards to help them relax!

■ **The Federal Republic of Germany came into being in 1949 and has proved remarkably durable, being responsible for bringing the West German people from a state of near ruin to their present prosperous condition. It has seen the collapse of the Communist system in the former GDR, absorbed that state, and is now struggling to bring equal prosperity and democracy to the whole of Germany. ...■**

18

The German political structure is based around its constitution – the *Grundgesetz* (basic law), which includes human rights guarantees. It is often used as an excuse for inactivity by German politicians although it has been amended more than 30 times. During the Gulf War of 1991 politicians in Bonn argued that they could not commit troops outside Nato territory without changing the *Grundgesetz*.

The Bundestag The German parliament has two chambers. The Bundestag, the lower chamber, carries more weight in decision-making. It is directly elected to a four-year term, though the government can call an election earlier after referring to the Federal constitutional court (see below). At the time of writing, the parties represented are: the Christian Democratic Union, the conservative party led by Chancellor Helmut Kohl; the Christian Social Union; the Free

Democratic Party, the liberal party of foreign minister Klaus Kinkel; the Social Democratic Party, former rulers under the past leadership of ex-Chancellors Willy Brandt and Helmut Schmidt; the Party of Democratic Socialism, the revamped Communists of eastern Germany; and the Bündnis Alliance 90, formed from pro-democracy civic groups in the former GDR and linked with the Green Party. The current government is a coalition of the Christian and Free Democrats.

The Bundesrat The upper house represents all 16 German *Länder* (states). Delegates are chosen by the *Länder* and always include state prime ministers. Under the *Grundgesetz*, the Bundesrat approves all laws that affect the states. Leadership of the Bundesrat is currently in the hands of the Social Democrats.

Top jobs The German chancellor, the leading figure in German politics, is not directly elected but holds the office as leader of the majority party in the Bundestag. The post of Federal President is mostly ceremonial; the President is elected for a five-year term of office.

The constitutional court Germany's judicial system is led by the *Bundesverfassungsgericht* (constitutional court), which has two chambers, one dealing with individual liberties, the other with political issues. Each court contains eight judges, elected by the Bundestag and Bundesrat.

The Bundestag in Bonn

<< Guest workers – the *Gastarbeiter* – mainly from Turkey and Yugoslavia, were encouraged to come to Germany during the years of economic revival to do menial jobs. Now, with rising unemployment, financial incentives have been introduced by the government to encourage them to leave. **>>**

Extremists out In Germany, the system of proportional representation allows every voter two votes, one for a constituency candidate and another for a political party. Any political party is excluded from the Bundestag if it polls less than five per cent of a party list vote – effectively keeping out independent candidates and extremist groups.

The economic miracle The rapid development of the economy after near total collapse at the end of World War II – the *Wirtschaftswunder* – transformed West Germany and gave its citizens the highest standard of living in the EC. This was despite strong bureaucratic controls which seemed to discourage private enterprise, minimal emphasis on customer service, relatively little use of high-tech equipment (although much of Europe's advanced technology is produced in Germany) and a telephone system which claims to be the best in the world, but simply does not live up to the boast. Some experts say economic success was

due to aid programmes such as the American Marshall Plan. Sociologists suggest that most Germans just wanted to forget the past and rebuild their country. They made sacrifices and today's generation is reaping the benefits.

Slow-down With the absorption of 17 million people from the former GDR and the world recession in the early 1990s, the miracle began to fade. As the economy stagnated, unemployment climbed – particularly in eastern Germany as it moved from a 'command' economy to a market economy.

Where the decisions are made: the Bundestag, or lower chamber

The Bundesbank Central to the German economy, the bank controls interest rates – and so inflation. The bank, an independent body, often opposes the economic policies of the Federal government.

■ **The West Germans have for many years been in the forefront of the environmental or 'Green' movement. 'Green' politics have been much more central to events in Germany than, for example, in the UK where the issues have been largely peripheral. The term 'environmentally friendly' was invented here in the mouthful *umweltfreundlich*. An aversion to atomic power provided the motive force for 10 years of student and youth activism. Habits which have become second nature to environment-conscious people – the trip to the bottle-bank, the separation of glass, paper and other waste – began here....■**

Legacy of pollution In the new Germany the political environment holds sway over the natural environment. In the GDR, heavy industry was seen as the economic saviour: its legacy of smoke, fumes and rivers streaked with chemicals suggests the opposite.After unification, the stream from east to west of two-stroke Trabant cars, with their billowing exhaust fumes, added insult to injury.

Then there is Bitterfeld, described by ecologists as a chemical time-bomb. For years, the 60,000 inhabitants lived in the shadow of two huge plants making herbicides, pesticides and paints. Since unification they have closed, but local rivers are ecologically dead, the victims of years of industrial sewage. A coal-burning power plant in Cottbus reportedly emits more sulphur dioxide than all the power plants in Norway and Denmark combined.

Tackling the problem Authorities in the new Germany are having to tackle this sort of ecological mess. Environmental union is even harder to manage than political union. The pre-unification Bonn administration maintained a careful environment programme, largely due to the growing influence of the Green Party. No such receptiveness to public opinion prevailed in the GDR. Now the Bonn politicians are promising to improve conditions all over Germany, knowing that the clean-up in eastern Germany will be costly and drawn out.

Public concern Some view the German interest in environmental issues with cynicism. The fact that the German student lobby, vocal on a whole range of issues since 1968, seems to shout loudest, makes suspicious observers doubt the extent of the concern. But a look at the age-range of those involved in demonstrations shows that environmental issues affect Germans on many levels and in many ways.

<< West Germans are particularly avid ecologists: they recycle 42 per cent of their waste paper and reprocess 50 per cent of their glass bottles and about 70 per cent of their tyres. >>

The question of acid rain and its effects on the German forests bears this out. For many Germans, their woodland is not just a set of surroundings, or even an economic resource. The forests are a refuge for recuperation; they are a place of leisure and – with more than 30 per cent of the country still occupied by woodland – an almost mythical retreat to the roots of the nation. This explains the horror that gripped communities, notably in the south, around the Schwarzwald (Black Forest), when it became clear that *der Wald stirbt* – 'the forest is dying'. Rain had once been an essential vital force for the wood, enabling it to survive, but the mixture of polluting agents inflicted by factories, power plants and cars turned the rain into an acid cocktail. Add to this the hurricane-style winds of early 1990, and it is easy to see why Germans are so concerned their woods should be protected. But there is a paradox here.

The car is king The logical solution would be for the Germans to limit use of their cars, but this would go against another tenet in modern German life which demands that citizens should drive as fast, as powerfully and, in the end, as damagingly as they like. '*Freie Fahrt für freie Bürger*' ('a free path for free citizens') is the cry of the car industry; but it is part of the German way of thinking too... and will take more than lead-free petrol to shift.

Hope for the future Western conservationists have rediscovered a forgotten landscape in the Lower Oder Valley National Park, near the Polish border. The River Oder flows through the middle, with Poland on one bank and Germany on the other. There are ospreys, sea-eagles and beavers. Several projects are being set up to conserve the diverse flora and fauna that have been discovered.

■ **The German film industry does not operate on the Hollywood scale and has not achieved the same worldwide success. Nevertheless, cinema is a respected art form, whose rule in modern culture is taken seriously. The reputation of German 'art house' films is undisputed and they are internationally acclaimed......■**

Directors rule It is the directors, rather than the actors, who get the accolades. Some, such as Rainer Werner Fassbinder, have deliberately cultivated their own protégés (though Hanna Schygulla has become a star in her own right). Fassbinder's determination to investigate controversial sexual and social themes – coupled with his own controversial life and death – did much to develop his high profile as a public figure. Wim Wenders has attracted interest for his serious, poetic, emotional visions of apparently well-known landscapes. An acclaimed example of this is *Der Himmel über Berlin* (*Wings of Desire*, 1987), in which modern Berlin is viewed through the eyes of two invisible angels, listening to the thoughts of anxious city-dwellers. In a sense, this sums up the '*Neues Deutsches Kino*' (New German Cinema), which promotes the validity of emotions in the face of modern reason.

International success These directors have earned a lasting reputation. Volker Schlöndorff, with his adaptations of literary works such as Günter Grass's *Die Blechtrommel (Tin Drum)*, has extended this type of

<< In 1962 the Oberhausen Manifesto announced the birth of the 'new German feature film'. Among its signatories was Edgar Reitz who in 1984 gained international renown for the TV series *Heimat*. >>

cinema on an international scale. It is often the quirky rather than the characteristic which gets the most prominence abroad. Werner Herzog is known for his remake of *Nosferatu*, and his exotic South American-based works *Aguirre, Wrath of God* and *Fitzcarraldo*. His vision of desperate individuals, underdogs at the mercy of Nature and Fate, is personal and poetic, and Herzog could hardly be regarded as part of a German 'trend'. Margarethe von Trotta (Schlöndorff's wife) is one director who has broached contemporary themes (the role of women, the importance of the family) in films such as *The German Sisters* (1981).

A scene from Himmel über Berlin *(Wings of Desire, 1987)*

■ **Some aspects of German culture, such as classical music, are known internationally; others are largely confined within the country's borders. Open a German television magazine, read about the trials and tribulations of the country's media stars, and marvel – you'll have heard of hardly any of them.....■**

Our unfamiliarity with Thomas Gottschalk and 'Blocky' Fuchsenberger (game-show idols in their own land) goes with the comparatively unusual choice of Germany as a holiday destination.

The famous in sport (Boris Becker, top) and in politics (Helmuts Schmidt, above left, and Kohl)

Political giants The figures who make an impression abroad do so for weightier reasons. Willy Brandt, former Chancellor, Mayor of Berlin and Nobel Peace Prize winner, stood out, until his recent death in October 1992, as a great European statesman, committed as much to a fair policy towards the Developing World as to untangling domestic problems. His successor as Chancellor, Helmut Schmidt, has to a lesser extent, taken on a similar role (as well as being a highly talented concert pianist).
Helmut Kohl, arguably less charismatic than Brandt, has been around at the right time, pressed home his advantage and grasped the mood of the nation. He seems clumsy (German magazines have seemed obsessed with his battle to control his wildly fluctuating weight, invoking improbable comparisons

with Elizabeth Taylor), but has held on. Never a model of elegance, he has acquired an air of solidity – and aroused adulation when he visited his new *Länder* in the old German Democratic Republic. For those citizens, in that country and at that time, he *was* unification.

Royalty-watching The weekly news magazines – *Bunte, Stern, Quick* – dote on anyone royal and regularly tell readers far more about the personal lives of the rich and regal than any palace-conscious editor could in Britain. As substitutes for the missing German royalty, tennis stars Boris Becker and Steffi Graf have played an important role. It's not so much the game – it's having home-grown stars of indisputably world class. Becker's personal fortunes are paraded for every German to enjoy. In truly royal terms, it's perhaps more Grimaldi (Monaco) than Windsor (Britain), but until Kaisers and princes return to Germany (and they won't), this is how Boris and Steffi will serve their nation.

23

■ **The first identifiable permanent settlers in the area that is now Germany were Celtic tribes in the 8th century. BC; the Rhineland was a key area of production in their industrial society. But new forces were developing in Europe. The Roman Empire was expanding, and Germanic peoples were on the move from Scandinavia. .....**■

Germanic tribes moved to lands east of the Rhine and north of the Black Sea, and their invasions and periodic uprisings created instability within the Roman Empire. Roman attempts to push across the Rhine failed to establish permanent occupation. They ended in AD9; after reaching the Elbe the Romans were pushed back by German tribes under the leadership of Arminus (Herman), who destroyed three legions.

G E R M A N I A

Charlemagne's coronation as Holy Roman Emperor marked a new era

Rise of the Franks By the time of Constantine, when the Empire's capital shifted to Byzantium in the east, Roman rule was beginning to break down. After the introduction of Christianity by Emperor Constantine, the Roman Empire disintegrated and the area that is now Germany was overrun by the Franks. When Charlemagne was crowned Holy Roman Emperor in 800, their influence stretched across most of Europe. Civil war followed Charlemagne's death; the Treaty of Verdun in 843 split the Empire into a Latin western section and a Germanic eastern part (led by Ludwig the German). Ludwig's appointment marked the emergence of a German identity.

The Saxon ascendancy In the 10th century, the area came under the rule of the Saxons. Otto the Great was faced with invading Magyars from the east, and a growing threat from duchies and principalities inside the eastern empire. After defeating the Magyars in 955, Otto strengthened his ties to the Papacy, which led to church dominance over much of the country. In 962, he was crowned Holy Roman Emperor.

The power of the princes The influence of powerful dynastic German families increased steadily. By the 13th century, the Holy Roman Emperor had little power against feudal princes. Many began to push eastwards, conquering Poland and setting up German communities in areas now in Russia and Romania. In 1356, the law regulating the election of an emperor (the Golden Bull) was introduced, based on the votes of four noble and three ecclesiastical electors, excluding the Papacy. In the 15th century, the Habsburgs were elected Holy Roman Emperors, and retained their title until it was abolished some 400 years later.

Germany in 1608, from **Geographiae Universae tum veteris, tum narae absolutissimum opus** *by Giovanni Magini (Köln)*

25

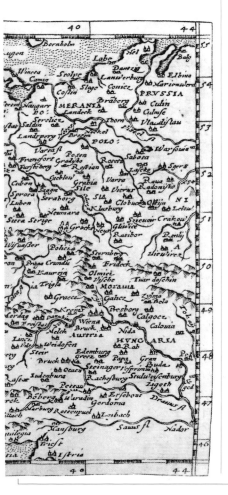

■ **In the 16th century Germany was suffering under a greedy and powerful aristocracy who appropriated land and held the oppressed peasantry in serfdom. This, alongside an equally grasping and cynical Church trading in 'indulgences', led to the religious upheaval of the Reformation in the 16th century. ......■**

Discontent with the church authorities increased. Martin Luther led accusations over corruption, nailing his '95 theses', an attack against papal abuses, to the door of Wittenberg church in 1517. Luther was excommunicated but politically powerful German princes were able to protect him from sentence of death.

Century of conflict After publication of Luther's translation of the Bible, the oppressed in Germany were ready to revolt. The Peasants' Rebellion of 1524–5 brought destruction of church properties, but was put down by princely armies. The period of the Reformation and Counter-Reformation created more than a century of strife between Catholics and Protestants and, by the early 17th century, Europe was embroiled in the Thirty Years' War. Many battles were fought on German lands, bringing extensive destruction. Negotiations to end the war began in 1643, culminating in the Peace of Westphalia in 1648. The treaty ended the conflict, reduced the status of Holy Roman Emperor and began the decline of the House of Hapsburg, while giving power to more than 300 principalities and other territories.

<< In the 16th century, German mercenaries led the way in high fashion. The style of 'slashing' clothes – cutting slits in the material and pulling the lining through for display – started with battlefield booty used to patch clothes and found its way to the French and English courts. >>

The rise of Brandenburg-Prussia By the end of the 17th century, a power in the area of Brandenburg-Prussia emerged. The Hohenzollern family, who held the Electorate of Brandenburg, defied the laws of the Holy Roman Empire and assumed the title of Kings of Prussia. Frederick William, the Great Elector, was the first; the dynasty consolidated itself in the early 18th century. Under Frederick the Great, the third Hohenzollern king, Prussia rose to be one of the dominant European powers by the middle of the century. Despite liberal laws at home, Frederick asserted Prussia's military authority and, after going to battle with Austria over Silesia, engaged in the Seven Years' War (1756–63). Frederick annexed much of Poland and established Prussia as a counter power to Austria. Prussia's power was tested during the Napoleonic Wars of the early 19th century but, in the Battle of Waterloo in 1815, Napoleon was defeated by the armies of Britain, Hanover and Prussia. The Congress of Vienna, which met that same year and created the Deutscher Bund (German Confederation), established Prussian dominance among some 40 states in the German world, alongside Austria.

German unification Now Germany began to experience the pains of the industrial revolution. Economic reforms and customs unions were introduced to ease the strains caused by the many protective borders in the German region. Also, a wage-earning class as well as a bourgeoisie emerged. Uprisings in 1848 demonstrated how serious the demands for the dissolution of an

older political order in Germany were becoming. In 1862, Prussia's Wilhelm I chose Otto von Bismarck as his Chancellor. Within a decade Bismarck united Germany under Prussian leadership. After a war with Denmark over Schleswig-Holstein in 1864, and the Bohemian War with Austria in 1866, all the German states north of the River Main were united.

To gain the support of German southern states (Bavaria, Baden and Württemberg), Bismarck provoked a war with France; after the Franco-Prussian War ended in 1871, Germany was united as the Second Reich with King Wilhelm of Prussia as Kaiser.

Below: the Rüdesheim Niederwald Monument celebrates German unification in 1871

Above: the Peasants' Rebellion, 1524–5. Below: Bismarck in 1915

World War I Bismarck then embarked on a number of liberal domestic reforms as well as creating alliances with Austria and Russia. After Wilhelm II – grandson of the British Queen Victoria – succeeded to the imperial throne, these alliances were tested. British and French suspicions were aroused by Germany's huge expansion of its navy. The two powers, allied with Russia, stood against the alliance of Germany and Austria in 1914, when World War I broke out over Habsburg claims in the Balkans. After three agonising years, Germany's defeat was hastened by the entry of the United States into the war.

■ **Germany's humiliating defeat in World War I was followed in 1919 by the founding of the Weimar Republic, based on a democratic constitution. That same year, Germany's new leaders were forced to sign the Treaty of Versailles, marking a radical shift in the European balance of power. It called for enormous war reparations as well as the confiscation of and withdrawal from territories that Germany had controlled, in some cases, for centuries. ....■**

Unemployment and inflation hit Europe after World War I and in almost every country, political movements on the extreme left and right began to gather strength and make themselves heard.

The Treaty of Versailles, finally signed and set out in 'The Golden Book', May 1919

The rise of the Nazis During the 1920s and early 1930s, Germany suffered galloping inflation. Due to the lack of central political strength in Germany, elections in 1930 allowed extremist parties to gain prominence, most noticeably the Nazi Party led by Adolf Hitler. This attracted the unemployed and destitute, and industrialists and other wealthy groups who saw the party's authoritarian policies as a return to the order that the country had known under the last Kaiser.

Adolf Hitler gained more power and was made Chancellor by the Republic's President, Paul von Hindenburg, in January 1933. On 27 February 1933, the Reichstag, the nation's parliament building, was set on fire, an incident orchestrated by the Nazis. Hindenburg declared a state of emergency.

The road to war The Nazi Party became the only legal party in the country and Hitler became President as well as Chancellor. Democracy was suppressed under Dr Joseph Goebbels' propaganda ministry. Many horrors occurred during Hitler's Third Reich. Jews were persecuted and murdered. The government and education systems were perverted. Many of the nation's most talented people – many of Jewish origin – emigrated and, gradually, the terms of the Treaty of Versailles were nullified. Hitler's plan for Europe became well understood, but the West was not ready to stand up to him until 1 September 1939, when Germany invaded Poland. Two days later, Britain and France declared war.

World War II and its aftermath The war and the vicious activities of Nazis against Jews, Slavs and others are well documented.
At first the war went well for the Nazis but their invasion of Russia in 1941 proved a turning-point. Defeats in North Africa and at Stalingrad followed in 1942 and 1943. A German resistance movement developed among the top army

<< The Nazi extermination programme involved the murder of an estimated 6 million Jews. Other groups which fell victim to the 'Final Solution' were Slavs, gypsies, homosexuals and mentally ill and handicapped people. >>

leadership and attempts were made on Hitler's life. Germany was totally defeated, and in 1945 Hitler committed suicide.

The legacy of the Third Reich and World War II will be a burden to Germany for decades to come. Six million Jews murdered in concentration camps have not been easily forgotten by the world. Those leaders held responsible were put on trial for war crimes and crimes against humanity; the civil service was purged of all Nazi sympathisers. The victorious Allies divided Germany into four occupied zones under Soviet, US, British and French control. Two separate political systems emerged; in May 1949 the territories occupied by the British, American and French were combined to form the Federal Republic of Germany. Four months later, the Russians created the German Democratic Republic. The two Germanies rivalled each other for more than 40 years, each trying to rebuild a nation out of the ruins and rubble of World War II. They came to represent the Cold War division of Europe, formalised by the erection of the Berlin Wall in 1961.

The years of division Throughout the Cold War period, both Germanies built strong economies. West Germany's economy became Europe's strongest, while East Germany's industriousness made it the most prosperous and productive country in Comecon, the Eastern Bloc's economic alliance.

By the 1970s, many Germans accepted the division, though they still hoped that Germany would be reunited. Unofficial recognition of the division occurred in the *Ostpolitik* policies of Willy Brandt, when he became Chancellor in 1969. Nevertheless, West German political parties, while attempting to work with the leaders of the GDR on some economic and social programmes, still insisted that unification was the ultimate aim. By the mid-1980s, however, many West Germans dismissed the idea.

Adolf Hitler at the Nazis' Parteitag, *a show of party strength in Nürnberg, 1933*

■ **On 9 November 1989 the momentous decision to open up the Berlin Wall was made. East Germans had spent days and nights peacefully demonstrating for political rights. The communist East German regime no longer had the steadfast military support of its closest ally the former Soviet Union. The government of the GDR finally gave way and opened up points on the Wall, allowing its citizens to step over into West Germany. ....■**

Some had never seen the west in their lifetime, but most had conjured up a picture in their minds from television programmes which had been beamed across the barbed wire.

One Germany Within months, a new democratically-elected Federal government had been set up with the task of uniting East and West Germany. At first, people thought the process would take several years, but the government moved quickly to merge the two economies, providing East Germans with Deutschmarks on 1 July 1990. The East German economy began to deteriorate due to the inability of the nation's industrial base to compete with western production standards. The Federal Republic's ruling coalition was compelled to move quickly and absorb the territory of the former East Germany into the Republic much faster than had been expected. On 3 October 1990, after more than four decades of division following Germany's defeat in World War II, a dream came true for many Germans – the country was reunited.

After euphoria The political leaders in east and west called on the nation to work together and to avoid treating the former East Germans as second class citizens. Sadly, the Wall still exists in many people's minds. Those from the east continue to complain that their country was simply annexed by the west, and accuse the West Germans of arrogance, while Germans in the west are angry that their taxes have been increased to pay for German unification (despite repeated assurances by Chancellor Helmut Kohl that this would not happen). Concern about high levels of unemployment in the eastern area has spurred violence against foreign refugees and immigrants to Germany. In 1990 some particularly fierce violence occurred in areas around Dresden. This has been countered by a number of national solidarity movements, but many social scientists claim that until the economy in eastern Germany has stabilised and eastern Germans fully appreciate the ways of democratic life, social unrest in eastern Germany will continue.

At the same time, neo-Nazis from the west canvassed for new members and the number of attacks against foreigners and Jewish memorials continued unabated. Even Germany's politicians in Bonn, aware of the country's Nazi past, failed to act quickly enough to stem the racist and fascist elements which began to emerge following reunification.

Return to Berlin With unification, the Federal government was faced with the important question: should the seat of government remain in Bonn, the former capital of western Germany, or return to Berlin, the historical seat of the German government? Parliament was besieged with concerns about the costs, questions about the necessity of such a move and fears that a return to Berlin could rekindle old

German militaristic attitudes about German leadership in Europe. Finally, it was agreed that, despite the enormous costs, government was obliged out of respect for German history to return to Berlin. In the meantime, the infrastructure development – roads, telephones, electricity, the clean-up of the environment and economic integration of the new areas – have become the main focus of the Federal government's policy. Special federal taxes have been introduced to pay for the very costly work.

The European goal Since the Federal Republic of Germany (West Germany) was founded in 1949, German national policy has passionately supported European integration. At first through common agricultural and trade policies, and now through economic and political integration, German politicians have used the banner of the European Community as a standard for the next generation. This policy is often at odds with the other European countries, particularly Britain – and some opponents fear German dominance of the Community. Others argue that European unity is needed to prevent the rise of extremist movements; neo-Nazi riots in Rostock in 1992 fuelled this argument. In any event, the German government seems set to support a politically unified Europe.

Berlin's Brandenburg Gate. Top: packaged pieces of the Berlin Wall

■ A strong tradition of stories and poetry undoubtedly existed in the German language long before written literature. The one tantalising glimpse of this that was written down is the *Hildebrandslied* (The Lay of Hildebrand), a 9th-century fragment of an alliterative heroic poem. Otherwise, the earliest German manuscripts were of a religious nature, written and preserved as part of the Christian monastic tradition of learning. .....■

By the 12th century, literature had passed from the monasteries to the courts. German versions of French romances, such as the tale of Tristan and Isolde and the Arthurian stories, were written and, in about 1200, tales of the hero Siegfried took form in the anonymous *Nibelungenlied*. *Minnesang* (lyrical love songs) also flourished in the 12th century.

The literary renaissance Luther's translation of the Bible (1534) is often regarded as the first great modern German work of literature, but not until the 18th century did German writings – notably those of Johann von Goethe and Friedrich von Schiller – reach a level comparable to that of the Middle Ages. A meeting between Herder and Goethe led to the *Sturm und Drang* (Storm and Stress) movement. Weimar, where

Luther, father of modern literature

<< Philosopher and mathematician Gottfried von Leibniz (1646–1716) is remembered for the development of differential calculus, for which his notation is still used. His ideas of expressing 'all truth' in terms of simple statements using symbols was a foretaste of modern mathematical logic. >>

Goethe and Schiller spent much of their lives, became synonymous with their writing – Schiller's poetry and many dramas and Goethe's dramas (notably *Faust*), novels, poetry and philosophical works.

From romanticism to naturalism The German romantic movement started around 1790. It had a profound effect throughout Europe, and romantic ideas dominated

<< Georg Wilhelm Friedrich Hegel (1770–1831) put forward the theory that history, which he called the *Weltgeist* (World Spirit), was a developing process of 'consciousness of freedom', from the 'Oriental' through the 'Greek' to the 'Christian–German' period. He saw the process paralleled in three stages of awareness, from 'awareness of objects' through 'awareness of self' to 'awareness of reason'. >>

<< The philosopher Immanuel Kant (1724–1804) greatly influenced the 18th-century Weimar literary school with his emphasis on moral duty and aesthetics. >>

German literature up to the mid-19th century, with 'folk' poetry and tales (such as those of the Brothers Grimm) being an important element.

Transition The poet and political radical Heinrich Heine marks a transition from romanticism to realism. Contemporary life became the theme of writers at the end of the 19th century, as in the stories of Gottfried Keller and Theodor Storm, and the plays of Gerhart Hauptmann.

The 20th century At the turn of the century there was a reaction to naturalism in the Nietzsche-inspired poetry of Richard Dehmel and the aestheticism of Stefan George.

The greatest German poet of the 20th century was undoubtedly Czech-born Rainer Maria Rilke, whose intense poetic world was spun almost entirely out of his own psyche. Another Czech-born 20th-century giant was Franz Kafka, whose novels shed a grotesque and often absurd light on human experiences. The novelist Thomas Mann explored the contrast between solid bourgeois insensitivity and the fragile world of the artist.

In 1947 Gruppe 47 was formed, a group of politically left-wing writers, some of whom have gained international status, including Heinrich Böll (winner of the Nobel Prize for Literature in 1972) and Günter Grass, best known for *The Tin Drum*.

Martin Heidegger's (1889–1976) philosophy was a form of early existentialism. His ideas had great influence in Germany in the first half of this century.

Notable among writers of the former GDR are the innovative dramatist Bertolt Brecht, who died in East Berlin in 1956, and the novelist Christa Wolf.

<< The reputation of Friedrich Wilhelm Nietzsche (1844–1900) has suffered as a result of Nazi enthusiasm for his philosophy. His concept of the *Übermensch* (superman) is to blame for this, though he himself in no way connected it with the Aryan myth. For Nietzsche the basic motive of human action was the will to power (he despised Christianity for its morality based on humility). He saw the superman as one who succeeds in overcoming himself. >>

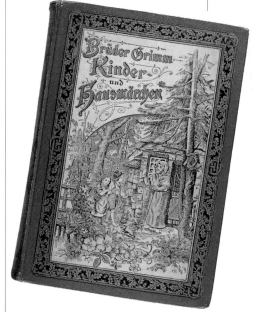

The cover of Hansel and Gretel *by the Brothers Grimm, 1892*

■ **The first architectural style to emerge in medieval Germany – the Romanesque – owed much to the traditions of Rome. The Rhineland has relics of Roman buildings – notably at Trier, where the great Porta Nigra, a gateway in the Roman city walls, still stands. The Roman basilica (meeting hall) inspired many Romanesque churches and cathedrals. ....■**

Romanesque and Gothic Fine cathedrals arose during the 11th to 15th centuries: Romanesque Speyer, Mainz and Worms, then the soaring Gothic splendours of Bamberg, Cologne, Ulm and Freiburg. Sculpture in stone and wood was used to complement architecture. Painting, too, often done anonymously, can be seen in altarpiece panels and manuscript illuminations.

34

Porta Nigra, Trier

<< The sculptor Tilman Riemenschneider – the 'Master of Würzburg' – bridged the Gothic and Renaissance in Germany. He was one of the first German sculptors not to use gilding or colour. >>

Renaissance In the late 15th to early 17th centuries, architecture took a back seat, as the influence of the Church waned and the wealthy middle classes asserted themselves. Many notable buildings show Italian

<< The rococo style - a kind of ultra-baroque - emerged in Germany in the mid-18th century. A French invention, it is characterised by dainty and irregular *'Louis Quinze'* motifs. Sanssouci Palace at Potsdam and Cuvillié's Amalienburg in Munich are examples. >>

influence. Some of the great names of German art belong to this time, including the Renaissance painter, draughtsman and engraver Albrecht Dürer, and the mystical painter Matthias Grünewald. In this period Lucas Cranach the Elder painted the portraits of the leaders of the Reformation, and the two Holbeins, Elder and Younger, were prominent.

Baroque and neo-classicism The 17th and 18th centuries arguably produced very few distinguished artists, but saw a brilliant age of baroque architecture by Lukas von Hildebrandt, Balthasar Neumann, Andreas Schlüter and others. During the Age of Enlightenment, Frederick the Great employed Georg Wenzeslaus von Knobelsdorff to help design official buildings for Berlin, and the Prussian capital continued its prominence as an architectural centre into the 19th century, as the neo-classicism of Karl Friedrich Schinkel made its mark.

Romanticism As in music and literature, the trend towards romanticism is seen in art and architecture in the 19th century. Otto Runge and Caspar David Friedrich,

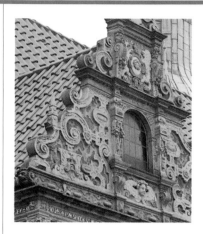

comic expressions of everyday life. After World War I, the Bauhaus (literally 'Building House') movement developed. Its founder in Weimar, Walter Gropius, envisaged co-operation between art and industry, and the name Bauhaus became synonymous with austere functionalism. Nazi hostility led to its dissolution in 1933; members of the movement settled in other countries and continued to influence architectural developments.

The contemporary scene Today, German painters are again prominent figures in the international art world. The current German movement, influenced by the flourishing avant-

Above: The Garden Café, *by Ludwig Kirchner (1880–1938)*
Top: People by the Pool, *by August Macke (1887–1914)*

who worked in Dresden, were the finest of the German romantic painters. In architecture, romanticism is found to an almost absurd degree in castles built for King Ludwig II of Bavaria: the baroque-style Linderhof, the mini-Versailles of Herrenchiemsee and the 'Disneyland' Neuschwanstein.

The modern age At the end of the last century, many German painters adopted the Impressionist style of France, and painters such as the portraitist Max Liebermann had strong support from the emerging German bourgeoisie. *Jugendstil*, the German form of *art nouveau*, was emerging. By the beginning of the 20th century, the Expressionist school was in full swing with the founding in Dresden and Munich of Die Brücke (The Bridge) and later Der Blaue Reiter (The Blue Rider) groups. This historic era inspired powerful works, some hauntingly apocalyptic; others wonderfully

garde interpretations of social and cultural life in a prosperous modern society, has been referred to as neo-expressionism.
Post-war Germany's best-known artists include Georg Baselitz and Anselm Kiefer.

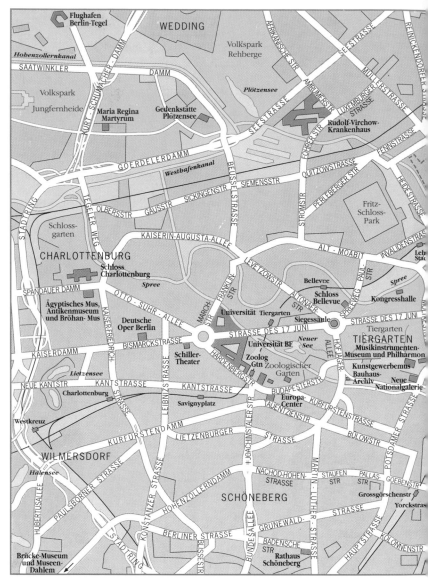

Since the Berlin Wall began to crumble on that extraordinary night in November 1989, the city's two halves have slowly and painfully attempted to fuse. Berlin is now just as fascinating for a visitor as it ever was in the midst of the Cold War. The minor thrill of crossing Checkpoint Charlie (and wondering if you would ever return) has vanished, and you can now drive unhindered across the Glienicke Bridge (where once only spies set foot) but Berlin remains a compelling city. As it struggles to regain its former status as the capital of a reunited Germany, Berlin is perhaps a litmus test for relations between East and West. Berlin has always been a place on the fringe, bursting with *avant-garde*

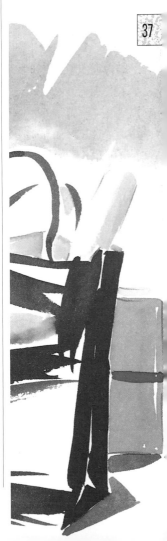

BERLIN

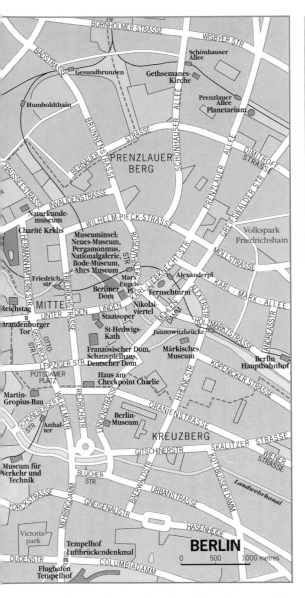

BORNHOLMER STRASSE
WISBYER STR
BADSTRASSE
Schönhauser Allee
Gesundbrunnen
Gethsemanes-Kirche
Humboldthain
Prenzlauer Allee Planetarium
BERNAUER STRASSE
BRUNNENSTRASSE
HAUSSEESTRASSE
PRENZLAUER BERG
SCHÖNHAUSER ALLEE
PRENZLAUER ALLEE
GREIFSWALDER STR
DIMITROFF-STRASSE
INVALIDENSTRASSE
Naturkunde-museum
Charité Krkhs
WILHELM-PIECK-STRASSE
ROSENTHALER STR
Volkspark Friedrichshain
HERMANN-MATERN-STR
Museuminsel: Neues-Museum, Pergamonmus, Nationalgalerie, Bode-Museum, Altes Museum
Friedrich-str
FRIEDRICHSTRASSE
Berliner Dom
Marx-Engels-Pl.
KARL-LIEBKNECHT-STR
Alexanderpl
Fernsehturm
KARL-MARX-ALLEE
MOLLSTRASSE
Reichstag
UNTER DEN LINDEN
Nikolai-viertel
MÜHLEN DAMM
ALEXANDERSTR
Brandenburger Tor
GROTEWOHL
OTTO
Staatsoper
St-Hedwigs-Kath
Jannowitzbrücke
HOLZMARKTSTRASSE
ANDREASSTR
LEIPZIGER STR
Französischer Dom, Schauspielhaus, Deutscher Dom
Märkisches Museum
Berlin Hauptbahnhof
POTSDAMER PLATZ
WILHELMSTR
Haus am Checkpoint Charlie
HEINE STR
KÖPENICKER STRASSE
Martin-Gropius-Bau
FRIEDRICHSTR
Berlin-Museum
ORANIENSTRASSE
SCHÖNEBERGER STR
Anhal-ter
KREUZBERG
SKALITZER STRASSE
WIENER STRASSE
GITSCHINERSTR
Museum für Verkehr und Technik
BLUCHER-STR
BAERWALDSTR
URBANSTRASSE
KOTTBUSSER DAMM
Landwehrkanal
MEHRINGDAMM
YORCKSTRASSE
GNEISENAUSTR
HASENHEIDE
Victoria-park
Tempelhof Luftbrückendenkmal
BERLIN
DUDENSTR
Flughafen Tempelhof
COLUMBIADAMM
0   500   1000 metres

ideas and sometimes subversive culture. Its reputation for decadence, even vice, is not unfounded – mostly a legacy from the Weimar years of the 1920s. It's a city of youth, and a cosmopolitan one. In the late 1960s and 1970s, young people flocked here to study on advantageous government grants, or to avoid military service, from which Berliners were exempt. A large number of foreigners have settled here – many as *Gastarbeiter* (guest workers). This has enriched Berlin's culture but has resulted in ugly racial confrontations, as unemployment and pressures on housing increase. Older residents believe much of the goodwill behind Berlin's laconic sense of humour has disappeared.

BERLIN

Berliners are renowned for their sense of humour, their *Berliner Schnauze*, a kind of gritty, quick-witted irreverence which can sometimes sound cynical or slightly aggressive. Every monument in the city is given a typical Berlinerisch nickname (the modern church on Ku'damm is 'The Lipstick and the Powderpuff'; the Berlin Philharmonic Orchestra's striking concert-hall, which looks like a yellow tent, was of course immediately christened 'Karajan's Circus'). Berlin also has its own dialect, with a characteristic harsh 'k' sound (icke instead of ich) and its own rules of grammar.

More Turks live in Berlin than in any other city outside Turkey. Many arrived originally as *Gastarbeiter* (guest workers) to do the jobs that few Berliners wanted to do. Now many of them are second and third generation citizens who want their fair share of the city's resources. A high proportion of Berlin's Turkish immigrants live in Kreuzberg.

Fabrics at the Turkish market, Maybachufer

Berlin, large even when divided, is now vast – Munich, Frankfurt and Hamburg could all fit within it. Its population is currently 'only' 4 million, and huge tracts of the city consist of forests, lakes, even farmland, contrasting oddly with the intense urbanisation of other areas. The West, all but razed by the Allies during Hitler's last-ditch stand in 1945, is almost entirely modern. Frequently meretricious and ill-conceived, the best of post-war West Berlin is a *tour de force*, studded with startling examples of art, architecture and design. East Berlin, also badly mauled by the bombs, has been reconstructed in two bizarrely conflicting styles: drab, Stalinist functionalism on one hand and a painstakingly accurate reproduction of grandiose monuments on the other. Two former working-class districts with some intact (or carefully renovated) architecture give a more realistic picture of pre-war Berlin: Kreuzberg in the West and Prenzlauer Berg in the East both display a volatile mixture of bohemian lifestyles and 'alternative' culture.

Berlin gives visitors a sense of double vision. Most cultural venues are duplicated on the other side of the city (two national galleries; two Egyptian museums etc), with sometimes an extra added for good measure (*three* symphony orchestras, universities etc). The city has about 60 museums, some world-class, although their contents may be uncomfortably split; rationalisation is bound to occur over the coming years.

Meanwhile, the Wall has been ripped away and the last chunks of rubble lie unheeded in a fenced 'graveyard' outside Spandau – but the scar tissue of No Man's Land still disfigures Berlin, marked in places by the crosses of those killed as they attempted to escape westwards. The mental lesions between East and West may take longer to heal.

▶ ▶ ▶   Ägyptisches (Egyptian) Museum
Schlossstrasse 70
This collection is housed in an officers' barracks and the Old Royal Stables opposite the Charlottenburg Palace. Star exhibit is a bust of Nefertiti, other fine pieces include smiling mummies, a flying scarab, a carving of the Priest Tenti and his wife holding hands, and a strange blue hedgehog. The 2,000-year-old Kalabscha Gate was a gift from the Egyptian government in 1973. *Open*: daily except Friday. Entrance free.

▶ ▶ ▶   Alexanderplatz
Before World War II, 'Alex' was the hub of the Mitte district, the historic core of old Berlin. After war-time damage many of its damaged buildings were replaced by truly ghastly architecture. The Alexander-Haus and Berolina-Haus are examples of an earlier 'objective' style, dating from the late 1920s. Since the Wall came down, the square's antiseptic dreariness has been exchanged for a patina of graffiti and litter, though street artists add a human touch. East Berlin's first department store, Zentrum, is fronted by the People's Friendship Fountain and the Weltzeituhr (world chronometer) which tells the time in Ulan-Bator, amongst other places. The square has several times seen revolutionary happenings, including the pro-democracy rallies of 1989

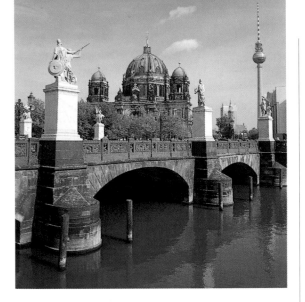

Museuminsel, from Unter den Linden

which toppled the regime of East Germany. The history of the square is depicted in eight panels in a pedestrian subway near the 30-storey Hotel Stadt Berlin. The Fernsehturm now dwarfs Berlin's second oldest parish church, the Marienkirche. Restored in 1950, its best feature is a Dance of Death fresco near the organ.

Southwest of Alexanderplatz is the Rotes Rathaus (Red Town Hall). A 74m tower dominates this neo-Renaissance building, decorated by 36 lively terracotta reliefs depicting Berlin's history. Near its entrance is the bronze Neptunbrunnen (Neptune Fountain).

▶ ▶ ▷   Bauhaus-Archiv
Klingelhöferstrasse 13
This distinctive building beside the Landwehrkanal holds a variety of exhibits showing how widely the Bauhaus Movement has influenced 20th-century design, from architecture to typography. Plans and models of Mies van der Rohe's box-like buildings, period coffee sets and desk lamps, paintings by Kandinsky and Klee, and Marcel Breuer's famously uncomfortable-looking chair are all on display. Computerised information is available (in English) summarising the ideas and achievements of the Bauhaus artists. (See also Dessau, page 135).
Open: daily except Tuesday from 11.00hrs.

▶ ▷ ▷   Berliner Dom
Museumsinsel
The protestant cathedral is one of the main landmarks of east Berlin. It was built at the turn of the century by Julius Carl Raschdorff, in heavy neo-baroque surmounted by an imposing dome. Massive restoration has recently been completed. Inside are tombs of the Hohenzollerns and the Imperial Staircase leading to the Parish Church, where an exhibition is housed.
Open: Monday – Wednesday, Friday, 12.00–16.00hrs; Sunday 12.00–14.00hrs. Entrance charge.

Alexanderplatz's most unmissable structure is the 365m-high Fernsehturm (TV Tower), like a cricket ball stuck on a skewer. The Berliners call it Telespargel (tele-asparagus). A lift takes visitors to a viewing platform at the top (40km views on a clear day) and a revolving restaurant. At its base is a useful tourist information centre.

39

Queen Nefertiti was the wife of the unorthodox Pharaoh Akhenaton who ruled Egypt from 1375 to 1358BC. The famous limestone bust in the Ägyptisches Museum shows her as a remarkably beautiful woman by today's Western standards (best seen in profile), but the first thing you notice is that she has only one eye. Some historians believe Nefertiti may have suffered from a cataract, a common disease in ancient Egypt. The bust was unearthed by a German archaeologist in 1912, during excavations of Akhenaton's royal capital. Towards the end of World War II it was removed from the Neues Museum on Museumsinsel to keep it out of Soviet hands. The bust may soon rejoin other Egyptian antiquities currently housed in the Bode-Museum in eastern Berlin.

Alfred Döblin drew on his experiences as a doctor in one of Berlin's low-life districts for his novel *Berlin Alexanderplatz* (later filmed by Fassbinder). A pioneer stream-of-consciousness novel, often compared to James Joyce's *Ulysses*, it tells the grim story of an ex-convict, released from prison after being wrongly accused of murdering a prostitute, and trying to build a new life in the Berlin of the 1920s. His efforts lead him to a spell in a lunatic asylum, and, eventually, a bottom-of-the-heap job as a porter.

Sculptor Gottfried Schadow's Quadriga, the four-horse chariot that crowns the Brandenburger Tor, was recast in copper from moulds found in West Berlin after the original was destroyed in World War II. It was vandalised at the end of 1989, as crowds marked the peaceful revolution in East Germany. The Quadriga was fit again by August 1991 – just in time for the gate's 200th anniversary.

Brandenburger Tor from the East German side

▶ ▶ ▷ Berlin-Museum

Lindenstrasse 14

Housed in the 1735 Altes Kammergericht (former Supreme Court building), the collection here outlines Berlin's history and culture since the mid-17th century. The paintings range from Berlin street scenes by Expressionist painter Max Beckmann, to scenes of everyday domestic life. Additional displays include porcelain, glass and Biedermeier furnishings, and there is an excellent restaurant, Das Altes Weissbierstube.

Open: daily except Monday, 10.00–22.00hrs.

▶ ▶ ▶ Brandenburger Tor

After the erection of the Berlin Wall, the Brandenburg Gate – stranded in No Man's Land – symbolised the division of Germany. Modelled on the Propylaea (entrance gate) to the Acropolis in Athens, it was built in 1788–91 as a triumphal arch for Friedrich Wilhelm II of Prussia by Langhans the Elder. Six tall Doric columns, front and back, form five passages. During the period of the Prussian empire, the gate made a spectacular theatre for military parades. Draped in swastikas, it also became a symbol of Nazi Germany. Hitler enjoyed driving convertibles through the wide middle archway.

▷ ▷ ▷ Brücke-Museum

Bussardsteig 9

This tiny museum in the leafy Berlin suburb of Dahlem is difficult to get to, but worth the trouble for those interested in 20th-century German art. Opened in 1967, it was built specifically for the work of Die Brücke (The Bridge), Expressionist painters who included Emil Nolde, Ernst Ludwig Kirchner and Karl Schmidt-Rottluff.

Open: daily except Tuesday, 11.00–17.00hrs.

▶ ▶ ▷ Charlottenburg Museums

Antikenmuseum (*Schlossstrasse 1*) An excellent display of antiquities containing objects of great aesthetic appeal as well as scholarly interest. Contents include Roman bronzes and Etruscan vases, Minoan carvings and Greek helmets. Downstairs is a treasure-

trove of Roman silver, the Hildesheim collection, dating from the time of Caesar Augustus.
Open: Monday–Thursday, 09.00–17.00hrs; Saturday and Sunday 10.00–17.00hrs. Entrance free.

Bröhan Museum (*Schlossstrasse 1a*) This museum, next to the Antikenmuseum, houses a collection of Art Nouveau and Art Deco *objets d'art*: ceramics and glass, silver, paintings and furniture. The top floor (coffee sets, cigarette cases, cutlery etc) is worth the climb.
Open: daily except Monday, 10.00–18.00hrs (until 20.00hrs on Thursday). Entrance charge.

Museum für Vor- und Frühgeschichte (*Langhans (West) Wing, Schloss Charlottenburg, Spandauer Damm*) Excellently organised material from early Palaeolithic cultures through the Bronze and Iron Ages. Though depleted after World War II, what remains of Schliemann's Trojan finds is still remarkable.
Open: daily except Friday, 10.00 –18.00hrs. Entrance free.

►►► Museen-Dahlem
Arnimallee 23–27
Dahlem, home of the Free University and a residential area, is known for its important group of museums. The **Gemäldegalerie** (picture gallery) houses a huge range of European paintings from the Middle Ages to the end of the 19th century. The German section includes works by Dürer, Altdorfer, Cranach and Holbein the Younger. The Dutch section has works by Rembrandt and Bosch. There is also a fine collection of Islamic art. In the **Skulpturengalerie** (Sculpture Gallery) is work by the 15th-century master woodcarver, Riemenschneider. The **Museum für Indische Kunst** (Museum of Indian Art) has one of Europe's largest collections, with bronzes, woodcarving and early Sanskrit manuscripts. The **Museum für Völkerkunde** (Ethnographic Museum), near the main complex, covers cultures from around the world.
Open: daily except Monday, 10.00–17.00hrs. Entrance free. (All Dahlem museums.)

►►▷ Haus am Checkpoint Charlie
Friedrichstrasse 44
The hut where East German border guards kept watch was moved to the Deutsches Historisches Museum (on the west side of the Wall) in 1990. The 'House at Checkpoint Charlie' stands near the former crossing point. It gives a history of the wall, with photographs and biographies of those who tried to escape to the west.
Open: daily until 22.00hrs.

►►▷ Kunstgewerbemuseum
Tiergartenstrasse 6
The Applied Art Museum stands in the new Kemperplatz (Culture Forum) of buildings, the most eye-catching of which is the tent-like Philharmonic Hall. Inside is a host of beautiful objects from all over Europe: silver, gold, bronze, glass, jewellery, porcelain, furniture, textiles and much more, dating from medieval times to the present.
Open: Tuesday–Friday, 09.00–17.00hrs, Saturday and Sunday, 10.00–17.00hrs. Entrance free.

The eight-year association of the artists who called themselves Die Brücke (The Bridge) was unusually coherent. Four young artists, Kirchner, Heckel, Schmidt-Rottluff and Bleyl, founded the group in Dresden in 1905. They wanted to get away from the dull, imitative German painting of the 19th century, and painted in a deliberately crude style using distortion and harsh clashing colours in order to express emotions rather than verisimilitude – hence the name of this school of art, Expressionism.

The huge areas of woodland in the Grunewald and around the River Havel are a fascinating nature reserve. Before the wall came down, West Berlin was largely protected from the danger of rabies, so prevalent among East European wildlife. With the demolition of the wall this is no longer the case; infected foxes and, even more alarmingly, wolves have managed to swim the River Oder from Poland and now colonise Berlin's forests.

BERLIN

The Museum für Verkehr und Technik (Museum of Transport and Technology), at Trebbinerstrasse 9, Kreuzberg, explains the history of aviation, railroads, cars, shipbuilding, printing, computers and much more – although exhibits could be better displayed. It is housed in market buildings and old workshops of the Anhalter Bahnhof. There is a remarkable Klaus Buscher mural on one external wall.(*Open*: Tuesday and Wednesday, 09.00–17.50hrs: Thursday and Friday, 09.00–21.00hrs; Saturday and Sunday, 10.00–18.00hrs.)

▶ ▶ ▶ Kurfürstendamm

The famous 'Ku'damm' (Elector's Causeway) dates back to the 16th century, when it was a bridleway by which the Prussian kings reached their hunting-lodges in the Grunewald. It became a favoured address for Berlin's smart set. In 1871 Bismarck, impressed by the *Champs Elysées,* remodelled it. In World War II virtually all its great houses were destroyed and its 3.5km length became a parade of pubs and shops. The most striking landmark is the ruined tower of the Kaiser Wilhelm Gedächtniskirche (memorial church), bombed in 1943 but left as a reminder of the horrors of war. Inside is an exhibition, with references to cities such as Coventry (in England) that suffered similarly. A modern glass and concrete church stands alongside. Near by is the tall, black plate-glass slab, the Europa-Center (*see* Shopping), surmounted by a whirling Mercedes logo. The area at this top end of the Ku'damm is fairly seedy at night, a haunt of homeless youngsters and loitering prostitutes.

The Museum für Verkehr und Technik

▶ ▶ ▶ Museumsinsel

Friedrich Wilhelm IV of Prussia in 1841 designated Museumsinsel (Museum Island) 'an open space for art and science'. This complex of museums – including Berlin's oldest, the Altes – stands on an island in the River Spree. The first building you will notice is the ruined Neues-Museum (there are plans to restore the complex to its pre-war grandeur). If you only have time to visit one museum, make it the Pergamon.

The **Altes Museum** on Marx-Engels Platz was built in 1824–30 by Schinkel, Friedrich Wilhelm III's architect, to look like a Greek temple. Completely destroyed during World War II, it was rebuilt in 1966 and houses the 20th-century collection of the National Gallery and the Kupferstichkabinett (print cabinet) which contains illustrations by Botticelli for Dante's *Divina Commedia.*

The **Bode-Museum**, formerly the Kaiser Friedrich Museum, was the final addition to Museumsinsel. It was renamed in 1956 after its founder, Wilhelm von Bode, and includes the Ägyptisches (Egyptian) Museum. The Bode also houses the Museum für Ur- und Frühgeschichte (museum of pre- and early history),

The Reichstag

notable for antiquities unearthed by Heinrich Schliemann at the site of ancient Troy, and the Münzkabinett, one of the world's largest coin collections.
Open: Wednesday to Sunday, 10.00–18.00hrs (all museums).

Three great wonders of the ancient world are housed in the **Pergamonmuseum**, which had to be constructed around them. The colossal Pergamon Altar, after which the museum is named, is a temple of Zeus and Athena from Asia Minor (what is now Bergama in Turkey) dating from about 180–160BC. Marble steps ascend to a wide colonnade; gods and giants writhe in complex friezes around the plinths. Next is the huge Roman Market Gate from Miletus. Third is the most startling exhibit of all – Nebuchadnezzar's Ishtar Gate and Processional Way from Babylon, with lions striding towering walls of azure tiles. Upstairs is the Pergamon's Islamic collection. Don't miss the Mshatta Gate from Jordan, smothered with carvings, and the panelled Aleppo Room.
Open: daily 09.00–18.00hrs (Friday 10.00–18.00hrs). Major exhibits only are open on Monday and Tuesday.

▶▶▷   Neue Nationalgalerie
Potsdamer Strasse 50
The glass and steel New National Gallery was designed by Mies van der Rohe and completed in 1968. The collection of paintings, drawings and sculpture from the 19th and 20th centuries has works by Kokoschka, Klee, Picasso, Beckmann, von Menzel, Corot and Courbet.
Open: Tuesday–Friday, 09.00–17.00 hrs; Saturday and Sunday, 10.00–17.00hrs. Entrance free.

▶▶▷   Reichstag
Platz der Republik
The original parliament building was damaged in the notorious fire of 1933 and then by bombs in World War II. The restored building houses an exhibition called *Fragen an die Deutsche Geschichte* (Questions about German History), with sections on the Third Reich and reunification. The dedication, '*Dem deutschen Volk*' (to the German people), is visible on the façade.

Nikolaiviertel
This area southwest of Alexanderplatz and centred on Berlin's oldest recorded building, the 13th-century Nikolaikirche, is a creation of the post-war planners of East Berlin. Destroyed in 1944, it is now a renovated quarter with restaurants and shops, masquerading as medieval Berlin. Some buildings are replicas of originals; others, modern in style, were designed to blend with the surroundings.

A bright and cheerful museum, the Musikinstrumenten-Museum (Museum of Musical Instruments), at Tiergartenstrasse 1, is right next door to the Philharmonie (Philharmonic Hall). It features instruments and their manufacture from the 16th century to the present day, from an ancient set of bagpipes to synthesisers. There are occasional demonstrations of instruments and special tours at 11.00 on Saturday mornings. (*Open*: Tuesday–Friday, 09.00–17.00 hrs; Saturday and Sunday, 10.00–17.00hrs. Entrance charge.)

BERLIN

Sachsenhausen was the first Nazi concentration camp to be constructed, and it stands right in the middle of an otherwise pleasant suburb. Now the place is oddly peaceful and birds sing, but during the war thousands of 'undesirables', or Untermenschen, were herded here – liberals, pacifists, communists, homosexuals, as well as Jews and captured Allies. Sachsenhausen charts a patch of Berlin's history that should never be forgotten.

The head of a dying warrior at the former Zaughaus

▶ ▶ ▷   Sachsenhausen

Strasse der Nationen, Oranienburg (take S-Bahn to Oranienburg).

Sachsenhausen Concentration Camp has recently been opened as a memorial after 45 years in East German hands. Visitors wander round the camp in increasing horror. First you see the boot-testing track, where prisoners were forced to run on different surfaces carrying heavy weights until they dropped (when they were shot where they lay); then the accommodation blocks; the cell-blocks in which prisoners languished in darkness for months until they died; and the 'hospital' where the most perverse experiments were conducted. The site of the 'shower rooms' and ovens is the final stop. Displays are mostly photographs and information boards. One of the most horrifying is a prisoner hurling himself against the electrified perimeter fence.

Open: daily except Monday. Entrance free.

▶ ▶ ▶   Schloss Charlottenburg

Luisenplatz

This vast palace started out in 1695 as a modest home for Sophie-Charlotte, wife of the future Friedrich I of Prussia. Eventually it became a grand baroque summer residence for the Prussian kings. The rococo-style Neuer Flügel (New – or Knobelsdorff – Wing) was built for Frederick the Great. The central section of the palace, with a domed clock tower, contains the sumptuous royal apartments of Sophie-Charlotte and her husband.

The gardens were first laid out in 1697 in the French style, but were transformed into an English-style garden in the early 19th century. Look out for the Schinkel Pavilion, the Mausoleum and the Belvedere, with its fine collection of porcelain (Meissen and Berlin's home-grown KPM, the Königliche Porzellan Manufaktur). Note the Iron Cross on Frederick's dinner plates.

Open: Tuesday–Sunday, 10.00–17.00hrs (until 20.00hrs, Thursday).

▶ ▶ ▶   Unter den Linden

Berlin's famous thoroughfare – the name means 'under the lime trees' – was a royal mall. Frederick the Great's bronze equestrian statue, backed by the Brandenburger Tor, looks down on the swirling traffic from the centre of his great avenue. The statue was turned by the former communist authorities so that Frederick appears to ride eastwards, rather than bearing down on the Brandenburger Tor. The 'Linden' runs from the Brandenburg Gate to the river. Walking east you reach, on the left, the neo-classical palace of the **Humboldt University** building. The former **Zeughaus** (Arsenal), near the eastern end, houses the Museum für Deutsche Geschichte (open daily except Wednesday). The 22 heads of dying warriors in the inner courtyard, by the great baroque sculptor Andreas Schlüter, are particularly outstanding examples of German monumental sculpture. Other buildings to look out for are Schinkel's neo-classical **Neue Wache** (New Guardhouse), the restored baroque **Alte Bibliothek** and the **Deutsche Staatsoper**, a splendid neo-classical opera house. New shops, such as a Meissen showroom, are opening here.

Excursion

▶ ▶ ▶ Potsdam

Public transport and organised bus tours allow fairly easy access to Potsdam. Its main claim to fame is **Schloss Sanssouci**, summer home of Frederick the Great of Prussia, whose aim was to indulge in cultural pursuits *sans souci* – 'without care'. This example of German architecture – arguably the finest example of rococo in Europe – is open to the public. In 1945 the town's **Cecilienhof** – an English-looking, 1916 mock-Tudor building – hosted the Potsdam Conference, when Churchill (then Attlee), Truman and Stalin met to decide Germany's future. Part of the building is now a hotel; some rooms, unchanged since 1945, can be visited.
Open: daily, 09.00–17.00hrs, but closed the second and fourth Monday of each month.
The ostentatious **Neues Palais** (New Palace), which Frederick the Great built after the Seven Years' War, is under restoration. Look out for the huge Marble Hall and, beneath it, a fine indoor grotto, encrusted with shells and minerals. In the park is the 18th-century **Chinesisches Teehaus** (Chinese Teahouse). Additionally there is the restored 18th-century theatre, and the lovely **Belvedere**, shelled by the Russians in 1945 but restored in time for Potsdam's 1,000th anniversary in 1993.
Open: as for Schloss Sanssouci. **In the town** Try to see the fine classical **Nikolaikirche** (St Nicholas Church) by Schinkel and Persius, restored after war damage, and the 18th-century **Holländisches Viertel** (Dutch Quarter).

Potsdam: Frederick the Great's summer home

Thanks to reunification, Frederick the Great's family were able, in 1991, to carry out the king's wishes and rebury his remains, which had lain at Burg Hohenzollern near Stuttgart, at Sanssouci, next to his 13 greyhounds. Frederick wrote: 'Let me be taken by the light of a single lantern, with no cortège, to Sanssouci, and buried simply on the right hand side of the terrace.' His wishes had not been carried out at the time since his family were appalled at the prospect of his lying in unconsecrated ground. The evocative reinterment ceremony on the 205th anniversary of Frederick's death – 18 August 1991 – caused controversy since it was seen by some as a revival of Prussian-style nationalism.

45

The influx of tourists since 1990 has brought its share of problems to Sanssouci. Pieces of gilt stucco have been stolen, and an enterprising group, working at night, made off with a bronze sea nymph, complete with sea horses, from a fountain in the park.

Shopping

Weekend itinerary
Saturday
Morning: Ku'damm.
Investigate the old quarters either side of the Ku'damm, such as around Savignyplatz or the Jewish quarter on Fasanenstrasse. Stop for coffee at Leysieffer's, diagonally opposite the Kempinski Hotel. Visit Kaiser Wilhelm Gedächtniskirche. On to KaDeWe for lunch on the 6th floor.
Afternoon: Neue Nationalgalerie in Tiergarten, perhaps also Kunstgewerbemuseum or Musikinstrumenten-Museum; take a stroll round the restored area of Nikolaiviertel then a short walk to Potsdamerplatz. Take in the Brandenburgertor and the Reichstag, before walking down Unter den Linden. Take a break at the Opern Café next door to the Staatsoper.
Evening: (try to) get tickets for the Deutsche Oper (Bismarckstrasse). Dine at one of several Italian restaurants within walking distance.
Sunday
Morning: The Zoo (Budapesterstrasse), followed by lunch at Café Einstein (Kurfürstenstrasse 58).
Afternoon: Walk through Tiergarten to open-air market on Strasse des 17 Juni (crafts, antiques, porcelain and silver). Refreshments at the Berlin Pavilion, next to Tiergarten underground station.

There is only one store that is an absolute must – the famous **KaDeWe** (Kaufhaus des Westens, 'Store of the West'), said to be Europe's largest department store. Its food hall is arguably more sumptuous than that of Harrods in London. Don't waste much time in other departments, but head for the *Feinschmecker Etage* (gourmet floor) – an express elevator takes you non-stop to the 6th floor.

Not far from the KaDeWe, on Tauentzienstrasse, is the **Europa-Center**. Although it has more than 70 shops and restaurants, there is little of startling interest for the tourist. Shop-owners have the reputation of being abrupt and unfriendly; you may want to give it a miss.

For fashion, the area to frequent is the Kurfürstendamm and its side-streets, particularly Uhlandstrasse and Fasanenstrasse, where exclusive (and expensive) shops sell the latest creations of Berlin's top designers. Fashion of yesteryear is also a Berlin speciality, in the form of stylish second-hand clothing on sale in flea markets; at the **Garage** (Ahornstrasse 2, opens at 11.00hrs), once an underground car park, now a vast clothes emporium, items are sold by the kilo; and in many other shops in the Kreuzberg, Schöneberg, Charlottenburg and Prenzlauer Berg districts.

Elegant Unter den Linden, the pre-war shopping Mecca of the well-heeled, is again developing into an exciting area for shoppers, with new stores opening all the time. The same applies to the revived old centre of Spandau, a select residential suburb. Rather than the inevitable bear, you might choose Berlin porcelain as a souvenir of your visit. Attractive, if pricey, it is available from the Ku'damm showroom. If you prefer the 'opposition', try the Meissen showroom on Under den Linden.

Markets Lovers of markets are well served in Berlin, where local markets abound. For bric-à-brac, **Trödelmarkt** in Prenzlauer Berg can produce a bargain, as can the **Nollendorf fleamarket**, under cover in the old Nollendorf S-Bahn (not Tuesday), while **Strasse des 17 Juni** has a colourful weekend flea market. For a glimpse of the Orient, visit the **Turkish market** on Maybachufer, in Neukölln (Tuesday and Friday afternoons).

Food and Drink

Where to eat German food is frequently somewhat heavy, but with a degree of Austrian influence, and a dash of German creativity, a new generation of chefs have come up with *neue Deutsche Küche* – Germany's version of *nouvelle cuisine* (not cheap). Highly recommended is **Trio** at Klausenerplatz 14 (closed Wednesdays and Thursdays); **November** at Schönberger Ufer 65 offers similar food. If money is no object, the **Bamberger Reiter**, Regensburgerstrasse 7, is your best bet. At **Mernik's** (Kantstrasse 53), you're guaranteed a good time if you like fish. The Merniks are Russian émigrés who came to Berlin about 20 years ago, and have created this successful eatery; try their smoked fish and homemade borsch. The **Mövenpick** (Europa-Center) is a Swiss restaurant, divided into a good many themed sections, all differently decorated, so you could have *Schnitzel mit Rösti* in one bit, *Kaffee und Kuchen* here, pizza or pasta there, beers and drinks somewhere else. Well-run and friendly, it sells all its sumptuous cakes at half price after 19.00hrs.

In an unsung but appealing part of the city, **Martin Gropius Kneipe** (Martin-Gropius Bau, Stresemanstrasse 110) is a most handsome building, now devoted to exhibitions of art, Jewish life, and so forth; the attractive white-painted café with baroque music and imaginative health foods is a welcome change from the meat-based dishes of most Berlin restaurants – good *Apfelstrudel*, too.

Alter Dorfkrug Lubars (Alt Lubars 8, 1000–Berlin 28), miles from the centre, is a little oasis out among fields. The restaurant looks like something Bavarian, and makes a very nice (if touristy) lunchtime venue on sunny days. **Cafe Einstein** (Kurfürstenstrasse 58) is a popular (and crowded) re-creation of Viennese coffee-house culture, with gardens to the rear.

The department store **KaDeWe** has a number of counters where you can enjoy a typical Berliner lunch that won't break your budget. A place which is worth trying is the Schnitzel bar, overlooking the Tauentzienstrasse; an enormous *Wiener Schnitzel* with potato salad (reasonably priced) will keep you satisfied for the rest of the day. Other counters serve fish or German specialities such as *Sülze* (cold meat in aspic) or herring with *Bratkartoffel* (fried potatoes).

The Café Kranzler in Ku'damm

Where the trendies go
Yuppies – the Germans call them 'schickie mickies' – are rather looked down upon. Their habitat is the posher suburbs like Grunewald or Dahlem and they usually shun the tourist spots. You're likely to find creative and arty types in the bars and coffee shops of the Savignyplatz area. But so many students frequent these places too, that the trendies are not easy to distinguish. Shell, on the north end of Savignyplatz at Knesebeckstrasse 22, is the place to be seen on a weekday morning when everyone else is at work. Cour Carree, at Savignyplatz 5, with its spreading vines, is a summer meeting place.

A popular summer drink is Berliner Weisse mit Schuss – light beer with a shot of raspberry syrup or liqueur, which turns it pink, or extract of the plant woodruff, which makes it green. This 'champagne of the north' was concocted by Huguenots in the 17th century, when they found the local beer too bitter.

Nightlife

Week's itinerary

Monday
Morning: Ku'damm and Kaiser Wilhelm Gedächtniskirche; explore side-street shops.
Afternoon: bus tour to Potsdam (but check opening times).

Tuesday
Morning: Dahlem museums, lunch in museum café.
Afternoon: Finish Dahlem museums or wander round Dahlem village and its small church.

Wednesday
Morning: Zoo; Neue Nationalgalerie; Musikinstrumenten-Museum; Kunstgewerbemuseum .
Afternoon: Martin-Gropius-Bau (Stresemannstrasse, Kreuzberg, tea at café/restaurant), and walk along the Schöneberger Ufer.

Thursday
Morning: Schloss Charlottenburg; walk through the extensive gardens at the back of the castle.
Afternoon: Ägyptisches Museum and Bröhan Museum.

Friday
Morning: go round the Reichstag; Brandenburgertor; Alexanderplatz; Nikolaiviertel.
Afternoon: Shopping/leisure or, if exhaustion allows, Museumsinsel.

Saturday
Morning: coffee on the Ku'damm then on to the open-air market at Winterfelderplatz.
Afternoon: walk in the Tiergarten; market on Strasse des 17 Juni.

Sunday
Morning: breakfast at Savignyplatz, visit to an art gallery or museum (eg Bauhaus-Archiv).
Afternoon: walk around Englischer Garten, part of the grounds of the Schloss Bellevue; alternatively look out at Berlin from the train window on the S-bahn line to Sachsenhausen, getting off for a wander here and there.

Like New York, Berlin is a city that never sleeps, and certainly not at night. The nightlife only starts in the early hours of the morning, so if you're someone who needs a good night's rest, you'll probably miss out on the more exciting (if seedier) aspects of the city. (Despite its lively feel, Berlin can also be surprisingly quiet at night.)

Nothing ever gets going before midnight at least, and while prowling round the discos at 23.00hrs will get you an entrance ticket, once inside you'll find you're the only one there. Young Germans living in Hamburg or Munich often come to Berlin for a weekend of clubbing; there are no laws for closing hours and many bars and discos stay open until 06.00hrs. You might consider the **Friedrichstadt Palast** (Friedrichstrasse 107), highly recommended for all sorts of nightshows and revues.

One popular night-time activity is to stay out all night and then meet at a fashionable bistro, such as **Shell** on Savignyplatz (generally without much to recommend it) for early morning breakfast and a glass of freshly squeezed orange juice.

The Ku'damm – equivalent to London's Oxford Street and just as touristy – is by day a fashionable shopping street; by night it is the haunt of prostitutes. In Kreuzberg, Berlin's East Village of Manhattan, there are a variety of leather bars, discos and strip joints making up the city's 'alternative' scene.

Cabaret, folk music and dance clubs are scattered throughout the city. For jazz lovers, the **Quasimodo Club** on Kantstrasse near the Bahnhof Zoo is an absolute must. Magazines such as *Berlin-Program* (published monthly by the tourist office), *Tip* and *Zitty* (published in alternate weeks), for sale at every newspaper kiosk, provide details on what's on where and what's in vogue. On a different level, there are three opera houses, three symphony orchestras and enough cabaret and theatre to keep you occupied for months on end. In the summer, the **Waldbühne**, the city's open air arena in the shadow of the Olympic stadium, hosts classical concerts and international pop stars.

Dressing for a night out? T-shirts ready for sale

Accommodation

There are some ambitious hotel projects in the east, notably the palatial Grand just off Friedrichstrasse, and the luxury Hilton in the shell of the old Dom hotel in Mohrenstrasse. West Berlin, however, remains the most convenient and lively place to stay, with a greater choice of nightlife and restaurants when dark falls. Until the wrangles over land ownership between east and west are settled, there is unlikely to be much investment in the east, leaving the west's hotels in this increasingly popular city with a captive market of regular business visitors, a booming conference trade and a growing number of tourists. Berlin may not (yet) be a capital city, but its prices certainly are. Increasingly, tourists find themselves using small pensions and bed and breakfast accommodation, or staying some way out of town. Since public transport is so efficient, the last is quite feasible if you have the time and don't mind quiet evenings or travelling to the centre at night; there are several peaceful hotels in the Grunewald area near the Wannsee.

Following the collapse of the Communist regime, many hard currency hotels were closed for several days so that corridor cameras could be taken out, bedrooms debugged and secret police rooms converted to hotel use.

Where the rich & famous go
The best place to observe the rich and famous is at the Deutsche Oper on Bismarckstrasse – spend the intervals celebrity-spotting in the bars. Between January and March the fashionable world takes to the dance floor in balls, including the Press Ball, usually attended by the Chancellor and Foreign Minister. The most sought after and elegant of all is organised by the wealthy business community. Top shopping spot is along the western end of the Ku'damm, while top people dine at the Grand Slam restaurant in Zehlendorff or in the heart of the Grunewald at the Landhaus Bott.

49

Möhring café, Ku'damm

Other options for budget travellers are a number of youth hostels and hotels designed with students in mind. The Tourist Office provides a list of these free of charge. Accommodation is basic, possibly without a bath or shower, but civilised. There's one on a side-street near Schöneberg Town Hall off Martin-Luther Strasse, another towards the Wilmersdorf end of the Ku'damm. If you like more idiosyncratic accommodation, try a pension or small hotel on or just off the Ku'damm in the older houses that escaped RAF bombs. These are often family-run, with characterful rooms, some retaining original art deco or *Jugendstil* (art nouveau) features. There are several in Wielandstrasse, others in Meinikestrasse. Most hotels, however, lie clustered around the Europa-Center, and are a dullish lot. Though generally in good condition, with most facilities and sparklingly clean, they now look quite *passé*.

It's as well to note that a surprising number of 'health-conscious' Germans smoke, and hotel bedrooms may smell of stale tobacco. Ask for non-smoking rooms, if they are available.

Berlin's transport system is highly efficient; there are few areas you cannot reach easily. Compared with many European cities, traffic congestion is low; buses are thus able to move at speed and keep to timetables. Since reunification the city's twin transport networks (formerly impeded by the Wall) have been merged, and many of the old underground routes and stations reopened. Berlin has an underground rail U-Bahn system (11 lines, excellent for the central areas), an S-Bahn system (ten lines) serving more outlying areas, and a conventional rail network for the distant suburbs. An excellent bus system operates throughout the city, with night services too. There are some ferries, and the east has a few trams (there are plans to improve the network, perhaps

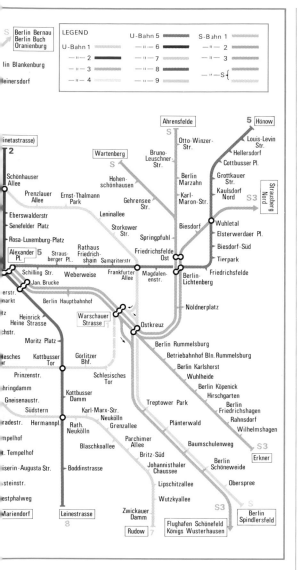

LEGEND

U-Bahn 1		U-Bahn 5		S-Bahn 1	
— " — 2		— " — 6		— " — 2	
— " — 3		— " — 7		— " — 3	
— " — 4		— " — 8		— " — S {	
		— " — 9			

Map stations:

Berlin Bernau / Berlin Buch / Oranienburg
lin Blankenburg
einersdorf
inetastrasse)
2
Schönhauser Allee
Prenzlauer Allee
Ernst-Thälmann Park
Eberswalderstr
Senefelder Platz
Rosa-Luxemburg-Platz
Alexander Pl. 5
Strausberger Pl.
Rathaus Friedrich-shain
Schilling Str.
Weberweise
Samariterstr
Jan. Brucke
erstr
narkt
Berlin Hauptbahnhof
tz
Heinrich Heine Strasse
chstr.
Moritz Platz
lesches r
Kottbusser Tor
Görlitzer Bhf.
Prinzenstr.
Schlesisches Tor
hringdamm
Gneisenaustr.
Kottbusser Damm
Südstern
Karl-Marx-Str.
Neukölln
radestr.
Hermannpl.
Rath. Neukölln
Grenzallee
mpelhof
t. Tempelhof
Blaschkoallee
Parchimer Allee
iserin-Augusta Str.
Boddinstrasse
Britz-Süd
Johannisthaler Chaussee
steinstr.
Lipschitzallee
estphalweg
Wutzkyallee
Mariendorf
Leinestrasse
8
Leinestrasse
Zwickauer Damm
Rudow 7
Wartenberg
Hohen-schönhausen
Gehrensee Str.
Leninallee
Storkower Str.
Springpfuhl
Friedrichsfelde Ost
Frankfurter Allee
Magdalen-enstr.
Warschauer Strasse
Ostkreuz
Ahrensfelde
S
Otto-Winzer-Str.
Bruno-Leuschner-Str.
Berlin Marzahn
Karl-Maron-Str.
Biesdorf
Berlin-Lichtenberg
Nöldnerplatz
Berlin Rummelsburg
Betriebbahnhof Bln. Rummelsburg
Berlin Karlshorst
Wuhlheide
Berlin Köpenick
Hirschgarten
Treptower Park
Berlin Friedrichshagen
Plänterwald
Rahnsdorf
Wilhelmshagen
Baumschulenweg S3
Berlin Schöneweide Erkner
Oberspree
S3
Berlin Spindlersfeld
Flughafen Schönefeld / Königs Wusterhausen
5 Hönow
Louis-Levin Str.
Hellersdorf
Cottbusser Pl.
Grottkauer Str.
Kaulsdorf Nord S3
Strausberg Nord
Wuhletal
Elsterwerdaer Pl.
Biesdorf-Süd
Tierpark
Friedrichsfelde

One bus route of particular interest to visitors is Bus No 100, from outside the tourist office past many of Berlin's main sights to Alexanderplatz. With a pass, you can hop on and off as you like and see much of the city. Several companies offer city bus tours, and excursions to Potsdam or Dresden; in summer boats ply the lakes and canals. Private cars are as unwelcome in central Berlin as in most major cities.

There is a local Verkehrsamt (tourist office) in the Europa-Centre with its entrance on Budapesterstrasse (tel (262) 6031) which is near to the main train station and KaDeWe. Here you can pick up a good bus map. Amerika Haus and the British Council are both located near by, on Hardenbergerstrasse, if you want to inquire about English-speaking events in town or simply browse around the library and read newspapers or magazines from home. The local tourist offices are open from 08.00hrs until 23.00hrs.

51

even in the west side of Berlin). Standard fares operate for buses, U-Bahn, and S-Bahn (cheaper for short hops, or *Kurzstrecke*, and children). Tickets are valid for two hours and can be used on any system within that time. Before your journey you must validate each ticket by punching it into a machine to stamp the time. For most visitors planning to explore Berlin extensively, it is cheaper and more convenient to buy a pass allowing unlimited travel on any of the systems, lasting 24 hours, or longer.

Ask for details of inclusive or family tickets at main transport offices (the companies serving the two halves of the city are BVG and BVB), for example outside Zoo Station, or at Alexanderplatz S-Bahn).

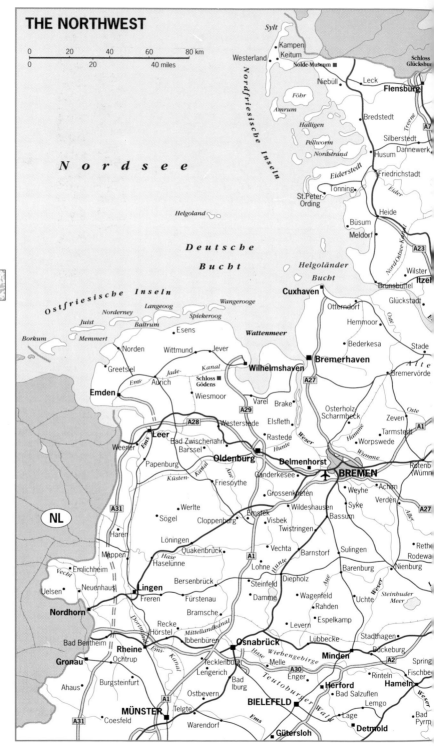

THE NORTHWEST

0   20   40   60   80 km
0   20   40 miles

Nordsee

Deutsche Bucht

Helgoländer Bucht

Sylt
Kampen
Keitum
Westerland   Nolde-Museum ■
Niebüll   Leck
Bredstedt   Flensburg
Schloss Glücksbur
A7
Silberstedt   Dannewerk
Husum
Friedrichstadt
Eiderstedt   Eider
Tönning
St.Peter-Ording   Heide
Büsum
Meldorf   A23
Wilster   Itzel
Brunsbüttel
Glückstadt

Nordfriesische Inseln

Föhr
Amrum
Halligen
Pellworm
Nordstrand

Helgoland

Cuxhaven
Otterndorf
Hemmoor
Bederkesa   Stade
Bremerhaven   Bremervörde
Alte
Oste

Ostfriesische Inseln

Langeoog   Wangerooge
Norderney   Spiekeroog
Juist   Baltrum   Esens
Borkum   Memmert
Norden   Wittmund   Jever
Greetsiel   Jade-Kanal   **Wilhelmshaven**
Emden   Aurich   Schloss Gödens ■   A27
Wiesmoor   Varel   Brake
Ems   Westerstede   A29   Elsfleth   Osterholz-Scharmbeck   Zeven
Leer   Bad Zwischenahn   Rastede   A1
Weener   Barssel   Weser   Tarmstedt
Papenburg   **Oldenburg**   Hunte   Worpswede
Küsten-   Aue   **Delmenhorst**   Wimme
Friesoythe   Ganderkesee   **BREMEN**   Rotenb
A31   Grossenkneten   Weyhe   Wümm
Werlte   Wildeshausen   Syke   Achim
NL   Sögel   Cloppenburg   Emstek   Visbek   Bassum   Verden
Haren   Löningen   Twistringen   A27
Mappen   Quakenbrück   A1   Vechta   Sulingen   Rethe
Hase   Lohne   Barnstorf   Rodewa
Vecht   Emlichheim   Haselünne   Hunte   Barenburg   Nienburg
Uelsen   Neuenhaus   Bersenbrück   Steinfeld   Diepholz   Aue   Steinhuder
Nordhorn   Freren   Fürstenau   Damme   Wagenfeld   Uchte   Meer
Bad Bentheim   Recke   Bramsche   Rahden   Stadthagen
Gronau   Hörstel   Ibbenbüren   Mittellandkanal   Levern   Espelkamp   Bückeburg
Ochtrup   Tecklenburg   **Osnabrück**   Lübbecke   **Minden**   A2
Ahaus   Lengerich   Melle   A30   Rinteln   Spring
Burgsteinfurt   Bad Iburg   Enger   **Herford**   **Hameln**
A1   Ostbevern   **BIELEFELD**   Bad Salzuflen   Fischbe
MÜNSTER   Telgte   Lemgo   Lage   Bad
A31   Coesfeld   Warendorf   **Gütersloh**   **Detmold**   Pyrm

Weser
Weser
Leine (Aller)
Ems
Dortmund-Ems-Kanal
Ems
Hase
Teutoburger Wald
Wiehengebirge
Wattenmeer

52

NORTHWEST GERMANY

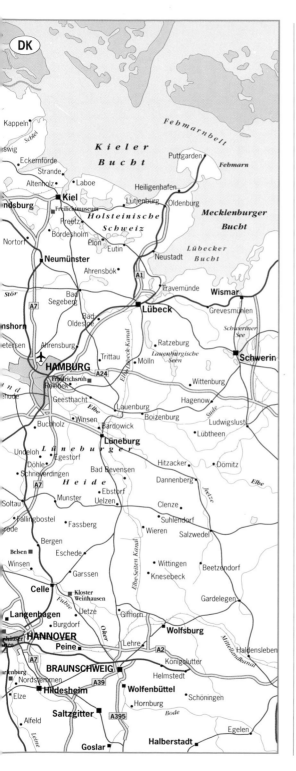

DK

Kappeln
swig
Eckernförde
Strande
Altenholz •
• Laboe
Kiel
ndsburg
Freilichtmuseum
Preetz
• Bordesholm
Nortorf
Plön
Eutin
Neumünster
Ahrensbök •

Kieler
Bucht
Puttgarden
Heiligenhafen
Lütjenburg
Oldenburg
Febmarnbelt
Febmarn

Holsteinische
Schweiz

Mecklenburger
Bucht

Neustadt
Lübecker
Bucht

A1
• Travemünde
Wismar

Stör
A7
Bad
Segeberg
Bad
Oldesloe
Lübeck
Grevesmühlen

nshorn
etersen
Ahrensburg •
Trittau •
Mölln •
Lauenburgische
Seen
Ratzeburg •
Schweriner
See
Schwerin

HAMBURG
A24
Friedrichsruh
Reinbek
Geesthacht
Elbe-Lübeck-Kanal
Wittenburg •
Hagenow •
Sude

nd
hude
• Buchholz
• Winsen
Lauenburg
Bardowick
Boizenburg
Ludwigslust •
• Lübtheen

Lüneburg

Undeloh
Döhle •
• Schneverdingen
Lüneburger
• Egestorf
Bad Bevensen •
Hitzacker •
• Dömitz
Elbe
A7
Heide
• Ebstorf
Soltau
• Munster
Uelzen •
Clenze •
Dannenberg •
Jeetze

• Fallingbostel
rode
Bergen
• Fassberg
Wieren •
Suhlendorf •
Salzwedel

Belsen ▪
Eschede •
Winsen

Celle
Fubse
Garssen •
Kloster
Weinhausen
Wittingen •
Knesebeck •
Beetzendorf •

Langenhagen
• Burgdorf
Uetze •
Gifhorn •
Oker
Gardelegen •

HANNOVER
Peine •
Lehre •
A2
Wolfsburg
Mittellandkanal
Haldensleben •

A7
BRAUNSCHWEIG
Königslutter
Helmstedt •
arenburg
• Nordstemmen
A39
Wolfenbüttel
Hildesheim
• Elze
Hornburg •
Schöningen •

Saltzgitter
A395
Bode
Egelen •

Alfeld
Leine
Goslar ▪
Halberstadt •

The northwest includes the two great Hanseatic seaports of **Hamburg** and **Bremen**, each a semi-autonomous *Land* (administrative region) on its own, as well as the whole of the *Land* of Schleswig-Holstein and nearly all of Niedersachsen (Lower Saxony). The area lacks the scenic wonders of the south, but it has its own quiet beauties, such as the **Lüneburg Heath**, and many historic and picturesque towns with buildings of mellow red brick, half-timbers and stepped gables.

Some areas show the Hanseatic merchant tradition; others are influenced by great princely houses such as the Guelphs and Brunswicks. The farms on the rolling plains tend to be large, rich and modern. **Schleswig**, long fought over between Germany and Denmark, did not become part of Prussia until 1864, and still has some Danish character. In 1945 the two former dukedoms of Schleswig and Holstein merged to form one *Land* with its capital at **Kiel** (but **Lübeck** is much the more interesting town). The coastlines of the two *Länder* are very different; the Baltic coast is gently pastoral, cut by low fjords and backed by wooded hills, while the North Sea coast is more flat and stark, buffeted by winds and storms that erode the coast. Major holiday resorts include the offshore island of **Sylt**.

Lower Saxony is misleadingly named, for its Saxon tribes emigrated in the Dark Ages and today it has no connection with the true Saxony area around Leipzig (see page 155). It has handsome old towns, such as **Celle**, **Lüneburg** and **Stade**, and much modern industry, notably around **Hannover**, its capital. In the coastal area, **Friesland**, which extends up into Schleswig, people keep their own culture and dialect, and their own dour temperament.

Catherinekirche – St Catherine's church – in Braunschweig

One of the most powerful families in the Holy Roman Empire, the Welfen (Guelph) were a thorn in the side of the Imperial family, challenging their power and policy. Heinrich der Löwe (Henry the Lion) was one of the most powerful Imperial princes, but was forced to retire to Braunschweig by his cousin the Emperor – a close childhood friend who became a rival in adulthood.

▶ ▷ ▷ Braunschweig (Brunswick)

An historic city with royal connections: in the 12th century it was the seat of Germany's most powerful ruler, the Guelph prince Henry the Lion. His symbol, a bronze statue of a lion, still standing in the Bergplatz, was erected in his own day (1166). Later the dukes of Brunswick resided here in 1753–1918. The city was heavily bombed and then none too prettily rebuilt. Today it is mainly industrial (trucks, machinery, etc) but some fine old buildings survive – notably the half-timbered Gothic and Renaissance houses on the Altstadtmarkt, and Henry's Romanesque cathedral. This contains his gift of a big seven-branch candelabra, the splendid Imervard Crucifix (1150), and the tomb of Henry and his English wife Mathilda. The Herzog Anton Ulrich museum has paintings by Rembrandt, Rubens, Cranach etc.

▶ ▶ ▷ Bremen

Germany's largest port after Hamburg is a fascinating old Hanseatic city with a quirky, individualistic personality. Like its bigger rival, it has a long history of independence and so today is a *Land* on its own. Its people are maritime, outward-looking and liberal-minded. Its port expanded in the 19th century, as a centre for coffee and cotton imports. Although it is 60km upstream from the mouth of the Weser, it can take ocean-going ships, and still handles much of the German intake of raw materials (it is well worth taking a boat-trip). Sadly, like Hamburg, the port is today in trouble. Its shipyards have declined and, despite the arrival of new modern industries (notably aerospace and electronics), many people are out of work. The new university began life in the 1970s, in a blaze of radical leftism. It has now grown milder but remains interestingly innovative.

Despite being a northern city, Bremen is full of colourful outdoor life – markets, buskers, street-festivals. In the Marktplatz you might find men in sailors' dress singing sea-shanties, or see a man in top hat and tails sweeping rubbish from the cathedral steps (it's a local custom that a man still unwed on his 30th birthday must do this, then marry the first girl who kisses him). The buildings are pleasingly varied – tall mansions in Weser Renaissance style, newer *Jugendstil* villas with oddly-shaped gables, even a windmill on a grassy hill made from part of the old ramparts that enclose the Altstadt.

55

Rebuilt after the bombing, much of the Altstadt is traffic-free and best toured on foot. The twin-towered cathedral is a Romanesque/Gothic mix and has a 13th-century bronze font. The arcaded Rathaus, also Gothic, with a rich Renaissance façade, has a noble banqueting hall. Its basement Ratskeller serves no French wines, only German (a custom kept from Napoleonic days) and has 17th-century cubicles for private parties. (If a woman and a man dine in one alone, they must keep the door open.) Outside stand two famous statues. One, built in 1404 as a symbol of independence, is a 10m figure of Charlemagne's nephew, the Knight Roland. The other is modern: a bronze pyramid of a cock on a cat on a dog on a donkey, depicting a Grimm's folk-tale.

The Böttcherstrasse, leading off the Marktplatz, is a *Jugendstil* alleyway designed in the 1920s by the offbeat Worpswede architect Bernhard Hoetger. Its gabled houses form a shopping arcade with stylish

Bremen: the statue of the Knight Roland (above) and the imposing Marktplatz (below)

In the North Sea, 90km northwest of Bremerhaven, **Heligoland** is an unspectacular small sandstone island. Its strategic position, however, commanding the sea lanes to the North Sea ports, made it a valuable possession. Germany eventually gained possession in 1890 by swapping it with Britain for the island of Zanzibar.

Celle's town crest

boutiques. There are also two small museums, one of medieval art, one devoted to the Worpswede painter Paula Modersohn-Becker. The nearby Schnoor district is a 'village' of narrow streets lined with old fishermen's cottages. It is now very touristy, full of craft shops, cafés and boutiques, but still engaging.

The main museums are outside the Altstadt. The large Focke Museum gives a wonderful idea of Bremen's history with maps, paintings, photos, model ships and much else. The Überseemuseum is devoted to Asian and African ethnography. The excellent Kunsthalle's varied paintings range from Cranach and Altdorfer via Brueghel and Delacroix to the Worpswede school.

 Bremerhaven

This big workaday port, 60km downstream from Bremen at the mouth of the Weser, was created in 1827 as Bremen's deep sea port. It is still busy but the Columbuskaje (quay), where ocean liners used to berth, is now used only by ferries and cruise ships. This is also Germany's leading fishing port and has interesting museums: an aquarium and fishing museum, an outdoor museum with 17th-century peasant houses, and a Deutsches Schiffahrtsmuseum, a big museum of maritime history with models of old boats and harbours, plus a genuine Hanseatic trading vessel of 1380, found in Bremen harbour in 1962.

► ► ▷ **Celle**

This is a stately old town, one of north Germany's finest, with a princely history. It has a neat, grid-like Altstadt of 16th- to 18th-century red and white gabled, half-timbered houses, some with upper floors quaintly overhanging. In the Celle region, orchids are grown and horses are bred. The parade of stallions through Celle in early autumn is well worth seeing.

The Lüneburg branch of the Guelph dynasty, vaguely related to the British royal family, ruled here from 1378 to 1705. Their handsome white Schloss, enclosed by a swan-filled moat, has a 17th-century theatre which is still used for staging classic plays. The lovely vaulted 15th-century chapel has rich Renaissance décor, while the state rooms are Italian baroque. Near by, note the biblical quotes on the decorated facade of the Lateinschule (1602), a former college, and the *trompe-l'oeil* façade of the old grey Rathaus (1579). To keep alive so much history and tradition, every day at 07.30 and 18.30hrs the town's bugler mounts the 235 steps of the Gothic Stadtkirche to blow his horn.

Southeast of Celle is a true marvel – the big 13th-century Cistercian abbey of **Wienhausen**, warmly evocative of medieval times. Since the Reformation it has been a kind of retirement home for elderly lay Protestant ladies, who will escort you round. The stunning medieval tapestries are on display only around Whitsun but you can see the 14th-century murals in the chapel and other curiosities – above all the tiny museum containing 15th-century scissors, knives, nail-files, spectacles, notebooks, etc, all found under the chapel floorboards in 1953 and supposed to have been hidden or dropped there by the nuns before the Reformation!

The harbour at Emden, from the viewing deck of the Rathaus tower

▷ ▷ ▷ Emden

Emden is situated on the Ems estuary and is a herring-fishing centre and industrial port for the Ruhr via the Ems-Dortmund canal. The Landesmuseum has displays of weapons and of local history. The windy Friesland plain round here is mainly dull but **Greetsiel** is a pretty, if touristy, fishing village. To the east, in the quiet **Grossefehn** area where wooden bridges span canals, are five 19th-century windmills. Two have been restored and are again grinding corn – mainly to attract tourists.

▶ ▷ ▷ Flensburg

Set on a fjord by the Danish border, this handsome old port was long part of Denmark and still has a Danish look and ambience. Its fine buildings include the 15th-century Gothic Nikolaikirche and the 16th-century Nordertor (north gate). For local history visit the Städtisches Museum. Flensburg used to be a wealthy merchant centre based on Caribbean sugar imports. The trade still continues, and rum is still made here.

Out on an islet in the fjord to the northeast is majestic white-walled **Glücksburg Castle**, a northern Renaissance jewel. It contains mementos of its former owners, relatives of the Danish royal family, as well as Gobelin tapestries and a richly decorated banqueting hall. A pretty coastal route leads east to the old port of **Kappeln**, through the Angeln country that gave its name to England, for it was from here in the 5th and 6th centuries that the Angles went colonising.

West of Flensburg, near the Danish border north of Niebüll is the former **home of Emil Nolde**, the expressionist artist. It is now a museum of his colourful, anguished work – powerful, but maybe not to all tastes.

Although he joined the Nazis in 1920, the painter Emil Hanse (called Emil Nolde after his birthplace) was forced into internal exile by the Third Reich. His intense expressionistic style of painting was considered degenerate by the Nazis.

HAMBURG

(map labels)
AMANDASTRASSE · ALTONAER STR. · SCHRÖDER STIFTSTRASSE · RENTZEL STR. · BUNDESSTR. · GRINDEL ALLEE · Univers
Sternschanzen-park · AN DER VERBINDUNGSBAHN
Sternschanze · Fernsehturm · Congress Centrum Hamburg
Hagenbecks Tierpark · MAX-BRAUER-ALLEE · SCHULTERBLATT
STRESEMANNSTRASSE · KAROLINENSTRASSE · Planten un Blomen
Messegelände · Alter Botanisc Garter
Friedhof Norderreihe · Neuer Pferdemarkt · NEUER KAMP · FELDSTRASSE · SIEVEKINGPLATZ · Kleine Wallanlagen · GORCH-FOCK-WALL
Justizgebäude · KARL MUCK-PL. · Musikhalle · KAISER-WILHELM-STR.
BUDAPESTER STRASSE · Heiligengeistfeld · Grosse Wallanlagen
HOLSTENSTR. · GLACISCHAUSSEE · HOLSTENWALL · ENCKE-PLATZ · NEUSTADT
ST. - PAULI · SIMON-VON-UTRECHT-STRASSE · MILLERNTOR PLATZ · Museum für Hamburgische Geschichte · GROSS-NEUMARKT
KÖNIGSTR. · REEPERBAHN · St.-Pauli-Theater · HELGOLÄNDER ALLEE · Elbpark · ZEUGHAUS-MARKT · OST-WEST-STRASSE
PEPERMÖLENBEK · Bismarck-denkmal · Michaeliskirche · SCHAAR MARKT · SCHAARSTEINWEG
Nord-Deutsches Landesmuseum · ST.PAULI-HAFENSTR. · ST.PAULI LANDUNGSBR. · Jugenherberge · DITMAR-KOEL-STR. · KAJE
Fischmarkt · Norderelbe · ST.PAULI-ELBTUNNEL · JOHANNIS-BOLLWERK · Niederhafen · VORSETZEN · Binn
0 200 400 600 metres

▶ ▶ ▶ **Hamburg**

Germany's second largest city and major port is the proud heir of a great merchant seafaring tradition dating from Hanseatic days. A cultured as well as an industrial city (it has probably the best opera in Germany), Hamburg is an unusually spacious and civilised place that delights nearly all its visitors. For centuries it was a Free Imperial City and today is a *Land* on its own, an autonomous city state; its most famous son in post-war times is ex-Chancellor Helmut Schmidt, a former city senator.

Set by the broad Elbe some 100km upstream from the sea, it's a town of water – the river, the huge port, the many canals (it has more bridges than any other world city, 2,195 against Venice's 400), and the big and beautiful Alster lake, in its very heart. As it was never a royal or episcopal town but a merchant one, it has few grand or distinguished buildings compared, say, with Munich. Overall, however, it is pleasingly harmonious and after massive wartime destruction has been tactfully

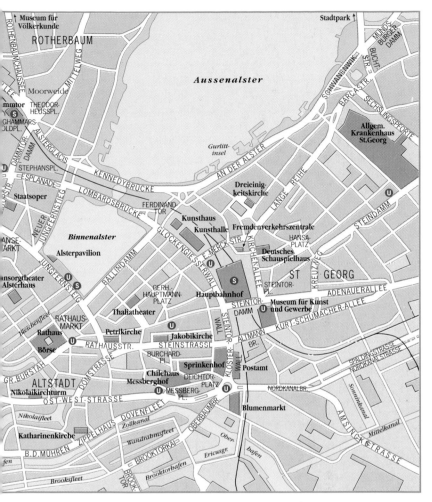

Museum für
Völkerkunde

ROTHERBAUM

Moorweide

mmtor THEODOR-
HEUSSPL.

GHAMMARS-
OLDPL.

STEPHANSPL.

ESPLANADE

Staatsoper

ANSE-
ARKT

Binnenalster

Alsterpavilion

nsorgtheater
Alsterhaus

RATHAUS-
MARKT

Rathaus

Börse

ALTSTADT

Nikolaikirchturm

OST-WEST-STRASSE

Nikolaifleet

Katharinenkirche

B.D.MUHREN

fen

Brooksfleet

Aussenalster

Gurlitt-
insel

AN DER ALSTER

Stadtpark

MUNDS-
BURGER
DAMM

Allgem.
Krankenhaus
St.Georg

Dreieinig-
keitskirche

Kunsthaus
Kunsthalle

Fremdenverkehrszentrale

HANSA-
PLATZ

Deutsches
Schauspielhaus

ST GEORG

STEINTOR-
PL.

Hauptbahnhof

STEINTOR-
DAMM

Museum für Kunst
und Gewerbe

ADENAUERALLEE

KURT-SCHUMACHER-ALLEE

Thaliatheater

GERH.-
HAUPTMANN-
PLATZ

Petrikirche

Jakobikirche

STEINSTRASSE

BURCHARD-
PL.

Chilehaus

Messberghof

Sprinkenhof

DEICHTOR-
PLATZ

Postamt

MESSBERG-
PL.

NORDKANALBR.

SPALDINGSTRASSE

NORDKANALSTRASSE

Blumenmarkt

AMSINCK STRASSE

Zollkanal

Wandrahmsfleet

BROOKTORKAI

Ober-

Ericusgr.

bafen

Brooktorbafen

Mittelkanal

rebuilt, mostly in local redbrick style, avoiding the concrete harshness of so many German towns. There are no skyscrapers to spoil the elegant skyline of green-copper spires by the Alster. In the suburbs are charming *Jugendstil* wrought-iron balconies, parks and gardens, even old timbered farmsteads and leafy lanes within the city's wide borders. Some streets retain odd names, such as Ole Hoop.

The people, often tall, lean and blond, have real style in their own Nordic way; some men wear the local blue sailors' caps that Helmut Schmidt favours. They are cautious and reserved, not exuberant like Bavarians but direct, businesslike and very polite to visitors. Theirs is a tolerant, liberal spirit, cosmopolitan and anglophile. Hamburg has been called the most English of German towns, still proud of the historic trade links; as the old saying goes, 'When it rains in London, Hamburgers open their umbrellas.'

Hamburg has long been a major commercial centre. First established as a port in 1189, then a leader of the

Hanseatic League, it created Germany's first stock exchange in 1558 and was a Free Imperial City from 1618. Wrecked by a huge fire in 1842, it was then rebuilt on the spacious scale it still enjoys. Its major growth came in the late 19th century, due to sea trade with America. Later, this free-thinking town was less welcoming to Hitler than other towns were, and the Nazis never held major rallies there – but it was to suffer badly from British RAF fire-raids in 1943.

Since the war, although it has shared in the economic miracle it has ceased to be Germany's richest city, overtaken by others as German industry has shifted to the south. This huge port has suffered as a result of Rotterdam's better situation for the Atlantic trade. The once-mighty shipyards, such as Blohm und Voss, have been forced to contract, close or diversify, like so many others in Europe. Although new modern industry has arrived, notably in electronics (Philips, etc) and aeronautics (huge Lufthansa repair yards, MBB factories working on Airbus, etc), unemployment remains high. After 1945 Hamburg was cut off from its natural markets in the GDR and Poland, but today it is eagerly reclaiming them, and its prospects have improved.

Despite the decline of the merchant firms, there is still much wealth in Hamburg. With its musical tradition – it is the home town of Brahms and of the first German opera house (1677) – there is a culture, too. Since World War II both opera and ballet have been as good as any in

The city of Hamburg, viewed from the harbour

Hamburg's wealth is based on trade and commerce. One important source of earnings is the Freihafen (free port), which is a customs-exempt area where goods can be stored in transit or processed for re-export without attracting duty.

Germany, the former under the great Rolf Libermann (now retired), the latter under John Neumeier. Theatre has shone under Peter Zadek and Michael Bogdanov. Since its merchant rulers were less concerned with collecting art treasures than were the aristocrats of South Germany, Hamburg has few major art museums. However, it is a key German centre for press and media, above all for weekly magazines (*Der Spiegel*, *Die Zeit* and *Stern* are all here), record companies and TV news.

The port and city centre With annual traffic of some 60 million tonnes, this is Europe's fourth biggest port, taking vessels of up to 110,000 tonnes. Its terminals can load or unload very fast, using few workers. This has put many dockers out of work but it suits the owners of the containers, as port dues are high.

A guided boat-tour of the port (starting from the Landungsbrücken in St Pauli) is a good way to start a city visit. You'll be shown the 68km of quays, the 4km Kohlbrand suspension bridge (1975), and the protective

walls built after the 1962 floods which caused 350 deaths. Near the eastern side of the port, Speikerstadt is an impressive group of high gabled brick warehouses by canals. Built in the 1880s, they are still used for storing spices, tobacco, silk, etc.

Near by is what remains of the Altstadt after the 1842 and 1943 fires. Here St Catherine's Church is Gothic with a baroque tower; St Nicholas', with its slim spire, has been left partly in ruins as a war memorial. Attractive gabled warehouses line the Nikolai fleet canal, and many of the 17th-century merchants' houses off the narrow Deichstrasse are now atmospheric restaurants To the west, the baroque church of St Michael, large and stately, has a famous tall green tower (with a good view from its platform). The nearby Krämeramtswohnungen, an alley of 17th-century almshouses, is a most picturesque surviving corner of old Hamburg.

Glance at the high-pedestalled statue of an arrogant Bismarck with sword and spiked helmet, in a park by St Pauli. Move on to the dullish Hamburg history museum, which has photos and models of city and port, and a large model railway. Further along the broad inner ringway you'll come to the rebuilt Opera House, then to an area of new shopping arcades, wonderfully stylish and luxurious, with startling window displays – Hanse Viertel and Galleria are the best. The massive Rathaus, with its heavy, lavish interiors, was built in 1897 in the neo-Renaissance style and seems symbolic of the city's proud heyday. The broad square and the canal beside it are attractive; so are St Jacob's late Gothic hall-church, and St Peter's with its high 14th-century tower. Beyond

A boat tour round the harbour at Hamburg offers interesting views

Hamburg beer is known for being cold, with a good head (like its citizens, some would say) – and it's also strong. A specialisation in the harbour district is *Lütt um Lütt* – beer fortified with schnapps; not a drink for the faint-hearted.

Flowers that bloom in the Planten und Blomen flower park

the ringway looms the glass vaulted roof of the Hauptbahnhof (station), next to the Museum für Kunst und Gewerbe (arts and crafts), which has Renaissance furniture, *Jugendstil* ornaments, etc, and even lays on authentic Japanese tea-ceremonies in a real tea-house. The Kunsthalle, the city's main art museum, offers a huge but confusingly presented array, from North German primitives via European masters to the romantic Caspar David Friedrich, and Dix and Klee.

Alster and the north side The Aussenalster, the much larger outer lake, is a lovely shimmering focus of the city's life, much used for recreation. Against a setting of elegant spires, handsome villas and weeping willows, white sails glide and Hamburgers stride the shore paths with their dogs. There are outdoor cafés for summer; and in winter it often freezes so hard that, despite police warnings, stalls selling *Glühwein* are put up on the ice.

The up-market residential district of Harvestehude, on the lake's west side, contains the charming village of Poseldorf, a mini-Chelsea of bistros and bars frequented by media folk and the smart set. At the Museum für Volkerkunde (ethnology) do not miss the Javanese shadow-puppets among the displays of Developing World folk-art brought to Hamburg by past explorers. Close by is the huge university, curiously quite recent (1919) and, further on, the attractive Planten und Blomen flower park, the Botanical Garden (illuminated fountains play on summer nights), and the 271m TV tower (with a fine view from its top). Out to the north, the big Hagenbeck Zoo was the pioneer of the civilised trend of letting animals live outdoors in some freedom.

St Pauli and Altona The suburb of St Pauli, a former fishing village, is best known for its garish main street, the notorious Reeperbahn, which has thrice changed its nature. It began in the 19th century as a fairly respectable amusement district for the new transatlantic passenger trade, full of terrace cafés with live orchestras; the sailors' brothels were in side-alleys. After the war, as the liner age waned, it slid down-market into sex and voyeurism for tourists and businessmen. Today, due in part to AIDS, it is moving back to 'decency': the biggest brothel has closed, smart restaurants are opening. But if you wish you can still spot the women in the pink-lit windows of the Herbertstrasse. But the Star Club where the Beatles first won fame, is no more.

The nearby Hafenstrasse, high above the Elbe, won a different notoriety in the mid-1980s as the scene of a militant Leftist squat, which the police took years to evict. On the quayside below, the traditional St Pauli Fischmarkt (fish market) is held every Sunday from 05.00 to 10.00hrs. Now mainly a flea-cum-food market, it does sell some fish. Go afterwards to the exuberant Fischerhaus restaurant for a Hamburg breakfast of eel and plum soup, herring and beer.

The big suburb of Altona, Danish until 1864, still feels like a separate town. It has stately white patrician houses and a fine view of the river from the Altonaer Balkon (Altona Balcony). Its Nord-Deutches Landesmuseum, rebuilt after a recent fire, is Hamburg's nicest museum, with splendid old ships' figureheads and fishing-boats, local costumes, rural interiors and paintings of Schleswig scenes. Beyond Altona, you can stroll under trees by the river at idyllic Övelgönne, then visit the neo-classical Villa Jenisch (with superbly furnished interiors) and the Ernst-Barlach Haus (works by the sculptor), both in a pretty park. Finally you reach the former fishing village of Blankinese, with steep alleys and riverside pubs.

All life meets at St Pauli's Fischmarkt between 5 and 10 every Sunday morning. Revellers partying into the small hours mix with market workers tucking into a hearty breakfast in the bars and restaurants and early-morning shoppers buying fish, fruit and vegetables or browsing in the fleamarket.

63

Signs from the Reeperbahn area

▶ ▶ ▷   **Hannover (Hanover)**

A dynamic and prosperous commercial city, Hannover is the home of automobile and audio-visual industries as well as of Europe's leading annual trade fair. It is also a place of great historic importance, with much worth seeing. It was the princely seat of the House of Brunswick from the 17th century, and the House of Hannover inherited the British throne in 1714 through a Stuart connection. Hannover became a kingdom itself until its absorption by Prussia in 1866. Its people, somewhat reserved, speak the most correct, accentless German.

The modern central area, around the broad Kröpcke square and the imposing opera house, is affluent and spacious. From here you can stroll through the rebuilt but picturesque Altstadt, full of interest, the half-timbered Ballhof (1650), now a theatre, the historical museum, with old maps and four state coaches, the busy taverns of the narrow Krämerstrasse, the high gabled facade of the 15th-century Altes Rathaus, and the Gothic Marktkirche with its superb stained glass. On the banks of the little River Leine, opposite the neo-classical Leineschloss (now housing the Landtag) are three unusual pop-art sculptures, the Nanas, by the French artist Niki de St-Phalle. The Gothic Aegidienkirche with its blue tower has been deliberately kept half-ruined after the bombing, as a memorial – like Berlin's Gedächtniskirche.

The grandiose neo-Gothic Neues Rathaus (1913), across the ringway, has scale models of what the city was like before the bombing. The adjacent Kestner Museum, covered in an odd honeycomb of concrete, contains Greco-Roman antiquities and much medieval art. Further on, close to the Maschsee (a lake created in the Nazi

The baroque gardens of Herrenhausen, in Hannover's western suburbs

period and still used for watersports), are two other major museums: the Landesmuseum (paintings of many periods, notably German late 19th-century) and the Sprengel Museum, excellent for modern art (eg Klee, Picasso, lots of Germans such as Dix and Beckmann, and the Hannover-born surrealist Kurt Schwitters).

In the western suburbs are the famous and masterly baroque **Herrenhausen**, the former royal gardens of the Brunswicks. The main one, the Grosser Garten, is formal and French, with a maze, statues, and fountains sometimes lit up (one jet rises to 82m). Concerts and plays are given here in summer. The Georgengarten contains a museum devoted to the hugely popular cartoonist and poet Wilhelm Busch (1832–1908). Near the botanical Berggarten are the remains of the former royal palace, mostly bombed to bits; little survives save the mausoleum of George I.

The Electors of Hannover became heirs to the British throne through a strategic marriage to the royal house of Stuart. From 1714 the Elector also ruled in London. However, in 1837, with the accession of Queen Victoria, Hannover passed from the British royal family, as the title could not be inherited by a woman.

Michaeliskirche, one of Hildesheim's two restored Romanesque churches

▶ ▶ ▷ Hildesheim

Apart from the 15th-century Templarhaus, few of the many old buildings of this distinguished town survived the war. Some have been well restored, notably the Gothic Rathaus and two Romanesque churches: the Michaeliskirche and the cathedral, where the art works include an 11th-century carved bronze column, with biblical scenes. Legend has it that the celebrated rose tree in its cloister dates from AD815. After the 1945 air raid it began to flower again, adding to the local belief in its miraculous powers.

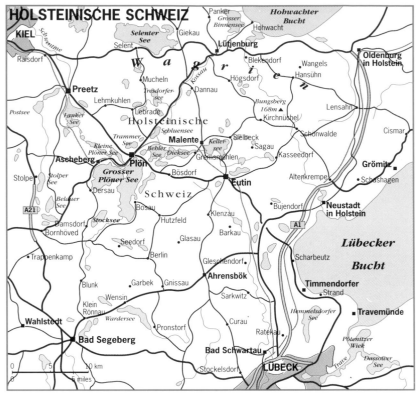

HOLSTEINISCHE SCHWEIZ

KIEL · Raisdorf · Preetz · Lehmkuhlen · Postsee · Lanker See · Muchela · Tresdorfersee · Liebrade · Holsteinische · Schlensee · Trammer See · Kleine Plöner See · Bebler See · Malente · Keller See · Dieksee · Ascheberg · Plön · Grosser Plöner See · Bösdorf · Stolper See · Dersau · Schweiz · Belauer See · A21 · Bosau · Damsdorf · Stocksee · Bornhöved · Seedorf · Trappenkamp · Berlin · Blunk · Garbek · Gnissau · Klein Ronnau · Wensin · Wardersee · Pronstorf · Wahlstedt · Bad Segeberg · Panker · Grosser Binnensee · Hohwachter Bucht · Selenter See · Giekau · Selent · Lütjenburg · Hohwacht · Blekendorf · Wangels · Oldenburg in Holstein · Högsdorf · Hansühn · Dannau · Bungsberg 168m ▲ · Lensahn · Kirchnüchel · Sielbeck · Sagau · Schönwalde · Cismar · Gremsmühlen · Kasseedorf · Grömitz · Altenkrempe · Schashagen · Eutin · Klenzau · Bujendorf · Neustadt in Holstein · Hutzfeld · Barkau · A1 · Glasau · Gleschendorf · Scharbeutz · Lübecker Bucht · Ahrensbök · Sarkwitz · Timmendorfer Strand · Curau · Hemmelsdorfer See · Travemünde · Ratekau · Pollnitzer Wiek · Dassower See · Bad Schwartau · Stockelsdorf · LÜBECK · Trave

0 5 10 km
0 6 miles

▷ ▷ ▷   Holsteinische Schweiz

This is a gentle region of woods and low hills good for walking, and of pretty lakes good for sailing and bathing. Its nickname, Holstein Switzerland, was given it locally in the last century to attract tourism, but it's a misnomer, for none of the hills rises above 168m. You can tour the lakes by excursion boat from Plön, an old water-girt town with a big white baroque hilltop castle that formerly housed a Prussian army college. At Eutin, a pleasant town of 18th-century brick buildings, there's another baroque castle, with a moat and bronze cupola. In summer, its pink courtyard hosts the operas of Carl Maria von Weber (1786-1826), born in Eutin. Malente, near by, is a delightful little lakeside resort where water galas are held. Best of the nearby Baltic seaside resorts is Hohwacht.

▷ ▷ ▷   Husum

This graceful old North Sea fishing port and market town is known for its horse fairs, and is close to a region of polders. The history of these, of the land reclamation and the age-old battle against sea and storm is well recorded in the Nissenhaus Museum. Another museum is in the home of Theodor Storm (1817–88), a suitably named poet and novelist whose work movingly evokes the life of this strange, flat, melancholy region.

Friedrichstadt, to the south, was built in the 17th century by Dutch Protestant refugees. It's a picturesque little

Dutch-looking town of stepped gables, canals and cobbled streets. On the long peninsula to the west is St Peter Ordning, a resort with good sandy beaches, known for its sulphur cures.

▶ ▷ ▷ Jever

This brewery town is known for its Pilsener beer and for its delightful pink hunting-Schloss set in a moated park. This once belonged to the Russian Tsars, hence the portraits of Catherine the Great, alongside local costumes, toys, furniture, etc, in its interesting museum. On the wall of the café by its gates is an old *Glockenspiel* where figurines of Catherine and others do an hourly dance. In the Marktplatz, note the superb Renaissance sarcophagus with marble statues, situated in the belfry next to a modern church.

▶ ▷ ▷ Kiel

At the head of a broad fjord, always lively with shipping, stands Schleswig-Holstein's capital, formerly the leading German naval base. Badly bombed in World War II, it has been gracelessly rebuilt and has few notable buildings except for the restored *Jugendstil* Rathaus (1911), with a 106m tower. Shipping is still a major activity. The 100km

Northwest of Husum, around Bredstedt, you can explore some of the polders – areas of low-lying land reclaimed from the sea – known here as Köge (singular Koog); typical examples are St-Cecilien and Sonke-Nissen. The people tend to be taciturn and dour, due maybe to the incessant howling winds. They live in houses with flat green tin roofs and go in for breeding sheep, which sometimes graze even on the seaward side of the dykes.

The Olympiahafen (harbour) at Kiel

Kiel Canal, opened in 1985 to link the Baltic with the North Sea, remains the world's busiest with 50,000 ships a year – ahead of Panama or Suez. There's a fine sea walk along the Hindenburgufer (quay) to the Holtenau locks where the passage of ships between canal and sound is an impressive sight. At **Laboe**, the high brick tower shaped like a ship's stern is Germany's main naval war memorial (climb to its roof for a fine view). The museum inside includes a model of the Battle of Jutland.

To the southwest, at Molfsee, the Schleswig-Holsteinisches Freilichtmuseum is one of the best of the new German outdoor museums of rural life. About 30 old buildings, half-timbered and red brick in the regional style – including three windmills, a watermill, a 16th-century vicarage, and an 18th-century manor (note its 1817 school timetable) – are set in a pleasant park; bakers, carvers and potters work here and sell their products.

Kiel is a mecca for watersport enthusiasts. Since 1882 the Kieler Wache (sailing regatta) has been an annual event (in late June, early July). It's also been the watersports centre for two Olympics – 1936 (Berlin) and 1972 (Munich).

Thomas Mann's family. left Lübeck for Munich in 1891 when Thomas was 16, but he recorded his youth in his masterly novel *Buddenbrooks* (1901), which gives a vivid portrait of the city's upper-crust society. Mann was awarded the freedom of the city in 1955.

Detail of architecture in the Altstadt (old town) area of Lübeck

► ► ► **Lübeck**

This Baltic river port, and former leader of the Hanseatic League (see page 75), is a stately old city with tremendous local pride and a lovely relaxed, civilised ambience. Though badly bombed and then rebuilt, its main streets still evoke its wealthy merchant heyday. Here you will see those high zigzag gabled façades often thought of as Dutch, though in fact the old builders of Lübeck invented this style which the Dutch later copied. Some old houses also have the unusual Lübeck brickwork: alternating strips of red unglazed and black glazed brick. Behind the brick street fronts you'll find many small houses amid greenery, for surprisingly Lübeck is secretly a very verdant city, full of enclosed gardens.

In the Middle Ages this 'Queen of the Hanse' was the main business centre of north Europe and Germany's largest town after Köln (Cologne). Later it lost ground to Bremen and Hamburg but it still handles a lot of cargo, and has some big industries. Its position on the old GDR border was a handicap but today it is reforging links with its natural Mecklenburg hinterland.

Some of the old merchant families still flourish today. One leading family was the Manns, wealthy grain-dealers, who produced two great writers, Thomas and Heinrich (see panel, left). The family's old home and the model for the Buddenbrookhaus, at Mengestrasse 4, was badly bombed and only its façade survives, but the museum in the Drägerhaus has many Mann souvenirs.

Lübeck's medieval centre lies between two arms of the River Trave and is best visited on foot. The grander quarter, with fine old houses, is west of the central Breitstrasse, the artisan quarter is to the east. To make a circular tour, enter by the Holstentor, an imposing red twin-towered gateway housing a museum of history. Here by the river are some 16th- to 17th-century gabled warehouses, used to store salt in transit from the Lüneburg mines to Sweden. Crossing the river, you can visit the Gothic Petrikirche and the beautiful Music Academy converted from 22 merchant homes (concerts are often held here). In the narrow street oddly named Kolk, the marionette theatre and puppet museum have a

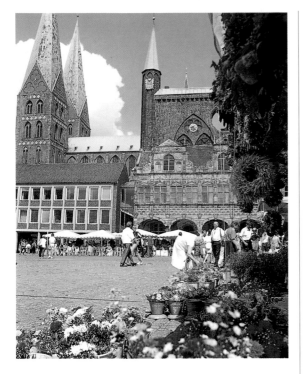

The Marktplatz at Lübeck, with the impressive Marienkirche in the background

South of Lübeck are two charming old towns. Ratzeburg, on a lake, has a tall red-brick Romanesque cathedral on its outskirts. Mölln, with its 14th-century Rathaus, is where the folk hero Till Eulenspiegel is said to have died of the plague in 1350. Touching the thumb of his statue (in the market) is supposed to bring good luck. Before reunification Ratzeburg was the archetypal frontier town. Until recently the eastern shore of the lake near the town (which is built on an island) was fenced off, forming the border between West and East Germany.

splendid and intriguing collection of exotic oriental puppets.

To the southeast, the double-towered cathedral (1173) is Romanesque with a Gothic chancel; the nearby St Annen museum contains relics of old Lübeck. Just to the north, in an area of mews-like alleys, are two fine 17th-century almshouses, Fucthtingshof and Glandorpshof, built for the widows of merchants and craftsmen and still used as homes for the elderly. On the 14th-century façade of the Katharinenkirche (now a museum), are fine modern statues, three of them by Barlach. The nearby Behnhaus and Drägerhaus are elegant houses, now small museums showing Mann souvenirs and paintings by Munch.

The Heiligen-Geist-Hospital, built c1280 as an old people's home, has a superb vaulted Gothic chapel with old frescos. In the Gothic Jakobkirche are 17th-century organ lofts. Just opposite, the tall step-gabled Haus der Fischergesellschaft, a Renaissance mansion built for the Fishermen's Guild, today serves as a tavern, very popular with tourists, but atmospheric. The lofty Marienkirche, with the highest brick nave in the world, was the main church of the merchant rulers. Badly bombed, it has now been skillfully restored in its original style.

The handsome Gothic/Renaissance Rathaus should be seen for its council chamber and the memorial to eight citizens shot as anti-Nazis.

Finally, pay a visit to the famous Niederegger marzipan store, which sells this local delicacy in every bizarre size and shape conceivable.

Lüneburg

This is a distinguished old town with handsome red-brick buildings in the local style. In the Middle Ages it grew prosperous from its salt deposits, which it sold to Scandinavia and the Baltic towns. Lining the broad street called Am Sande are tall houses with oddly-shaped stepped gables; some, as in Holland, still have the iron bars near the roof that were used for pulling up furniture. The big yellowish Rathaus (13th- to 16th-century) has a superbly ornate interior: a Renaissance council chamber with detailed wood carvings, and a Gothic Fürstensaal (princes' chamber) with lamps made from stags' antlers. Close by is the highly picturesque Wasserviertel, the old river port, with a gabled Renaissance brewery, a half-timbered millhouse by the water and an 18th-century crane.

At **Ebstorf**, to the south, little remains of its 14th-century Benedictine abbey save a Gothic gallery and cloister. Its main attraction is a copy of a 13th-century map of the world, the original of which was destroyed in the war.

The Rathaus at Lüneburg

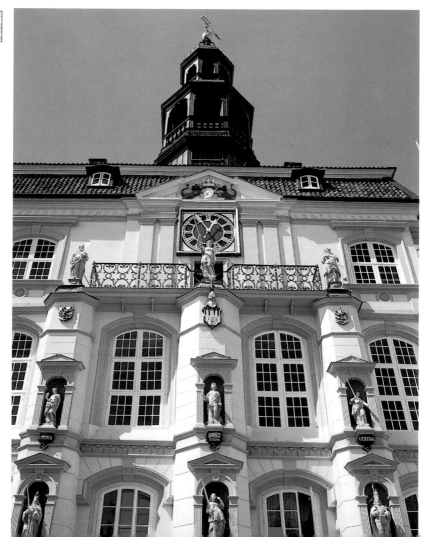

▶ ▶ ▷ **Lüneburger Heide (Lüneburg Heath)**

The famous Lüneburger Heide, not flat but gently undulating, is a large and subtly beautiful area stretching from the Elbe down to the River Aller, near Celle. It is best visited in August or September when the juniper shrubs are in leaf and the vast tracts of heather are in bloom – but in any season this varied landscape has its charms. You'll find low valleys, marshy ponds, pasture full of sheep and forests rich in game. In the three big nature reserves, cars must stay on the main road but you could hire a horse and cart, horse or bicycle and go meandering down quiet, clearly signposted paths. In some places, cross-country skiing is possible in winter. The sheep that browse on the juniper and heather yield a delicious fragrant mutton, known as Heidschnucken, that finds its way onto many local menus.

The main nature reserve is just west of the Hannover-Hamburg Autobahn and has several entry points. Among them are Undeloh to the north and Döhle to the east, two pretty villages reachable by car. From either you can hike or ride to the Wilseder Berg, a 169m hill that offers a wide view of the heath – even as far as the spires of Hamburg on a clear day (with field-glasses). The rolling heathland is covered with oaks, pines, birches and red-berried junipers, and above all with heather. Here there are large, thatched, smelly sheepfolds where the animals spend the night.

Heather is omnipresent. The villages have stalls selling heather bouquets (in season) and kitschy heather ornaments of all kinds. At Egestorf, a picturesque village east of Undeloh, heather is used to decorate the altar of the Protestant Heidekirche, an odd half-timbered structure that – from outside – looks less like a church, more like a dwelling.

The former Belsen concentration camp is next to a big British army barracks southwest of Bergen. Here 50,000 Nazi victims died, 30,000 of them Jewish, as the camp's museum relates in stark detail. You can also see the heather-covered mounds on the site of the mass graves, and the obelisk in honour of the victims. Near here, on 4 May 1945, in the presence of Montgomery, the German High Command signed its unconditional surrender. The area has since been a major British army base, within NATO, though this is now being much reduced.

71

Heathland at Lüneburg

The glories of the Heide were extolled sentimentally in poetry by Hermann Löns, whose memorial tomb stands alone in an area of cairns and ancient chamber-tombs near Fallingsbostel, southwest of Soltau. Further west is the huge Vogelpark Walsrode (bird sanctuary), where parrots, flamingos, cranes and ostriches are among the huge variety of species of birds from the world over that live and fly freely here. There's a playground for children at the sanctuary.

▶ ▷ ▷   Minden

This busy junction town on the Weser has a huge Schachtschleuse (lock), 85m long, that links the river with the Mittelland canal; a small museum describes its workings and the Weser area. The cathedral has a Romanesque façade and a striking 11th-century crucifix. At the Porta Westfalica, a scenic spot to the south, the river Weser has forced its way between two wooded hills. On each stands an unlovely memorial of Wilhelmine times: a tower dedicated to Wilhelm I, and a statue of Bismarck.

▶ ▶ ▷   Nordfriesische Inseln (North Friesian Islands)

This low-lying archipelago off the west coast of Schleswig is popular with holidaymakers. There are hotels on Amrum and Fohr – islands served by ferry – but the biggest and by far the best-known island is Sylt, a long strip of land linked to the mainland by a causeway that bears a railway but no road. Cars must board the train shuttle at Niebüll, and fares are high. Sylt is a legend in Germany for showy jet-set tourism. Its windy but bracing climate has made it a smart resort since the 19th century; Thomas Mann and Marlene Dietrich used to holiday here. In the 1960s it became a venue of wealthy playboys and filmstars, the 'St Tropez of the North'. That heyday is past but it remains a haunt of senior tycoons, politicians, editors, etc, seeking privacy. Sylt's history far pre-dates tourism: witness the 12th-century church at Keitum, and the Altfriesisches Haus, an old farmhouse now a museum of local lore and history.

The remorseless wind from the North Sea whips the clouds into odd shapes, causing shifting patterns of light, and this lends Sylt a special beauty. The North Sea coast has high dunes in the form of reddish cliffs, above a long and broad sandy beach. Coastal erosion is a serious problem but Sylt is a paradise for bathing and surfing, as well as for cycling, riding and jogging, and it attracts huge numbers of sport-lovers and health freaks, from all social classes – almost all of them Germans. It has nine separate resorts: Westerland is the biggest, but not the smartest. Of the others, Keitum is the prettiest, a showpiece full of boutiques, galleries and thatched cottages; Kampen is the trendiest, where bars and nightclubs try to keep alive the glory of the sixties. Kupferkanne, a former wartime bunker on the cliffs, is still popular as a disco and bistro, with a lovely garden-café.

▶ ▷ ▷   Oldenburg

A modern, spacious town with a new university and a river port linked to the North Sea by a tributary of the Weser, it is also the market centre of a rich farming region, noted for horse and cattle breeding. In the small water-girt Altstadt, agreeably closed to traffic, some handsome older buildings remain, notably the Gothic Lambertikirche and the 15th-century Lappan tower. The nearby Schlossgarten has splendid trees. Of the three museums, the Augusteum has paintings from the Worpswede colony (see page 77), the Landesmuseum, in the former ducal palace, contains works by Tischbein and interesting reconstructed farmhouse interiors and the natural history museum has displays of 2,400-year-old corpses which were preserved over the centuries in nearby peat-bogs.

Bad Zwischenahn, to the west, is one of the most fashionable of North German spas and a large summer resort, beside a big lake much used for watersports. The Johanniskirche is an exceptionally lovely church, with charming paintings on its wooden gallery, 16th-century frescos on its wooden ceiling and a fine painted altar. The well-kept lakeside gardens contain, curiously, an outdoor rural museum with a real windmill, old cottages and a superbly restored 17th-century red-brick farmhouse from the plain near by: humans and animals lived together in its one huge room.

▶ ▷ ▷ Osnabrück

Today heavily industrial, producing paper, textiles and metalwork, this town of 150,000 people is also strongly historical, a bishopric since 785. Here, and in Münster, the 1648 Peace of Westphalia was negotiated – in a room in the Rathaus now called the Friedenssaal (peace hall). The town has three fine old churches but is mostly modern. Curiously, its daily paper, the *Osnabrücker Nachrichten*, is renowned in Germany for its high-level political interviews and scoops in Bonn.

A fountain in Osnabrück, showing intricately detailed workmanship

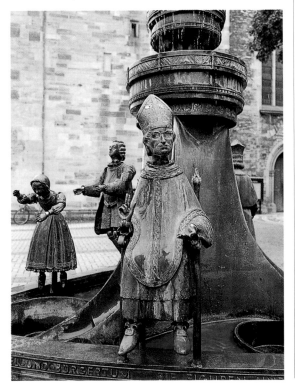

The Treaty of Osnabrück (1648) was part of the Peace of Westphalia, which ended the civil war of religion, the Thirty Years' War. Among the treaty's provisions was one that the bishopric of Osnabrück should be administered alternately by a Catholic bishop and a Protestant appointed by the Welf family.

The Friesians first settled in the Netherlands and on Germany's west coast in prehistoric times, driving out their Celtic predecessors. They were eventually conquered and converted to Christianity by Charlemagne.

▶ ▶ ▷ Ostfriesische Inseln (East Friesian Islands)

This is the eastern half of a long string of offshore islands that extends into Holland. Unsurprisingly the mainland of this part of Friesland is quite like Holland, with windmills, dykes and black-and-white Friesian cows.

The seven German islands, all inhabited and all reachable by ferry, are popular for summer holidays, thanks to their bracing climate and broad sandy beaches, backed by high dunes. Langeoog has an important bird sanctuary; the old church on Spiekeroog has mementos of the Spanish Armada; and Borkum and Juist are lively family resorts, good for horse-riding and sailing.

The most populous island and biggest resort is Norderney, 12km long. It is reached by regular ferries from Norddeich which will take cars but, to dissuade motorists, the fares are set high, so for a short stay it might be best to park at Norddeich, then go by foot or taxi on the island. Norderney is not a fashionable resort but it has an elegant-looking casino and lots of amenities. The little Fischerhaus museum gives details of the island's history and folklore; it has been a resort since 1797. The town and hotels are at its western end; the rest is rolling dune, much of it covered with wild grass or scrub. The interior has the feel of desolate moorland, with the sea out of sight behind the dunes, but the long sandy beaches are excellent. The insistent wind is a problem, as in other North Sea resorts; the beaches are neatly dotted with big hooded wicker chairs that give protection. As on Sylt, coastal erosion from the wind is a menace, and breakwaters are being built to check it.

▶ ▶ ▷ Schleswig

Starting life as a Viking trade centre, this attractive old seaport stands at the head of the Schlei, a long, low fjord, filled with small boats. Just to the south is a new museum of Viking culture and history, the **Haithabu**. The town's towering red-brick Gothic cathedral contains the beautiful Bordesholm Altar (1521); in the nearby Holm district you'll find little streets of old fishermen's cottages, a bit too neatly restored.

Continued on page 76

A cottage in Schleswig

The Hanseatic League

■ **At a time when Germany had yet to become a single political unit, its cities and merchant groups, benefiting from lively international trade, formed a wealthy and influential sector of medieval society. When these groups joined together they became an impressive force. The Hanseatic League was a union of 150 mainly north German towns, and the most powerful economic and political power of the region.....■**

Having started in the mid-14th century as a loose association for the protection of German tradesmen, the league created a single market which covered all trade between the North and Baltic Seas, a market which it fully controlled under the leadership of the town of Lübeck.

Top: The League's ships
Above: Danzig in the 16th century

Member cities followed the decisions of the Hansetag, the league's representative assembly. Any breaches of these decisions by a city would bring on the process of Verhansung, the boycott of the city by all others. No trade would take place with the boycotted city, nor could it use the league's common facilities abroad until it was brought back into line. By using such measures, the league managed to influence the economic and political development of each individual city as it wished. But this defect in the system – a loss of individual sovereignty – was compensated for by the enormous advantages of membership: no customs duties, common protection against competition, harmonised units of measurement, to name but a few. The parallels with the modern European Community and its Single Market, together with the possibility of introducing a single currency, are remarkable.

By 1370 the league was so strong it could afford to wage war against Denmark, in order to gain free access to the Baltic Sea. However, with the development in the 16th century of nation-states such as Sweden and Russia, the influence of the Hanseatic League began to wane and, by the time of the Thirty Years War, its useful life had ended.

Lübeck (above) and Danzig were both chief cities within the League

Close to Schleswig, the 8th-to 9th-century Viking settlement of Haithabu was a major trading centre.Trade in Scandinavian furs and marine ivory and slaves from east of the Baltic passed through the settlement on the way to Western Europe and Arab territories.

Continued from page 74

Schleswig's main glory is the moated white Scloss Gottorf (16th- to 18th-century), former home of the Holstein-Gottorp family which acceded to the Russian throne in 1762. It is full of riches – an ornate Gothic hall with a painted ceiling, a splendid Renaissance chapel with a carved ducal gallery and a Schleswig regional museum. Next door, do not miss the fabulous Nyddam Boat, one of the world's oldest surviving vessels, dating from the fourth century. This elegant 23m oaken craft, manned by 36 oarsmen, was found, well preserved, in the Danish marshes in 1863. In another room are the gruesome and unforgettable 'moor corpses' – skeletons of those who, 2,000 years ago, were tied up blindfold and left to die slowly on the marshes, as a punishment.

▶ ▷ ▷ **Stade**

This is a carefully restored old Hanseatic port near the Elbe west of Hamburg. A curious wooden crane, formerly used for unloading grain, stands by the narrow curving harbour, bordered with handsome old houses; best is the white and pink Renaissance one, number 23. Upstream is the Altes Land, a picturesque, pastoral district of cherry and apple orchards, best seen in blossom time. The old brick farmhouses, many thatched and timbered, are lovely too.

▶ ▷ ▷ **Visbek**

Down a woodland path, near this village south of Oldenburg, are some curious megaliths which Stone Age man created from granite boulders left by the Ice Age. One long double line of stones, forming a funeral chamber with adjacent 'sacrificial' table, is known as the Visbeker Bräutigam (bridegroom). Similar but smaller is the Visbeker Braut (bride).

To the west, at Cloppenburg, the Niedersächsiches Freilicht museum is one of the best of the many museums of traditional rural life, so popular in Germany today. In a big park, farmhouses and other old buildings from all over the *Land* have been rebuilt to look like a real old village. There's a tiny school, a church, a manor, live ducks and sheep in a pen, plus an old pub.

▶ ▶ ▷ **Wolfenbüttel**

A dignified old town, for three centuries this was the residence of the Dukes of Brunswick. Chief relic of that time is the great white Schloss, with a fine Renaissance tower and baroque additions. Handsome old half-timbered houses line the Stadtmarkt and Holzmarkt. The Herzog-August-Bibliothek, where the six million volumes include precious medieval illuminated manuscripts, was Europe's leading library in the 17th century. Its librarian in 1770–81 was the playwright Lessing, whose home next door is now a museum of his life and work.

▶ ▷ ▷ **Wolfsburg**

The principal factory of Volkswagen is here, founded by Hitler in 1938 to produce the 'people's car'. Today the firm employs 60,000 people in this town of 130,000 — a true 'company town'. The factory pioneered industrial

robots; you can go on a guided tour to watch these strange orange creatures performing precise balletic movements, as they assemble Golfs and Jettas.

▶ ▶ ▷ **Worpswede**

An intriguing village north of Bremen, Worpswede will fascinate art-lovers. In the 1880s it was colonised by a group of gifted young artists and writers from Berlin and Munich, who were drawn by the melancholy beauty of the moorlands. Later they left, and the odd houses they built began to crumble. Now they have been restored and Worpswede is trendily tourist. The museum has works by these artists, who were close to the pre-Raphaelites in ideas: Fritz Mackensen, Otto Modersohn, Paula Modersohn-Becker (the best), and the eccentric romantic poseur Heinrich Vogeler are all represented. The architect Bernhard Hoetger has left several off-beat buildings and sculptures, such as the Villa Mackensen, and the Kaffee Worpswede with its cheeky statuette of a grinning bonze – an Oriental Buddhist priest.

The old harbour in Stade

77

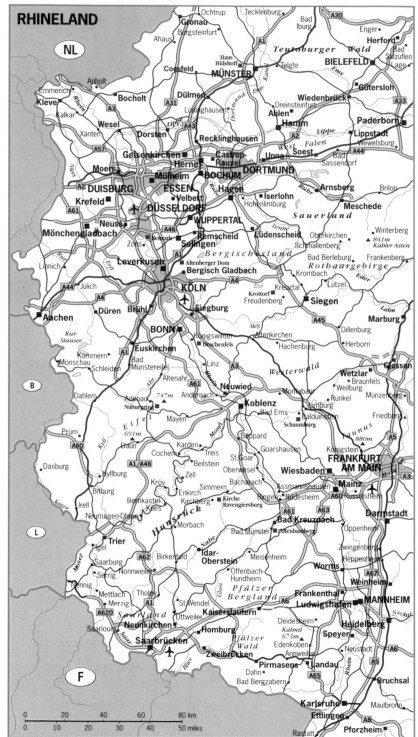

RHINELAND

NL

B

L

F

78

| 0 | 20 | 40 | 60 | 80 km |
| 0 | 10 | 20 | 30 | 40 | 50 miles |

This westernmost part of Germany focuses on the mighty Rhine and its tributaries, some of them scenic rivers in their own right – the **Mosel, Lahn** and **Ahr** – while others – the **Saar** and above all the **Ruhr** – have given their name to great industrial conurbations.

This is a region of contrasts. The Ruhr cities, comparatively new have their own identity and high cultural status, but none compares with the richness of 2,000-year-old **Köln** (Cologne), one of the great cities of Europe. Sophisticated **Düsseldorf** is the capital of the *Land* of Nordrhein-Westfalen, relaxed **Mainz** of the *Land* of Rheinland Pfalz, while **Bonn** – soon to be capital of nowhere – is vigorously looking for a new role.

To the west, the **Eifel** and the **Hunsrück** have some of Germany's loneliest and most rugged landscapes. To the southeast, the Palatinate wears a kindlier air, perhaps due to the warm red sandstone from which many of its buildings are made. Beyond the deep trench of the Rhine gorge are further uplands, of which the Sauerland is the most extensive, its rivers and woods a haven for the crowded populations of nearby cities.

To the north, the hills give way to the rich agricultural countryside of the **North German Plain**, where riverside poplars take the place of beech and spruce forests.

The region's vineyards are the world's northernmost, with delightful wine-villages and cheerful cellars and taverns. Life is taken less seriously here than in other parts of Germany, particularly in the Catholic cities of Cologne and Mainz, where exuberance knows no bounds during the pre-Lenten carnival period. This was the most Romanised part of Germany, with the Rhine forming the frontier of the Empire for centuries. Potent reminders of the Roman presence exist in **Trier**, with the greatest concentration of Roman monuments north of the Alps. French influence has been felt constantly, as kings, revolutionaries, an emperor, and republican governments all sought to push their frontier eastwards. The **Saarland** was only definitively returned to Germany in the late 1950s.

Today, no other part of Germany is so intimately tied to its neighbours across the unguarded frontiers, in links aptly symbolised by the joint administration of Nature Parks along the Belgian and Luxembourg borders.

Rüdesheim, seen from the Niederwald Monument

THE RHINELAND

The spa in Aachen's suburb of Burtscheid, with a water temperature of 76°C, is the hottest in Central Europe.

The Rathaus at Aachen

▶ ▶ ▷   **Aachen**

Germany's westernmost city, the country's gateway to many visitors from Great Britain and Belgium, Aachen deserves more than passing attention.

The city limits extend to the frontiers of both Belgium and Holland; a popular local excursion is to the Dreiländereck, the wooded hills where the three countries meet. In the late 9th century, Aachen's favourable location attracted Charlemagne (Karl der Grosse or Charles the Great), who built a fine palace here from which to rule the Frankish Empire which extended over most of Western Europe. Aachen's hot springs may have influenced the Emperor's choice; he was a notable bather. Though Aachen is still a spa town, with a good reputation in the treatment of rheumatism and similar afflictions, empire and palace have long since crumbled away, save for the Imperial Chapel. But what a chapel!

Forming the centrepiece of the city's Dom (cathedral), Charlemagne's octagonal chapel is one of the key monuments of Early Christian Europe. It has a two-storied arcaded gallery and is embellished with marble brought from Italy. The huge 12th-century chandelier hanging from its dome is one of the many treasures which make the cathedral such a storehouse of ecclesiastical art. In the light and airy 14th-century Gothic chancel is the Ambo, an extraordinarily ornate pulpit, as well as the gorgeous altar front known as the Pala d'Oro and the golden shrine containing Charlemagne's mortal remains. In the gallery is the imposing stone throne, on which some 30 German kings were crowned. An incomparable array of precious objects, crucifixes, chasubles, reliquaries fills the Schatzkammer (Cathedral Treasury).

The first German city to be taken by the Americans in late 1944, Aachen sustained severe damage, but enough of the Altstadt remains to remind us that this is an ancient and lived-in place. Appropriately for a spa town, water features prominently in the townscape; the light-hearted Puppenbrunnen (Dolls Fountain) has figures with movable limbs, while the thermal springs themselves are housed in neo-classical pavilions designed by the great Prussian architect Schinkel. Dominating the marketplace is the fortress-like Rathaus; its splendid Kaisersaal is decorated with 19th-century paintings of episodes in Charlemagne's career and houses reproductions of the Crown Jewels (the Habsburgs made off with the originals to Vienna).

Museums The city's museums are varied; the Suermondt-Ludwig-Museum has Old Masters as well as a medley of medieval sculpture, while the Sammlung Ludwig specialises in more modern work. The Couven Museum has well-appointed interiors showing how the comfortable classes lived in the 18th and 19th century. More unusual is the Internationales Zeitungsmuseum (International Newspaper Museum), commemorating Paul Julius von Reuter's early days, when his news service depended on carrier pigeons; its intriguing displays reveal how the news has been reported – or misreported – over the years.

▶ ▷ ▷ Bocholt

This cotton town close to the Dutch border is graced by two architectural landmarks. Dedicated to St George, the late Gothic hall church has a spectacular west window and a high altar with a fine 15th-century depiction of the Crucifixion by a Cologne master. The gabled and arcaded Renaissance Rathaus is one of the best preserved of its kind in the country.

Wasserburg Anholt stands right on the frontier with Holland 17km west of the town. The origins of this moated stronghold go back to the 13th century when the squat tower known as the Dicker Turm was built. The castle now houses the local museum.

▶ ▶ ▷ Bonn

For centuries, the old city of Bonn languished in pleasant provincial obscurity on the west bank of the Rhine at the point where the great river flows past the Seven Mountains into the flatlands around Cologne. In 1949, the committee assembled here to draft the constitution of the new West German state decided that the city should be made the capital of the Federal Republic. Far from the border with East Germany and with no metropolitan pretensions of its own which might upset more obvious candidates, such as Frankfurt, Bonn had the advantage of being within a short ferry ride across the Rhine from the Königswinter home of Konrad Adenauer, the elderly but immensely shrewd Chancellor of the newborn state.

Express trains were persuaded to stop, rather than steaming straight through, and an influx of civil servants and diplomats helped double the population. The notion that these arrangements were temporary and that one day Berlin would resume its rightful place as the nation's capital inhibited grandiloquent government building;

Relaxing at Aachen

Bonn's most famous son, Ludwig van Beethoven (1770–1827) left the place at the age of 22 for Vienna, never to return. He is commemorated by a statue, the Beethovenhalle (a modern concert hall), and an annual international festival. His birthplace contains an exemplary display of memorabilia, including, most poignantly, the ear trumpets which failed to breach the barrier of the composer's advancing deafness.

Parliament was housed in a teachers' training college, the Chancellor in the 19th-century Villa Hammerschmidt. By the 1970s, hopes for reunification were fading, and lumpy modern 'official' buildings began to transform the townscape. Some such are still being built, their future – like that of Bonn itself – in some doubt now that Berlin is to become the seat of government again. Look for the spectacular complexes housing the City Art Museum and the National Art and Exhibition Centre, the latter's 16 rusty columns symbolising the German *Länder*.

The government quarter extends southwards from the city centre, 2,000 years ago the site of a Roman fort defending the Rhine crossing. Much damaged in the last war, Bonn's old core still contains plenty of evidence of its long past. Prehistoric, Roman and Frankish remains are in the Landesmuseum, where the star exhibit is the skull of Neanderthal Man, found near Düsseldorf in 1856 (page 83). The late Romanesque/early Gothic Münster with its immensely tall central tower, airy interior and splendid cloisters, is one of the finest of many such churches in the Rhineland. The prince-bishops of Cologne preferred to reside in backwater Bonn rather than among the more rowdy citizens of their cathedral city; their contributions to the urban scene include the pink rococo Rathaus as well as the Residenz and the Poppelsdorfer Schloss, both part of the university.

Its setting is one of Bonn's great assets (its humid climate less so). The vast new Rheinauen Park links the city to the river and gives fine views of the Drachenfels and the Seven Mountains. Southward lies the old spa of Bad Godesberg with a particularly pleasant riverside promenade, while the very best panorama can be enjoyed from the terrace of the Godesburg, the ruined castle high above the town.

▶ ▶ ▶   Düsseldorf

Capital of Nordrhein-Westfalen, Germany's most populous *Land*, money-conscious Düsseldorf is the showcase in which the country's wealth is dazzlingly displayed. The city's skyline is dominated less by its numerous old churches than by such monuments of modern commerce as the coldly elegant Thyssen skyscraper. As well as the headquarters of many of the great Ruhr industrial concerns, Düsseldorf has also attracted numerous Japanese firms, which have made it the base of their overseas operations; the city's Japanese community is the largest in Europe.

Private affluence is balanced by a strong sense of civic pride, dating back to the city's rule by its Electors, the most notable of whom was Johann Wilhelm (1679-1716). Known affectionately as Jan Wellem, he laid out the spacious new districts beyond the Altstadt and attracted artists to the city; he is commemorated by a statue in front of the Renaissance Rathaus. Modern Düsseldorf is well endowed with parks, gardens and landscaped pedestrian areas which make it possible to stroll for hours across the city without crossing a road.

Theatre, music, opera and cabaret all thrive here, and the city's galleries are outstanding; the collection of Paul Klee paintings in the Kunstsammlung Nordrhein-Westfalen is the biggest in the country.

Excursions

Schloss Benrath, a sumptuous rococo palace in its fine park, is a favourite local outing. It was built in the mid-18th century by a French architect for one of Jan Wellem's successors.

The **River Wupper** snakes through a steep-sided valley to the east of Düsseldorf. Wuppertal is the string of industrial towns which form a linear city. They boast an outstanding collection of 19th and 20th-century German and French art in the Von der Heydt Museum, though this region is perhaps better known for its unique Schwebebahn, the overhead railway which has stitched its disparate communities together since 1901. Downstream, the valley is crossed by a more conventional railway line, carried 107m above the river on the Müngstenerbrücke, Europe's highest railway bridge. This links the timber-framed and slate-roofed town of Remscheid with Solingen, Germany's Sheffield, where the Klingenmuseum displays every possible kind of cutlery, from kitchen-knife to dueller's blade. Further downstream still, high above the river, is the spectacularly sited castle of Burg an der Wupper, housing the local history museum.

▶ ▶ ▷   The Eifel

Bounded by the Rhine, the Moselle and the country's border with Belgium and Luxembourg, the rugged Eifel is the northwesternmost of Germany's upland massifs. In spite of its proximity to great centres of population, its sweeping heights, vast forests and deep valleys offer endless opportunities for escaping the crowds.

The area's core is formed by the Hohe Eifel, composed of ancient volcanoes. Its highest point is the Hohe Acht, a basalt peak of 747m. The hills are pitted with strange circular lakes known as *Maare*, formed by violent volcanic explosions, which also left other curiosities in the shape of 'bombs' like the one near the little spa

Königsallee in Düsseldorf

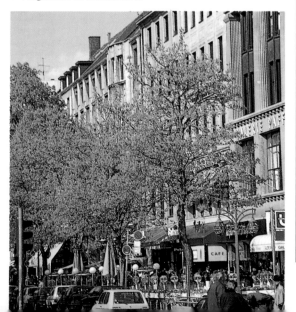

Writers, artists, and musicians have long been associated with Düsseldorf; the poet Heine was born here, Brahms, Mendelssohn and Schumann all found the atmosphere congenial, as did (in his own way) the ex-Messerschmitt pilot and postwar *enfant terrible* Josef Beuys (1986), whose felt and fat sculptures won international attention, if not always approval.

Düsseldorf brews an unusual beer, 'Alt', not unlike a pale ale, consumed in large quantities in the Altstadt. Echoes of the days when the city was no more than a riverside fishing village can still be picked up here, among the many bars, pubs, restaurants and discos which virtually guarantee a memorable night out.

The valley of the little Düssel river was a favourite retreat of the poet Joachim Neander, who gave it his name. The site of the cave where the skeletal remains of Neanderthal Man were found in 1856 is marked by a plaque. The famous skull is now in the Landesmuseum in Bonn, but there is a small museum here with displays on life 60 000 years ago.

About 17km south of Düsseldorf, on the west bank of the Rhine, is Zons, a fortified village built in the 14th century to control traffic on the river.

THE RHINELAND

The Ahr Valley in Eifel

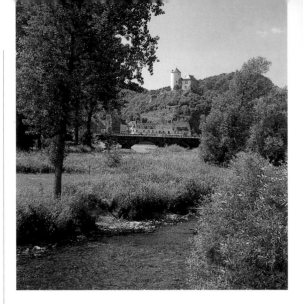

Bad Neuenahr
While ancient Ahrweiler has kept its town wall with towers and gates, the spa town of Bad Neuenahr is a 19th-century creation, dating from the discovery of medicinal springs here in 1861. Parks and gardens provide a manicured setting for visitors taking their cure and there is that characteristic feature of such places, a Spielbank (casino).

In a wooded setting on the edge of Mechernich-Kommern, the Rheinisches Freilichtmuseum (Rhineland Open Air Museum) is an extensive collection of carefully re-erected traditional buildings of the countryside, including wind and water mills and workshops as well as cottages and farmsteads

town of Daun. Perhaps the loneliest part of the Eifel is the Schnee-Eifel to the west, where cross-border Nature Parks merge with the Belgian and Luxembourg Ardennes. To the north is a 'Lake District', formed by the damming of the Rur and Erft rivers, and very popular with holidaymakers from across the Dutch and Belgian borders. More popular still is the pretty valley of the River Ahr, descending eastwards through a series of picturesque wine-villages to the Rhine.
An entire holiday could easily be spent in these attractive uplands, particularly by lovers of fresh air and exercise. Some of the Eifel's characteristic landscapes and little towns can be visited as an alternative to the Autobahn on the way southeast.

Monschau Overlooked by its medieval castle, and generally agreed to be the prettiest place in the Eifel, Monschau winds along the steep-sided valley of the River Rhur. Among its black and white houses stands the grand red-brick residence known as the Rotes Haus, its interior evocative of the comfortable life-style of its 18th-century proprietor, a dealer in the cloth for which the town was famous.

Bad Münstereifel With its walls still enclosing an intricate web of cobbled streets and alleyways, this is one of Germany's best-preserved medieval small towns. Castle remains guard one side of the valley, the buildings of the town's renowned spa the other, while the River Erft chatters alongside the main street. The best townscape is to be seen in the Orchheimer Strasse, where the high-gabled and intriguingly carved Windeckhaus forms a perfect composition with its neighbours.
On the lonely plateau to the east of the town is a great surprise – the utterly un-medieval structure of the Eifelsberg radio-telescope, the largest in the world.
The country road to the east drops down into the romantic valley of the River Ahr, a delightful miniature version of the Rhine gorge.

Altenahr A pretty little place, dominated by its castle ruin and with many inviting wine-cellars, Altenahr marks the western end of Germany's northernmost wine-growing area. Sheltered by the Hohe Eifel, the slatey slopes rising precipitously from the twisting river provide excellent growing conditions for vines. The local *Spätburgunder*, a 'velvety, noble wine', is reckoned by many to be easily the best of the country's otherwise rather undistinguished reds.

Maria Laach This splendid Benedictine abbey stands in what was once a remote setting beside the largest of all the volcanic lakes in the Eifel, the Laacher See. Founded in 1093, the great six-towered abbey church is one of the grandest and most harmonious Romanesque buildings in Germany. After the dissolution of the country's monasteries in 1802, its numerous art treasures disappeared, leaving the interior bare but dignified.

Schloss Bürresheim
The castle, southwest of Maria Laach, owes its exceptionally picturesque appearance to successive waves of building and rebuilding from the 12th to the 19th centuries.. The interior, unusually for Germany, is well furnished and there is an attractive formal garden with high hedges.

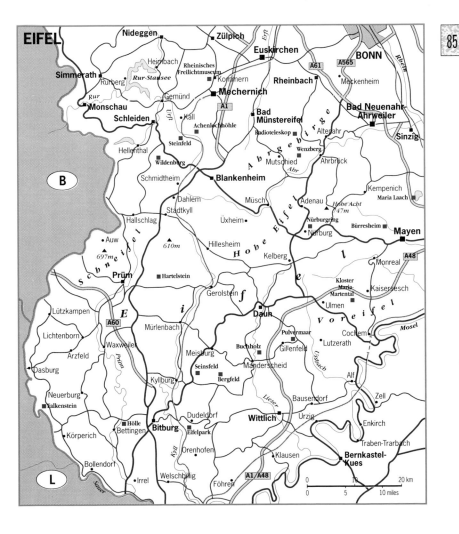

THE RHINELAND

Daughter of one of Kleve's dukes, Anne of Cleves (1515-57) became Henry VIII's fourth wife in 1539. Their marriage was intended to consolidate an alliance of Protestant rulers, but Henry took against the meek and unprepossessing 'Mare of Flanders' and had their unconsummated union annulled after only six months.

▶ ▷ ▷   Kleve (Cleves)

The last substantial place on the west bank of the Rhine before the Dutch border, Kleve (Cleves) is an ancient ducal residence whose Oberstadt (Upper Town) is built on the low hills rising over the flood plain of the great river. To the southwest is the vast forest tract known as the Reichswald, the scene of bitter fighting as the Allied armies prepared to cross the Rhine in early 1945. To the northeast stretch watery flatlands where the Rhine once wandered at will before being confined behind its present high embankments.

The medieval counts of Kleve eventually rose to the rank of duke, though their bid for even more enhanced status by marrying into the English royal family came to nothing (see panel). Though virtually destroyed in the last war, the town is still marked by their castle, the Schwanenburg, and by the fine parks and gardens they laid out.

Excursions

Emmerich, 9km east, is reached from Kleve by the country's longest suspension bridge. The brick-built port of Emmerich makes its living from the river and celebrates this long-standing connection in its Rheinmuseum.

Kalkar, 12km southeast, was famous in the late Middle Ages for its talented woodcarvers. This small town boasts a brick church with an astonishing array of fine altarpieces as well as a number of houses with stepped gables and a solid 15th century Rathaus.

Xanten, 27km southeast, was rebuilt after its near-destruction in early 1945. This is a neat little town which has conserved stretches of medieval fortifications (including the picturesque Kleve Gate) and a cathedral crammed with splendid art works. The town lies between two Roman settlements, civilian Colonia Trojana to the north, military Castra Vetera to the south. The civilian town is now an archaeological park, with thorough reconstructions of fortifications and buildings in an attempt to bring the days of Roman occupation back to life.

▶ ▶ ▶   Köln (Cologne)

With the twin spires of its glorious cathedral visible far away across the surrounding plain, this is one of Germany's great metropolitan cities, a centre of culture, arts and learning as well as industry and commerce.

First founded by the Romans in 33BC, 'Colonia' achieved city status under Emperor Claudius in AD40. Its importance at this time is reflected in the superb Dionysus Mosaic forming the centrepiece of the splendid modern Römisch-Germanisches Museum in the city's heart. By the Middle Ages, Cologne had become the largest city in Germany, with no fewer than 150 churches. The Altstadt is consequently huge, extending to the semi-circular Ring, a boulevard laid out along the line of fortifications demolished in the 19th century but still punctuated at intervals by the surviving city gates (Eigelstein Tor, Hahnentor, St Severins Tor).

The city suffered the RAF's first 1,000-bomber raid in 1942, and in the course of the war nine-tenths of the buildings in the centre were destroyed; their replacements may not always be of the highest architectural quality, but planners' retention of the ancient street pattern has helped maintain something of the spirit of 2,000 years of history.

Cologne's atmosphere is that of a city state, its strong local patriotism expressed in its own impenetrable *kölsch* (dialect). Its sociable people seem smaller and swarthier than the German norm, their enjoyment of malicious wisecracking best exemplified by the pot-bellied waiters serving the distinctive bitter beer (also called *kölsch*) in the numerous pubs and beerhalls. Local liking for a good time reaches its peak during Karneval,

In the 18th century an Italian resident distilled an astringent liquid from flower blossom. Intended originally as an aphrodisiac, the famous Kölnisch Wasser (Eau de Cologne) is more commonly used as toilet water.

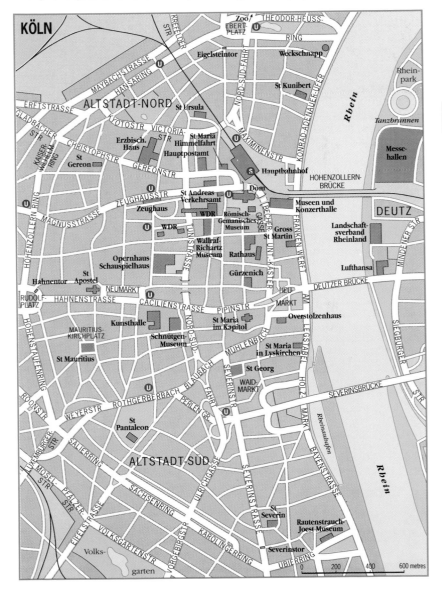

THE RHINELAND

The River Rhine and the cathedral at Köln

St Ursula
Daughter of a 4th-century British king, the virginal St Ursula is reputed to have been murdered in Cologne by rampaging Huns, along with 11,000 other Christian maidens. This spectacular end led to her beatification and commemoration in the city's coat of arms as well as in the church which bears her name.

the great pre-Lenten festival celebrated more boisterously here than in any other part of Catholic Germany. The revels unfold for several days (and nights!) around the seventh Sunday before Easter, starting on the Thursday with Weiberfastnacht when no man's tie is safe from scissor-wielding females, climaxing in the great parade of Rosenmontag (Rose Monday), and winding down with hangover suppers on Ash Wednesday. Merry-making knows few bounds – adultery over Karneval is considered unconvincing grounds for a divorce petition!

Most visitors probably get their first glimpse of Cologne from the hall of the main station whose high windows frame the cliff-like side of the cathedral. Walk out along the railway bridge (Höhenzollernbrücke) to savour the city's silhouette rising over the bustle of traffic on and alongside the Rhine.

The Dom (cathedral) itself is one of the world's great Gothic structures. Begun in the 13th century, it was completed only in the 19th, still in faithful accord with the intentions of its medieval architects whose original drawings had miraculously survived. Externally its sheer mass is relieved by the lace-like delicacy of its masonry, while the vast interior contains such incomparable works of art as the majestic golden shrine of the Magi, the 9th-century Gero Crucifix, the glorious 15th-century Cologne School altarpiece painted by Stefan Lochner and superb stained glass. A stiff climb up the south tower is rewarded by a fine panorama over the city centre.

The well designed pedestrian spaces characteristic of so many German cities invite exploration. To the southeast of the Dom, beyond the Römisch-Germanisches Museum, is the modern complex housing the Philharmonie, the central concert hall, as well as the Wallraf-Richard and Ludwig Museums with their major collections of German and international art. Not to be missed are the exquisite late medieval paintings of the Cologne School or the array of works by such early 20th-century masters as Dix, Beckmann, Kirchner and

Barlach. This is also a good place to ponder the Americana of the postwar Pop artists – Roy Lichtenstein and Andy Warhol.

Straying southwards is the Hohe Strasse, the city's main shopping street. Other streets and passageways lead Rhinewards into the core of the Altstadt centred on the Alter Markt and the14th-century Gothic Rathaus, with its Renaissance loggia. Before the completion of the Dom, the distinctive four-turreted tower of the Romanesque church of Gross St Martin dominated the skyline; completed in 1172, this is one of the city's several pre-Gothic churches, a grouping unique in Europe, each with its own special features. St Pantaleon, from the 10th century, is the oldest, St Gereon the most spectacular, with a superb delicately ribbed, ten-sided tower, the Decagon, while St Maria im Kapitol is richly furnished, with remarkable 11th-century carved doors. The best place to see religious art and furnishings is in the deconsecrated church housing the Schnütgen Museum; the squeamish should avoid the exquisitely carved *memento mori* (corpses in the last stages of decay).

Cologne continues to be a churchy place, many striking places of worship having been built this century, notably St Gertrud north of the Ring, or Neu St Alban to the west, with a dimly lit, highly atmospheric interior. Nearby is the Fernmeldeturm (Telecommunications Tower), 242m high, offering a vast panorama over city and surroundings. It rises over the Stadtgarten, one of the many fine parks of which the city is justifiably proud. On the far bank of the river, reached by cable car, is the Rheinpark, its centrepiece the Tanzbrunnen, a vast fountain above which floats a canopied dance floor.

Excursion

Altenberger Dom is about 17km northeast of Cologne among the lush woodlands of the hilly countryside known as the Bergisches Länd. This is no cathedral, but a former Cistercian monastery, one of the finest examples of Gothic architecture in Germany, restored in the last century. It is, unusually, worshipped in by both Catholics and Protestants.

Cafés in Köln

The Express feels its way and pushes the darkness along... Then suddenly the ground roars like a sea: we are flying, suspended, royally through air seized from the night, high above the current... Rushing like torches. – Ernst Stadler, *Journey over the Rhine bridge at Cologne by night*

89

Brühl, 14km southwest of Cologne, has Germany's largest theme park, Phantasieland, as well as the pleasure gardens from an earlier time which surround Schloss Augustusburg, the sumptuous Rococo palace of the Archbishops of Cologne. Often used for state receptions (and consequently liable to be closed to the public), this echo of Bavarian lightheartedness has an incredibly ornate staircase by the great South German architect Balthasar Neumann.

Germany's greatest writer came to Wetzlar as a young man to attend a session of the Imperial Courts. He fell, passionately, for a local girl, Charlotte Buff, already betrothed to another man, who subsequently killed himself. The experience of this tragedy was distilled by Goethe into *The Sorrows of Young Werther*, a key work of German Romanticism. Charlotte's house (Lottehaus) is now the museum of the sad affair, with many personal and literary memorabilia.

▶ ▷ ▷ **Lahn Valley**

Rising in the Rothaargebirge and flowing for much of its length through a wooded gorge, the Lahn winds past picturesquely sited castles, ruined like Balduinstein, or romantically rebuilt like Schaumburg and Braunfels, before joining the Rhine near Koblenz. The valley can be explored by car – but also along riverside footpaths and cycleways, by steamer, canoe and raft. The railway often hugs the river more closely than the road.

Each of the Lahn towns has a highly individual character. The classic spa town of **Bad Ems** was the favoured resort of Kaiser Wilhelm I; his statue stands in the immaculate riverside gardens. As well as haughty hotels, aristocratic Ems has a casino, an onion-domed Russian Orthodox church, and a cable-hauled railway to hoist the health-seekers up to the modern spa installations on the heights above the narrow valley.

Both Nassau and Diez, the latter with a high-walled castle, are associated with the Orange-Nassau dynasty. **Limburg** stands in a more open part of the valley. The town has won prizes for its careful conservation work and the results can be enjoyed among the picturesque timber-framed old houses of the medieval centre. Alleyways lead up to Limburg's cathedral, prominently positioned on a rocky spur overlooking the river. With its exterior repainted in the bright orange and white livery of medieval times, the cathedral is a fine example of the transition from Romanesque to Gothic. The cool interior has unique 12th-century wall-paintings, while the Diocesan Museum and Treasury house further ecclesiastical art objects.

The biggest castle along the Lahn was once the medieval Burg at **Runkel**; its rugged walls still rise imposingly over the old village with its bridge and weir. The stronghold at **Weilburg** is different altogether – an elegant Renaissance residence constructed by the

Top: the tranquil spa town of Bad Ems
Left: a quiet street in Limburg

Counts of Nassau. Ornate interiors are complemented by terraced gardens stepping down to the river, which almost encircles the spur on which castle and its dependent little baroque town are built. Boat traffic can take a short cut through the promontory via a 210m tunnel, the longest of its kind in Germany.

Wetzlar's industries make an array of products, of which Leica cameras may be the most famous. But this is an historic town too, for over 100 years the seat of the Law Courts of the Holy Roman Empire. Towering over the old houses that step down to the seven-arched bridge over the Lahn is the unfinished cathedral, a strange amalgam of Romanesque and Gothic.

▶ ▷ ▷ Mainz

Seat of the government of Rheinland-Pfalz, 2,000-year-old Mainz is endowed with most of the good things to be expected of a lively provincial capital: a cathedral, an archbishop's palace, an ancient university, museums, an attractive Altstadt... Its position on the banks of the Rhine and its exceptionally mild climate may explain its cheerful atmosphere; its great pre-Lenten Karneval is second only to Cologne's for high spirits, and there are more jollifications like Johannisnacht in March and a big wine festival in August/September.

The great red sandstone cathedral with its six towers looms over the largely pedestrianised city centre. Essentially Romanesque though with many later additions, it has a spacious interior containing the splendid tombs of its powerful prince-bishops. The Diocesan Museum off the Gothic cloisters houses some of the wonderfully sensitive sculpture of the mysterious medieval mason – the Master of Naumburg.

A short walk from the cathedral, the banks of the Rhine hold a medley of public buildings, ancient and modern, including the exuberant Renaissance-baroque Schloss housing the Römisch-Germanisches Zentralmuseum, though there are more spectacular Roman artefacts in the Landesmuseum near by. Start a stroll 'inland', through the Altstadt with its half-timbered houses and wine taverns, at the Marktbrunnen, the delightful Renaissance fountain. Perhaps the outstanding work of modern art in Mainz is to be found in the Stefanskirche; the church's stained glass, glowing with visionary intensity, is the work of the great Russian Jewish artist, Marc Chagall, who took as his theme 'Reconciliation'.

▶ ▶ ▷ Marburg

With half-timbered houses clustering around the castle high above the River Lahn, a great church dedicated to St Elisabeth, and a venerable university, Marburg seems to represent the very essence of medieval Germany..

The focal point of Marburg's Altstadt, particularly in university term-time, is the Marktplatz with its late-Gothic Rathaus and St George fountain. In this part of town, the steep streets are supplemented by stairways. One leads up to the Schloss, the residence of Elisabeth's descendants, the Landgraves. Built from about 1260 on, it has a three-storey Rittersaal (Knights' Hall) and houses part of the outstanding collections of the Universitätsmuseum (University Museum).

A window by Chagall in Stefanskirche, Mainz

A native of Mainz,Johannes Gutenberg revolutionised communication by elaborating the idea of printing using movable metal type, rendering the painstaking work of the medieval scribe obsolete at a stroke. Between 1452 and 1455 he printed some 200 Bibles, one of which can be seen in the fascinating Gutenberg Museum. Housed in the elegant Renaissance mansion known as the Römischer Kaiser, the museum has much else besides, including a replica of his original workshop with an operating press.

Hounded by a grasping partner, Gutenberg made no money from his discoveries, though in later life he was elevated to the petty nobility and given a pension by the Elector of Nassau.

While it's possible to drive the whole length of the signposted *Moselweinstrasse*, it's more fun to do at least part of the trip by steamer. Various permutations of car, boat and even train are possible and can be investigated locally (a good one is train from Cochem to Traben-Trarbach and return by steamer). Feet can be brought into play too, particularly for climbing up to the viewpoints offered by the many castles – intact or in ruins – along the route. Though extremely popular, the Mosel is less commercialised than its counterpart, the Rhine gorge. River traffic is less intense, and the railway runs along only one bank, often wandering off altogether. You can always get away from the crowds by taking to the footpaths or coming out of season – vineyards in winter have a special charm!

▶ ▶ ▶ **Mosel Valley**

Rising high up in France's Vosges mountains, the Mosel (Moselle) forms the boundary between Germany and Luxembourg before reaching the ancient city of Trier. From here to its confluence with the Rhine at Koblenz, the river cuts through the Hunsrück and Eifel uplands in extraordinary loops and bends. Every square metre of steep slope able to catch the sun is completely covered with a forest of poles to hold the vines steady in the rather slatey soil. The wines yielded are delicate, sometimes with a touch of sharpness which nicely matches the elegant green bottles in which they are presented.

It was the Romans who brought the vine to this northeastern extremity of their empire. A replica of the famous Roman wine-ship (the original is in the Landesmuseum in Trier) stands in the Peterskapelle in Neumagen, the town where it was found. Downstream is the charming double town of **Bernkastel-Kues**, renowned for its Doktor vineyard. Colourful Renaissance houses line the sloping market square with its fountain, while the odd-shaped Spitzgielbelhaus near by comes straight out of a picture book. Among the vines above the town stand the ruins of Landshut castle. On the far bank, Kues has a Gothic almshouse still serving its original purpose; in the chapel is a fine 15th-century altarpiece.

Another double town spanning the river is the resort of **Traben-Trarbach**, not particularly attractive, but a useful urban centre. Zell has two trademarks, the round tower forming part of its medieval defences and the Schwarze Katz, a legendary black cat, whose statue stands in the square. Fortified **Beilstein** is dominated by the massive ruined castle once owned by Chancellor Metternich. **Cochem**'s picturesque setting, with its romantically rebuilt castle crowning a vine-clad knoll, has inevitably made it one of the most-visited places along the river. Equally popular is **Burg Eltz**, a short distance up a deeply

The River Mosel at Zell

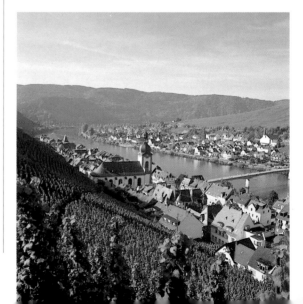

The 514km Mosel river rises in eastern France. For 34km it forms the border between Luxembourg and Germany; it then travels 242km in Germany, ending its course in the Rhine at Koblenz.

Cochem, with its romantic castle overlooking the Mosel river

wooded side valley. This is one of Germany's dream castles, its sheer walls rising spectacularly through the trees and capped by steep-pitched slate roofs and an array of turrets. The intimate interior is stuffed with medieval furniture.

Further castles follow, one at **Thurant**, two at **Kobern-Gondorf** before the river flows beneath the great autobahn bridge which marks the approach to Koblenz and the river's junction with the Rhine.

▶ ▷ ▷ Münster

The historic capital of Westphalia, Münster is a prosperous university city, proud of its strongly Catholic identity in an otherwise largely Protestant province. Its splendidly varied architectural heritage suffered badly in World War II, but local pride has expressed itself in the loving restoration and reconstruction.

The bustle on the Domplatz is presided over by the handsome, twin-towered cathedral, built in the early 13th century in the transitional style between Romanesque and Gothic. The interior is richly endowed with statuary, tombs and altars, and has a remarkable astronomical clock of 1540, with automata which bestir themselves daily at noon for the benefit of the assembled crowds. The foundations of the present building's 8th-century predecessor can be seen in the cloisters; beyond is the treasury, which includes in its precious objects an 11th-century jewel-studded reliquary of St Paul.

As well as the cathedral, Münster has other remarkable churches including the 14th-century Überwasserkirche with an elaborately decorated tower, and the Gothic Lambertikirche. The three cages hanging from its tower once held the corpses of leading Anabaptists who unwisely overthrew Church rule and proclaimed the millennium. This rash act precipitated the massacre of the townsfolk and their own execution by mercenaries in the pay of the bishop. From the Lambertikirche, the city's main thoroughfare, the Prinzipalmarkt, is lined with

MOSEL VALLEY

Pfälzer Wald (Palatinate Forest)

The splendid forests of this upland country, much of it protected as a Nature Park, form the most extensive area of continuous woodland in the whole of Germany. To the east rises the high ridge – the Haardt – which then falls steeply to the vineyards lining the Wine Road. To the south, linking with the Vosges in Alsace, are the sandstone hills of the Wasgau, weirdly weathered into castle-crowned cones, cliffs and spikes.

With its timber-framed houses and millstream, the little town of Annweiler is a good centre for exploring the southern part of the Forest. Within easy reach is a whole clutch of castles. Overlooking the town itself is 11th century Trifels, where Richard Lionheart was imprisoned in 1193. Splendid views from the chapel tower include the lesser castles of Anebos and Scharfenberg. To the southwest is Berwartstein, typifying the 19th-century Romantic view of what a crag-top castle should look like. Nearby Drachenfels, now a ruin, had no need of walls, so sheer were its natural defences. Dahn is the best place to investigate the effects of wind and weather on the soft local sandstone. Eroded into strange shapes, it also formed the building material for Dahn's three castles, all of them erected within the same perimeter wall.

the arcaded and gabled Renaissance town houses, (mostly rebuilt) of prosperous merchants. At the far end is the superb Rathaus, with a wonderful panelled chamber – the Friedenssaal (Hall of Peace); this is where the Peace of Westphalia was signed in 1648, bringing to an end the disastrous Thirty Years War.

Less flamboyant than its south German equivalent, the baroque style evolved by the local architect Johann Schlaun resulted in a number of notable buildings such as the aristocratic mansion called the Erbdrostenhof, the unusual circular Clemenskirche and above all the huge palace of the prince-bishops, of 1767–73, now the main building of the university.

Two museums merit mention. Medieval sculpture and old masters feature in the Landesmuseum, while rural Westphalia has been recreated on the banks of the Aasee, city's big recreational lake; the Mühlenhof museum is one of the longest established of Germany's open-air museums, with a fascinating collection of old buildings, water-mills, windmills, timber-framed farmsteads...

The agriculturally rich and rather damp area around Münster – the Münsterland – is famous for its country houses, most of them moated. Nowhere else in Germany is there such a concentration of fine rural residences, most still in private hands. Ranging from the grandiose 'Westphalian Versailles' at Nordkirchen to the more homely Haus Rüschhaus just outside Münster, these delightful 'Wasserburgen' could hold your interest for several days. Start at the 700-year-old Burg Vischering (near Lüddenhausen) which conveniently houses an informative Münsterland museum.

▷ ▷ ▷ **Nahe Valley and the Hunsrück**

The idyllic valley of the Nahe runs northeastwards through a series of gorges to join the Rhine at Bingen. The products of the picturesque vineyards along its course are reckoned by some to combine the best qualities of German wine, full-flavoured yet fresh. Further north is the rugged Hunsrück, a high plateau of upland farms and extensive forests of beech and spruce.

Quaint old houses stand on the bridge at Bad Kreuznach, a good starting point for a tour of the Nahe. This pleasant spa town comes complete with casino, Kurpark and strange timber structures known as 'salinas' in which brine is vaporised for the benefit of health-seekers.

Bad Münster is another spa, south of Bad Dreuznach on the B48. It is overlooked by the lofty castle called the Ebernburg. To the west of Bad Münster on the riverside road, and shouldering the river aside, is the mighty cliff known as the Rotenfels. Vines flourish in the narrow strip of soil at its base, as they do on the slopes around the attractive villages which succeed one another upstream.

At Odernheim the valley of the Glan leads to medieval Meisenheim, which has an array of picturesque old houses and a fine stone church. The road along the Nahe can be rejoined near the abbey ruins at Disibodenberg.

Beyond the health resort of Sobernheim, the village of

Monzingen has particularly fine half-timbered houses, among them the Altes Haus of 1589. Off the main valley to the north the castle ruin of **Dhaun** affords a splendid panoramic viewpoint, while **Kirn** is dominated by another ruin, the **Kyrburg**. The steep rock-face at the jewellery town of **Idar-Oberstein** is also crowned with fragments of old fortress, but the real curiosity here is the Gothic church set spectacularly into the cliff itself, and reached via 214 steep steps from the town's market square. Much is made of Idar-Oberstein's long history of mining, cutting and polishing precious stones of all kinds; after visiting the Heimatmuseum, the Edelsteinmuseum (museum of precious stones - incongruously housed in a skyscraper) and the Steinkaulenberg mine, you should know more about gemology than most!

Half-an-hour's drive north from Idar-Oberstein will bring you on to the Hunsrück Höhenstrasse. This fine highway was built in the interwar period to relieve unemployment and help open up this inhospitable area, then one of Germany's poorest and most isolated regions. More prosperous today, the Hunsrück is still a lonely place, drawing to it city-dwellers in search of truly rural peace and quiet.

The Nahe Valley, near Bingen

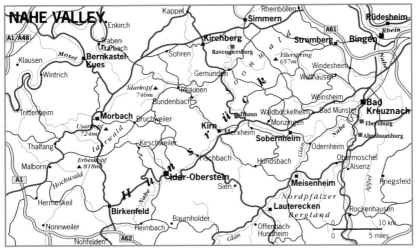

THE RHINELAND

The chairlift (top) and Drosselgasse (above) at Rüdesheim

▶ ▶ ▶ **Rheintal (The Rhine Valley)**

The Rhine invariably conjures up a string of clichés: a rocky gorge with a robber baron's castle clinging to each crag, vineyards growing precariously on the steep slopes, passengers waving at each other from the decks of white steamers, unbridled merriment in the cobbled streets of cheerful wine villages. Accurate enough, like all clichés, yet really only applicable to the Rhine Gorge, the relatively short Bingen-Koblenz stretch of the 1320km river. A mountain torrent near its source in the Swiss Alps and still pretty untamed at the great falls near Schaffhausen, for most of its length the Rhine is the watery equivalent of a many-laned motorway, a traffic artery tying together the canal and river systems of most of Europe. Below Lake Constance the river forms most of the boundary between Germany and Switzerland, turning north at Basle to flow across the broad plain between the French Vosges and the Black Forest. Its erratic past, when it wandered freely over its flood plain, means that most cities are built on one bank only or even a fair distance away like Strasbourg and Karlsruhe. Fed from the east by its tributaries the Main and Neckar, the Rhine near Mainz is up to 800m wide, a dimension it only attains again well below its gorge. Downstream from Bonn the river matures, carrying the heavy traffic of the industrial Ruhr across the flatlands linking northwest Germany and Holland to its ocean outlet at Rotterdam's Europoort.

Places of interest along the river (L = left bank, R = right bank) are described below from south to north (ie downstream), from Wiesbaden to Bonn.

Below Wiesbaden and Mainz the vines of the **Rheingau** (R) extend to the very top of the high south-facing slopes. Sheltered from the north by the wooded Taunus hills, this is one of Germany's most renowned wine-regions. It has its own scenic highway, the Rheingau-Riesling-Route, which hops up and down among the slopes taking in such pretty places as Kiedrich with a Gothic church full of fine furnishings. Eberbach Abbey has a splendid collection of wine presses, Johannisberg Castle a panoramic view. The Rheingau's 'capital' is Rüdesheim; the tavern-lined Drosselgasse alleyway

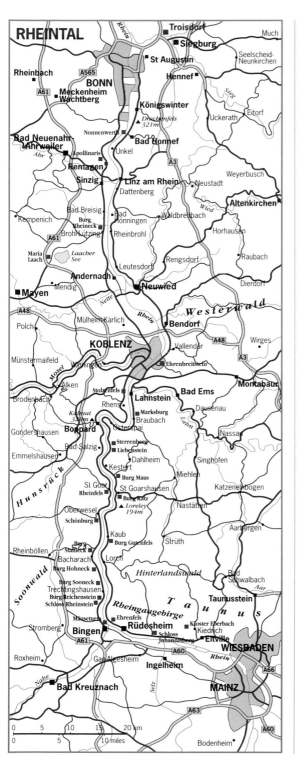

There are many ways of getting acquainted with the Rhine Valley's spectacular landscape. Even the hurried traveller should consider leaving the Autobahn and driving along one of the riverside roads. Until a new high speed railway line is built between Cologne and Frankfurt, expresses will continue to wend their way through the gorge, giving you the chance to view it in armchair comfort – but given the frequency of tunnels, it's especially dangerous to window-lean!. Motorists with time to spare can try the signposted scenic routes on either bank (Rheingoldstrasse on the left bank, Lorelei-Burgenstrasse on the right) which link minor roads together to give some of the best views down into the gorge. There's a high-level route for ramblers too, the Rheinhöhenweg, while cyclists can ride along sections of the old towpath. Remember that there are no bridges between Koblenz and Bingen, though there are plenty of ferries (some for foot passengers only). Perhaps the most relaxing and time-efficient mode of transport is to travel one way by boat (possibly downstream) and return by train (combined tickets available; see the helpful leaflet in English published by German Rhine Line).

THE RHINELAND

A particularly rugged section of the gorge leads to the high Loreley Rock, around which the river makes one of its more tortured twists. This legendary haunt of troglodytic dwarfs may be the place where the treasure of the Nibelungs lies buried, but it is known above all as the place from which a flaxen-haired temptress (the Lorelei herself) lured sailors to a watery grave with her seductive song (definitive version by the Romantic poet Heine). The danger to shipping is real enough; the river is forced by the rock to somehow squeeze itself through a gap only a third of its normal width and it is here that it reaches its greatest depth of 20 metres.

does its best to contain the high tide of tourists washing up from the landing stage. Genuine picturesqueness fights it out with the tackiness of take-aways and tawdry souvenir shops. High above the town stands the Niederwald memorial. Its massive figure of Germania celebrating the German unification which followed victory over the French in 1871 is in better shape than the crumbling remains of Ehrenfeld castle near by.

At the railway town of **Bingen** (L) the Rhine narrows and turns north to enter the gorge. This turbulent section is known as the Binger Loch (Bingen Hole), and still presents some difficulties to navigation, though the reefs of hard quartzite which once gave rise to dangerous rapids have long since been blown up.

A succession of strongholds now follows (L), Rheinstein, Reichenstein, Sooneck... Tiny fiefdoms, good defensive sites and the chance of extorting tolls from traffic on the river help explain the building of so many castles along the river. Many now stand in ruin, while most others were over-zealously restored in the 19th-century rush to recreate a more than medieval Middle Ages, a mania which went to the lengths of embellishing railway tunnels with turrets and battlements.

The view from the café at Boppard

Standing guard in the stream at Bingen is the 13th-century Mouse Tower. Legend has it that this is where Bishop Hatto of Mainz was eaten alive by mice in just retribution for a variety of misdeeds (hoarding grain in time of famine, burning bands of beggars to death...).

Attractive slate-roofed **Bacharach** (L) has its fortress too, Burg Stahleck, now a youth hostel. Towers and ramparts still protect this attractive little place; its main enemy is now the railway roaring past on its embankment. It's touristy to be sure, but there's lots to see along its cobbled streets and around the pretty market place.

Kaub (R) is overlooked by Gutenfels Castle, where the lords continued to exact tribute from passing traffic until well into the 19th century. Their instrument for doing so was the 14th century Pfalz, the extraordinary white toll-castle standing ship-like in the stream. **Oberwesel** (L) is dominated by verticals – the Ochsenturm near the waterfront, the red tower and slate steeple of the Liebfrauenkirche (Church of Our Lady), and the keeps and ramparts of Burg Schönburg high above.

St Goar (L) is overlooked by Rheinfels, a city-sized castle which French Revolutionaries did their best to demolish, without however quite succeeding. Burg Katz (Cat Castle) above **St Goarshausen** (R) can't match Rheinfels for sheer size; it was built in the late 14th

century by the Count of Katzenelnbogen to outface his territorial rival, the Bishop of Trier, whose own fortress just downstream he disdainfully nicknamed Burg Maus (Mouse Castle). Beyond is another brace of castles, Sterrenberg and Liebenstein (R), named the Warring Brothers after a 14th-century family feud.

As befits its origins – it was founded by the Romans – **Boppard** (L) is the most substantial place along the gorge, with two fine churches, remains of Roman and medieval defences, and a Heimatmuseum in the Archbishop's Castle. The town turns an attractive face to the Rhine; its long promenade dates from the 19th century when it first became popular as a place of retirement and refined tourism. Hotels abound, together with taverns dispensing the produce of the big Bopparder Hamm vineyard. Boppard is a good starting point for river trips and for excursions 'inland' as well; a branch railway winds up through the woods to the rugged Hunsrück region, or there is a chair lift up to the famous Vierseenblick viewpoint.

Old-fashioned **Rhens** (L) and **Braubach** (R) are both worth a visit. High above the latter is the imposing silhouette of Marksburg, the only medieval castle to have escaped ruin or wholesale restoration, and consequently able to give a truly authentic feel of life along the medieval Rhine. **Stolzenfels** (L), opposite Marksburg, is one of the more thoroughgoing efforts at making a ruined castle better than new.

The city of **Koblenz** has made the most of its position at the confluence of the Rhine and Mosel since Roman times. Four-fifths flattened in World War II, the town is still worth a stroll, starting perhaps at the Deutsches Eck, the promontory between Rhine and Mosel. A massive masonry plinth once carried a statue of Kaiser Wilhelm I, now controversially awaiting reinstatement. The riverside promenades enfold the old town with its

The Burg Stahleck, overlooking the Rhine

THE RHINELAND

In early 1945, the Ludendorff railway bridge at Remagen was the only bridge to survive the German defenders' attempts to blow up all the Rhine crossings. Rushed by a company of infantry from the American 9th Armoured Division, the bridge resisted bombing, shelling, attack by V2 rocket and frogmen, for 10 days, before dropping into the river with acute metal fatigue. By this time it had enabled several divisions to establish a bridgehead on the far bank of Germany's last natural barrier to invasion. It has not been rebuilt, though the abutment on the left bank houses a small Peace Museum.

Siegfried, the hero of the Ring saga (Nibelungenlied), is associated with the Drachenfels. Legend has it that he killed a dragon that lived on the rock, and bathed in its blood. This made him invincible, except for an area between his shoulders where a leaf had fallen while he bathed.

Koblenz, where the Rhine and the Mosel meet

two fine twin-towered churches, Romanesque St Kastor and the Liebfrauenkirche. Crowning the heights on the far side of the Rhine is the vast fortress of Ehrenbreitstein, an impressive setting for the August firework extravaganza – 'The Rhine in Flames'.

Between Koblenz and Bonn the riverside scenery is perhaps slightly less spectacular than in the gorge proper, but more varied and equally interesting. Riverside towns, all of them worth disembarking for, include **Andernach** (L), Roman and medieval, **Linz** (R) with many cheerfully coloured half-timbered houses, and **Sinzig** (L), with a perfect example of a Rhineland Romanesque church. High above Remagen (famous for its bridge) stands a virtual scale model of Cologne Cathedral, the pilgrimage church dedicated to St Apollinaris. Downstream, the river divides to flow past Nonnenwörth (Nuns Island), overlooked by the ruins of **Rolandsbogen** (L), supposedly built by the paladin Roland to give him an occasional glimpse of his fiancee who turned nun on the (false) news of his death, commands a fine panorama of the old volcanic hills on the far bank collectively called the Siebengebirge (Seven Mountains). These myth-encrusted heights have long furnished the stuff of fairytales and legends, the most potent story being that of the dragon that met its end at the hands of Siegfried; today the 'castled crag of Drachenfels' (Byron) is Europe's most popular summit, climbed by 3 million visitors every year (on foot or by rack railway). Walkers can try to escape the crowds among the lovely woodlands of these miniature mountains with their 30-odd (not seven) peaks, many of them topped by castle ruins. At their base lie the riverside resorts of **Bad Honnef** and **Königswinter**, the latter with the Konrad Adenauer Museum. This is housed in the former residence of Federal Germany's first and doughtiest Chancellor, whose liking for his home ground seems to have borne some relation to the choice of Bonn – just downstream – as the country's provisional capital.

FOCUS ON *Wine*

■ **Germany's 11 main wine-growing areas follow the valleys of the Rhine and its tributaries, Mosel and Main, Nahe and Neckar; the former GDR has some little-known vineyards around Naumburg and Dresden.** The mild climate, and 2,000 years' expertise – the Romans introduced the vine to these parts – means that these vineyards are further north than any other major vineyard, yielding some of the world's greatest (and most expensive) wines. .....■

Most German wine is light, largely from the Riesling, Müller-Thurgau and Silvaner grapes, but about one-eighth of the total production is red, little known abroad but much appreciated at home.

Wine production has created some spectacular landscapes. The need to capture as much sunshine as possible explains the remarkable terracing on the steep sides of the valleys, where even the most inaccessible south- or west-facing slope is cultivated. Good conditions for the vine favour fruit production, too, and some wine-producing areas (Pfalz, Main, Baden) are glorious with blossom in spring. Wines are always best tasted where they are made, but nowhere more so than in Germany, particularly at vintage and festival times.

New tastes German wines are traditionally sweet, but recent hankering after a more 'sophisticated' taste has encouraged a range of *trocken* (dry) or *halb-trocken* (medium-dry) wines. Categorisation and labelling is strictly regulated, producing useful information about the area of origin and standard of a particular bottle. A *Deutscher Tafelwein* (German table wine) is a pleasant, unpretentious product from one of five main areas. A *Qualitätswein* (quality wine), of a higher standard, must be characteristic of both grape type and one of the 11 main regions. A *Qualitätswein mit Prädikat* (quality wine with distinctive features) has special attributes; the grapes must be fully mature and the wine have a 10 per cent alcohol content without added sugar. All wines within this category (beginning with those designated *Kabinett*) come from one district. The very best wines are those made with ripe and over-ripe grapes, selected specially, either in the vineyard (*Spätlese, Auslese*) or in the vat room (*Beerenauslese, Trockenbeerenauslese*); the last-names is the summit of German wine culture, made from raisin-like grapes affected by the mould unappetisingly known as 'noble rot' and picked as autumn expires. A rarity is *Eiswein* (ice wine), based on the intensely sweet liquor yielded by grapes frozen by the first frosts of winter. *Sekt* (sparkling wine), the best made as carefully as any champagne, should undoubtedly be tried.

Only a fraction of Germany's wine is produced by the red grape – but red wine is well liked within Germany

THE RHINELAND

Sauerland and Rothaargebirge

Little known abroad, these green hills make a wonderful playground for the cities of the Rhine and Ruhr. Consisting of forested ridges broken by sometimes gorge-like valleys, the area is an important water-gathering ground, with many reservoirs providing endless opportunities for watersports enthusiasts. Outdoor life isn't confined to one season: the chief resort, Winterberg, has probably the best winter sports facilities north of the Alps.

The hills are attractive rather than spectacular, the more or less continuous forest cover making for a certain monotony. The most comprehensive view is from the bare summit of the Kahler Asten (841m) in the Rothaargebirge (Redhead Heights), the easternmost of the four Nature Parks making up the area. With abundant ores and minerals beneath the surface, wood for fuel and rushing streams for power, the valleys attracted metalworkers long before the Ruhr was industrialised. Some spots have the dismal air of a workplace past its prime, but elsewhere the longstanding industrial tradition has been turned to advantage, with good examples of industrial archaeology. The building tradition is a distinctive one, with many fine old timber-framed and whitewashed houses under steep slate roofs making a harmonious picture against the invariably green background. Few places could be described as particularly picturesque but there are sturdy upland villages around the Kahler Asten (Nordenau, Oberkirchen, Grafschaft...), and most of the towns have some features of interest – such as Altena dominated by its massive castle.

▶ ▷ ▷ The Ruhr

Named after the river running along its southern boundary to join the Rhine near Duisburg, Germany's 'Kohlenpott' or Black Country is still Europe's greatest industrial agglomeration, though coal and steel are no longer as important as they once were. Population, though still an impressive 5.5 million, has declined – spread over a strange combination of varied settlements, ranging from such great cities as **Essen** and **Dortmund** to picturesque little riverside places like **Kettwig**. As well as industrial sprawl, there is attractive countryside, especially along the often wooded banks of the Ruhr itself, with a series of artificial lakes, and the romantic crag-top castle at **Blankenstein**.

The Ruhr was never a continuously built-up area, and sensible planning has ensured that the whole conurbation is now interspersed with green spaces, threaded by footpaths and cycleways which connect city centres with splendid new parks (like Essen's Grugapark) and with the open countryside.

It is still industry which characterises the scene, and most visitors are there for business rather than pleasure. Urban pleasures are plenty, however, and should not be neglected. Each city proclaims its own identity and boasts an enviable array of cultural facilities. Galleries abound, foremost among them the Museum Folkwang in Essen, with superb collections of 19th- and 20th-century painting. **Recklinghausen** has a rarity, a museum devoted almost entirely to icons. **Bochum**'s modern wedge-shaped Städtisches Schauspielhaus (City Theatre) enjoys an international reputation for its classical and avant-garde productions.

Bochum's Bergbaumuseum (Mining Museum), with its excellent displays and its 2.5km of underground galleries, is outstanding, and the city also has an Eisenbahnmuseum (Railway Museum). Industrial history can be enjoyed in the open air too, notably in the Muttental near **Witten**. Here there is a Bergbauhistorischer Rundwanderweg (Mining Heritage Trail), featuring horse-operated pithead gear as well as the chapel where the miners gathered to pray and be counted before descending into the perilous depths.

With the digging of coal went the drinking of beer, and brews evolved to slake the miners' thirst taste just as good today, with a more distinctive character than their Bavarian counterparts. Some, like Dortmunder Union, travel the world, while others, of no less quality, remain a local secret (willingly shared with visitors!).

▶ ▷ ▷ Saarland

Like the Mosel, the Saar rises in the Vosges Mountains in France, joining the larger river just above **Trier**. It has given its name to Germany's smallest *Land*. Long disputed between Germany and France, and still with a Gallic air about it, the Saarland and its capital, **Saarbrücken**, look to the future rather than back to their grimy past of rustbelt industries based on coal and steel. Thus while Saarbrücken makes the most of its definitely limited architectural heritage (18th-century Schloss and Rathaus), it promotes itself as a business and cultural centre, and is cultivates its 'green' image. It celebrates

Saarbrücken

this – and the healing of old rifts – in the Deutsch-Französischer Garten (Franco-German Park).

Industry extends downriver to **Saarlouis**, founded by Louis XIV as one of the fortresses consolidating his hold on France's eastern frontier; the town's market square still has the air of a parade ground.

Below **Merzig** the valley narrows and begins to run through a wild, spectacular defile. **Mettlach** is an important centre of the ceramics industry, part of which occupies the palace-like buildings of the 18th-century Benedictine Abbey. The viewpoint at **Cloef** overlooks the great loop in the river – the Saarschleife. Downstream from **Serrig**, scrub and woodland give way to vines, and from here onwards the valley takes on an attractive Mosel-like character; vineyards climb the steep slopes, yielding lively wines which are dispensed in the taverns of such villages las Ayl and Ockfen, Wavern and Wiltingen. Centre of this little wine region is 1,000-year-old **Saarburg**, with a castle and a stream dropping precipitously past houses and vineyards.

The countryside between Saar and Mosel was much favoured by the Romans. Among the 50 or so villas which have been excavated, the one at Nennig (19km west of Mettlach, overlooking the Mosel and the Luxembourg border) has the largest mosaic floor north of the Alps, with scenes of the hunt and of gladiators.

Other extensive Roman remains, with reconstructions of original buildings, can be seen in the Römisches Freilichtmuseum Schwarzenacker, a big open air museum near Homburg east of Saarbrücken. To the north, **Ottweiler** has a carefully conserved Altstadt and St Wendel, a three-towered church, while near **Nonnweiler** is the Hunnenring, the spectacular remains of a Celtic fortified settlement. A world away from the industries of the southern Saarland are the vast woodlands of the Hochwald, rich in deer and wild boar.

Drive **Route north from steelmaking Siegen to medieval Soest**

The old core of Siegen with its Schloss sits on a spur of land overlooking the Sieg. Rubens was born here and there are several of his paintings in the castle's Siegerland museum.

To the northwest Freudenberg's black and white houses step harmoniously up the hill. Beyond Olpe is the largest of the region's lakes, the Biggesee. The landscape varies from rocky (at Attendorn) to industrial (around Rönkhausen), to grandiose in the Lenne Mountains.

To the west of the Sorpe dam is the Luisenhütte, Germany's oldest blast

furnace, dating from 1732. Arnsberg, an ancient centre of administration, rises in tiers over the River Ruhr. Like the Sorpe and Eder dams, the Möhne dam was attacked by the RAF on the night of 16–17 May 1943. After five attempts, the masonry wall of the dam, 34m thick at its base, was breached, flooding a vast area and disrupting water supplies to the armament industries of the Ruhr. Long since repaired, the dam holds back a 10km lake for the pleasure of watersports enthusiasts (north shore) and birds (south shore).

Soest is approached from the south across the Kassel-Ruhr Autobahn.

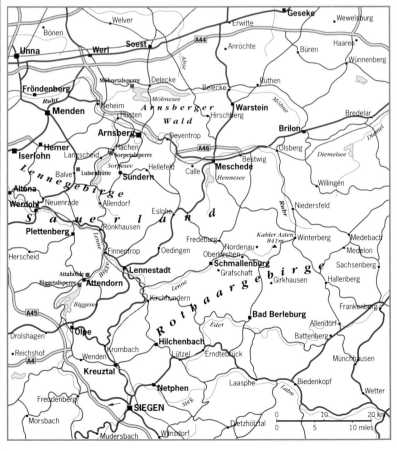

*Old buildings at
Soest*

▶ ▶ ▷   **Soest**

In the Middle Ages Soest was the most important city in
Westphalia, making good use of its position on the
Hellweg (the ancient highway running right across
northern Germany) to trade with Novgorod and Milan,
Bruges and London. Having escaped the industrialisation
which befell Dortmund, its old rival, Soest still wears an
attractive medieval air, with many redroofed and timber-
framed housed lining the labyrinthine streets behind the
surviving ramparts.

Stroll in any direction from the Marktplatz and take in
some of the little city's array of fine places of worship.
Near the baroque Rathaus stands a sturdy pair of
Romanesque churches, each with an impressive
westwork, topped, in the case of the St-Patrokli-Münster
by a formidable tower. The Petrikirche has frescos
attributed to a local master of medieval times, Konrad
von Soest, who also painted the altar in the nearby
chapel dedicated to St Nicholas.

Reflected in the waters of the pretty little lake – the
Grosser Teich – are the twin spires of the Gothic
Wiesenkirche (Our Lady of the Meadows). The stained
glass of the splendidly light interior includes a depiction
of the Last Supper with typical Westphalian
refreshments on the table – ham, beer and
pumpernickel, the local black rye bread and Steinhäger,
the local schnapps. On rising ground near by is St Maria
zur Höhe (Our Lady of the Heights) with original
Romanesque wall paintings.

Soest's attractive ambience seems to have drawn
artists; the work of two local men, Heinrich Aldegrever
(a follower of Dürer) and Wilhelm Morgner (a
contemporary of the Expressionist Emil Nolde) is shown
in the modern Wilhelm-Morgner Haus. The municipal
museum is in the 16th-century Burghof, attached to
which is a real rarity, a town house dating back to the
12th century.

THE RHINELAND

First established by the Celtic Treveri peoples, Trier was called Augusta Treverorum in 15BC, becoming one of the most important Roman cities north of the Alps. With a population of 80,000 – close to today's total – it flourished as an Imperial residence and capital of the western part of the Empire. Emperor Constantine made it Germany's first bishopric. By the Middle Ages, its prince-bishops were among the most powerful of German rulers – but the city's most influential son, for good or ill, was Karl Marx, born here in 1818.

Ancient Trier

▶ ▶ ▷ **Trier**

Trier, situated among the vineyards of the Mosel valley close to the Luxembourg border, is probably the oldest city in Germany. Its heritage of buildings spanning two millennia makes it irresistible for visitors.

Start exploring Trier's compact centre at the massive Porta Nigra, the biggest and best preserved Roman gateway in Europe, so named because of the blackened appearance of the huge blocks of limestone from which it is made. Its ingenious construction as well as its sheer scale foiled all attacks by besieging armies. In the Middle Ages it was converted into a church in honour of St Simeon; the nearby monastery bearing his name has a unique, delightful courtyard with two-storey cloisters.

The traffic-free Simeonsstrasse leads to the Hauptmarkt, with an ornate Renaissance fountain as its focal point. On the rise to the east is the huge cathedral, begun by Constantine but predominantly Romanesque with a baroquified interior.

Part of Constantine's great Imperial palace, the brick-built Konstantinsbasilika, survives as an awesome and austere Protestant church; apart from the Pantheon in Rome it is the biggest enclosed space to survive from the days of antiquity. Next door, in total contrast, is the light-hearted strawberry and vanilla façade of the rococo Prince-Bishop's Palace; its formal garden extends south to Trier's third great Roman monument, the Kaiserthermen (Imperial Baths). In a better state of preservation are some of the Roman artefacts in the Landesmuseum, among them the famous stone Wine Ship with its grinning oarsman.

Trier's further delights include a Roman 20,000-seater amphitheatre, the piers of a bridge over the Mosel, the Bischöfliches (Episcopal) Museum, the medieval interior of St Matthias Church, St Paulin Church by Balthasar Neumann, and modern Karl Marx Haus.

The Weinstrasse

■ **At the foot of the Haardt Mountains forming the eastern rim of the vast Palatinate Forest lies a cheerful, sun-drenched countryside which produced fine wines for the Romans. Today the delightful wine towns and villages of the Rheinpfalz are linked by one of Germany's best known touring routes, the Deutsche Weinstrasse, the Wine Road. Some 80km long, it links Bockenheim in the north to the border with Alsace in the south. .....■**

Rheinpfalz wines are made from a variety of grapes; the whites span the whole quality range from everyday table wines to the most exquisite *Trockenbeerenauslese*. Reds are produced, too, from the Portugieser grape, but account for only one-tenth of total production. No-one should miss tasting the wines offered in traditional vintners' houses opening off cobbled village streets.

Every place along the route has something special to offer: charming, half-timbered or mellow red sandstone houses; the remains of medieval fortifications; a ruined castle on a hill... The landscape gives continual pleasure, too, with ever-changing views of hills and broad plains. The benevolent climate means that not only vines, but other southern plants also thrive, such as fig, almond and chestnut trees, tobacco and maize. Kallstadt is proud of its local speciality, Saumagen (sow's belly in wine – give it a try!). Bad Dürkheim celebrates the vintage with Germany's biggest wine festival, the Wurstmarkt. Deidesheim has one of the best arrays of restaurants and inns, including the oldest tavern in the Palatinate. Medieval Neustadt, with its viticultural institute, is the region's miniature metropolis, while nearby Hambach Castle is where Germany's black-red-gold tricolour was raised by patriots for the first time in 1832. There are stunning panoramas from the Kalmit summit (673m), a short way into the hills, or from Bavarian King Ludwig I's summer residence, Schloss Ludwigshohe. The fantastic turrets and ramparts of another castle, Madenburg, loom over Eschbach. Beyond the resort of Bad Bergzabern, the route's terminus is marked by the huge Weintor gateway.

Weinstrasse vineyards

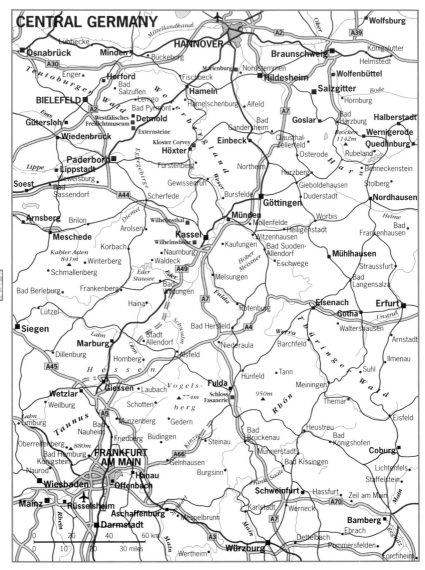

The Germans tend to keep the charms of Central Germany to themselves. Only a handful of towns, such as **Hameln** (Hamelin), with its Pied Piper fable and spectacular Weser Renaissance houses, are on the international tourist circuit. Although it has none of the drama of the Alps, it can be rewarding making your own discoveries in the numerous attractive small towns and rolling, forested uplands. **Hessen**, crossed by the Main and with **Frankfurt** as its chief city, was founded by the Americans as an administrative centre after World War II, and it is very much the centre of Germany. It did, however, exist long before the Americans came along, although it was fragmented along geographical and religious lines. In 1866 Hessen was incorporated in the

Alsfeld's town square, with the Rathaus in the background

Kingdom of Prussia and five years later became part of the Greater German Reich.

While Frankfurt, banking capital of Germany, remains the heart of the country's economic wealth, other towns, notably **Kassel** in north Hessen, generate enormous wealth from industrial output. Not far away from the urban landscapes of the 20th century are reminders of slower-moving times in old towns such as **Marburg** and **Alsfeld**. For lovers of the countryside , the **Vogelsberg**, a plateau created by a volcanic eruption 30 million years ago, is a little-developed area of hills and forests. But best of all, this is the land of the Brothers Grimm, whose often chilling and disturbing tales evoke a landscape of forests, rivers, lakes and castles. The region stretches from **Göttingen** up into the **Weserbergland**. The River Weser, one of the loveliest rivers in Germany, is flanked on both banks by the green hills of the Weserbergland which rise to a height of some 500m. It is difficult to imagine this region 500 years ago, when it was the centre of battle, and generals made it their meeting point to discuss their strategy. **Hanau**, near Frankfurt, where the Grimm Brothers were born, is about two hours from Göttingen and it's from here that the **Deutsche Märchenstrasse** (Fairy Tale Road) begins, continuing on to the coastal town of **Bremerhaven**. The **Harz** mountains comprise the highest ground in the region. Once harshly divided by the East-West German border, they now offer some good opportunities for discovering the lesser-known Germany.

Alsfeld: door detail

▶ ▶ ▷ Alsfeld

Set amid the rolling wooded Vögelsberg hills, Alsfeld is a picturesque old town with some fine half-timbered Renaissance buildings. It is set on the uppercourse of the River Schwalm, where the folk traditions inspired the Grimm brothers. At summer festivals girls still wear the local red folk-dresses. Outside the Walpurgiskirche is a fountain with a figure of a goosegirl in the style of costume worn by Little Red Riding Hood.

In the Marktplatz the tiny, quaint Rathaus (1516) stands above arcades where markets were once held. Opposite is the Renaissance-style Hochzeithaus built for weddings as its name implies. Fine examples of baroque architecture can be seen in the Rittergasse, notably the Neurath Haus at number 3 and the Minnigerode Haus at number 5. In Hersfelderstrasse, numbers 10 and 12 are among Germany's oldest half-timbered buildings.

▷ ▷ ▷ Bielefeld

This big industrial town has manufactured linen since the 16th century. Today it is also a centre for engineering, electronics and food-processing. Of the two museums of interest, the Kunsthalle has some German expressionist works (Beckmann, etc), and sculptures by Rodin, Moore and others; the Bauernhaus Museum is devoted to traditional farm life.

Herford near by, an old Hanseatic town, has a late Romanesque Münster and a number of Gothic churches; of these, the Johanniskirche has notable 17th-century woodwork and stained glass windows. **Gütersloh** (pop. 82,000) contains the headquarters of Bertelsmann, the world's largest publishing firm, and is a true company town, swarming with printers and editors.

▶ ▷ ▷ Darmstadt

This otherwise dullish industrial town is best known as the heartland of the *Jugendstil* (art nouveau) movement in the early 1900s. An artists' colony was established on the low hill of Mathildenhöhe, and their *Jugendstil* buildings still stand there (see panel): the Ernst-Ludwig-Haus with its Adam and Eve figures on the portal, the Behrens Haus, and the Hochzeitturm (wedding tower), designed for the wedding of Grand Duke Ernst Ludwig in 1905. The spectacular Russian Orthodox chapel with its gilded domes dates from the 1890s. A collection of *Jugendstil* artefacts is displayed in the Landesmuseum near the reconstructed 18th-century Schloss. The rococo Prinz Georg Palais holds a notable collection of porcelain given by various members of European royal families.

Darmstadt was a centre of the *Jugendstil* – German *art nouveau*. The style began as quite floral and naturalistic but after the 1900s it increasingly took on an abstract form. The architect Peter Behrens, who built a house for himself in the Mathildenhöhe, was an exponent of the late *Jugendstil*.

▶ ▷ ▷ Detmold

Until 1918 this town was capital of the principality of Lippe and it still has a strong sense of its own identity. Its noble 16th-century castle has Brussels tapestries and souvenirs of the family of Prince Bernhard of the Netherlands whose seat was here. There are British Army barracks in the town, nicknamed 'Little London'.

To the south is the Teutoburger Wald, a long narrow range of wooded hills with two interesting sights on its crest. One is the Hermannsdenkmal, a 26m green-

Duedstadt's town hall

copper statue of Arminius, the local chieftain who in about AD9 rallied the Germanic tribes to oppose Rome's rule and defeated its legions on this spot. Erected under Bismarck, the memorial became a focus of German nationalism, and the Nazis held rallies here. The Externsteine near by is a cluster of high rocks in strange, toothy shapes, once used as a place of worship by pagan tribes, later by Christians. The summer solstice used to be celebrated here, as the sun rose between the rocks. Note the amazing 12th-century Romanesque bas-relief carved on one rock, and the chapels and pulpit also hewn from the rock. For a closer view you can climb up new stairways in the rock. On the plain below is a large ornithological park, and the Westfälisches Freilichtsmuseum, an open-air museum with nearly 100 reassembled farm buildings from the region.

▶ ▷ ▷ Duderstadt

Only 20km east of the university town of Göttingen Duderstadt has a successful blend of Renaissance and Gothic architecture, which can be seen both on Hinterstrasse and in the Rathaus. The Westertorturm (gate tower) is notable for its curiously twisted narrow roof. The town contains two worthwhile churches: the Gothic St Cyriakuskirche, decorated in ostentatious baroque style, and St Servatiuskirche, refurbished in the art nouveau manner after a fire in 1915.

▶ ▷ ▷ Einbeck

A small town (pop. 29,000), Einbeck was known in the Middle Ages for its beer-making. There were no fewer than 700 breweries then but only one survives today, producing a well-known strong beer. Around the cobbled Marktplatz and in the Tidexerstrasse are half-timbered Gothic and Renaissance houses. In the Stiftskirche St Alexandri is the oldest choir stall in Germany (1288).

During World War II Einbeck would have been levelled to the ground had it not been for the persuasive skills of one Heinrich Keim, who later became Bürgermeister of the town. He talked a Nazi officer out of destroying this medieval gem.

CENTRAL GERMANY

A trade centre since Roman days, Frankfurt has played a major role in German history. Barbarossa and other early German kings were elected here, and from 1562 to 1806 the Holy Roman Emperors were crowned here. Goethe, born in the city, called it 'Germany's secret capital' (perhaps it still is?), and the first pan-German parliament met here in 1848–9. The city began to mint its own money in the 16th century; then in the 19th century local financiers such as Rothschild made it into a key world centre of banking. After 1945 it was proposed as the new federal capital, but Adenauer insisted on Bonn – a pity, very many people think. Today, together with Hannover, it is Germany's major trade fair venue and has the country's leading international airport. Industry includes machine tools and chemicals (Hoechst).

▶ ▶ ▷ **Frankfurt-am-Main**

Europe's tallest office building (254m) rises up in the heart of downtown Frankfurt (pop. 627,000), a city that is the home of the mighty Bundesbank and has branches of some 390 world banks. It is Germany's well-established financial capital, and its battalions of skyscrapers near the river Main have lent it the nickname of 'Mainhattan'. Its image of a dull, heartless money-making place is far from the whole truth: there's a great deal for the tourist to see, including some of Germany's best museums. Because the city is rich, it has the money to spend on culture, such as high-class opera, and at its annual Book Fair – the world's largest – literature and commerce join hands.

Frankfurt has a metropolitan, outward-looking ambience, largely due to all the high-profile international activity. It is also a city of tensions, with relatively high levels of crime and drug abuse and a large immigrant population, 22 per cent of the total. Politically, it is polarised: Green and left-wing protest has habitually been sharper here than in other cities (except Berlin), maybe because these militants react against the banks' assertive capitalism. Today – ironically – this city of bankers is ruled by an SPD/Green coalition: one of its councillors is Danny Cohn Bendit, once a May '68 rebel and now a local Green.

One local hotbed of Leftism has been the famous university (45,000 students), where radical philosophers such as Habermas and Adorno once propounded new ideas. This city of money is also a lively centre of the alternative avant-garde, with many fringe theatres: controversial film director Rainer Werner Fassbinder once worked here.

Frankfurt is a major publishing centre and has two of Germany's leading dailies, the *Allgemeine* and the *Rundschau* – in short, no mean city.

The main sights are central, and many can be toured on foot. Near to the Messegelände (exhibition centre) and the central station is the financial district, where the 24-storey Deutsche Bank building with its gleaming grey-blue glass façade is the most graceful of the city's skyscrapers (the Bundesbank itself is out in the suburbs). Much of this central area was gracelessly rebuilt after wartime bombing (witness Zeil, the hideous main shopping mall) but some older buildings have been well restored, notably the big neo-classical opera house

Opposite page: a river scene in Frankfurt
Above: the neo-classical opera house, no longer the venue for operas but an architectural attraction
Below right: Frankfurt cathedral, where Holy Roman Emperors were once crowned

(but the operas are now staged elsewhere). The imposing 15th-century Eschenheimer Turm is one of the 42 towers that used to ring the city; near by is the Börse (stock exchange), and the 18th-century baroque Hauptwache. The Goethehaus, the handsome family house where the poet was born and brought up, has been well restored after wartime damage and now houses a museum, full of memorabilia.

Frankfurt before the bombing had the biggest medieval Altstadt in Germany. Little now survives save for a carefully restored sector around the cathedral and the Römerberg, a cobbled square lined with fine half-timbered houses that used to be the city's focus for festivals and royal ceremonies. Here the Römer, a group of 15th-century houses that once formed the Rathaus, has a Renaissance stairway leading to the stately Kaisersaal. Across the square is the tiny Gothic Nikolaikirche, and the History Museum which includes scale models of how the Altstadt used to look, and photos of what the Allied bombers did. Just to the east is a fascinating hotch-potch zone where new modernistic buildings have purposely been put up next

The Rothschilds
The name of this great banking family comes from the words *rother Schild* (red shield), after the shield that hung on the family's house in the ghetto in Frankfurt-am-Main. Born in 1743 in Frankfurt, Mayer Amschel Rothschild was the founder in 1766 of the Rothschild bank. It handled the fortunes of Europe's royalty and played a large part in financing the Napoleonic wars. Mayer Amschel's elder son, Nathan Mayer, founded the British branch of the family bank in Manchester in 1800, and the second son, James Mayer, developed the French side of the family's business in Paris.

Once the setting for royal ceremonies: Frankfurt's cobbled square, Römerberg

Born in Frankfurt-am-Main in 1749, Goethe is undoubtedly Germany's greatest literary figure – and a lifelong lover of women. The young Johann reluctantly studied law in Leipzig where he met his first love Kätchen Schönkopf. He continued his law studies in Strasbourg, where he had another love affair and met the German writer and thinker, Herder. With Herder's help, Goethe became part of the Sturm und Drang (Storm and Stress) movement. In 1771 he returned to Frankfurt and became a newspaper critic.

to ancient ones. The new glass-walled Kultur-Schirn, an arts centre, gives on to the ruins of a Carolingian palace and of a Roman bath (around AD100) beside St Bartholomew's Cathedral, with its lofty Gothic tower (the view from the top is splendid). The emperors were crowned in this austere-looking reddish church which has interesting medieval murals and choirstalls. In the adjacent Wahlkapelle the Holy Roman Empire's seven Electors chose their king, and the cathedral's little museum displays the adornments they wore. The 15th-century St Leonard's Church has impressive stained glass.

Down by the river, on Untermainkai, the remarkable new Jewish Museum expounds the history of the city's once so influential Jewish community. The Nazi period is dealt with very discreetly. There are books from the Rothschild library, and details of Jewish life. Just across the river are six other excellent museums, some quite new. From west to east they are: (1) the Liebig museum of sculpture, ranging from ancient Egypt to the baroque; (2) the important Stadel Museum of art, with a large if somewhat muddled collection containing works by, among others, Holbein and Cranach, Tintoretto and Rembrandt, Renoir and Monet; the rich array of German painting includes, suitably, Tischbein's memorable portrait of Goethe sitting pensively near Rome; (3) the Postal Museum, with details of stamps, mail-coaches, also telephones; (4) the Cinema Museum, mostly technical and scientific, with not much about individual films; (5) the Museum of Ethnography, with objects from native tribes; (6) the Museum of Applied Art, displaying a striking collection of glass, porcelain, *Jugendstil* furniture, a good oriental and Islamic section and more, all in a lovely new building.

This south side of the Main is Sachsenhausen, a

residential area with some 16th- and 17th-century houses and a lot of cider-pubs and other evening jollity. At the eastern end, near the Alte Brücke, one group of narrow streets is now full of discos, pubs and cheap restaurants, which look amusing but have grown tacky, and many are full of exuberant US soldiers at the weekend. Back north of the river, Frankfurt's large zoo has lovely rare fish and a special section on nocturnal creatures. Dead or extinct animals, such as dinosaurs, can be studied in the Senckenberg natural history museum, which is near the university and the large Grüneburg Park, containing botanical and tropical gardens.

Two towns near Frankfurt are well worth a visit. **Offenbach**, Germany's chief leather-making centre, has a big museum devoted to that subject. **Höchst**, home of the giant Hoechst chemicals firm, has a charming undamaged Altstadt and several fine old buildings such as the baroque Bolongaro Palace and a red-brick Renaissance palace. Höchst's historic porcelain industry is now being revived and is on display at the Dalberhaus.

Frankfurters cross the river to let their hair down in the cider-houses of Sachsenhausen. *Apfelwein* is the local speciality, but if you're not used to this cider the first quaff could take your breath away – it's dry, almost vinegary and very strong.

115

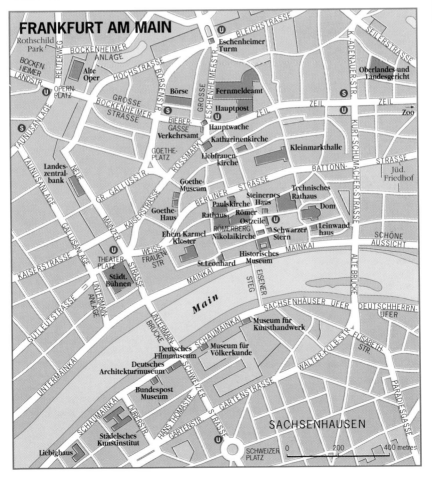

CENTRAL GERMANY

If you haven't yet had your fill of baroque, visit Schloss Fasanerie (guided tours April to October, closed Mondays), south of Fulda and built for the 18th-century Prince bishops of Fulda. Its sumptuous décor and sheer size are almost overpowering, but the park offers a relaxing respite. Near the town is the Kirche auf dem Petersberg (Petersberg church) built on a 400m-high rock and visible from afar.

Friedburg's old town

▶ ▷ ▷ **Friedberg**

There are a few Jewish baths remaining in Germany, and Friedberg houses one of them. The Judenbad here is a particularly fine example of such a ritual bathing place for women. Built in the 13th century, it descends 25m below ground level – reached by 74 steps. The Burg (Imperial Town) was built by the Emperor Frederick Barbarossa in 1180 and today still remains a separate community as it was in medieval times. The opposition of church and state is apparent, with the other main part of town being focused on the Stadtkirche, dating from the 13th and 14th centuries.

▶ ▶ ▷ **Fulda**

Ever since the 8th century, Fulda has been one of the most important centres for Catholic religious instruction in Germany. It all began when a Benedictine abbey was founded here by St Boniface, an English missionary to the pagan Germanic tribes. The abbey became famous for culture and learning throughout the Christian world.

Today the town contains a variety of architectural styles, above all a wealth of baroque, a style that extends to the huge palace (now a museum) and even the former police station. The main Dom (cathedral) was rebuilt by Johann Dientzenhofer (one of a family of architects much in demand) at the beginning of the 18th century, having been inspired by Italian baroque architecture; in fact he worked from a model copy of St Peter's in Rome. The Michaelskirche is one of the oldest churches in Germany, with a crypt dating from 822.

The Hanauisches Amtshaus at **Steinau**, about 25km southwest of Fulda, was the boyhood home of the Brothers Grimm; a puppet theatre re-enacts their fairy tales, and the much-fortified Schloss (open daily except Christmas and Mondays) contains a monument to the Grimms.

▶ ▷ ▷ **Gelnhausen**

The town is said to have been founded by Emperor Frederick Barbarossa in 1170 (it is sometimes called Barbarossa Stadt). It stands on a slope of the Kinzig valley (close to the Naturpark Hessischer Spessart, good walking country with its forested hills). The town was built as a military foundation and is still partly surrounded by fortifications. The Marienkirche (St Mary's) is a multi-towered Romanesque church that looks over Gelnhausen from its heightened position. The best feature of the interior is the chancel with the high altar and the shrine depicting the Madonna with four saints. The unusual choir stalls are ornately decorated and there are two well-preserved tapestries. Barbarossa's castle, the Kaiserpfalz, stands ruined on an island in the River Kinzig (open daily except Monday).

Büdingen, about 10km north of Gelnhausen, possesses an intact town wall, dating from the 15th and 16th centuries, distinguished by squat towers and pierced by elaborate Gothic gateways. Guided tours of the Schloss (14.00–16.00hrs, March to October) take you over a still-inhabited 12th- to 17th-century building ranged round a courtyard.

The old town at Goslar

▶ ▶ ▷ Goslar

One of the loveliest towns in north Germany, Goslar is also a winter sports resort, popular with Berliners. It was a seat of the Salian emperors in the 11th century, then a Free Imperial City. In the Middle Ages it became a centre of silver and lead mining. Merchants began to pour in, lead and silver were increasingly mined and refined and this led to a building boom around the 16th century, the peak of Goslar's prosperity. This explains its legacy of fine buildings from different epochs – Gothic, Renaissance, baroque – all close together in the centre. Many are half-timbered or of stone, rather than the usual north German red brick. The mines ultimately went bankrupt, but some are still worked today, in the hills south of the town. By the 19th century Goslar was prospering again under Prussian domination.

The Altstadt is full of interest. The traffic-free, cobbled Marktplatz (Market Square), surrounded by dignified stone and half-timbered houses with elaborate slate roofs, has a quaint chiming clock (modern) on the treasurer's building which performs four times a day – 09.00, 12.00, 15.00 and 18.00hrs – with scenes outlining the mining history of the town dating back to the Middle Ages. In the old arcaded Rathaus, a fine Gothic building, the Huldigungssaal is covered from floor to ceiling with splendid coloured frescos of around 1500; it also holds the Goslar Gospel (1230). Across the square, the 15th-century Kaiserworth, once a guildhouse, is now a hotel: on one corner gable is a cheeky statue of a boy ejecting a coin from his backside (symbolic of Goslar's former right to mint coins). The square also has a fountain with two large bronze basins surmounted by an imperial eagle with wings spread. Many of the houses in the streets off the square are half-timbered (Fachwerkhäuser). The Siemenshaus (Schreiberstrasse 12), which has daily guided tours, was built in 1693 by Hans Siemens, an ancestor of the Berlin industrialist who created the Siemens empire. The Goslarer Museum (Königstrasse 1) contains a detailed outline of the artistic and cultural history of the Harz, and models of the town. The Mönchehaus (Mönchestrasse 3) contains a modest collection of modern art.

At Friedland, near the former GDR border south of Göttingen, there used to be a large transit camp for political refugees arriving not from the GDR but from other east European countries. Here they stayed while their papers were processed, before moving on to a new life in some West German town.

The Gänselieselbrunnen at Göttingen

▶ ▷ ▷ Göttingen

Göttingen is first and foremost a university town. The university, named after its founder the Elector of Hannover, who was also George II, King of Great Britain and Ireland, has given the town a hallowed reputation as a leading place of learning. The university has produced several Nobel Prize winners, and it is the headquarters of the Max Planck-Institut, comprising some 50 scientific groups. Max Planck, the father of modern physics, is buried in Göttingen.

The 30,000 university students bring added life and colour to the town which prides itself on the Gothic churches and neo-classical buildings, such as the Aula, or Great Hall, scattered about the campus. The students have made the town hall area and its Ratskeller (cellars) the hub of activity. Even during vacations you will find throngs of young people milling about. Nightlife is always interesting, and many students are keen to talk to foreign visitors. There is a tradition for students to visit the Gänselieselbrunnen ('Goose Lizzie's fountain') in the centre of town in front of the Rathaus, once they've completed their examinations, and to give the bronze statue a kiss.

The Vierkirchenblick, viewpoint of four churches, is a memorable sight. Stand at the southeast corner of the Markt and you will see: to the east the 15th-century St Albanus, to the south St Michael, to the west, the two octagonal towers of the Johanniskirche, and to the north St Jakobi, the tallest, which stands at 72m. In the old quarter of the town, there are half-timbered houses to be seen; one dating from 1563, northeast of the Markt, houses the old pharmacy.

▶ ▶ ▷   Hameln (Hamelin)

There is more to Hameln than just the legend of a man in a strange costume and a plague of rats. There are many attractive half-timbered buildings left, despite severe damage done during the Thirty Years War (World War II fortunately had less impact).

The town is a treasure house of immaculately restored buildings in the so-called Weser Renaissance style of the 16th and 17th centuries. Typically this makes use of scroll decorations and pinnacles on gables, carved stone banding and large bay windows. The Rattenfängerhaus (Ratcatcher's House), at Osterstrasse 28, dates back to 1603 and is a good example. Its carved stonework is embellished with busts and heads, and there is an inscription about the Pied Piper on the side; the house was actually built for a councillor. The Hochzeitshaus (Wedding House), at Osterstrasse 2, was built between 1610 and 1617 and was used for burghers' weddings. You will easily recognise it since today it is the town hall and library. On the side facing the Marktplatz, the Pied Piper clock features mechanical figures which appear three times a day – at 13.05, 15.35 and 17.35hrs.

A wander through the streets will reveal other beautiful old buildings. Two in Osterstrasse house the Museum Hameln (open daily except Monday) with a collection of religious art, local history and Pied Piper lore.

Excursion

Hämelschenburg, about 11km south of Hameln, is a magnificent example of the Weser Renaissance style. The castle (guided tours April to October, closed Mondays) was built between 1588 and 1618 in a horseshoe shape.

North of Hameln is **Fischbeck** (8km), where there is a convent dating from the 10th century. The church is 12th-century and has a fine Romanesque crypt.

The poet Max Herrmann Neisse used the story of the Pied Piper to express the sorrow of the wartime evacuation of children: 'So dead are squares and gardens now like Hameln after the ratcatcher's revenge: the children have all left us, a mother's heart is trembling under every roof'.

'Rat pastries'

Thanks to the Pied Piper legend, immortalised by Goethe and then in verse by the English poet Robert Browning, Hameln has become famous far beyond Germany. Every Sunday afternoon from mid-May to mid-September, between 12.00 and 12.30hrs, a Pied Piper play is performed on the terrace of the Hochzeitshaus.

The Harz is famed for its witch legends. The eve of 1 May is believed to be the *Walpurgisnacht,* the night of the witches' sabbath on the Brocken (1,142m), the highest mountain in the region; this occasion features as an episode in Goethe's *Faust.*

There is a strange mixture of the comic and the tragic in German folklore – the piper of Hameln who charmed the rats away, then because he was not properly paid, took the children with him too; Tannhäuser, the knight who abandoned his vows and went into a strange mountain to spend the rest of his days in the company of Venus. The most celebrated mountain in Germany is the Kyffhauser, east of Göttingen, where the emperor Frederik Barbarossa slumbers in a hidden cavern, radiant with gold and jewels. His great red beard has grown almost three times around the stone table at which he sits. A shepherd once strayed into the cavern and spoke to the emperor, who told him that he must remain there until the ravens cease to fly around the peak outside.

Traditionally, the 16th-century Dr Johann Faust, a mountebank who travelled throughout Germany but who is particularly associated with the city of Erfurt, sold his soul to the devil in return for knowledge of science and alchemy, and died with his neck being wrung by an archdemon. The devil was, however, outwitted at Cologne, for the great cathedral was built there according to a plan drafted by him as a lure to gain the soul of the architect. The clever architect came to a rendezvous carrying a crucifix, which kept the devil at bay while he snatched the expert document.

In many parts of the country there are traditions of the *Wilde Jagd,* the Wild Hunt, a ghostly cavalry crashing through the forests to the accompaniment of trumpets and shouts. This is a survival of the cult of the great Teutonic deity Odin.

The transfer from paganism to Christianity, too, is represented in various legends, such as that of the Drachenfels, a mountain near Bonn, where a wicked fire-breathing dragon tried to seize a beautiful Christian maiden but was hurled by her prayers into the river below.

The Rhine is the most venerable of European rivers. According to legend, a treasure trove lies hidden in it; the secret was known only to the last two Nibelung heroes, who refused to divulge it despite torture and death. When the sun shines on the Rhine the reflection of this treasure can be seen, but none of it càn be found. Old lore also tells of Charlemagne, who was especially

Figures from German folklore: Red Riding Hood (opposite page); the Valiant Tailor and Giant (left); and the Goose Girl (above) – all from the brothers Grimm

partial to a castle which he had at Ingelheim. When he noticed that the snow melted quickly on the hills of Rüdesheim, west of Mainz, he established fine vineyards there, and now his spirit can be seen on spring nights, blessing the vines. A predilection for wine was also shown by the 14th-century Emperor Wenzel, who once feasted in a beautiful meadow at Rhens, south of Koblenz, and was so impressed with a cask of fiery wine from Bacharach that he sold his realm for it.

At Bingen, in the 10th century, lived Hatto, a bishop who was so rapacious that in time of famine, he refused food to the starving multitude. By divine punishment his palace was infested with mice. To escape the pests, he retired to a tower in the Rhine, but he was pursued there by the mice and devoured by them. More fortunate was a prisoner in Frankfurt long ago, who was offered his freedom if he could hit a weathercock on a tower in the wall of that city with nine consecutive shots from his musket. He succeeded, leaving holes in the weathercock in the perfect shape of the figure 9.

At Darmstadt, a story is told of a poor and inept knight stopping to pray at a roadside statue of the Virgin Mary. He fell into a faint and, while he remained there, the Virgin took on his appearance and won the laurels at a great tournament.

A fine deed was performed by the women of Weisberg, north of Stuttgart, whose town was besieged during the civil wars of the 12th century. They begged to be allowed to depart in safety with whatever they could carry with them. This request was granted, and they walked unmolested through the enemy lines, each lady carrying her husband on her back!

Goethe in *Faust* describes the sorcery associated with the Brocken in folklore: 'And when we sail around the top, first skim the ground, then fill it up, that all the Brocken height may be smothered in swarms of witchery'.

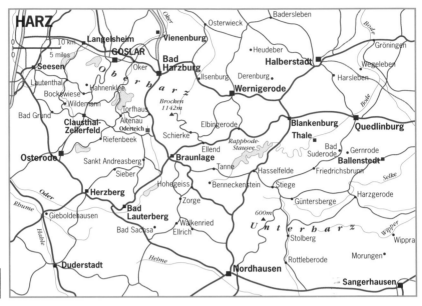

HARZ

The Harz region has a strong mining tradition associated with gold and silver, and for this reason the mountains were once known as the 'Treasury of the Emperors'. Clausthal-Zellerfeld was a busy mining town until the last mine closed in 1931. Its Oberharzer Museum (Museum of the Upper Harz – closed on Mondays) has displays of tools and explanations of some unusual local mining methods. The local church was built of wood in the 17th century. Amazingly, since its interior furnishings are also all wooden, it has escaped destruction by fire. At Sankt Andreasberg, the Silberbergwerk (silver mine) known as Grube Samson (the Samson pit) arranges guided tours (daily except mid-November to mid-December). The mine was in operation from 1521 to 1910. It was re-opened in 1951 as a museum.

▶ ▶ ▷   **Harz**

Straddling the old East-West German border, the Harz mountains, the highest land in northern and central Germany, are a rewarding area for exploration. Summits rise to over 1,000m, and while the 'Little Switzerland' nickname may be an exaggeration, it contrasts strikingly with the surrounding plains.

On the west side, hotels are efficiently run, restaurants and cafés plentiful, buildings immaculately restored and neat pine forests crossed by well signposted paths and skiing routes. In the east, everything lags about 40 years behind, although tourism is likely to change that.

Bad Harzburg's high street

The Harz region comprises two distinct areas – the **Oberharz** (Upper Harz) in the west, containing vast areas of delightful forests and valleys for long refreshing walks, and the **Unterharz** (Lower Harz) in the east, which has more open land scattered with beech forests.

CENTRAL GERMANY

The Brocken was just east of the boundary between the former German Democratic Republic and the Federal Republic. It is still possible to spot the old border posts where East German guards stood on the lookout for those trying to escape to the west. Bleak, unpainted houses in the eastern region make it fairly easy to detect the former boundary.

Because it is relatively easy to get to the Harz from a number of large German cities, it has become a popular tourist destination, both in the summer and winter. An unpredictable climate, often damp and cold, does not deter the visitors who come for the walking, skiing and spas. They follow in the footsteps of 19th-century romantics, who saw the Harz mountains as the epitome of poetic, myth-steeped landscape.

Since reunification, many previously unvisited Harz towns are being swamped by curious tourists. **Wernigerode**, a well-preserved 14th-century town with a quaint walled Rathaus and other half-timbered houses with ornate façades, is packed every weekend, even when the weather is not too good. In a few years' time, with some coats of paint and badly needed renovations, this town and others like it, such as **Elbingerode**, which has a timber-framing museum, **Quedlinburg** and **Blankenburg**, will add to the charm of the region. For the moment, however, such Unterharz towns still look rather bleak and depressing. The spa and health resort of **Bad Harzburg**, a short drive from Goslar, is a good base from which to explore the Harz region.

The highest point of the Harz, the **Brocken** (1,142m), was in the old forbidden zone close to the border: but now it can be visited again, and it offers a good view. You can go up by cable car to the Hexentanzplatz (witches' dance floor) which features in Goethe's *Faust*. The lovely **Bode** valley south of Thale, and the giant caves at **Rübeland** with their stalagmites and stalactites, are also worth exploring.

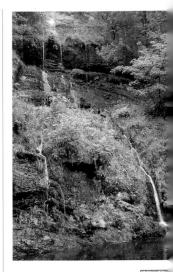

The Romerkalle Falls in the Harz

Walk From Bad Harzburg (about 20km)

Starting point: Railway station at Bad Harzburg. Head for the large car park at the cable-car. Look for signs to Papenberg (7F, red triangle), then Ahrendsberger Weg to Brockenblick (17K, yellow triangle). From Eiserner Weg to the B4 road to Bastesiedlung, pass along Grenzweg and Kaiserweg (35E, blue dot inside triangle) to Molkenhaus (11A, blue cross) and then return to the car park.

Walk Goslar to Altenau (about 30km)

Starting point: Goslar (50A, blue point) – Bad Harzburg – Panenberg – then look for 71F, red triangle to Ahrendsberger footpath – Salzsteig – Ahrendsberg (17M, green point) – Kalbetal – Kellwassertal – Schwarzenberg – Schultal – and finally Altenau. Take a knapsack with refreshments. It is possible to stay overnight at Altenau (several youth hostels, reasonable pensions and hotels).

From the rear of Schloss Hohenlohe there's a fine view over the Wilhelmshohe Schlosspark, as splendid a Romantic landscaped park as any in Europe, built soon after 1700. It is crowned by a vast Hercules statue (copy of the Farnese Hercules in Naples) atop a towering 70m grey granite monument. Below it are waterfalls and fountains (activated on certain days in summer) and some charming 18th-century follies – Pluto's Grotto, Devil's Bridge, baroque temples, and the startling grey-pinnacled castle of Löwenburg which may look medieval but is pure Romantic fake.

Just north of Kassel, the pretty rococo Schloss Wilhelmsthal is worth a visit: its ornate interior, designed by Cuvilliés, contains Tischbein portraits of ladies.

▶ ▷ ▷ **Kassel**

Badly bombed in 1943, and rebuilt in a dull style, the principal city of north Hesse is today an industrial centre for engineering, chemicals, etc, and has little charm (its Altstadt is vanished). But its setting amid wooded hills is pleasant, and it is worth visiting for the extravagantly romantic Wilhelmshöhe park, and for its excellent museums.

The Landgraves of Hesse developed Kassel in the 17th and 18th centuries, creating the great park and encouraging industry. They were keen art collectors – a tradition today kept up with the famous avant-garde and multi-media Dokumenta exhibition, held every five years since 1955 (next in 1995). One of its patrons was the late Joseph Beuys, who planted 7,000 oak trees in Kassel as an action sculpture. In the town centre is the Dokumenta's main venue, the opera house and the curiously shaped Ottoneum, Germany's oldest theatre (1606). Best of the nearby museums is the Landesmuseum (early astronomical and scientific instruments, prehistory, and an unusual display of wallpapers dating from the 16th century). A small museum near by is devoted to the Brothers Grimm, who lived and worked in Kassel. The Neue Galerie has 19th and 20th century paintings, few of them notable, but there are some attractive canvases by Tischbein, who was born near Kassel.

In the western suburbs is the pink-granite **Schloss Hohenlohe** where the Westphalian king Jerome Bonaparte held lavish court in 1807–13. The Schloss contains a large and excellent museum, notable less for its Egyptian, Greek and Roman antiquities than for its excellent range of paintings, especially Italian, Flemish and Dutch (note Teniers' *Peasants' Dance*). Napoleon III was interned here in 1870: as he passed through Aachen the crowd jeered, *Ab nach Kassel!* – the origin of today's German phrase which means 'Off we go!'.

Kassel's Hesse museum

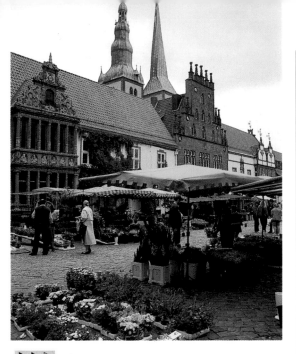

Market day at
Lemgo's Marktplatz

The Staatliche
Kunstsammlungen in Kassel
has an outstanding
collection of paintings by
Rembrandt. The gallery once
boasted 17 canvases by the
artist but six of these are
now of disputed origin. An
undisputed masterpiece is
*Jacob Blessing the Sons of
Joseph,* a late work of
remarkable tenderness.

▶ ▶ ▷   Lemgo

One of the best-preserved towns in northern and central Germany and formerly a member of the Hanseatic League, Lemgo was once known as the Leipzig of Westphalia because of its printing presses (Leipzig was the publishing capital of Germany). In the 15th and 16th centuries trade with Flanders and England brought wealth to Lemgo; today signs of this early prosperity are much in evidence, particularly as the town escaped damage in World War II. You'll find many half-timbered houses with a rich variety of façades in Breitestrasse, the town's main street. At number 19 there is the Hexenbürgermeisterhaus (House of the Witches' Mayor) completed in 1568 and a famous example of the Weser Renaissance style with characteristic oriel windows. The house gets its name from Hermann Cothmann who sentenced 90 women to death for witchcraft, when he was Mayor of Lemgo from 1666 to 1681. It houses a Heimatmuseum (local history museum), with a display relating to law and punishment as they were applied to witchcraft, including a macabre display of instruments of torture.

The Marienkirche is a Gothic hall church with a Renaissance organ still in excellent shape, both in sound and appearance. Take advantage of any concert being put on in the church. The 13th-century Nickolaikirche shows both Romanesque and Gothic work.

▶ ▶ ▷   Münden (Hannoversch Münden)

A delightful old town of narrow streets and black and white half-timbered houses, in the words of a well-known poem, Münden stands 'where Werra and Fulda kiss each other' – for these rivers meet here, and the Weserstein, a monumental stone, marks the spot. The bridge over the Werra behind the Schloss is 14th century or earlier. In the Marktplatz are buildings in

CENTRAL GERMANY

Münden's most famous son, Johann Andreas Eisenbart, was an 18th-century doctor with allegedly miraculous powers. A costume play commemorating his life is performed out of doors on Sundays from mid-May to the end of August.

126

The front entrance of Münden's Rathaus (above); and (left) buildings at Münden

Weser Renaissance style, including the handsome gabled Rathaus. The St Blasiuskirche is a Gothic hall church with a bronze font dating from 1392.

▶ ▷ ▷ Münzenberg

Plan your visit to Schloss Münzenberg, about 30km north of Frankfurt-am-Main, between March and October, as these impressive ruins are closed from November until February. You will be able to visit the grounds and the fortifications and living quarters. The latter are heavily decorated in the Romanesque style, especially apparent in the windows and the gallery. There is a keep at each end of the complex. The well maintained grounds are pleasant for a leisurely stroll, and there is a magnificent view from the top of the east tower, which takes in the low-lying Welterau, a region between two upland massifs, the Taunus and the Vogelberg.

▷ ▷ ▷   Paderborn

This ancient Westphalian town (pop. 123,000) is an active commercial and industrial centre. It entered history in 799, when Charlemagne had an important meeting here with Pope Leo III, reaching an agreement which led the following year to the creation of the Holy Roman Empire. The site of the palace where the meeting took place came to light during the rebuilding of the city after World War II. Paderborn's main landmark is its cathedral, which dates mainly from the 13th century: its Romanesque tower has become the city's emblem. The Bartolomäuskapelle (St Bartholomew's Chapel), a separate structure north of the cathedral, was Germany's first hall church (11th century). On the exterior of the cathedral, note the Paradiesportal, a 13th-century porch on the south side. Another porch, the Brautportal, bears sculpted scenes from the life of Christ. Just below the church of the Abdinghof monastery are more than 200 warm springs, the source of the little River Pader.

▶ ▷ ▷   Taunus

Densely clothed in forests, the rolling hills of the Taunus are Germany's richest region of mineral springs. This has resulted in the opening up of several famous spas. The region's proximity to Wiesbaden, Mainz and Frankfurt-am-Main has helped in its development. There are several good roads giving easy access to the peaks, of which the highest is the **Grosser Feldberg**, an important telecommunications centre at 880m. You can drive near the summit, then climb the tower on top (167 steps) for a grand view, as far as Frankfurt to the south and the heights of the Westerwald to the north.

The little town of **Königstein im Taunus** is situated on a height well away from the main slope. Its most interesting feature is Burg Königstein, a mighty ruined castle with 16th-century bastions and 17th-century projecting defences. Built around 1200, it was finally destroyed in 1796.

Bad Homburg, in the foothills of the Taunus, used to be one of Europe's most fashionable spas, visited by the Kaiser, the Prince of Wales and others (Dostoevsky set *The Gambler* here). Today it has moved somewhat downmarket but the big Kurpark is still attractive, with a Russian chapel and a Thai temple, gifts from former royal visitors from those lands. In the centre are the medicinal springs and lawns and walks. The stately white high-towered 17th-century Schloss (open daily except Monday) was the residence of the Landgraves of Hesse-Homburg and subsequently summer palace of the Kings of Prussia.

North of Bad Homburg, amid pleasant forests, is the *in situ* reconstruction of **Saalburg** Roman Camp (open daily), originally guarding the adjacent Limes fortifications which demarcated the northern extent of Roman occupation (still visible, in varying degrees). Just outside the village of Neu Anspach is the **Freilicht Museum Hessenpark** (open daily except Monday, March to October), where reconstructed Hessian buildings include a functioning bakery, and workshops produce crafts.

Paderborn cathedral

Bad Homburg claims a number of 'firsts' – the Spiel Kasino, the first casino and inspiration for Monte Carlo; the first water closet in Germany; and the famous 'Homburg' hat.

CENTRAL GERMANY

▶ ▷ ▷ **Waldeck**

Thanks largely to the spa resort of Bad Wildungen, the Waldeck region, just southwest of Kassel, has become one of the most popular tourist areas of central Germany. The countryside is attractive, with dense forests and gentle hills cut through by the course of the River Eder. The most spectacular feature is the great lake formed behind the Edertalsperre (Eder Dam).

The waters of **Bad Wildungen** are used mainly to treat kidney and gall bladder complaints, and problems of hypertension and metabolism. Peaceful walks cross the Kurpark to the Georg Viktor spring. The Evangelische Stadtkirche (Protestant church), famed for its altarpiece of 1403 by Konrad von Soest, has a 14th-century tower that overlooks the rest of the town. Further east, the fortified town of **Fritzlar** occupies a site above the River Eder. Dom St Petri, founded by St Boniface in 724, is

Above and left: Burg Waldeck, the castle of the Waldeck princes

essentially late Romanesque with baroque additions; the huge crypts are the main feature of the building, predating its reconstruction in 1180. The Marktplatz contains an appealing range of half-timbered buildings.

In the town of **Waldeck** itself, part of the castle of the Waldeck Princes (Burg Waldeck) is now a hotel, and down in the vaults is a museum, set up as a tribute to the House of Waldeck. One of Germany's largest feudal castles, Burg Waldeck was built in the late 12th century and was much added to in subsequent centuries. It was abandoned by the House of Waldeck in the 17th century. The view from the castle terrace is particularly impressive. Below the castle is the Eder Dam and the artificial lake with its wooded shores.

About an hour's drive away is **Korbach**, with its many old timber houses. The town was formed after two fortified settlements, Altstadt and Neustadt ('old town' and 'new town'), amalgamated. North of Korbach is **Arolsen**, its regular plan very much the creation of the Waldeck princes who lived here. Their baroque-styled Schloss (guided tours May to September) is easily found at the eastern end of the main street. Built between 1714 and 1724, the palace was inspired by Versailles; some of the rooms were not decorated until 1811.

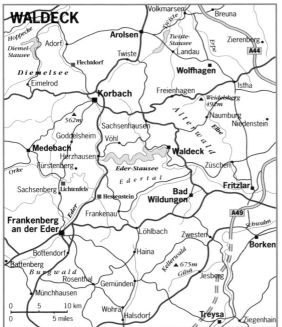

A view from Waldeck's castle towards Eder Dam

CENTRAL GERMANY

Weserbergland

▶ ▶ ▷ Weserbergland

The Weserbergland is a region of green hills lining both banks of the River Weser. This is one of Germany's most picturesque river valleys, and it is well worth taking four or five days to follow the river's course north. You can either take the passenger boats that glide downstream, or drive along one of two roads: either the Wesertalstrasse (Weser Valley Road) or, on the other side of the river, the B80, called the Deutsche Märchenstrasse (Fairy Tale Road) because it was the route the Brothers Grimm took when they gathered their famous fairy tales. The towns and villages along the way are characterised by the Weser Renaissance style of architecture.

A recommendable route starts at the old town of **Münden**, founded in 1170 by Henry the Lion (see page 125). From there, go through the beautiful Kaufunger Wald, a forest south of Münden, part of which is a nature park, and on to **Mollenfelde**, with its unique Europäisches Brotmuseum (European bread museum). You can trace the history of bread from Ancient Egyptian days to the present. Now go north to the romantic 14th-century **Schloss Sababurg**, where the Brothers Grimm used to come on hunting parties. It is said to have been the model for the castle in *The Sleeping Beauty*, and is now a hotel. The nearby zoo, with bears, penguins, etc, is Germany's oldest (1571). Further on, **Bad Karlshafen** is a beautiful white town, founded in 1699 for French Huguenot settlers, while **Höxter** has a townscape of elaborately painted and carved façades, and a magnificent Renaissance alabaster pulpit in the twin-towered Kilianikirche. The Dechanei (Deanery) and Rathaus are two of the most eye-catching buildings, and busy Westerbachstrasse is perhaps the finest street. Near by, at **Corvey** you can see the Imperial Abbey (822) with a rare example of an original Carolingian west end. It was in the abbey (now converted to secular use) that the poet Hoffmann von Fallersleben composed the German national anthem.

Continuing north, the Rathaus at **Bodenwerder** was once the home of Baron Münchhausen, famous for tall stories about his unbelievable feats (he did actually live, but his true exploits were somewhat tamer than the tales). The building houses a small museum commemorating him. At **Hämelschenburg**, you can visit the splendid Weser-Renaissance castle (1588-1610), while the nearby town of **Hameln** is famous for its story of the Pied Piper (see page 119). At the Porta Westfalica, the Weser breaks through the mountains into the north German lowlands and continues north through Bremen and Bremerhaven (see pages 54–56), before flowing into the North Sea.

▶ ▷ ▷   **Wiesbaden**

The capital of Hessen and an important spa, Wiesbaden lies between the Rheingau wine region and the Taunus mountains. Its 26 hot springs have long attracted visitors, and today it is popular with jet-setters, artists and business people, and there is a distinct whiff of wealth. There are countless literary and musical associations. Goethe came here, as did the Russian writers Turgenev and Dostoevsky. Brahms, Wagner and Robert and Clara Schumann were also visitors.

Wiesbaden hosts a series of annual events, ranging from horseriding competitions to wine-tasting. In May an important festival attracts top foreign theatre companies.

Other sights in the town include the Stadtschloss, which became a royal castle in 1866, but today is the seat of the Hessen state parliament. There is an old town hall; and the Städtisches Museum (town museum) contains paintings by, among others, expressionist artist Alexei von Jawlensky, who worked with the Russian artist Kandinsky in Munich and later settled in Wiesbaden, where he died in 1941.

Wiesbaden's neo-classical spa building, the Kurhaus, which stands in the pleasant Kurpark

Taking the cure
Wiesbaden's neo-classical Kurhaus was built in 1906 and is a showy venue. It houses the Wiesbaden casino – the Spielbank (note the portico with six Ionic columns).
Many thermal baths are located inside hotels, but two can be visited without an overnight stay: the Kaiser Friedrich Bad in Langgasse (where you can bathe in a mock-Roman pool) and the Thermalbad Wiesbaden in Leibnizstrasse (which is less expensive). Towels are usually included in the cost. . Be warned that saunas in Germany are often for mixed sexes, so if you are not used to this, check with the reception beforehand. Make an appointment for a massage in advance if possible, since the masseurs often tend to be booked up.

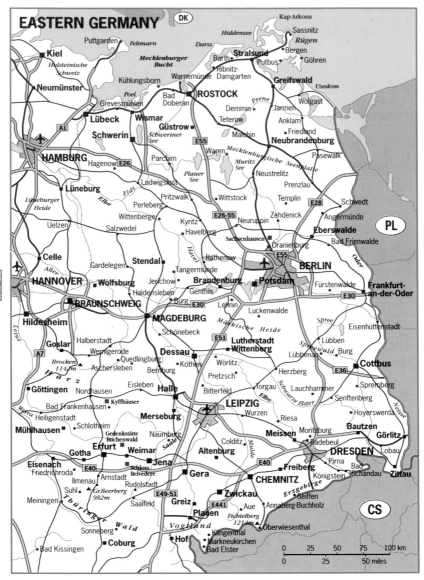

132

With the Iron Curtain (quite literally) dismantled, it's now easy to visit the former German Democratic Republic – a country that used to do everything it could to make life hard for tourists by hedging them round with visa restrictions, controls on where they could go, fierce customs checks, and police registration requirements.

It's now a very rewarding area to tour, provided you're willing to make certain allowances. Despite the near-collapse of the economy which followed the momentous events of 1989, and the grim underlying realities of unemployment, pollution and dereliction which face much of the country, it is changing amazingly fast and offers a fascinating contrast to the West.

EASTERN GERMANY

The biggest problem is the chaotic traffic clogging up an antiquated road system which is virtually being rebuilt from scratch. Signposting is often poor and driving standards erratic, among people more used to driving Trabants and Wartburgs than Audis and Mercedes. Petrol is now widely available, from smart new filling stations being erected on the edge of many towns and cities along with supermarkets and industrial estates.

Another problem for visitors is the shortage of accommodation in the middle price range. Many of the bigger hotels have already been modernised to a high standard, and – especially in rural areas – good family pensions are appearing but, if you're on a budget, in many areas you'll have to rely on private rooms, booked through the tourist office. There are still some old-style basic hotels around the less-visited areas (though these are neither cheap nor good value).

The third point for visitors is the language. Russian was the main foreign language for most East Germans, although many are now trying to learn more English.

The East is much poorer than the rest of Germany – but it's much less frenetic, and people can be very friendly and willing to help. One result of high unemployment is that casual economy is booming – right down to the small snack stalls and barbecues you'll see on many country roads and town squares.

Eastern Germany has great cultural and historical importance, reflected in many cities, castles and historic houses which have survived. The painters Albrecht Dürer, Hans Holbein and Otto Dix, and the composers Johann Sebastian Bach, George Frederick Handel, Robert Schumann and Richard Wagner were all born here. Modern German literature had its beginnings in the Wartburg castle at Eisenach, where Martin Luther translated the Bible into German. And, in Weimar, Germany has a literary centre of worldwide importance, home of Goethe, Schiller and Herder, as well as the one-time capital of the ill-fated republic that bore its name.

Woodlands of Vogtland (see page 166)

▶ ▷ ▷ Bernburg

Bernburg is interesting mainly for its huge Renaissance castle, with buildings of different styles and ages grouped round a large irregular courtyard; on one side, steep wooded slopes extend down to the river Saale and the lower town. It also boasts, in both the lower and upper towns, well-kept town walls and streets of 16th- to 18th-century town houses. The outskirts, though, are scruffy and industrial.

There's another Renaissance palace at **Köthen**, 20km to the east. J S Bach worked for six years as *Kapellmeister* in the Ludwigsban part of the town; there's a small museum dedicated to him here. Köthen also has some fine aristocratic houses dotted around its centre.

In the other direction, 20km west of Bernburg, **Aschersleben** clusters below the 80m tower of St Stephen's church, a fine 15th-century Gothic hall church. There are several attractive burghers' houses in the ancient town centre.

▶ ▶ ▷ Brandenburg

Brandenburg is surrounded by numerous attractive lakes along and around the River Havel, an area popular for excursions known as Havelland and famous for its birdlife – reed warblers, marsh harriers, bitterns, storks, herons and cranes are to be observed in abundance.

Both town and *Land* take their name from the castle known as the Brandenburg, first mentioned in AD948. It took 200 years before this seemingly impregnable fortress was finally overcome by a warrior prince with the delightful name of Albrecht the Bear. Both the Old and New towns remained separate members of the Hanseatic League until 1518 and only joined together in 1715. Huguenot settlers increased the town's prosperity, and in the 20th century it became a major industrial centre, consequently heavily bombed in World War II.

Brandenburg's cathedral took no fewer than seven centuries to complete. It has a 14th-century Bohemian altar, a 13th-century Saxon crucifix, as well as countless valuable manuscripts. The town hall, built around 1480, has a 5m figure of Roland dating from 1474, a symbol of civic rights.

Bernburg's castle courtyard

▶▷▷ Colditz

The old town of Colditz, on the River Mulde in Central Saxony, has a picturesque town centre with an attractive town hall, market place and a 13th-century parish church. The ancient castle on a hill overlooking the town achieved notoriety during World War II as a formidable prisoner of war camp from where a number of British officers made well publicised escapes. Though used as a hospital for many years, there are plans to transform the castle into a luxury hotel. Mementoes of escapees are kept in the museum, including some false German uniforms, photographic material and an illicit printing press.

▷▷▷ Dessau

Dessau is world-famous among architects and designers as the home of the Bauhaus movement (see panel). The building from which it gets is name was built by Walter Gropius in 1925–26 and still stands – restored in 1977 to something like its former glory – in a suburban avenue 2km northwest of the centre. A downstairs bar is open

Above: the White Bridge at Dessau
Top right: Colditz castle

to the public, and there are occasional performances and lectures. There are also examples of Bauhaus architecture on the outskirts, including a 300-dwelling housing estate at Dessau-Törten to the south, but they are hard to find and the buildings themselves are not well preserved.

Much of the centre of the city – which was also famous as the site of the Junkers aircraft factory – was destroyed in the war and has been rebuilt in blocky modern style.

For light relief, make for the baroque castle at **Mosigkau** (9km southwest), where a guided tour will take you round a fine collection of furniture, porcelain and Dutch paintings; or head for **Wörlizter Park** (15km east) which was modelled in the 18th century on English landscape gardens, dotted with picturesque buildings and criss-crossed with canals and lakes.

The Bauhaus movement was founded by the German architect Walter Gropius in Weimar in 1919. His school of art (which moved to Dessau in 1925) became an experimental laboratory for architects, engineers, painters, sculptors and designers. Gropius's central idea was to bring together aesthetics with the needs of an industrial civilisation. The function of an object should control the design of its structure. Thus the courses at the Bauhaus school were directed at the creation of forms suitable for mass production.

Semper Opera House, Dresden

▶ ▶ ▶ **Dresden**

The city's name is indelibly linked with the events of 13–14 February 1945, when a devastating Anglo-American air attack turned the whole of the centre into a blazing inferno, destroying thousands of ancient buildings and taking an estimated 35,000 lives. In the 1950s and 60s, much of the city was rebuilt in a blocky, Stalinist style, impressive in its scale and self-confidence, but not much fun to explore. Even today, many of the outlying areas are grimy and industrial, with more than their fair share of dereliction.

For all this, Dresden is not to be missed. Enough of its enormous cultural heritage remains, providing plenty of worthwhile sights and famous works of art, most of them dating back to the city's heyday as capital of Saxony, and especially to the reign of the aptly-named August the Strong in the late 17th and early 18th centuries, and to a long period of prosperity in the 19th century. Even at the height of the Cold War, considerable efforts were made by the East German authorities to restore the most important of those monuments which were not smashed to pieces. Since unification, this process has accelerated. Encouraged by Dresden's revived status as capital of the province of Saxony, western investors have poured money into building projects, which are beginning to transform the centre and give the city a renewed claim to its long-standing reputation for culture, commerce and gracious living.

What to see The Brühlsche Terrasse, a gracious, elevated terrace on the south bank of the Elbe, and known locally as 'Europe's balcony', lies at the heart of the historic part of Dresden, surrounded by gaunt, dignified buildings in a range of styles. Immediately behind it, the stark, windowless remains of the 18th-century **Stadtschloss** are a reminder of the reconstruction work yet to be done – the castle is due to be reopened for Dresden's 800th anniversary in 2006. The neighbouring **Frauenkirche** (Church of Our Lady) will have even less to look forward to because it is to remain permanently in its ruined state, as a reminder of the horrors of World War II. A kinder fate has befallen the nearby **Hofkirche** (royal cathedral) which was built in 1739–55 in Italian baroque style and contains a fine mid-18th-century organ by Silbermann.

Facing the cathedral across the square stand the **Semper Opera House**, first built by Gottfried Semper in 1838–41 and subject to a huge restoration programme by the German Democratic Republic. It was eventually reopened in 1985 to reveal a very high standard of comfort and facilities as well as painstaking attention to period detail.

A few steps away is Dresden's most famous sight, the **Zwinger** (keep), a complex of Baroque-style pavilions grouped round a graceful, relaxed courtyard. It gets its name from the ancient fortifications that used to occupy

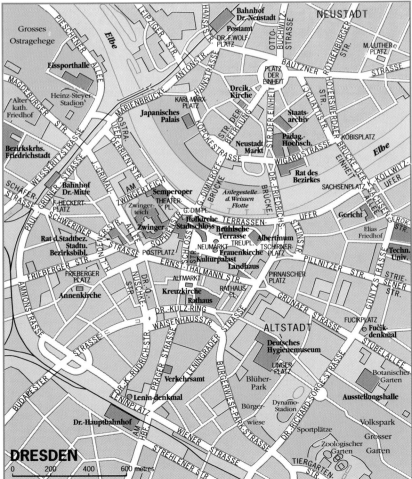

DRESDEN REGION

138

Detail from the Zwinger

the site: the buildings themselves date from 1711 to 1728 but have been added to and altered over the years. They contain a treasure-house of museums (closed Mondays), including a world-famous porcelain collection, and museums of science and zoology; the Gemäldegalerie Alter Meister (Gallery of Old Masters) will also return here from its temporary home in the Albertinum (see below) when restoration work is complete.

Behind the Zwinger, you will find the **Langer Gang** (long passage), a 16th-century arcade with Italian-style white pillars. On the outside, it bears a huge 19th-century porcelain frieze depicting Saxon princes. Near by are two more museums, of geology and transport.

Back by the Brühlsche Terrasse stands one of Dresden's most important galleries, the **Albertinum**, a 16th-century building that once served as an arsenal and which currently contains one of the world's most impressive art collections. One part of the building houses the Gemäldegalerie Neuer Meister (Gallery of New Masters, closed Mondays), which includes pictures by Dix, Liebermann and several French impressionists. Another, the Grünes Gewölbe (Green Vault, closed Tuesdays) contains the royal collection of silver, gold and jewellery as well as the star of the show, *The Court of Delhi on the Birthday of the Great Mogul*, a set of 132 gold, enamel and bejewelled painted figures. And a third provides a temporary setting for the Gemäldegalerie Alter Meister (closed Mondays, and due to be rehoused in the Zwinger, see above). The collection includes Raphael's *Sistine Madonna*, Giorgione's *Sleeping Venus* and works by Canaletto (many of them scenes painted on his visits to Dresden), Rembrandt, Vermeer and Titian. Further exhibitions include one of the most valuable sculpture collections outside Italy as well as over 200,000 coins, medals, notes and seals (both closed Tuesdays).

Further away from the river, the scene becomes bleaker, marked by big blocks and wide open spaces. One of these, the **Altmarkt**, was the bustling centre of a great city before it was razed to the ground in 1945; it has now recovered some of its bustle, but the charm will be harder to restore. In its southeast corner stands the **Kreuzkirche** (Church of the Holy Cross) which dates

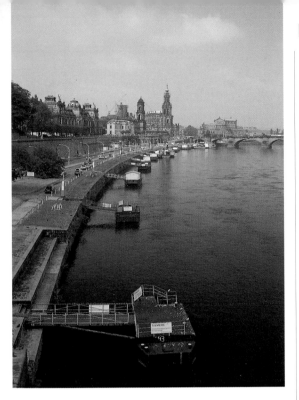

*A city view of
Dresden*

back to 1764–92 and is the oldest church within the line of the city walls. It is home to Dresden's famous choir, the Kreuzchor, who perform here most Saturday afternoons. To the south of the Altmarkt, you can continue along modern pedestrianised **Prager Strasse**, which houses the city's larger restaurants and hotels.

There's a little more of the flavour of pre-war Dresden across the Elbe in **Dresden-Neustadt**, which has many imposing 19th-century buildings, and is centred round a car-free main boulevard, the Hauptstrasse.

Excursions The best bet is to take a paddle-steamer (the **Weisse Flotte** steamers leave from the landing platforms by Terrassenufer) along the Elbe to some of the worthwhile destinations just outside Dresden. One option is the old town of **Meissen** (see page 152).

A very pleasant alternative is to go upstream to **Schloss Pillnitz** (10km southeast), a charmingly relaxed grouping of summer palaces built in Chinese style for the King of Saxony, and dating from 1723; it's set in a beautiful wooded section of the Elbe Valley, and is surrounded by a small park (closed Monday). Further upstream brings you to **Pirna** (20km from Dresden), an ancient market town straddling the river. Its market place boasts fine medieval houses, and the Marienkirche (St Mary's Church) is one of the finest late Gothic hall churches in Saxony. Pirna is known as the gateway to Saxon Switzerland (Sächsische Schweiz; see pages 155–6).

The **Dresdener Heide** (Dresden Heath) starts on the northeastern edge of town, and is easily reached by public transport. It's a relaxed area of common and open woodland, crossed with well-marked paths.

The Grosser Garten (or Volkspark), a large 17th-century park is about 1.5km southeast of the centre of Dresden, and includes a baroque pleasure palace and the city's zoo. Running through the park is the Parkeisenbahn, an enormous model railway with five stations and 5.6km of track. The Deutsches Hygiene Museum, built for the 2nd International Hygiene Exhibition (held in Dresden in 1930), is best known for its glass models of a woman, a cow and a horse (open Saturday to Thursday).

▶ ▶ ▷ Eisenach

Despite its small size, this city, nestling in wooded hills at the northwest end of the Thüringer Wald, has an enormous importance in the history of German civilisation. This is because of its position at the foot of the **Wartburg**, a spectacular hilltop castle dating back to the 11th century. It became an early centre for music and poetry, hosting the traditional *Sängerkrieg*, a competition for singer-poets, in the early 13th century – subsequently immortalised by Richard Wagner in his opera *Tannhäuser*. It was also famous as the residence of Martin Luther when he was preparing the first German language translation of the Bible. It's quite a stiff climb to the top from the town, but car parking near the castle is restricted (and gets very full); an alternative is to travel by special shuttle bus (the Wartburg-Express) or more traditional donkey. At the top, one ticket will get you into the inner courtyard and up the South Tower for a spectacular view; a second ticket is needed for a guided tour of the interior (long waits at busy periods), taking in Luther's study, the castle's art collection and various halls including the enormous Festsaal (banqueting hall) decorated with murals by Moritz von Schwind in the 19th century.

Back down in the town, a major point of interest is the J S Bach house commemorating the birthplace of Eisenach's most famous son. As well as a collection of music and instruments, and a very pretty garden, the museum offers short recitals on some of the keyboard instruments. A short distance away lies a small Luther museum containing a room Luther used as a student. In a completely different vein, Eisenach also has an automobile museum housed in a small pavilion close to the centre, containing examples of Wartburg cars which were produced here over the years (the factory has now been taken over by Opel).

One of Eisenach's attractions is its big squares surrounded by graceful houses: in the centre of the largest of these (the Markt) stands St George's church, which has an unusual galleried interior, decorated with murals.

Cars on display in the Automobile Museum of the old Wartburg factory, Eisenach

An Erfurt street

▶ ▶ ▷   Erfurt

The capital and largest town of Thuringia, Erfurt has its fair share of dereliction and hideous development. But at its core lies an extensive and, for the most part, well-preserved medieval core, crowned by its imposing cathedral and neighbouring St Severin's church with pointed spires which loom large over the large, irregularly-shaped Domplatz (cathedral square), which is used for fairs and markets of all sorts.

The cathedral, reached up a flight of 70 steps from the square, dates back to the mid-12th century and was built in the form of a Romanesque basilica, though it gained a Gothic choir in the mid-14th century. It contains some fine works of art, including a Romanesque altar, carved wooden stalls and 14th- to 15th-century stained glass. The largest bell in eastern Germany, the 'Gloriosa', hangs in the middle tower. The 14th-century St Severin's church boasts some of Germany's finest early Gothic architecture and a splendid 15th-century font.

Down in the town, there's a wealth of fine buildings and streets to see. Some of the ancient houses are in poor shape, especially away from the main streets, but the showpieces around the pedestrianised centre have been well looked after. The highlight of these is the Krämerbrücke (Shopkeeper bridge), an extremely pretty bridge over the wide and shallow River Gera, lined with tall, narrow half-timbered houses. It is the only bridge of its kind north of the Alps. Nowadays, humbler trades in

Old Erfurt

the narrow cobbled street that passes between them have given way to antique shops. A few streets away is the restored 13th-century Augustiner church and monastery which had Martin Luther among its novices.

A couple of kilometres southwest of the centre, the 15th-century (but much altered) Cyriaksburg castle stands in leafy grounds, part of which are given over to a large permanent museum and exhibition devoted to all forms of gardening and horticulture – a long-established Thuringian local industry.

▶ ▷ ▷ **Erzgebirge**

The Erzgebirge is a range of mountains stretching for 140km along the Czech frontier from the Vogtland (see page 166) to Saxon Switzerland (see pages 155–6). It includes the highest point in eastern Germany, the Fichtelberg (1,214m).

The western part of the range is characterised by steep-sided valleys and thick forests, dotted with villages and small industrial towns; the eastern part, to the east of the River Flöha, consists mainly of high plateaux and is more open in appearance. The whole area gets its name (Erz means ore) from the mineral ores which have been mined here since the 12th century, starting with silver. Sadly, more recently, open cast lignite mining (mostly on the Czech side of the frontier) has led to very high levels of pollution, and many trees have, unfortunately, become diseased.

As successive mines became exhausted, local inhabitants turned their hands to a variety of crafts, and the area is particularly well-known for its toy-making industry.

What to see Annaberg-Buchholz is the biggest town in the area and has a large and spectacular hall church, the biggest in Saxony, dating from 1499–1525, with a fine main portal and several beautiful altars. Nearby **Frohnau** (2km west) has an unusual industrial museum, Frohnauer Hammer (closed Mondays, except June–August) which was originally (1436) a corn mill, converted to a silver and iron forge in 1621. Twenty-four km to the south, **Ober-Wiesenthal** is a winter sports and mountain resort at the foot of the Fichtelberg; the 1,214m summit can be reached by cable car for a fine panoramic view.

In the eastern part of the Erzgebirge, **Seiffen** has been the centre of the Saxon toy industry since the 18th century. Its main points of interest are its two museums: one, the Spielzeugmuseum (Toy Museum, open daily) documents the history of local toy making, and shows many of the traditional items made in the area; a second, the Freilichtmuseum (Open Air Museum, open daily except in winter), on the Deutscheinsiedel road out of town, shows furniture and folk history of the region.

A view of the Obermarktplatz (upper market place) buildings in Görlitz

▶ ▶ ▷   **Görlitz**

Görlitz is a large and extremely ancient city which once spread across both banks of the River Neisse but which, following World War II, found itself straddling the German-Polish border.

The German part of town contains most of the old centre, which – though shabby in parts – has many crooked, narrow streets spectacularly rich in medieval buildings, both secular and religious. The most interesting examples are grouped around the part-arcaded Untermarkt (lower market place), which has a notably fine collection of Renaissance and baroque town houses; look out particularly for the house at no. 22 which has an unusual portal.

In nearby Neissestrasse, house no 29 (the 'Biblische

The town hall clock in Görlitz

Haus') dates from 1570 and bears relief scenes from the Old and New Testaments. The Rathaus (town hall) is in an unusual mixture of styles dating mostly from the 14th and 16th centuries.

▶ ▷ ▷ **Gotha**

The centre of Gotha is dominated by the 360-room 17th-century baroque castle of Friedenstein, which stands on a hill above the main square. Ranged around a large square courtyard, the massive white-painted, arcaded buildings incorporate a local history and cartography museum, a theatre and a library. The town's other main highlight is the long, narrow Hauptmarkt (market square), which stretches down the hill. At the top of the square is a group of restored Renaissance buildings, and the neo-Renaissance red and white town hall.

Excursion

Friedrichroda is a small, relaxed resort on the edge of the Thüringian Forest: a 17km ride on the narrow-gauge Waldbahn (forest train) takes you through the fields and back gardens of this pretty and unspoiled area.

▶ ▷ ▷ **Greifswald and Usedom**

Greifswald lies on the eastern side of Mecklenburg-Vorpommern, not far from the Greifswalder Bodden, a shallow, virtually tideless bay of the Baltic. In the 13th century monks founded this settlement near their coastal monastery of Eldena. In 1278 the town became part of the Hansa League. In 1648, after the Thirty Years' War, Greifswald was granted to Sweden, only to return to Germany in 1815 under Prussian rule.

Greifswald has some fine buildings, notably an originally Gothic town hall, rebuilt in the 18th century after a fire, the 13th-century Marienkirche, half-timbered St Spiritus Hospital and town houses with elegant gabled façades. The painter David Caspar Friedrich was born here in 1774; his highly evocative paintings of coastal seascapes and the ruins of Eldena Monastery provide a record of the landscape as it was early last century.

Usedom Not far from Greifswald across the straits of the Peene Strom lies Usedom, a curiously shaped island which extends over the Polish-German border. Wollin, the eastern part of the island, is Polish territory. There are excellent bathing beaches, with small seaside resorts at Bansin, Heringsdorf, Ahlbeck and Zinnowitz, overlooked by a castle, and attractive inland lakes such as the Gothenesee and the Schmollensee. Eighty-five per cent of the surface area of Usedom, predominately meadowland, woods, bays and dunes, is protected landscape, much of it nature reserve. The area enjoys considerable peace and tranquillity. In clear weather there are views to the southeast tip of Rügen, while the border crossing at Ahlbeck brings neighbouring Poland's Swinemunde within easy access.

Peenemunde, on the northern extremity of Usedom, was the unlikely place where, during World War II, the physicist Werner von Braun developed and tested the notorious V1 and V2 rockets. This high technology was put to rather better use in post-war times when von Braun, now part of the United States Space Research team, helped to develop starter rockets for the US space programme and successful first flight to the moon.

145

A rooftop view of Griefswald

The Rathaus in Halle

▶ ▷ ▷ Halle

Now a major industrial and cultural centre, Halle is one of central Germany's oldest cities, and was the birthplace of the composer Händel (see page 147). Its wealth came originally from the mining of the salt. The city's Halloren and Saline Museum brings much of that past to life. Halle's most striking landmark is the four-towered,16th-century church of Unser Lieben Frauen in the market place. Close by is the Roter Turm (Red Tower) which became a symbol to Halle people of their struggle against feudal domination. The Moritzburg, now the city's art gallery, is a late 15th-century Gothic fortress, built as a stronghold for the powerful Archbishops of Magdeburg against such insurrection.

▶ ▷ ▷ Heiligenstadt

A small, quiet resort on the River Leine, Heiligenstadt's long, partly pedestrianised main street is dominated by the parish church of St Martin. The centre was partly destroyed by fire in 1759, but several half-timbered and Renaissance houses survive from earlier times, among them the 15th-century Mainzer house and the baroque Rathaus.

Set at the centre of the hilly and part-forested Eichsfeld region, Heiligenstadt has long been popular as a place for recuperation. It also has a famous son: the great 16th-century wood carver and sculptor, Tilman Riemenschneider.

Händel

■   **Georg Friedrich Händel was born in the city of Halle, where his statue now surveys the market square, in 1685 (the same year as J S Bach). His complete mastery of composition is evident from the fact that he wrote 46 operas, over 30 oratorios and a large number of cantatas, concerti grossi, sacred music and various other instrumental and vocal works. .....■**

Against the wishes of his father, a noted barber-surgeon, Händel became organist at Halle Cathedral at the age of 17, while studying law. In 1706 he went to Italy for four years, where he became known as a virtuoso harpsichordist and violinist, so earning himself the title of *il caro Sassone* ('the dear Saxon'). He also wrote his first operas – including *Almira* – in the Italian style. Despite giving a poor impression (he was always in London) to the Elector of Hannover, to whose court he had been appointed *Kapellmeister* in 1710, Händel followed his master when the Elector succeeded Queen Anne to the English throne as George I in 1714. The *Water Music* may even have been written to appease his patron. If this was the composer's aim, he was certainly successful since, on his succession to the monarchy, George I doubled his pension.

In London Händel busied himself in the composition of more operas, with mixed fortunes. This patchy operatic success caused him to experiment with a new musical form, the oratorio. In this new area success was immediate and undoubted; Händel conducted no fewer than 15 separate oratorio concerts in 1735 alone but in 1737 he suffered a stroke. Nevertheless, the next five years saw him complete many of his finest works, including *Saul* (1739), *Israel in Egypt* (1739) and *The Messiah* (1742). His health continued to deteriorate and in 1759 he died; he was buried in Poet's Corner in Westminster Abbey.

Right: Georg Friedrich Händel, master of the oratorio

Above: Händel's house in Halle, where the composer was born in 1685

▷ ▷ ▷ Jena

The vast modern housing estate of Lobeda, which marches along the valley connecting the centre of Jena with the motorway, makes a sad introduction to this ancient university town, famous also for its optical industry started by Carl Zeiss in the mid-19th century. Zeiss' name and work is commemorated in the planetarium (the world's oldest working one), located in the botanic garden just north of the centre; the city also has an optical museum.

Jena has illustrious associations with some of the greatest figures in German culture: Hegel and Schiller taught at the university, and Goethe was a frequent visitor to the city.

One end of the enormous market place, lined by the 14th-century town hall and Gothic St Michael's church, has some charm, but with most of the rest of the centre rebuilt in monumental modern style, topped by a 26-storey cylindrical university building, the city is heavily dependent on its past glories.

 Old and new architecture in Jena

▶ ▶ ▶ Leipzig

Founded by Slavic settlers in the 7th and 8th centuries, by the 10th century Urbs Libzi, or the town by the lime trees, had become a German stronghold and flourishing centre where the great east–west and north–south trade routes intersected on the Thuringian-Saxon plain. Today Leipzig is Saxony's largest city, a major industrial, shopping, cultural and administrative centre with 550,000 inhabitants, renowned for its long associations with trade, science, humanism, music and publishing, and its twice yearly Trade Fair.

Leipzig's university was founded in 1409. Martin Luther preached here many times and disputed passionately with his opponents. Books were printed for the first time in Leipzig in 1481, laying the foundations for its long publishing tradition. Music was first printed in the city in 1754. Johann Sebastian Bach worked as cantor and director of music at the Thomaskirche for the last 27 years of his life until his death in the city in 1750. A bronze plaque in the church marks his grave. Richard Wagner was born in the city in 1813 but later had to flee

Instant art: a street artist produces a portrait to order in Leipzig town, where there are long-established links with many branches of the arts

EASTERN GERMANY

Looking towards Leipzig's Marktplatz

Protest against the 40-year-long communist dictatorship in East Germany came to a head in the late 1980s in Leipzig in regular prayers for peace at the Nikolaikirche led by Neues Forum – New Forum – an alliance of Christian and liberal-democratic protesters. Candles were lit and carried by thousands of people of the city as a potent symbol of peaceful protest which helped to bring about the downfall of the hated Honecker regime. Prominent among dissidents was the celebrated Leipzig conductor Kurt Masur. The Nikolaikirche, built between the 13th and 16th centuries, has an inspiring 18th-century interior that symbolises hope – elegant white columns soaring upwards and bursting into delicate green palm fronds at their apex, crowned by a ceiling in shades of pink and green, complemented by stately white pews.

149

for his life for supporting radical views. The world famous Leipzig Gewandhaus orchestra is based in the city at the Neues Gewandhaus concert hall.

Much of the city centre is now traffic free, with fine old squares, gardens, courtyards and shopping arcades opening out of the centralised pedestrianised areas. Despite some brutal rebuilding of office blocks, apartments and the university in modern concrete, many superb buildings remain. The richly decorated railway station is one of the most impressive in Germany. The Old Town Hall houses the Alte Börse, the old Stock Exchange, built between 1678 and 1687 and one of the city's loveliest baroque buildings. Many other fine 18th-century baroque façades can be seen in the city centre, for example in the Katherinenstrasse.

Goethe studied law in Leipzig as a young man and set a scene of *Faust* in Auerbach's Cellar, still to be found in the Madlerpassage, where Mephistopheles is made to ride out on a barrel of wine. Goethe was also one of the celebrated visitors to the famous coffee house called the Kaffeebaum in the Kleine Fleischergasse.

Sculpture in Leipzig's shopping area

The Magdeburg hemispheres
A 17th-century experiment by Magdeburg's scientific mayor, the physicist Otto von Gueriche (1602–86), who wanted to prove the strength of atmospheric pressure (the force exerted by the air around us), has ensured that Magdeburg's fame has spread worldwide. Von Gueriche put together two metal hemispheres and removed the air from inside them, to form a vacuum. When 16 horses (eight tied to each hemisphere) failed to pull them apart, this conclusively proved his thesis.

▶ ▷ ▷   **Magdeburg**

As early as AD968, this Archbishop's seat was the centre of the Church's mission to Christianise the Slavic population. The city's original constitution of the same date became known as the Magdeburg Laws and was used as a model for the establishment of numerous other towns in eastern Germany. Magdeburg's 13th-century cathedral was the first Gothic cathedral on the Elbe, its scale a testimony to the power and influence of the city in the middle ages. Around 90 per cent of Magdeburg, including part of the cathedral itself, was destroyed in World War II, though its central areas have been rebuilt and elegantly laid out with boulevards and shops, with many of the historic buildings carefully reconstructed or restored.

The Monastery of Our Lady, north of the Domplatz, now houses a collection of medieval wood sculptures and also the national collection of contemporary small-scale sculptures. A wine cellar in the Buttergasse dates from 1200 and was only discovered by chance during rebuilding operations.

In the old market place, the former heart of the city, is a baroque town hall and the Eulenspiegel Fountain, a modern tribute to the famous medieval folk hero and prankster Till Eulenspiegel. The baroque composer Georg Philipp Telemann (1671–1767) was born in Magdeburg, and the present day concert hall bears his name.

Links between the River Elbe and the Mittellandkanal in the 1930s allowed river traffic from the Ruhr to the Elbe and Magdeburg became an important inland port, increasing its trading and industrial base. Cruise boats of the Weisse Flotte now operate from and through the city between Hamburg and Dresden.

▶ ▶ ▷   **The Mecklenburgische Seenplatte and Muritz National Park**

The Mecklenburgische Seenplatte (Mecklenburg Lake Plateau) consists of over a thousand lakes, residue from the last Ice Age when retreating glaciers left great moraines, banks of sand and pebble-like detritus. The ice also carved out channels and basins through which ecaping water formed runnels and waterfalls. Storms carried loose sand into hilly dunes which, as the climate warmed, became carpeted with woodland to create a distinctive undulating lowland landscape patterned with small lakes.

The 310sq km Müritz National Park was founded in October 1990 from Germany's largest nature reserve. It extends from Waren to beyond Neustrelitz and from the Müritzsee's eastern shore to the source of the Havel. Sixty-five per cent of the area is forest, 25 per cent moorland and water, six per cent meadow and grazing land and around four per cent is currently under cultivation. About 200 years ago the River Elbe was widened and deepened causing the water level of the Müritzsee to sink by 2m, so that the low-lying eastern banks of the lake dried out, with consequent changes to the natural flora.

The Müritzsee, or 'Morcze' (small sea), as it was known by the Slavs, is one of 117 lakes in the national park. It is 6m deep and 27km long and is Germany's second largest lake. Conditions on the lake area can be very severe, particularly in February when blocks of floating ice are a common occurrence; heavy thunderstorms and impenetrable mist can also be a hazard at other times of the year. Carpets of beautiful white water lilies cover stretches of water in the summer months. The lake

Archaeological remains indicate that the Mecklenburgische Seenplatte was already settled by Mesolithic (Middle Stone Age) times while Neolithic stone graves, pottery and flint axes and Bronze Age jewellery, a Roman import of a richly decorated silver bowl in Iron Age times and 7th-century evidence of Slavic settlement, point to the area having a complex history of settlement and resettlement. Among especially attractive townships in the area, many of them of Slav origin, are Neustrelitz, Feldberg, Mirow and Weserberg.

The medieval Monastery of Our Lady in Magdeburg: an exterior view (above left) and the monastery's doorway (below)

boasts 700 varieties of plants and grasses, 800 varieties of butterfly and countless varieties of insects and is particularly noted for its orchids, gentians, sundew and rare grasses, especially in the area known as the Spukloch (the Spook's Hole). Only Scandinavian Fjallrinder or white unhorned cattle, sheep and horses are allowed to graze in this very vulnerable area. Rare birds such as cranes, white-tailed eagles and black storks enjoy the strictly protected habitat. The shore woodland consists of alders, birches, oaks, beeches and fir. There are wild deer in the forest, who can at times cause problems by over-grazing.

Despite the emphasis on nature protection, there are plenty of well marked paths for walkers, riders and cyclists to enjoy. The lake is also available for boating and sailing, though part of the lake and its shore is restricted to exclude boats so that the breeding of the most vulnerable bird species will not be affected.

A craftswoman at work producing the internationally famous Meissen porcelain

▶ ▶ ▷   Meissen

Meissen's castle – the Albrechtsburg, which stands on a rock rising above the broad River Elbe – was the birthplace of the European porcelain industry in 1710; ever since, the town's name has been closely linked with the finest decorative tableware. The factory, at 9 Talstrasse, offers a demonstration workshop and showroom (closed Mondays), but the town's main attractions are on and around the Albrechtsburg. The castle itself (closed Mondays) dates back to the late 15th century and is a showpiece of late Gothic. The neighbouring Dom (cathedral), which shares the triangular hilltop site, is older still, dating from the mid-12th century, though its soaring twin spires, which dominate the whole area, are early 20th century. Down in the town centre, around the picturesque market place, you'll find numerous medieval town houses and a Renaissance brewery.

About 17km east, standing in pleasant informal parkland, is **Moritzburg Castle** (closed Mondays), an outstandingly well preserved early 18th-century hunting lodge containing a collection of baroque furniture and exhibits of the history of hunting.

▶ ▷ ▷ **Mühlhausen**

Mühlhausen's old town is quiet and remarkably well-preserved, encircled by town walls which you can still walk around; they're punctuated by towers and gateways leading to murky cobbled streets lined with ancient houses. In the centre are several impressive churches, including the enormous hall church of St Marien (the second largest in Thuringia, after Erfurt Cathedral), as well as Renaissance mansions. The part-Gothic town hall has an attractive inner courtyard and incorporates a 16th-century church.

The town's main historical claim to fame is its association with Thomas Müntzer, a leader of the Peasants' Revolt which was organised from here in 1524–5; he was seen by the former East German regime as an early revolutionary (though Martin Luther warned against him!). The town has attracted several monuments and memorials, including one to Müntzer himself in the St Marien church, and to the Peasants' Revolt in the Barfüsser Monastery church.

Scholtheim (17km east) has fine half-timbered houses, a baroque castle of 1773 and a Romanesque church.

▶ ▷ ▷ **Nordhausen**

Nordhausen lies on a sloping site above the River Zorge, and forms the southern terminus of the narrow-gauge railway crossing the Harz (the Harzquerbahn), which is partly operated by steam trains. Dating back over 1,000 years, the centre is still partly encircled by walls. The attractive, irregularly-shaped market square is lined with half-timbered houses and overlooked by the twin towers of St Basil's parish church, an imposing and spacious late 15th-century Gothic building. A couple of blocks away, the modest Dom zum Heiligen Kreuz (Cathedral of the Holy Cross) dates back to the 13th century, with a Romanesque crypt and a 14th-century nave lined with massive octagonal pillars.

Parts of the centre were damaged by heavy air strikes late in World War II, but numerous half-timbered houses survive, notably along the Barfüsser Strasse, at the top of which stands the Flohburg, a large black and white structure dating back to 1500. The large stone Renaissance town hall bears a colourful figure of Roland, a long-established symbol of the town.

To the southeast of Nordhausen (approx 20km) lies the **Kyffhäuser Natural Park**, an area of modest but very striking wooded hills rising to 477m on the Kulpenberg, topped with a TV transmitter. The slightly lower Kyffhäuser (453m) bears an 80m monument to Kaiser Wilhelm. Legend has it that one of his predecessors, Friedrich I, dreamt of German unity on this site, and would sleep until the day it came – but there have so far been no reports of his waking up. On the western edge of Kyffhäuser, there's bathing at the Kelbra reservoir, and the ruins of nearby Rothenburg castle lie in a secluded wooded setting. To the south lies the small town of **Bad Frankenhausen** which has mineral springs, a spectacularly leaning church (more precarious even than the Leaning Tower of Pisa) and a panoramic modern mural commemorating the decisive battle of the Peasants' Revolt in 1525, on the Schlachtberg.

In August 1992 refugee hostel residents in Rostock's bleak Lichtenhagen housing estate came under attack from neo-Nazi rioters, cheered on by local residents. Faced with West Germans' questions about the ability and willingness of Easterners to pull their economic weight, Easterners in their turn have sought someone to blame for post-unification unemployment and inflation. The collapse of the Wall brought an influx of refugees to the new Germany, many fleeing racial intolerance. The extreme right wing has found them an easy scapegoat for the East's fall from economic grace.

154

▶ ▶ ▷ Rostock

The city of Rostock has a long history. Originally a Slavonic coastal fortress, after being sacked in 1161 by King Waldemar of Denmark, it was settled and developed in the 13th century by German merchants and soon became a prosperous port, part of the famous Hanseatic trading league. In 1419 one of the first universities in Northern Europe was founded in Rostock and the city became a centre for learning and culture, though from the 17th century onwards its economic importance declined compared with the rapidly growing rival ports of Hamburg and Kiel.

Sadly, much of the older part of this strategically situated Baltic port was destroyed in World War II – only four of the 22 former ancient city gateways remain, but these include the handsome 54m Kropliner Gate, dating from the 13th century. Several of the city's medieval churches have been restored, and there are some attractive gabled merchants' houses.

The city grew rapidly in importance during the immediate post-war years, being developed into a major Eastern Bloc shipbuilding and industrial centre and becoming East Germany's main sea port and means of access to the outside world. The port was particularly significant in terms of trade to and from the former Soviet Union, traffic which has now virtually disappeared. There are impressive museums of shipbuilding and shipping, and a large zoological garden and botanic gardens.

Excursions

Rostock is a conveniently situated centre to reach a number of small but attractive seaside resorts along the Baltic coast. It's worth making the trip to the graceful old spa town of **Bad Doberan**, with its celebrated 14th-century Cistercian monastery, if only to take the narrow gauge steam railway with the charming nickname of 'Molli'. This little railway links Bad Doberan with **Ostseebad Heiligendamm**, Germany's oldest seaside resort which was founded in 1793. It is celebrated for its charming period cottages which resulted in the village being known as 'The white town by the sea'. There is a lovely neo-classical spa building or Kurhaus in the village centre. Close by is the Conventer Lake Nature Reserve, a wildlife reserve.

Kühlungsborn, also linked to Bad Doberan by 'Molli', is a far newer seaside resort, developed from three villages linked together during the 1930s. As well as a heated seawater bathing pool, the town has 4km of sandy beach. Notable features are an early Gothic church with a wooden tower, and a 19th-century windmill.

▶ ▷ ▷ Rudolstadt

Rudolstadt nestles in the pretty valley of the River Saale, on the eastern fringes of the Thuringian forest. Its wide, pleasant main square, flanked on one side by an imposing medieval town hall and clock tower, is thankfully bypassed by the traffic which thunders through this town; from here it's a short, steep climb up to Schloss Heidecksburg, a graceful baroque hilltop

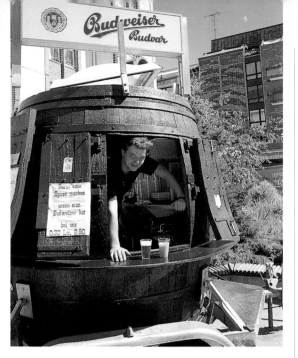

A beerstand in Rostock

palace ranged around three sides of a courtyard. It houses collections of furniture, painting and weapons, and hosts baroque music concerts in summer.

Further cultural attractions are provided by the small Thuringian Landestheater (provincial theatre), which was founded by Goethe, a frequent visitor to the town (as was Schiller, who met his wife Charlotte here).

Across the river from the castle and main historic centre is the Thuringian Farm Museum (Volkskundemuseum) where two fine half-timbered farmhouses are displayed in a parkland setting.

Excursions

About 8km to the northeast of Rudolstadt lies **Kochberg** which has a castle owned by the von Stein family whom Goethe often visited. Many of its rooms have been restored to what they were in Goethe's time. **Paulinzella** (23km west) has romantic 12th-century monastic ruins in a wooded setting.

▶ ▶ ▶ Sächsische Schweiz

A short way upstream along the Elbe from the outskirts of Dresden, between the city and the Czech border, lies some of Germany's most dramatic scenery: Saxon Switzerland National Park, also known as the Elbe Sandstone District.

High sandstone cliffs and crags, forming a deep gorge through which the River Elbe flows, have been exposed, weathered and worn over millennia by frost, wind and rain into a series of fantastic sculptured shapes – pillars, towers, arches and stacks towering some 300m above the river. In places they are exposed as bleak, bare crags, a kind of central European Grand Canyon. In other places trees and shrubs twist out of cracks, cling to crevices, crowd onto summits and form the kind of

fantastic landscape that inspired such painters as the great 19th-century romantic Caspar Friedrich. Ancient woodlands – pine, beech, oak, maple, fir – flourish around and between the craggy rocks, forming a dense green backcloth to the sculptured formations.

Between the crags wind deep, narrow gorges, some of them barely a couple of metres wide, cool and shady on even the hottest summer day, many of them penetrated by winding footpaths which suddenly emerge into full daylight at thrilling viewpoints. Narrow tributary valleys of the Elbe, especially the Polenz, the Sebnitz and the Kirnitz, also create dramatic features within this unique area of natural beauty.

At Bastei (road access and car park), a pedestrian bridge was built from stone in the 1850s, 194m above the Elbe, creating a remarkable viewpoint. It is linked to a series of pedestrian walkways across the crag summits, all with safety rails.

Across the river at Königstein a massive crag has been used as the base of a great medieval fortress, strategically placed to defend the valley and dating back to the 14th century.

Although the area is now strictly protected as a national park and nature reserve, access is easy from Dresden by road along the B172 or by suburban railway, with a series of ferries crossing the river to such small riverside resorts as Stadt Wehlen, Kurort Rathen, Schmilka and Bad Schandau. In the summer months, the Weisse Flotte boat services operate a regular public passenger service along the river from Dresden.

Schwerin's castle, seen from the pleasure gardens

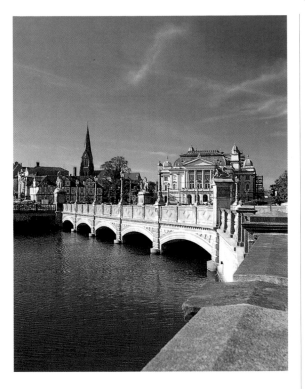

Looking across the Schwerin's castle bridge towards the state theatre

▶ ▶ ▷   Schwerin

The old city of Schwerin in Mecklenburg has some lovely half-timbered houses in its centre, and an imposing cathedral, founded in 1171. The town hall in the market square has a medieval core, though with a neo-Gothic facade of 1835. The early 18th-century Nikolaikirche, also called the Schelfkirche, is the finest of Mecklenburg's baroque churches, while the imposing Kollegiengebäude in Schloss Strasse is the administrative headquarters of the state government. Trip boats operate from the town centre across the Schweriner See to Zippendorf where the 138m television tower provides panoramic views of lake, city and countryside.

Schwerin's spectacularly beautiful castle is set on an island, joined to the mainland by twin bridges. Reminiscent of a Loire château, it was built for the Dukes of Mecklenburg in neo-Renaissance style, one of the architects being Gottfried Semper who designed Dresden's Semper Opera House. The castle now houses the Mecklenburg-Vorpommern State Parliament. In the north wing there is a beautiful church. To the south of the castle are baroque pleasure gardens with canals, groves and paths in formal geometric patterning. To the northwest, in the former castle garden, is the state theatre and the art gallery with a collection of important Dutch and Flemish masters.

The Sorbs are a Slavic people who have kept their own language and culture in two regions in Germany, in Lower Lusatia around the Spreewald and in Upper Lusatia in the southeast of Saxony east of Dresden. Signposts and official notices in both areas are in two languages – German and Sorbian – and Catholic churches use the Sorbian language in their liturgy. Ortenburg, a castle in the beautiful 1,000-year-old town of Bautzen, is said to be the place where their tribal fortress used to stand. Today Bautzen with its baroque- and Renaissance-style buildings is the centre of Sorbian culture and tradition, and the seat of the Sorbian national organisation, the Domowina. There is also a Sorbian publishing house, regular newspaper, comprehensive school and Sorbian-German folk theatre. Many Sorbian customs are preserved, such as Easter Riding, a mixture of the pagan and the Christian, while during Lent young people go from house to house playing bagpipes and fiddles, asking for eggs and bacon, and money. Straw brooms are burnt like the witches of old and Easter eggs are decorated with beautiful intricate designs. Sorbian national costume is generally now only worn for festivals and holidays and is extremely colourful with its intricate embroidery.

▶ ▶ ▶ The Spreewald

The River Spree southeast of Berlin, between Berlin and Cottbus, flows through an area of low-lying countryside, splitting into countless minor tributaries, creating the complex area of lakes, ponds, marsh, wetland and riverine woodland known as the Spreewald. There are also areas of low-lying farmland drained by a network of small canals and dykes.

This is an area which has a unique beauty, due to the effects of light both in early spring, when the birch trees lining its water channels are reflected in the water, and again in late summer and autumn when the luxurious vegetation and vivid colours makes the shortest excursion an adventure. Much of the area is now a Biosphere Reserve, reflecting both the natural beauty and wildlife interest of the area and its rich cultural associations, particularly linked with the Sorbian settlements in the area. The region is divided into the **Unterspreewald** north of Lübben, and the larger and better known **Oberspreewald**, north of Lübbenau. The whole of the Spreewald teems with game such as wild boar, deer, partridges and pheasants; white storks and herons can also be seen in abundance.

The area also had its own highly characteristic form of local transport, with narrow barges or punts carrying both people and goods along the myriad channels between villages and outlying farms in the forest. A favourite summer activity for visitors, including day trippers from Berlin, is to be punted along the various canals and canalised rivers and streams, though motors have replaced muscle power on most occasions.

The Lower Spreewald around the **Lübben** area is a large enclosed forest area with alder, birch and beech

Above and left: punting along the canals in the Spreewald

interspersed with areas of open, low-lying meadowland and watermeadows which provide an ideal habitat for numerous plants and animals, and biotopes for amphibians, water-loving insects, rare dragonflies, kingfishers and cranes.

The attractive Sorbian township of **Lübben** was founded in 1150, but its history goes back as far as mid-Stone Age times. Its castle, with richly decorated rooms, was built in the latter stages of the Renaissance and became the seat and capital of the Lower Lausatian government. The town is also the gateway to both Upper and Lower areas of the Spreewald, with motorised punt services into the forest.

From **Lübbenau**, a small tourist resort, there are splendid walks into the Oberspreewald along well signed paths over old canal-side dykes which go deep into the forest. Nearby **Lehde** has a fascinating open-air museum with traditional Sorbian farmhouses with their own distinctive waterside architecture, a kind of little Venice in the forest. In the summer months motorised barges link Lübbenau with the Lehde. The soil for the pleasure grounds of Lübbenau's early 19th-century castle had to be brought by barge. In the building itself is the old locomotive and carriage of the narrow gauge train the Spreewaldguste which ran for the last time in 1970.

The Oberspreewald has the historic town of **Burg** as its eastern gateway. There is another Biosphere Reserve here where eels, pike and plaice are available in abundance, while woodruff (used to colour the Berlin Weissbier bright green) also flourishes. Labyrinths of water channels are crossed by high wooden bridges, there being at least 300 around the town of Burg and its satellite parishes alone. Waterlilies bloom along quieter stretches of water; the whole area, with several nature reserves, is a paradise for the naturalist.

Market gardens in the area provide produce for nearby Berlin, Spreewald gherkins being a much prized delicacy. Plant extracts are also produced, used in a variety of homeopathic remedies.

▶ ▶ ▷ **Stralsund**

Stralsund occupies a defensive position on a small hillock between the Strelasund, the narrow strait which divides the Isle of Rügen from the mainland, and two attractive small lakes, the Knieper- and Frankenteichs. Like Rostock, this was a Hanseatic town, but between 1648 and 1815 it became part of Sweden before being reclaimed by Prussia. The old town and small harbour occupy this island, and boast particularly fine architecture, including impressive merchants' houses. In the Alt Markt is the remarkable reddish brick town hall, dating from the 13th century, with its high elegant façade. The Marienkirche dates from 1384, and two surviving towers are both 15th-century in origin. The town centre has an attractive pedestrianised market area, and scheduled passenger boats from the harbour link the mainland with the island of Hiddensee and with the Darss peninsula. The rail and road bridge linking Stralsund with the Isle of Rügen was built only in 1936. Stralsund is a stepping off point to explore the **Vorpommersche Boddenlandschaft National Park** – a coastal national park consisting of a long, mainly wooded coastline along the Baltic, close to such small fishing villages and quiet seaside resorts as **Pramont**, **Prerow**, **Zingst** and **Wiek**. This is an area of sand dunes, winding sandbanks, mudflats, and shallow seas, rich in birdlife, including many waders and coastal birds and for that reason strictly protected. The area also offers sanctuary for thousands of birds of passage, including some of the largest colonies of marine birds in northern Europe. The coast itself is famous for its ancient coastal woodlands, including rare shrubs and grasses.

Rügen The whole of the Isle of Rügen is fascinating. Putbus is a sleepy little inland resort deliberately planned by a local prince early last century to be like an English spa town with elegant houses round a green 'circus' in the style of Bath. There is a fine neo-classical theatre,

Stralsund, on its hill overlooking the Strelasund

There are fine stretches of virtually tideless bathing beach with clean sand around the small Stralsund resorts. A particular feature of the area is the many attractive thatched cottages and farmhouses along the Darss peninsula and in many of the villages, giving the area an 'English feel', though the style is markedly different.

The coastal road from Stralsund via Barth to Ribnitz Damgarten is a particularly attractive drive (also a bus service from Barth station). It follows the narrow peninsula between Darss and Fischland, the peninsula enclosing areas of quiet inland sea and saltwater marsh known as Bodden with their spectacular birdlife. There are well signed cycleways and walkways along the coast, especially along the raised defensive embankments, partially enclosed by woodland.

while the former Kurhaus in 'English' parkland, is the parish church. A narrow gauge steam railway, known as 'Rasender Roland' (Rushing Roland) links Putbus with the seaside resort of Göhren. It puffs its way through an idyllic landscape of old meadows, scattered woodlands, small lakes and storks' nests to the seaside resorts of Binz and Göhren with their fine sandy beaches.

The narrow peninsula to the south, known as **Mönchgut**, is also a protected landscape, this time a Biosphere Reserve, safeguarded as much for its cultural qualities as its landscape. It has old farmhouses and thatched fishermen's cottages, ancient meadows crowded with brilliant wildflowers, many of them rare, low coastal cliffs and pebbly beaches overlooking a distant coastline stretching away to Usedom and the Polish border. In the little museum in Göhren you'll find examples of early 19th-century Staffordshire ware, traded and brought back by sailors from England.

Sassnitz is an old port and ferry terminal on Rügen, where train and car ferries leave for Trelleborg in Sweden. Originally a small fishing port and quarry town, it later became a resort, and handsome 19th-century villas are still to be seen around the older part of the town. Immediately to the north of Sassnitz lies Jasmund National Park, with some of the most impressive coastal scenery in Germany. High chalk cliffs crowned by dense beechwoods overlook the quiet Baltic. Though thousands of tourists from coach and car park crowd the Kaiserstuhl, a tall chalk cliff and impressive viewpoint, a few hundred metres away along the coastal path all is quiet with impressive views. At Wissower Klinken, weather-carved chalk cliffs provide a dramatic feature which became the subject of one of the most famous of Caspar Friedrich's romantic paintings. The beechwoods, as well as the meadows and the heathland, provide a habitat for a rich flora, especially the orchids. Fauna include small reptiles and rare varieties of butterflies.

Despite the Thüringer Wald's many charms, it also has its sad side. Emissions from nearby open cast brown coal mines have caused dreadful air pollution in many parts, and a survey in 1989 showed that more than half the trees were affected. Some of the area's towns have suffered, too, from ramshackle industrial installations and aggressive modern development.

▶ ▶ ▷ **Thüringer Wald (Thuringian Forest)**

The Thüringer Wald covers an area of ancient hills stretching for about 100km southeastwards from Eisenach, and averaging about 30km wide. By German standards, the hills are not especially high – the highest point is the Grosser Beerberg at 982m – but the area is crossed by numerous narrow valleys, and is quite densely settled with old-fashioned villages and small industrial towns. The area is heavily forested, as its name implies, mostly with fir and beech trees, but the woodlands are interspersed with meadows and orchards, and there's plenty of variety from one kilometre to the next.

Because of its small scale and varied scenery, the Thüringer Wald is excellent walking country, and it has long been popular with East Germans for quiet country holidays and excursions. A long distance path – the Rennsteig – runs southeastwards from the Wartburg for 160km within the Thüringer Wald on its long journey heading for Budapest. Even for those not inclined to tackle its full length, it offers lots of opportunities to get into the countryside. Like many of the shorter paths which criss-cross the area, it's well-marked ('R' symbols on trees and signposts) and easy to follow.

Unusually for eastern Germany, the Thüringer Wald offers a reasonably good variety of accommodation. Proximity to western Germany has encouraged many

local people to try their hand at catering for tourists, and you'll find plenty of small pensions and *Zimmer frei* (rooms available) even in the villages, together with family-run restaurants and bars. There's plenty of Thüringer Bratwurst to go round, often from roadside barbecues.

What to see The best of the forest scenery in the Thüringer Wald lies along a line fairly close to the Rennsteig, and you willl have to come off the main roads to see it – see page 165 for a suggested route.

Of the smaller places towards the centre of the forest, it's worth making for **Schmalkalden** for its fine half-timbered houses grouped around an imposing irregular market square; nearby Schloss Wilhelmsburg dates back to the 1580s, and is one of Thuringia's most important Renaissance buildings. **Bad Liebenstein** has dignified spa buildings lining its leafy avenues; there are extensive views from the ruins of medieval Liebenstein castle, while nearby 18th-century Schloss Altenstein is set in an English-style park. **Wasungen**, set in the wooded Upper Werra valley, has numerous half-timbered buildings (including a fine three-storey town hall dating from 1533) in its specially-protected town

163

The ancient foothills of the small but diverse Thüringer Wald

Legacies of Cold War antagonisms in the Thüringer Wald countryside

centre. **Friedrichroda** (see also Gotha entry) is a relaxed forest resort with fine parks, an open-air swimming pool, a lake and a large early 19th-century castle, Reihhardsbrunn, once reserved for high Party officials and now a hotel. The nearby Marienglashöhle caves (closed Monday and Tuesday) boast unusual gypsum crystal formations. **Oberhof** is an important local winter-sports centre, dominated by the striking modern Hotel Panorama, built in the form of two ski-jumps. An alpine garden contains 1,500 specimens collected from all over the world (open from May to October).

A number of larger towns of historical and architectural interest ring the edge of the main forest area. **Suhl** was the capital of the whole region when this was part of the GDR, and gained tower blocks and an egg-box style shopping precinct. Famous since medieval times as a home of gun-making, the town also has a weapons museum (closed Monday and Tuesday) in the 17th-century malthouse building. The nearby old high street, the Steinweg, has been pedestrianised, and has several fine 18th-century houses.

Ilmenau, a glass- and porcelain-making town, was a favourite retreat of Goethe's, and has several places associated with him: the Amtshaus (official's house), Gabelbach hunting lodge, and the Goethe hut and Kickelhahn – all linked by a footpath called *Auf Goethes Spuren* (in Goethe's footsteps). **Arnstadt** gave J S Bach his first job as an organist, in the baroque church which now bears his name; a jaunty statue of the great man watches over the small market place of this very well preserved small town. The surrounding landscape of lush, gentle hills is exceptionally pretty, and is known for its botanical rarities, including German gentians.

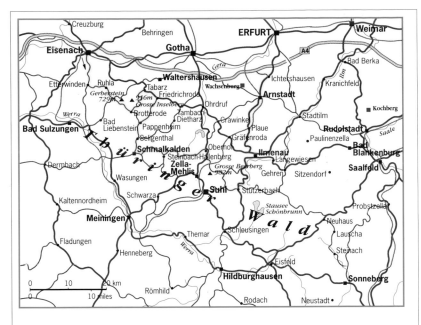

Drive **Thüringer Wald**

This 187km tour starts from Eisenach.

12km after leaving Eisenach on the D19 Meinigen road, turn left at Etterwinden, on an unclassified road to Ruhla and Brotterode. Here, turn left towards Tabarz.
After 4km you can park in the large car park on the right, to climb the Grosser Inselberg (approximately half an hour each way, on an easy path) for the mountain-top café, and a great view.

Continue to Tabarz, then right on the D88 road to Friedrichroda; leave by a minor road to Schmalkalden, then take minor roads to Steinbach-Hallenberg and Oberhof. Turn right on to the D247, then 1km south of the village, turn left on a minor road. This follows the Rennsteig and passes the Grosser Beerberg.

Continue to the main D4 road, turn left and return through Ilmenau and Arnstadt, to take the E40 motorway back to Eisenach.

▶ ▷ ▷ Vogtland

This hilly region of forests, steep-sided valleys, isolated rocks, lakes and dams extends along the southern frontier of the former GDR, up as far as the Erzgebirge on the Czech border (see page 142). The area is dotted with small, industrial towns – some of which are famous for musical instrument making – and with modest spas based on mineral-rich springs. The area's relaxed character and varied scenery make it a good choice for simple, open-air pursuits, notably walking on the many well-marked paths; there's some sailing on the lakes and reservoirs too.

Some of the best scenery is around **Klingenthal**, a straggling semi-industrial village right up against the Czech frontier and famous for its manufacture of harmonicas. 5km to the north lies **Schneckenstein**, the only place in Europe where topaz can be found – there are still some isolated rock formations in the area. **Schoeneck**, 12km to the northwest, marks the southern end of the dramatic, deeply cut valley of the Steinicht river. About 20km north of the town, around Schnarrtanne and Beerheide, you'll find some of the Vogtland's prettiest woodland scenery.

The biggest of the reservoirs is **Stausee Poehl** near the region's main town, Plauen, but there are lots of attractive small lakes in the area stretching south from here to Markneukirchen and Bad Elster.

Markneukirchen has been Germany's leading musical instrument making town since the early 19th century; it has a small baroque castle, the Paulusschloessel, which houses a collection of 1,000 musical instruments (closed Mondays). **Bad Elster**, in a quiet wooded side valley off the main road, has antique spa buildings dating from the mid-19th century. At **Landwuest,** 6km to the east, there's a small open-air folk museum with farm implements and local history collections (closed Mondays).

Tranquil scenery in Vogtland

▶ ▶ ▶ Weimar

Although only a modest-sized town, Weimar is one of Germany's greatest cultural treasures. With its fine public buildings, parks, squares and boulevards, it feels like a small capital city – which indeed it was, of Sachsen-Weimar from 1547 to 1870. Following a meeting of the German Parliament in the city in 1919, it gave its name to the ill-fated democratic republic that preceded the Hitler years. The city was lucky enough to be spared wartime destruction and for 40 years after World War II it managed to be spared the effects of mass international tourism. Now it's catching up fast, acquiring a Hilton hotel and plenty of bars and restaurants. Much of the older part of town is being spruced up with help from the German government.

Weimar's catalogue of cultural connections is almost limitless: Goethe spent most of his working life here, and his influence on the life of the city was immense; the writers Friedrich von Schiller and Johann Gottfried von Herder lived here; musical residents included Franz Liszt and Richard Strauss, who were both masters of music at the court; in the 20th century, Walter Gropius founded the Bauhaus Movement here.

There are lots of sights, many of them associated with Weimar's famous residents. Provided you can dodge seemingly endless building works, it can be a relaxing city, helped by its manageable size, its neat squares and outdoor cafés, and above all by the huge park which extends along the River Ilm almost to the town centre.

The **Goethehaus** on the Frauenplan (closed Mondays) will be top of most people's lists. This combines Goethe's own family house – still complete with his study, his books, furniture and collections of coins, minerals and art – with an imposing museum explaining the writer's life and influence (most explanations in German only). There's a charming small garden at the

Weimar: the Wittumspalais (top) and a flower stall in the market (above)

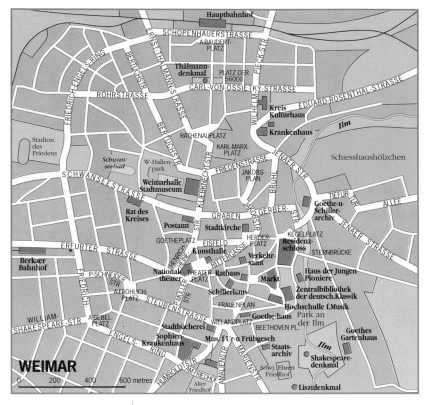

back. A few hundred metres away, in the Ilm Park, you can also visit **Goethe's Gartenhaus**, an idyllic rural retreat in which he lived for six years. The renovated **Schillerhaus** (closed Tuesdays), on Schillerstrasse, was lived in by Schiller for the last three years of his life, and incorporates many of his and his family's possessions; a modern museum annexe documents his work. The **Liszthaus** (closed Mondays), by the west entrance to the Ilm Park, was used by the composer as a summer residence for 17 years, and sets out his living and working quarters with many of his possessions, documents, pictures and mementoes.

Of the city's many palaces and castles, the **Wittumspalais** stands on the Theaterplatz, immediately opposite the National Theatre, with its famous double statue of Goethe and Schiller holding hands. The palace itself (closed Mondays, also Tuesdays in winter) was built for Duchess Anna Amalia in the 1770s when the main city palace burned down. It has been furnished in baroque style and has the atmosphere of a typical prosperous town house of the period. One room – the Tafelrundenzimmer (round table room) – was a popular meeting point for artists friendly with the court. In one wing of the palace there's a museum commemorating another famous Weimar resident, the writer von Herder. The main **Weimar Castle**, rebuilt in 1803, is an inspiring neo-baroque structure overlooking the Sternbrücke (Star Bridge) and River Ilm. It houses a collection of local paintings and fine arts (closed Monday). The nearby **Grünes Schloss** (Green Castle) houses the 900,000 volumes of the Library of the German Classics, many of which are extremely ancient. The best pieces are kept in the large Rococo Room decorated with busts of Weimar's literary giants.

Out of Town It's a very pleasant 20–minute walk along the River Ilm to the south of the town, through a large relaxed park, to the 'Roman House', a classical pavilion built in the 1790s, which enjoys a beautiful setting overlooking the river; inside there's a collection of local works of art (closed Tuesday). A further 5km out of town, in the same direction, brings you to **Schloss Belvedere**, a modest but charming country retreat and hunting lodge built in the 1730s, and flanked by two delightful single-storey pavilions (closed Monday and all winter); the surrounding park was landscaped in the early 19th century, when it acquired a large exotic plant collection kept in the Orangery and neighbouring glasshouses. About 5km to the northeast of the town, **Schloss Tiefurt**, built in 1760, became a major cultural centre in the late 18th century; the castle contains a collection of literary paintings and fine arts of the period, and stands in a finely-landscaped park stretching down to the banks of the Ilm.

On a much more sombre note, the stark remains of **Buchenwald concentration camp** stand 10km to the northwest of Weimar (open daily). There's a museum about the history of the camp (closed Monday) and a simple memorial to the 50,000 who were murdered there by the Nazis.

*Above: Duchess
Anna Amalia's home*

In 1346 a group of six towns from the Oberlausitz (Bautzen, Görlitz, Lobau, Laubau, Kamenz and Zittau) with imperial permission, banded together to further the development of cloth-making and linen weaving and to protect each other against attacks from robber knights and their followers. It has recently been decided to reconstitute this union as an aid to economic survival, an example of history partly repeating itself.

▶ ▶ ▷   Wernigerode

Wernigerode, strategically situated on the northern fringe of the Harz mountains, is famed for its richly coloured half-timbered houses and its elaborately carved, twin spired, late Gothic town hall. Wernigerode was granted its town charter in 1229 and in 1449 became the seat of the powerful Counts of Stolberg, and a prosperous trading centre. Its decline in later years perhaps helped to keep its medieval character. Inevitably the town suffered a number of fires in earlier periods, but miraculously its town hall, most of its charming streets and part of its defensive walls with impressive gates were spared. In the 18th century a number of baroque buildings were added. Overlooking the town, Wernigerode's castle, largely rebuilt in the mid 19th century, stands on the site of a much older fortress dating from 1121. It is rapidly being rediscovered as a tourist centre for the Harz, with several rebuilt and restored hotels. The town lies at the northern terminus of the Harzquerbahn narrow gauge steam railway to Nordhausen which gives access to superb walking country close by.

It's worth travelling just 50km east of Wernigerode to **Quedlingburg**, recently designated a UNESCO World Heritage Site because of its astonishing wealth of half-timbered houses along narrow streets and courtyards, with groups dating from the late Gothic (15th century) time onwards. One example, in Wordgasse, dating from the first half of the 14th century, is the oldest house in central Germany. With its narrow windows and uneven floors, it has been restored as a museum. The castle, built between the 16th and 17th centuries, also houses a museum. The Renaissance Town Hall with a statue of Roland dating from 1426 symbolising citizens' rights, overlooks a handsome pedestrianised square fringed by old inns, cafés and attractive shops.

The countryside surrounding Wittenberg

▶ ▷ ▷   Wittenberg

Lutherstadt Wittenberg is forever associated with Martin Luther, the great Protestant reformer, and his criticism of contemporary clergy and particularly of the sale of indulgences or pardons. As was then customary, in 1517 his 95 theses were nailed up on the town's church door. His ideas gained further prominence at Wittenberg's university (founded 1502), whence they spread throughout much of Europe. Luther's house is a museum and on the site of Luther's Oak, in front of which the Papal Bull was burned, a (later) oak tree

The Stadtkirche of St Mary in Wittenberg, where Luther often preached

stands. Close by is the Lutherhalle, the world's largest collection of exhibited material devoted to the Reformation. Famous Wittenberg contemporaries of Luther included court painter Lucas Cranach the Elder and theologian Philipp Melanchton, whose 16th-century dwelling is also a museum.

▶ ▷ ▷   Zittau

Zittau lies in the extreme southeast of Germany in the area known as Dreiländereck close to the Czech and Polish borders where lakes and heather predominate. The town dates from the 13th century, when it became an important trade centre under the protection of the Bohemian kings.

The town's former fortifications have now been replaced with green spaces and a flower clock which in winter is decorated with moss, pine cones and branches instead of flowering plants. The town has a market place with a Mars fountain dating from 1585 and an Italian-style town hall. The Marstall of 1511 (stables) dominates the Salzmarkt whilst the Dornsprachhaus is a lovely Renaissance building. The church of St Petri and St Pauli was originally an old Franciscan monastery church; the buildings now house the town's museum.

The 12km Zittauer narrow gauge steam railway, opened in 1890 to the spa towns of Oybin and Jonsdorf, passes beautiful rocky landscape in the Zittau mountains, a paradise for walkers and climbers. Oybin has a medieval castle, churches and monastery ruins on the Oybin Berg; Jonsdorf, a former weavers' village, has fine examples of the typical Oberlausitz Umbindehaus, a characteristic style of vernacular architecture with wooden arches over the housefront to support the weight of looms.

Zittau's relationship with its neighbours wasn't always peaceful. In the 15th century the town actually went to war over beer when townsmen of nearby Görlitz spilled several barrels of Zittau's celebrated beer at a place still known as the Beer Puddle.

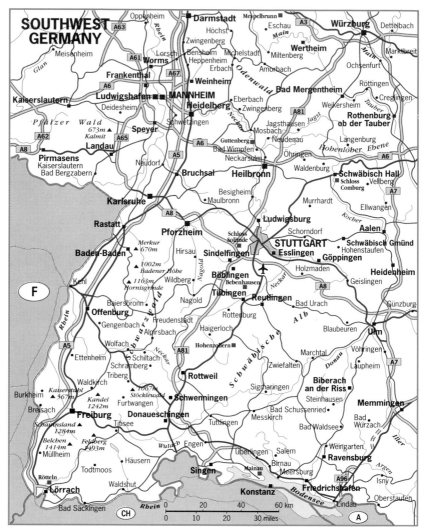

The southwest is an appealing region for gentle rural exploration, with plenty of peace and quiet, charming countryside, deep forests, wooden farmhouses and smart village resorts. There is excellent potential for walking, and sports facilities are plentiful. A wide range of accommodation exists, offering higher standards than in much of the rest of the country.

The region defined here incorporates **Baden-Württemberg**, one of the youngest of the German *Länder* – it was formed only in 1952 and still has two distinct characters. The people of Baden, most of them Catholic, are known for their friendly and relaxed dispositions, as opposed to their neighbours in Württemberg (or Swabia) who take life more seriously, and are reputed to be careful how and when they spend their money and to spend much of their spare time spring-cleaning their houses.

The Southwest is dominated by several upland masses, principally the **Schwarzwald** (Black Forest), which rises to over 1,200m. The **Danube** rises in the Schwarzwald and follows a course east, forming a deep gorge as it approaches the **Schwäbische Alb** (Swabian Jura), a less elevated and far less well known area of limestone ridges with clifftop castles, half-timbered villages and gushing waterfalls. The Rhine defines the western border with France. Germany's largest lake, the **Bodensee**, shared with Austria and Switzerland, is like an inland sea, and has a string of pretty resorts on its shores. Another river, the **Neckar**, is Swabia's main waterway. Flowing through a country of vineyards and fruit trees in its upper course, and through wooded valleys in its lower course, it passes through the lovely university towns of **Tübingen** and **Heidelberg**. More commercial and industrial centres such as **Stuttgart, Mannheim** and **Karlsruhe** constitute the modern face of Baden-Württemberg. The region's charms may be well known – Heidelberg and the main resorts of the Black Forest and Bodensee are the principal honeypots – but its attractions are well spread and it is always possible to escape peak-season crowds.

The battery above Baden-Baden

▶ ▶ ▶   Baden-Baden

Stylish Baden-Baden draws visitors from all over the world to its renowned spa and its casino, Germany's oldest. Not the least of its attractions is its position in the lush valley of the little river Oos on the fringe of the northern part of the Black Forest.

Though its heyday may be over, it remains a handsome place, with elegant 19th-century hotels, a *Jugendstil* (art nouveau) Trinkhalle where you can test the saline waters, a white neo-classical Kurhaus and a long park that looks as manicured as most of the visitors.

Baden-Baden's mild climate make it a pleasant place to visit all year round, but it is best known for its thermal springs, Europe's hottest, which gush out at 69°C (156° Fahrenheit). The Roman Emperor Caracalla bathed here in AD213 in the hope of finding a cure for his rheumatism – the remains of the Imperial Baths (open

Baden-Baden has long been a playground for the rich and famous – Brahms, Dostoevsky and Queen Victoria were among its many visitors.
By the 19th century Baden-Baden had become the place to be seen. Following the construction of the Kurhaus in the 1820s, the French impresario Jacques Benazet opened a casino, the first in Germany. Today's visitors to the Casino must wear formal dress (locals are officially prohibited from attending). The famous Iffezheim races began here in 1858, further enhancing Baden-Baden's prestige. The Lichtentaler Allee is the most glamorous thoroughfare. Scene of many an historic event, it has witnessed the future Edward VII of England riding along on his way to a party dressed as a ghost, and in 1861 was the scene of an attempt on the life of the King of Prussia.

The casino at Baden-Baden can accommodate 2,500 gamblers at 35 tables. According to Marlene Dietrich, 'The most beautiful casino in the world is at Baden-Baden – and I have seen them all.'

Baden-Baden town – still a fashionable and popular spa town

April to October) lie beneath the Stiftskirche.
The Lichtentaler Allee runs from the Kurgarten, site of both Trinkhalle and Kurhaus, to the old Cistercian monastery at Lichtental, passing on its way the Theatre, the International Club and the Kunsthalle (Art Gallery) where important temporary exhibitions are held.
Baden-Baden suffered a calamitous fire in 1689, which destroyed most of the old town. The Stiftskirche survived; inside is a huge sandstone crucifix, a masterpiece carved in 1467 by Nikolaus von Leyden.
The Renaissance/baroque Neues Schloss (guided tours May to September) stands at the top of steep steps and gives excellent views over the dramatic rooftops of the town to the Black Forest. It is still the residence of the Zähringen family who were once the Margraves – and for a time, Grand Dukes – of Baden. You could reward yourself after the climb by relaxing in the sumptuous Friedrichsbad or the modern (and cheaper) Caracalla Therm.

Excursion
The town of **Rastatt**, north of Baden-Baden, was rebuilt on uniform lines in the 18th century by Margrave Ludwig Wilhelm of Baden (nicknamed Louis the Turk because of his role in the anti-Turkish wars). Its massive red sandstone Schloss is Germany's first example of a palace in the style of Louis XIV's Versailles. It houses both the national Army Museum (with many of Ludwig Wilhelm's war trophies) and the Museum of Liberation (evolution of German Liberalism). Ludwig's widow, Sibylla, was responsible for the small-scale and deliciously ornate Schloss Favorite (open daily except Mondays), 5km outside town.

▶ ▷ ▷   **The Bergstrasse (Mountain Road)**

This long-established route (the Strata Montana of the Romans and today's B3) runs through the orchards at the foot of the forested Odenwald hills for 58km from Darmstadt to Heidelberg. The fruit trees and almonds come into blossom here earlier than anywhere else in Germany, making a spectacular display in late March/mid-April, while a string of picturesque little towns offers a welcome at all seasons.

South of Darmstadt is half-timbered **Zwingenberg**, the oldest place along the route, with steep alleyways and a pretty little market square overlooked by the 13th-century church. Near **Bensheim** is the Schloss at **Auerbach** (open daily except Monday) with the first of many viewpoints over the wide plain of the Rhine.

Fürstenlager Park was laid out in the 18th century with pavilions and garden monuments in the taste of the time. A trail is laid out among the exotic trees which flourish in the mild climate.

Heppenheim is dominated by the ruins of Schloss Starkenberg which contains an observatory and a youth hostel. The place has the cheerful air of a centre of wine production, with fine timber-framed buildings in the market square including an ancient apothecary's shop. The square is overlooked by the massive neo-Gothic church which is known as the 'Cathedral of the Bergstrasse'.

Weinheim has picturesque streets, an old tanners' quarter and a friendly market place. The town's inviting Schlosspark has many rare trees and near by, up in the valley of the Weschnitz, is the restored castle of Wachenburg with a fine panorama stretching westwards towards Mannheim and the Rhine.

175

A great Benedictine abbey once stood at Lorsch. Of it there remains the delightful little structure known as the Torhalle, Germany's oldest intact building, dating from the late 8th century and probably erected as a triumphal gateway for the emperor Charlemagne.

Windeck and castle, on the Bergstrasse

Seewein (lake wine) is a good reason for visiting the Bodensee. On the shores of the lake, Meersburg holds a wine festival every September, which is a good introduction to the region's wines.

► ► ► **Bodensee (Lake Constance)**

Fed by the Rhine and shared with Austria and Switzerland, the Bodensee is the second largest (after Lake Geneva) of the great Alpine lakes. Sometimes called the 'Swabian ocean', its sheer size (roughly 65km by 12km) gives it something of the character of an inland sea and this, together with the distant backdrop of the Alps and a mild climate which allows exotic vegetation to thrive, has made it a popular place for German holidaymakers who flock to the chain of pretty resorts along the north shore.

The historic town of **Konstanz** stands at the end of a peninsula astride the channel linking the main body of the lake – the Obersee – to the smaller Untersee with its attractively varied shoreline. The lakeside at Konstanz is attractive enough, with steamers tying up in the harbour, a verdant park (the Stadtgarten), old defensive towers and the venerable warehouse of 1388 known as the Konzil. In summer the traffic-free Altstadt has a bustling, almost Mediterranean atmosphere; there is a cathedral – the Münster – a fine Renaissance Rathaus and a pleasingly fusty local museum (Rosgartenmuseum). Now an elegant lakeside hotel, the town's 13th-century Dominican monastery was also the birthplace of Graf Zeppelin, the airship pioneer.

Mainau, reached by road and footbridge or by lake steamer, is a paradise island of tropical plants with a fairy-tale castle. Laid out by Grand Duke Friedrich I of Baden in the mid-19th century, it is now owned by the flamboyant Swedish Count Bernadotte.

Reichenau Island is accessible along its causeway or by boat. Less overcrowded than Mainau, it is of exceptional interest because of its Romanesque churches – testimony to an important monastic past. Look particularly for the 11th-century wall-paintings at Oberzell church. Mitterzell abbey dates from the 10th century and has Gothic reliquaries in its treasury.

Singen, further west, is dominated by the biggest castle ruin in Germany, Hohentwiel; the castle was razed by the French in 1801, but offering a terrific panorama of lake and Alp.

One-thousand-year-old **Meersburg**, easily reached by

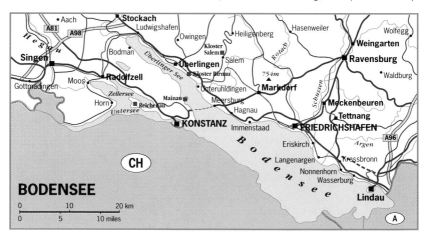

BODENSEE

0   10   20 km
0   5   10 miles

177

Bodensee

car ferry from Konstanz, is perhaps the prettiest place along the lake, with a formidable feudal castle, the Altes Schloss, and a baroque palace, the Neues Schloss, built for the Bishops of Konstanz who fled here when that town turned Protestant. The cliff-like shoreline between the Oberstadt (upper town) with its delightful Marktplatz and the Unterstadt (lower town) with its busy lakeside promenade also provides excellent growing conditions for the vines which stretch southward to Hagnau.

North of Meersburg the shore of the Überlingersee continues steep and rugged in places. At **Unteruhldingen** the prehistoric lake-dwellers' village has been imaginatively reconstructed. A short distance inland lies Schloss Salem, its Gothic church complemented by baroque abbey buildings. Since 1922 this has been Germany's most famous boarding school, numbering among its old boys the Duke of Edinburgh. One of the most appealing of all Germany's rococo buildings, the pilgrimage church at **Birnau** stands in a romantic setting among the vineyards overlooking the lake. Inside is a famous little figurine, a honey-stealing cherub licking his fingers.

Medieval **Überlingen** clinging to its steep lakeside site has maintained most of its fortifications and is dominated by its richly furnished, five-aisled late Gothic Münster.

From Meersburg to Lindau Southeast of Immenstaad the lakeside becomes flatter and the main points of interest are the lakeside settlements such as **Friedrichshafen** where Zeppelin based his great airships, little **Wasserburg** on its peninsula and, above all, **Lindau**. Built on the lake's largest island and connected to the mainland by two bridges, this ancient city is the southernmost in Germany, priding itself on its mild climate, its spectacular setting against the backdrop of the Alps and its high reputation as a summer resort. The monumental harbour entrance is guarded by the Lion of Bavaria and a lighthouse, the quayside by another lighthouse, the 13th-century Mangturm. Behind its traffic-free promenades, the Altstadt is full of interest, not least because of its happy blend of architectural styles, medieval painted houses, 15th-century Rathaus, baroque Cacazzen House (with a fine local museum) and *Jugendstil* station.

*The 'Swabian ocean':
Bodensee*

Apart from brewing, Donaueschingen prides itself on its annual music festival – the Donaueschinger Musiktage – featuring works by contemporary composers. The Donau (Danube) is Europe's second largest river after the Volga. It travels 2,859km from its source at Donauquelle to the Black Sea and on its course runs through three capital cities: Vienna, Budapest and Belgrade.

▶ ▷ ▷ **Donaueschingen**

High up among the rich farmlands of the Baar plateau between the Black Forest and Swabian Jura, little Donaueschingen owes its name to its position at the source of the Danube. The great river's starting point is marked by the monumental fountain standing in its Schlosspark, though the name Danube really only applies downstream from the confluence of two streams (the Breg and Brigach) just outside the town.

From 1723 Donaueschingen was the seat of the Princes of Furstenberg. Their Schloss (open April to September daily except Tuesdays) was rebuilt twice, in 1772 and 1893. It houses a sumptuous collection of porcelain, gold and silver plate, as well as Brussels tapestries. The Princes' rich art collections (open daily except Mondays) can be viewed in the Karlsbau. They include paintings by both Cranachs and by the Master of Messkirch, as well as by a number of 15th- and 16th-century Swabian masters.

Two views of Freiburg
Above: a street in the 'capital of the Black Forest'
Right: the old town's glory – the Münster

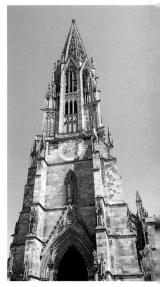

▶ ▶ ▷   **Freiburg**

Known as the capital of the Black Forest, Freiburg is famous for its Münster (cathedral), but for many Germans it conjures up images of youth: some 27,000 students are housed here, giving the town an unusually lively atmosphere all year round. The Albert Ludwig University was founded in 1457, the College of Education, State Music College and five technical colleges are more recent foundations.

What to see A walk through the squares and arcaded streets of the old town is delightful but the real glory of Freiburg is its red sandstone Münster, with a soaring tower that dominates the city. Colourful medieval and baroque houses (many being careful post-war reconstructions) fringe the cathedral square.
Begun as a ducal burial place by Bertold V of Zähringen, whose family founded the city in 1118–20, the Münster passed into the hands of the citizenry after the death of the last of the Zähringens died in 1218. To the late Romanesque east end were added the Gothic nave and the incomparable west tower. The desire of rich families for their own burial chapels determined the form of the late Gothic choir, begun in 1354. Its consecration in 1513 marked the completion of the minster. Since 1827 it has been the seat of an archbishop. The rich interior bears witness to the generosity and civic pride of local families: stained glass windows with coats of arms of patricians and guilds; the magnificent high altar triptych

A showcase for Baden wines, the Freiburger Weintage (Freiberg Wine Festival) is held in Münsterplatz in late June. Another city celebration with wine associations is the Fastnet (carnival) in February, when masks traditionally ward off evil spirits from the vines.

by Hans Baldung Grien; and the splendid furnishings of the choir chapels with their 16th-century windows and fine altars and monuments. The cathedral tower, with its traceried spire, has been described as the most beautiful tower in Christendom (you can climb the tower any day except Monday).

Augustinermuseum This owes its name to the former monastery of the Augustinian Hermits, going back to about 1300. Since 1923 the church and cloisters of the monastery buildings have housed the attractively displayed collections of the museum, which specialises in Upper Rhenish art from the Middle Ages to the baroque. Besides the medieval art treasures, there is a special section for southwest German baroque sculpture and a rich collection of *objets d'art*. The Augustiner also has a folk-art section holding a collection of clocks, local costume and folk art of the Black Forest. In the 19th century, artists became aware of the beauty of the Freiburg area and the Black Forest, and some of their canvases can be seen in the section devoted to Baden painters.
Remnants of the medieval town walls can still be seen south of the Augustinermuseum, while the old fishermen's quarter, known as the Insel (Island), has sensitively restored old buildings.

Other sights The colourful Münsterplatz is graced by the Gothic/Renaissance Kaufhaus (merchants' hall) with an arcaded façade which contains statues of Habsburg rulers; the baroque Erzbischöfliches Palais (Archbishop's Palace); the 18th-century Wenzingerhaus; and the restored 15th-century Kornhaus (destroyed in World War II).
A short distance away is Rathausplatz, pleasantly shaded by chestnut trees. It contains the Neues Rathaus (the present town hall), once the university's main building.

Excursions
If you have time, there are some worthwhile side-trips to be made to nearby places such as the fortified town of **Breisach**, which towers immediately above the Rhine and the French frontier; the **Kaiserstuhl**, a volcanic, vine-clad hill standing isolated in the plain; and the wine town of **Burkheim**.

▶ ▶ ▷   Haigerloch
This is one of southwestern Germany's most delightful small towns, a perfect synthesis of buildings and landscape at a point where the River Eyach has carved a deep double loop in the limestone of the Swabian Jura. The best panoramas of the town in its setting are to be had from the Kapf viewpoint, from the rococo St Anne's pilgrimage church and from the tower known as the Römerturm. The Hohenzollern Schloss dominates the place; its Gothic church has a resplendent rococo interior. A curiosity in this remote place is the Atommuseum, where German scientists tinkered (unsuccessfully) with a nuclear reactor in the last stages of World War II.

▶ ▶ ▷ **Heidelberg**

For people the world over, friendly Heidelberg is the very image of romantic Germany. The River Neckar flows through its deep wooded valley past ancient towers and bridges, the red sandstone castle ruin rises majestically over the roofs of the old town. This, and the sheer exuberance of the life led by the students of Germany's oldest and most tradition-bound university (immortalised in the ditties of Sigmund Romberg's operetta, *The Student Prince*), all combine to make the place quite irresistible to the countless thousands who flock here to prove to themselves that 'Old Germany' is still very much alive.

There are good views of Heidelberg as a whole from the graceful Alte Brücke (Old Bridge) spanning the fast-flowing waters. The bridge's gateway, its twin towers topped by spiky helmets, has long been one of the city's landmarks, a favourite subject of poets and painters, among them J M W Turner who came in 1836 and left many oils and watercolours of the city in its changing moods. If time permits, there are breathtaking views from the high-level Philosophenweg above the quayside, the 'philosophers' path' trod by many seeking inspiration from the incomparable panorama to the south.

Despite the romantic image of the city, Heidelberg is a major exporter of scientific know-how to countries throughout the world. Today 'Made in Heidelberg' is proof of excellent quality for a number of famous products. Research institutes include the European Molecular Biology Laboratory, the German Cancer Research Centre and the Max Planck Institutes. There is also a vigorous cultural life in Heidelberg, with more than 10 museums, several theatres, galleries, and an annual theatre festival which takes place in the castle in August.

181

Germany at its most romantic: Heidelberg's 17th-century castle and the River Neckar

The Grosses Fass (great vat) in the Fassbau in Heidelberg's castle, is a wine barrel with a capacity of 2,200 hectolitres, built in the 18th century to hold the tithe of Palatinate wines. On top of it is a platform used as a dance floor.

Fill me the beaker!
Now, Rhine and Nekkar,
Health to ye both, ye noble
streams!
Yours is a power,
To bring the hour
High above Wisdom's heavy
dreams – Gardens at
Heidelberg, Walter Savage
Landor

A generation or two ago, the caricature of a German male would show a reddened, almost bald pate with perhaps a few bristles adorning the roll of fat overlapping the collar, a monocle framing a glaring eye, and a scar or two adorning a cheek. Worn with pride, and known as a *Schmiss*, such facial scars would have been acquired in the course of the fencing bouts which were a feature of upper-class student life in the more tradition-bound universities. The contestants, wearing goggles and padding to protect their vital parts, would face each other in the company of their supporters and attendant medics. The liberal-minded students of the post-war generation were anxious to put such behaviour, with all its associations of fanaticism and militarism, behind them. But the tradition persisted among the right-wing student associations and has recently come into prominence again.

The Schloss High above the city's alleyways are the majestic ruins of the castle (guided tours daily), graced with fine terraced gardens, the creation of Friedrich V between 1616 and 1619. The princes of Pfalz (the Palatinate) lived here for 500 years; they included Friedrich V, who married the English princess Elizabeth Stuart, daughter of James I. It was for her that he built the Englischer Bau (English building) near the Dicker Turm, and the Elisabethentor (Elizabeth Gate) in the form of a classical triumphal arch. It was as a 17-year-old bride that Elizabeth came to the court over which she presided for five years before she was forced to flee to Prague, when Friedrich V, who was a Protestant, failed in an attempt to oust the Catholic Habsburgs from their supreme position. He was eventually stripped of his titles, and his machinations contributed to the outbreak of the Thirty Years' War. Later, the Schloss, and the city itself, suffered badly when Louis XIV attacked the Palatinate, to which he laid claim, in 1689 (four years later, a disastrous fire destroyed the old town). The castle fabric was much restored in the 19th century by Count de Graimberg, but numerous earlier features survive.

The Brown Hall contains Roman pillars brought from Charlemagne's palace at Ingelheim. Look too for the 16th-century Dicker Turm (fat tower) and the Glockenturm (bell tower), built for defence but with six subsequent residential floors added. The Deutsches Apotheken–Museum (German apothecary museum) within the castle complex provides a fascinating look into baroque and rococo workshops of German chemists from the early 17th century.

The University Heidelberg's is the oldest university in Germany, founded by Elector Ruprecht I von der Pfalz in 1386. It was badly neglected during the 18th century, but in 1803 Grand Duke Karl Friedrich declared it the first state university of Baden. One part of Universitätsplatz, dating back to the 18th century, is devoted to the Alte Universität (old university) while the rest of the square is taken up by university buildings of the 1930s. The Studentenkarzer (students' gaol; open daily except Sundays and holidays), in use from 1712 to 1914, was built for unruly students, whose graffiti are still in evidence. In the library (open daily except Sunday), the *Codex Manesse*, from the 14th century, a collection of Middle High German poetry, is illuminated with 137 exquisite miniatures. Here too is *Des Knaben Wunderhorn* (The Boy's Magic Horn), a collection of folk poetry which inspired the German romantic poets and also the composer Gustav Mahler.

Excursion
About 13km west, the town of **Schwetzingen** is known for its Schlosspark, a wonderfully fanciful 18th-century dreamland of romantic follies and eye-catchers. Beyond the formal French garden by the Schloss itself lie a Temple of Apollo, a statue of Pan playing the flute in a grotto, mock ruins, tricks of perspective and more. Mozart conducted an orchestral concert of his own works in the theatre here.

▶ ▶ ▷ **Karlsruhe**

Karlsruhe is the youngest of German cities. In 1715, tired of living in the much knocked-about medieval castle at nearby Durlach, Margrave Karl Wilhelm of Baden Durlach began building a new residence deep in the hunting forests of the Rhine plain. A city soon grew up, laid out in the shape of a fan, with the palace at its centre. This unusual pattern persists today, enhanced by the splendidly sober civic buildings in neo-classical style by Friedrich Weinbrenner. On his Marktplatz stands the famous pyramid where the town's founder is buried.

What to see Standing spick and span in its formal gardens facing the city centre, the Schloss is now the home of the Badisches Landesmuseum, where the rich and beautifully presented collections include the unique Türkenbeute, the booty won by Louis the Turk (see Rastatt) from his Ottoman opponents. Near by are the excellent galleries of the Kunsthalle (an array of superb Old Masters, including Grünewald's intensely moving *Crucifixion*, together with fine examples of German 19th-century painting) and of the Orangery (modern art since 1890, German and international).

Excursions

There are superb views of the surrounding area from the **Turmberg**, high above the Margrave's old castle at Durlach. Karlsruhe's smoothly functioning tramway system will whisk you out beyond the city to delightful half-timbered **Ettlingen**, also with a Schloss, or even further into the Black Forest itself, to the upland resort of **Bad Herrenalb**.

Karlsruhe

Students of Karlsruhe's School of Technology, established here in 1825, have included such illustrious names as Hertz, the discoverer of electromagnetic waves, Benz, inventor of the motor car, and Karl von Drais, who invented the bicycle.

183

Karlsruhe (Karl's rest) is no longer the capital of Baden, but its importance was confirmed by the siting here of Germany's Federal Constitutional Court.

■ **Intellectuals enjoy high status in Germany and many universities boast hundreds of years of tradition. Before World War II they tended to be elitist, conservative bastions – many German students and professors supported Hitler's rise to power. .....■**

Students busking in Tübingen

Involvement by the west since unification has had some negative consequences. For example, in Berlin, western authorities dismissed the popular head of the Humboldt University, the theologian Heinrich Fink, because of suspicions of secret police (Stasi) contacts under the communist regime. This unleashed a storm of student protests, particularly since it was suspected that many western academics were after positions in the better-known universities of eastern Germany.

The student movement and after Following the subdued period of the Wirtschaftswunder in the 1950s, a generation of post-war German youth began questioning the establishment – and the university system – in the student movement that exploded in 1968. Student self-governing committees were formed and curricula opened to all qualified school-leavers. Universities became vastly overcrowded and the quality of teaching – already affected by the civil service status of professors and the bureaucratic administration – fell. In addition, students extend their studies well into their 30s – supported by generous government grants. In German universities campus life, as found in Britain or the United States, hardly exists. Students rarely live on campus, although they eat together in a student Mensa or cafeteria.

Pressure to succeed is relatively low in German universities, with few exams before finals. In addition, as western German universities do not require compulsory attendance, many students do not take their studies very seriously. However, this may be changing: proposals to create more rigorous 'élite' universities are gaining ground, and a younger generation of competitive Germans has appeared.

In the east Under the communists, East German universities established their own traditions, with student admissions based on political criteria. The peaceful revolution in 1989 threw the universities into chaos, with large-scale firings of professors and restructuring of departments according to western standards.

▶ ▷ ▷   Mannheim

The second largest river port in Europe and an important industrial centre, Mannheim is situated at the meeting point of the Rhine and the Neckar. Like Karlsruhe, it is an 18th-century planned town, focused on its Schloss, a huge edifice which is now the seat of Mannheim's university. Laid out on a grid pattern, the streets define 144 city blocks, each of which is designated by a letter and a number, a logical system without parallel in Germany.

Mannheim is proud of its former eminence in the world of music and theatre, but little of its original 18th-century architectural elegance survives. The most striking part of the town is the *Jugendstil* Friedrichsplatz, laid out around a monster water tower. Here is the Kuntshalle, with one of Germany's leading displays of 19th- and 20th-century art. In the Zeughaus (arsenal) is the Reiss Museum, where the local collections evoke the look of the city before its industrialisation.

▶ ▷ ▷   Maulbronn

Maulbronn has one of the earliest Cistercian monasteries (founded in 1147) to survive as a superb and almost untouched example. As the locals tell it, a group of monks stopped by here to let their mules drink (the name means 'Mule Well'), and they stayed on forever. This story is depicted in sketches for a fresco on a wall of the Brunnenkapelle (well housc). Thc monastery church – consecrated in 1178 – is basically Romanesque with later Gothic additions. You can also see the cloisters with refectory and chapter house, early 15th-century chapels and a crucifix of 1473.

▶ ▶ ▶   Neckertal (Neckar Valley) and Odenwald

The Neckar rises in the Black Forest and runs for nearly 400km before entering the Rhine at Mannheim. Downstream from **Bad Wimpfen** it flows through charming countryside of orchards and vineyards before cutting its way through the Odenwald uplands in a deep wooded trench. The best way of enjoying its varied

Mannheim's Städtische Kunsthalle has an excellent collection of 19th-century French art, including Manet's *Execution of the Emperor Maximilian of Mexico*, a work exemplifying the artist's realism and the influence of Spanish painting on his style.

185

The Neckar Valley

Right: Bad Wimpfen
Below: Odenwald

Taken on a hunting trip to the Odenwald, Siegfried, the hero of the *Nibelungenlied*, was speared in the back by Hagen at a spring. Several springs in the area claim to be the *Siegfriedsquellen*.

landscapes, its attractive towns and castles is from a steamer (the river has been 'improved' for shipping up to Stuttgart), but road (the signposted touring route called the Burgenstrasse) and rail follow closely its winding course.

To the east of Heidelberg the road passes beneath the **Königstuhl** (658m) (King's Seat), crowned by a TV tower offering a panorama of the Neckar Valley and the Rhine Plain beyond. Equally dramatic views can be enjoyed from the castle ruins of **Dilsberg**, while Neckarsteinach is overlooked by no fewer than four castles. **Eberbach** has quaint inns and pubs, including the Wirtshaus Kraabbenstein, as well as Germany's oldest bathhouse (the 13th-century Altes Badhaus). The little resort of **Zwingenberg** has a splendid medieval castle; the Wolfsschlucht ravine inspired Weber's opera, *Der Freischütz*. Just off the main valley, **Mosbach** is well known for its fine collection of half-timbered buildings. Back on the Neckar again, **Burg Hornberg** (open daily April to October) dates back to 1148, while Burg **Guttenberg** (open daily March to November) is famous today for its birds of prey which are flown in public demonstrations.

Bad Wimpfen is the highlight of the valley. This fortified medieval town was once the imperial residence of the Hohenstaufens and retains an appealing mélange of half-timbering, narrow streets and stepped gables. The tall

tower known as the Blauer Turm stands squarely among the steep-pitched roofs and gives the best views over town and river.

Odenwald Stretching northwards from the Neckar, this wooded upland of beech and spruce contrasts strongly with the fertile landscapes of the Bergstrasse running along its western rim. It is traversed from west to east by the Niebelungenstrasse on its way from Worms to Wurzburg, an attractive touring route which passes through delightful **Michelstadt**. The little town's Rathaus with its stout oak columns and its corner turrets is almost too picturesque to be true. Michelstadt makes a good centre for visiting several of the Odenwald's other attractions: **Eulbach Park**, with ornamental hunting grounds dating from the 18th century, Renaissance **Schloss Fürstenau** in a pretty countryside setting, **Erbach**, also with a Schloss plus a unique museum of ivory carving, or the nearby Einhardsbasilika, like the Torhalle at Lorsch a striking example of Carolingian architecture, completed in the year 827.

The Rottweiler, a rugged cattle dog, is believed to have crossed the Alps from Italy with the Romans. Rottweilers were bred in the city as guard dogs. Their German name – *Metzerhund* (butcher's dog) – derives from the local butchers' practice of training the dogs to pull their carts.

▶ ▷ ▷   **Ravensburg**

187

This old town thrived in the Middle Ages, with its position on a great trade route connecting Northern Europe to Italy. Before the rise of the Fuggers of Augsburg, the Ravensburger Handelsgesellschaft was southern Germany's most important trading company. Ravensburg grew up at the foot of the Veitsburg, the fortified hill where Henry the Lion was born. The town walls are still mostly intact, with several gates and towers including the Mehlsack (flour sack tower) originally erected so the citizens could keep an eye on the Veitsburg. The Marienplatz is full of character, with another tall tower, the Blaserturm, a 15th-century Rathaus, and the Waaghaus, the focus of trading activity. Its hall once rang with the cries of foreign merchants promoting their wares, while weights and measures were checked on the ground floor.

▶ ▷ ▷   **Rottweil**

Rottweil enjoys a dramatic setting on a spur overlooking a bend in the upper Neckar. Its streets are a delight of fine old houses, mostly Renaissance and baroque, with features such as elaborate oriel windows or exuberant carving.
A further contribution to the townscape is made by four Renaissance fountains – the Marktbrunnen is the most splendid. The town's churches include the Kapellenkirche, baroquified inside but with a richly decorated Gothic tower, and the Heiligkreuz Minster with a Crucifixion above its high altar attributed to Ueit Stoss. The Lorenzkapelle houses a fine array of medieval sculpture.
The interesting local museum (Stadtmuseum) recalls the Roman presence here with a 2nd-century mosaic of Orpheus and also displays some of the weird and wonderful wooden masks worn at carnival time. Fastnet spans six days; the climax is the Narrensprung (Fools' Dance) on the Monday before Shrove Tuesday and on the Tuesday itself.

Ravensburg

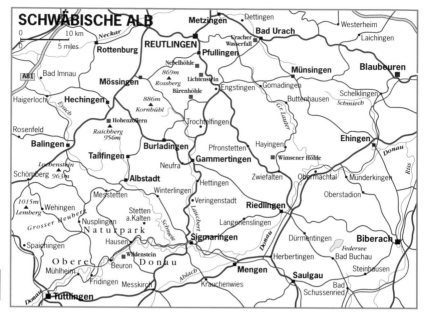

▶ ▷ ▷ **Schwäbische Alb (Swabian Jura)**

The Schwäbische Alb is a range of limestone hills to the east of the Black Forest, about 55km wide and 150km long. The young River Danube flows romantically through part of the region in a landscape of wooded limestone cliffs, crag-top castles and green meadows. The southwest part of the Schwäbische Alb has been designated the Naturpark Obere Donau (Upper Danube Nature Park).

The name of Hohenzollern is closely associated with this part of Germany – forged by the marriage of the Zollerns, originally Swabian overlords, to the Burgraves of Nuremberg. From the early 1700s, the family, as rulers of Brandenburg and Prussia, fought to establish a German Empire and finally achieved this in 1871 under Wilhelm I. In 1918, after defeat in World War I, Wilhelm II abdicated, but the family name and tradition continues. The present head of the family, who would have the title of Kaiser if the Empire had continued, is Prince Ludwig Ferdinand of Prussia, grandson of Wilhelm II.

In **Sigmaringen**, at the mouth of the Upper Danube gap, the Swabian Catholic branch of the family managed to hold on to its castle, which today is the product of several periods, most prominently of 19th-century romanticism. There are guided tours from February to November; you have to leave your car at the Rathaus and walk from there. During the height of the tourist season, there are vast crowds, but it is worth the wait. For those with a keen interest in European royalty this is a treasure trove, and there is perhaps the largest collection of armoury and weapons in Europe, with more than 3,000 items in one hoard. In the neo-Gothic hall a splendid collection of south German art of the 15th and 16th centuries includes works by the Master of Sigmaringen – actually two brothers, Hans and Jacob

The village of Beuron, west of Sigmaringen, clusters around its huge abbey. Founded by the Augustinians in the 11th century, Kloster Beuron now belongs to the Benedictines. It is celebrated for the monks' singing of the Gregorian chant (which can be heard by visitors at high mass and vespers), and for the Nazarenes, an early 19th-century group of artists who came here and adopted an early Christian art style (later known as the Beuron School). Male visitors might find accommodation in the abbey.

Strüb. The Johanniskirche, on the castle rock, is decorated with elaborate rococo stuccowork and houses the shrine of St Fidelio, a local martyr.

Between Sigmaringen and Tuttlingen the Danube flows through a superb gorge dominated by crags and lofty castles, including Burg Wildenstein (now a youth hostel), giving a spectacular view of the river, and the Knopfermacherfelsen, a magnificent viewpoint from a chaos of cliffs.

In a valley at the edge of the Schwäbische Alb lies **Zwiefalten**. The great Münster here rivals its Bavarian counterparts in splendour. The abbey church is largely the work of the South German 18th-century architect, J. M. Fischer. Its spacious interior is lavishly decorated in a whirl of white and gold, with stucco masquerading as marble, and the sculptures and large figures on the altar, set between pink and white columns, are by J. J. Christian. Among the many caves hollowed out in the soft limestone of the Alb, the **Wimsener Höhle** is perhaps the finest. It can be entered by boat. The church at **Obermachtal**, built 1686, displays stucco decoration and is an early example of wall-pillar construction, where a wall of internal buttresses represents a refinement to the medieval approach of using external flying buttresses.

Dettingen in the Schwaubisch Alb is famous for its Kirschgeist (cherry spirit). Selected cherries are cropped to make this strong, clear pick-me-up, which is drunk from thimble-sized glasses.

189

St Michael's church, Schwäbisch Hall (see page 190)

Burg Hohenzollern, the original seat of the Hohenzollern family, presents a spectacular outline, sited on a peak 850m above sea level near the town of Hechingen. There are guided tours from the beginning of April until the end of October. The castle was largely rebuilt in the mid-19th century, but the 12th-century Catholic chapel of St Michael, with beautiful stained glass, the oldest in Germany, remains. The Protestant chapel held the tomb of Frederick the Great until the mighty monarch's mortal remains were reburied at Potsdam in 1991 (see page 45). Many of his possessions, such as his uniforms and military decorations, can still be seen here.

Schloss Lichtenstein (open daily; weekends only November to March), a formidable 19th-century fortress, caps a craggy peak. Close by are several worthwhile caves, including the Nebelhöhle and the Bärenhöhle. Further west, Rossberg (869m) gives a vast panorama of the region from its viewing tower.

Bad Urach is a pleasant small resort sited in a narrow valley and endowed with a pleasing half-timbered square. Out of town to the west, **Urach Waterfall** is attractively set and is only a short walk from the main road.

▶ ▷ ▷ Schwäbisch Gmünd

This attractive town set in good walking country, just north of the Schwäbische Alb, is famous for its jewellery and silver tableware. The 14th-century master-builder Peter Parler was born here. One of the main works of the Parler family is the Heiligkreuzmünster (Cathedral of the Holy Cross). The attractive exterior includes fine tracery, pinnacles and a depiction of the Last Judgement in the south portal. The interior conforms to the Cistercian hall plan. Notice the magnificent vaulting, the Tree of Jesse altar in the Baptistery, and the carved choir stalls. The local museum (Johannisplatz 3) concentrates on late Gothic and baroque sculpture. The town maintains its craft traditions with its well known college of gold- and silversmithing.

A short distance south of Schwäbisch Gmünd are the **Kaiserberge**, three wooded hills once topped by castles. One of these, Hohenstaufen, was the original seat of the great imperial family. There are wide-ranging views from ruined **Hohenrechberg** which also has a baroque pilgrimage church.

▶ ▶ ▶ Schwäbisch Hall

One of the treasures of southwest Germany, this medieval town nestles in the heart of the Swabian forests, on the banks of the River Kocher, a tributary of the Neckar. Many of the houses and buildings are neatly arranged in tiers which overlook the ancient wooden bridges over the river. The site was already known for its saltwater springs in the 3rd century BC, and these encouraged a permanent Celtic settlement. During the Middle Ages, Schwäbisch Hall began to mint silver coins, first known as the Häller and then later renamed Heller (the name derives from Hall, meaning 'place of salt'). In the 13th century the town became a Free Imperial City.

Schwäbisch Gmünd was once the possession of the Hohenstaufen family, who ruled the Holy Roman Empire from 1138 to 1254 and marked a high point in German culture. When the family fell from power, Schwäbisch Gmünd became a Free Imperial City.

Its charming, sloping Marktplatz is often reckoned to be among the most stunning in Germany. It is used for theatrical performances (June to August). The baroque Rathaus, built 1730–5, has a palatial appearance and is architecturally one of the most important buildings of its time. It was rebuilt after war damage. The roof proudly displays a decorative clock and imperial eagle. The central part of the square is dominated by the

Timbered buildings in Schwäbisch Hall

SCHWÄBISCH HALL

- Ravenstein
- Assamstadt
- A81
- Krautheim
- Dörzbach
- Schöntal
- *Jagst*
- Mulfingen
- Möckmühl
- Jagsthausen
- Neudenau
- Forchtenberg
- Künzelsau
- Neuenstadt
- *Kocher*
- H o h e n l o h e r   E b e n e
- Langenburg
- Gerabronn
- Öhringen
- Neuenstein
- Kupferzell
- Neckarsulm
- Bretzfeld
- Waldenburg
- A6
- Braunsbach
- Pfedelbach
- *Waldenburger Berge*
- SCHWÄBISCH HALL
- Obersulm
- HEILBRONN
- Löwenstein
- Schloss Comburg
- Vellberg
- *L ö w e n s t e i n e r   B e r g e*
- Maishardt
- Oberstenfeld
- Wüstenrot
- Oberrot
- *Limpurger Berge*
- Sulzbach
- Gaildorf
- Bühlerzell
- Murrhardt
- *Kocher*

0   10 km
0   5 miles

Schwäbisch Hall's annual Whit Week festival recalls an occasion when salt workers saved the town's mill from fire, and is called the *Kuchen und Brunn en Fest de Haller Salzsieder* – the Cake and Fountain Festival of the Saltminers of Hall.

Schwäbisch Hall

Marktbrunnen, a 16th-century fountain which is adorned with statues of St Michael with St George and Samson. The old pillory forms part of the fountain's structure. The Pfarrkirche (St Michael's) adjoins the Marktplatz and you can reach it by mounting a wide flight of stairs. The church has hardly been touched since 1573 and, besides the tombs in the chapels, there are interesting furnishings in the choir stalls, tabernacle and altars.

The Keckenburg, once an aristocratic mansion, houses the Hällisch Fränkisches Museum (open daily except Monday), explaining the town's history.

About 30km north, the quiet countryside between the Swabian Forest and the Tauber valley is known as the Hohenloher Ebene, after one of the princely German families, the House of Hohenlohe; here the most common language is the Schwäbish (Swabian) dialect which even other Germans find difficult to understand.

At **Jagsthausen** is the much restored Götzenburg castle (now a hotel) which in 1480 was the birthplace of the knight Götz von Berlichingen – the Knight with the Iron Hand. Goethe wrote a drama about him and every summer a drama festival, including Goethe's play, is held in the courtyard of the castle. About 6km on is the Cistercian abbey of **Schöntal** in the the Jagst valley (guided tours daily in April to October). The church is famed for its 17th-century alabaster altarpieces.

At Öhringen the late Gothic Stiftskirche (dedicated to St Peter and St Paul), on the Marktplatz, contains tombs of members of the House of Hohenlohe. Note the monument to Philip of Hohenlohe, son-in-law of William the Silent, with detailed reliefs of battles from the Netherlands' War of Independence. Foremost among the furnishings is the high altar of around 1500.

The Schloss at **Neuenstein** (guided tours March to November) has been Hohenlohe family property since the 13th century, and displays a variety of styles – Renaissance, Romanesque and Gothic. **Waldenburg** was a fortified town, from which the princely family overlooked the plain and protected their empire.

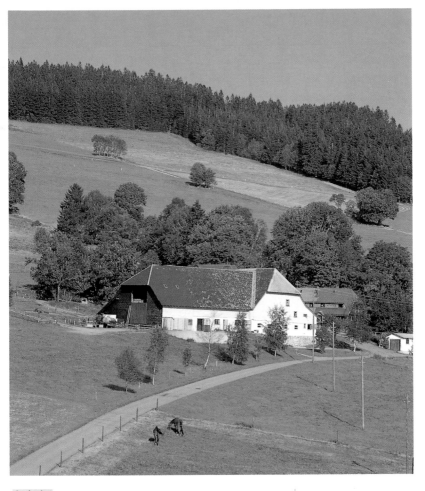

▶ ▶ ▶ Schwarzwald (Black Forest)

The highest land in southwest Germany, the Black Forest is a rewarding area for gentle exploration. Only in the gloom of its most inaccessible stands of spruce does the term 'black' seem appropriate, and by no means all of it is woodland. Picturesque wooden farmhouses and pleasantly unassuming villages nestling in green valleys are distinctive elements of the landscape; the terrain gets more open as you travel south into the orchards and farmlands of the Markgräfliches Land. The western slopes are dominated by vineyards; the **Badische Weinstrasse** (Baden Wine Road) winds through the Black Forest foothills. Development across the region is mostly low-key and small scale, with few big resorts.

Beneath all this is a thriving and well organised tourist industry, mostly catering to the Germans themselves who come for short breaks and non-medical 'cures'. Newish hotels in traditional style are found on the edges of many villages and are scattered around the country areas. Sports facilities (mostly one-to-one activities such

The Schwarzwald

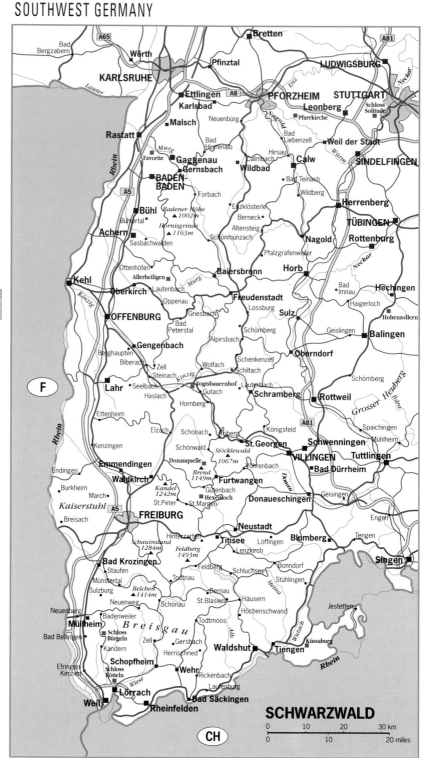

SOUTHWEST GERMANY

Bad Bergzabern
A65
Wörth
Bretten
A81

Pfinztal
LUDWIGSBURG

KARLSRUHE

Ettlingen
A8
PFORZHEIM
STUTTGART

Karlsbad
Leonberg
Schloss Solitude

Neuenbürg
Pfarrkirche

Malsch
Bad Liebenzell
Weil der Stadt

Rastatt
Bad Herrenalb
Hirsau
Calmbach
Calw
SINDELFINGEN

Favorite
Murg
Gaggenau
Wildbad
Bad Teinach

Gernsbach
Forbach
Wildberg
Herrenberg

BADEN-BADEN
Enzklösterle
TÜBINGEN

Bühl
Badener Höhe ▲1002m
Berneck
Nagold
Rottenburg

Bühlertal
Hornisgrinde ▲1163m
Altensteig

Achern
Schönmünzach
Pfalzgrafenweiler

Sasbachwalden
Baiersbronn
Horb

Ottenhöfen
Murg
Bad Imnau
Hechingen

Kehl
Allerheiligen
Freudenstadt
Haigerloch
Hohenzollern

Oberkirch
Lautenbach
Lossburg
Sulz
Geislingen
Balingen

Oppenau
Griesbach
Schömberg

OFFENBURG
Bad Peterstal
Alpirsbach
Oberndorf

Gengenbach
Schenkenzell
Schömberg

Berghaupten
Biberach
Wolfach
Schiltach

Zell
Steinach
Kinzig
Vogtsbauernhof
Lautenbach
Schramberg
Rottweil

Lahr
Seelbach
Gutach
Grosser Heuberg

Haslach
Hornberg

Ettenheim
Schonach
Triberg
Königsfeld
A81
Spaichingen

Elzach
Schönwald
St.Georgen
Schwenningen
Mühlheim

Kenzingen
Donauquelle
Stöcklewald 1067m
VILLINGEN
Tuttlingen

Emmendingen
Brend 1149m
Vöhrenbach
Bad Dürrheim

Waldkirch
Furtwangen

Endingen
Gutenbach
Donaueschingen
Geisingen

Burkheim
Kandel 1242m
Hexenloch

March
St.Peter
St.Margen
Engen

Kaiserstuhl
A5
FREIBURG
Neustadt

Breisach
Hinterzarten
Titisee
Blumberg
Tengen

Schauinsland 1284m
Löffingen

Feldberg 1493m
Lenzkirch
Singen

Bad Krozingen
Feldberg
Schluchsee
Bonndorf

Staufen
Stühlingen

Münstertal
Todtnau

Sulzburg
Belchen ▲1414m
Bernau

Neuenweg
Schönau
St.Blasien
Höchenschwand

Neuenburg
Badenweiler
Todtmoos
Jestetten

Mülheim
Breisgau

Bad Bellingen
Schloss Bürgeln
Zell
Gersbach

Kandern
Herrischried
Küssaburg

Efringen-Kirchen
Schopfheim
Waldshut
Tiengen

Schloss Rötteln
Wehr
Rickenbach
Rhein

Weil
Wiese
Lörrach
Lautenburg

Rheinfelden
Bad Säckingen
SCHWARZWALD

194

F

CH

0 10 20 30 km
0   10   20 miles

Rhein
Lauter
Enz
Nagold
Würm
Neckar
Kinzig
Steina
Wutach
Donau
Alb
Bibra

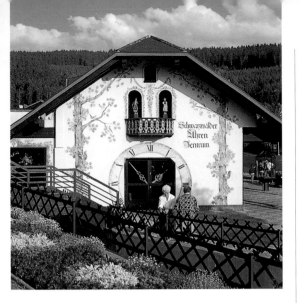

By the Titisee: a popular Black Forest lake set among woodlands

as tennis and squash) have been developed to an impressive degree, even in many smaller villages. The region excels as an area for outdoor pursuits, above all for walking; marked paths of varying degrees of difficulty (including many very easy ones) abound; signposting and tourist information are excellent. A useful tourist board scheme is *Wandern ohne Gepäck* (walking without luggage), where you can walk from village to village to pre-booked guesthouses and have your luggage transported by car. In winter, many come here for cross-country skiing.

Black Forest specialities are prolific. Most famous are undoubtedly the Schwarzwälder Kirschtorte (of which the ubiquitous factory-made Black Forest Gateau is a pale imitation), and the cuckoo clocks on sale in every souvenir shop. Zwiebelkuchen (onion cake) is often served accompanied by a young white wine. Black Forest smoked ham is best eaten sliced thin on locally made bread. In season, white asparagus, plums and cherries appear on the menu. Local drinks include the Baden wines and Kirschwasser, an unsweetened cherry brandy.

The heart of Black Forest clockmaking is around the industrial town and spa of **Triberg** (see pages 196–7). **Furtwangen** is the home of the Deutsches Uhrenmuseum (German clock museum), a must even for non-enthusiasts. There are also factories and workshops in the area, which will be only too pleased to give you a first-hand glimpse of local clock production in this region.

Southern Schwarzwald You will find this region one of the sunniest in Germany. The cherry trees display their blossoms in the early spring while the mountains are still topped with snow from the previous winter. Four of the region's tallest hills lie close to **Freiburg** – the **Feldberg, Schauinsland, Kandel** and the Belchen. All are easily

The tradition of Black Forest clockmaking goes back to 1667, when the wooden clock with foliot (weighted arm) was made for the first time in Waldau. Metal for the mechanisms was imported until 1787, when Leopold Hofmayer set up his brass foundry in Neustadt. Since then numerous variations have been produced, among them musical clocks with trumpeters or flutes, clocks with painted or lacquered shields, clocks to control watchmen, all leading to regulators, alarm clocks, even modern quartz-crystal clocks and radio clocks. As early as 1840, subsidiaries of the Black Forest clock traders existed in four continents and 23 countries. In 1845, 600,000 clocks were produced in the Black Forest – today the figure stands at 60 million a year!

As well as Schwarzwälds Kirschtorte (cherry cake), Black Foresters have other delicacies to tempt the sweet tooth at coffee time. Zwetschenkuchen (blue plums on a pastry base), Käsesahnekuchen (a rich cheesecake) and Johannisbeerenkuchen (a sponge base covered with redcurrants) are just a few.

reached from the road, but the Belchen has the best views; and just north of it is **Münstertal**, a deep and especially pretty valley, steep-sided and graced with the baroque church of St Trudpert. East of the Feldberg is one of the main resort areas; many come for the two lakes, the **Titisee** and the **Schluchsee**. Of these, the Titisee is the prettier, set among gentle woodlands, but the modern village on its northern side partly spoils the effect; the Schluchsee attracts older people and is less commercialised. More peaceful is **Hinterzarten**, an upmarket family resort.

The views are breathtaking in this area, whichever way you decide to travel. If it fits in with your plans, you might want to take a train ride from Freiburg to **Feldberg Bärental**, following a steep and winding route through the Höllental (Hell Valley) gorge. The station at Feldberg Bärental is proud of its special location, the highest railway station in Germany at 976m. If you prefer to put on your hiking boots, the nearby **Feldbergsee** lies at the end of an unspoilt romantic road only available to walkers.

Further south, the terrain is lower and less spectacular, but the country is more open – typically consisting of orchards, meadows and small, rounded hills of small-scale charm. There is less tourist development, and plenty of old-fashioned farmhouses have survived. Of the resorts, **Todtmoos** is especially pleasant, nicely placed amid gentle hills.

Not far from the Swiss border, half way between Freiburg and Basel, is **Badenweiler**, a popular tourist attraction, not only because of its spa, but also because of its fine views over the Rhine plain. The thermal springs here, well preserved since their rediscovery in 1784, have been flowing since Roman times. Today's inhabitants are intent on keeping things as clean and intact as possible, and you have to leave your car on the edge of town and walk in. There are open-air pavilions where numerous musical events are held throughout the summer months.

About 8km to the south of Badenweiler is **Schloss Bürgeln**, built in 1764 on orders of the abbot of the Benedictine abbey of St Blasien. From here you can obtain a spectacular view of the surroundings as far as the Swiss Alps.

Gutach and Kinzig valleys: the central Schwarzwald

A journey north through some fine towns and villages will bring you into the Gutach and Kinzig valleys. Here you will see examples of the distinctive Black Forest farmhouses with their low-hanging roofs, deep eaves and animal quarters under the roof, usually approached by an earth ramp. This is the heartland of Black Forest folk costume, such as the wide-brimmed hats with red pompoms worn by local girls. The **Schwarzwaldbahn** (Black Forest railway), with its 45 tunnels, crosses this landscape.

The highest waterfall in Germany (162m) is at **Triberg** (the Gutach falls). Cuckoo clock sceptics may be surprised that the business launched by Josef Weisser in 1824 in Triberg, called the 'Haus der 1000 Uhren' (House of 1,000 clocks), is still thriving. Triberg is not

Schwarzwald scenery

just clocks, however. It is a year-round spa, a winter sports resort and a relaxed sort of town. The forest at Triberg acts as a dust filter and visitors to the spa and health resort often remark on the purity of the air. In Triberg's Schwarzwald Museum you'll find a wide array of local costumes on display, as well as woodcarvings, ceramics and – of course – clockmaking memorabilia, which will give you an idea of the rural culture. **Gutach** is known for the Vogtsbauernhof, an imaginatively arranged open-air museum with an absorbing collection of reconstructed and traditionally furnished thatched farmhouses, complete with farm implements; in its country setting, the whole place has the feel of a real village.

Freudenstadt was badly damaged in World War II, and has little ancient character, but it has been carefully reconstructed and is now second only to Baden-Baden as a health resort. The town sits high on a plateau at the meeting point of all the main routes in the northern Schwarzwald. The arcaded market place, which is Germany's largest, has neatly laid out pavements and lawns.

To the south, **Schiltach** and **Wolfach**, both close to main roads, are among the prettiest Black Forest villages and boast half-timbered market squares.

Dying and diseased trees with yellowing needles and peeling bark are widespread in the forests. Acid rain, ozone fog and exhaust emissions are thought to be the culprits, and government pollution controls have been increased to curb the *Waldsterben* – Dying Forest Syndrome.

SOUTHWEST GERMANY

The northern Schwarzwald The B500 Schwarzwald Hochstrasse linking Freudenstadt with Baden-Baden is a popular road. It runs along almost the entire spine of the Black Forest. Numerous roadside stopping places will enable you to picnic al fresco and admire the view; or there are plenty of villages or hamlets for a meal or an overnight stay.

The drive along the Nagold valley from Freudenstadt (part of the Schwarzwald Bäderstrasse) brings you to **Pforzheim**, at the northern extremity of the Schwarzwald, some 30km north of Calw, with its half-timbered houses. At Pforzheim, the River Nagold joins the River Enz. As a centre of the jewellery trade, the town likes to think of itself as wealthy and has christened itself 'Goldstadt' ('town of gold'). The Schmuckmuseum (jewellery museum) is in the Reuchlinhaus in Jahnstrasse. Pforzheim is also the starting point for hikes into the northern tip of the Schwarzwald (see **Walks**, below, for possible walking routes).

198

Walks **Black Forest footpaths**

The Black Forest offers an excellent range of long distance walks, taking in viewpoints, unspoiled farmland, villages and wetlands. Signposting (look for diamond-shaped signposts) and path maintenance are of a high standard; there is plenty of good quality accommodation on the way and no shortage of refreshment facilities.

Long tracks divide into Hohenwege (hill paths), which take north–south courses along the footpaths, and Querweger (linking paths), which lead west–east. Of the four Hohenwege the longest is the 350km Pforzheim to Basel Westweg. The Querweger range from the 164km Freiburg to Bodensee Querweg to short expeditions such as the 48km Rheinfelden to Albbruck path.

Boats at Titisee

▶ ▶ ▷ **Speyer**

The Rhine town of Speyer possesses, in its cathedral, one of Europe's great Romanesque churches. Founded in 1030, it was remodelled at the end of the 11th century with four towers and two domes. Located in front is the Domnapf (cathedral bowl) of 1490, where wine is traditionally poured at the induction of a new bishop or for other special occasions, such as the 2,000th anniversary of the city in 1990. At the entrance to the vault of the emperors, or Kaisergruft, the name given to the huge 11th-century crypt (the largest of its period in Germany) where eight rulers were buried, is the 13th-century tomb of Rudolph of Hapsburg. From the cathedral's west front the broad Maximilianstrasse leads to the massive Altpörtel, the only city gateway to have survived.

At the Historisches Museum der Pfalz (Palatinate Museum – open daily) the Bronze Age 'Golden Hat' of Schifferstadt is the highlight of the collection which includes paintings and porcelain from ancient through to modern times. The Weinmuseum (Wine Museum) in the same building houses wine-making equipment with, amazingly, a 3rd-century bottle of wine (complete with contents).

The synagogue which once existed in Speyer has been destroyed, but 10m below ground level in Judenbadgasse is the Judenbad, a fine example of the ritual baths used by Jews for cleansing on important religious holidays and by brides prior to their wedding.

Speyer hosted 50 Imperial diets in the course of the Holy Roman Empire's history. As well as the Emperor and the six Electors, the diet was made up of 30 lay princes, 140 counts and lords, 120 bishops and archbishops and the representatives of 200 cities.

Steinhausen's Wallfahrtskirche

▶ ▷ ▷ **Steinhausen**

Steinhausen's Wallfahrtskirche (pilgrimage church), built between 1728 and 1733, is the work of two brothers – Dominikus and Johann Baptist Zimmermann – who perfected the baroque style in the churches they designed and decorated. Dominikus designed the building and Johann was the painter; both were involved in the stucco work. The airy oval nave with an encircling gallery above has been left as the brothers decorated it. Stucco flowers, insects, birds and squirrels form part of the composition. Not all the work originally intended was completed as the building cost four times as much as was estimated in 1727. Work ceased in 1733.

SOUTHWEST GERMANY

Stuttgart's prosperity is built on the work of Gottlieb Daimler, who developed the petrol engine and produced one of the world's first motor cars in the city in the 1880s. In 1926 the Daimler company merged with that of Carl Benz (another motor car pioneer) to form Daimler-Benz.

A café in Stuttgart

▶ ▶ ▷   **Stuttgart**

Capital of the *Land* of Baden-Württemberg, Stuttgart has an enviable valley setting among green hills. Home of charismatic names like Mercedes, Porsche, Bosch and Zeiss, the city is one of the most glittering jewels in the crown of industrial Germany, its standard of living one of the highest in the country. Cultural and environmental standards are high too, with splendid galleries and a park system which is a model of its kind.

Stuttgart's evolution was closely tied to the fortunes of the House of Württemberg, who made the city their seat in the 14th century. Under Napoleon, who made Württemberg a kingdom, the city became a royal capital, and though this only lasted a century, something of the feeling of royal splendour has persisted to the present. Stuttgart takes its name from a stud farm (Stutengarten) established in the 10th century by the Duke of Swabia, and a horse features in the city's coat of arms. In spite of being the focus of a metropolitan region of some two million people, the city has a relaxed air about it, possibly something to do with the abundance of vineyards within the municipal boundary; grapes grow within spitting distance of the central station.

Both the Porsche Museum and the splendid Daimler-Benz museum are outside the centre but easily accessible by the S-Bahn rapid transit system. Porsche features racing cars, Daimler-Benz all kinds of stars from the Mercedes stable, right down to the first 'Popemobile'.

A good way of starting your tour of Stuttgart is to ascend the tall TV Tower (Fernsehturm), completed in 1956 and the first of its kind in Germany, which rises above the woods in the south of the city. The viewing platform offers a magnificent panorama over Stuttgart, the Swabian Jura and, on a clear day, even the far-off Alps.

What to see The traffic-free main street, Königstrasse, runs south from the monumental railway station to the vast Schlossplatz. Here are some of Stuttgart's great civic buildings, such as the baroque Neues Schloss, last

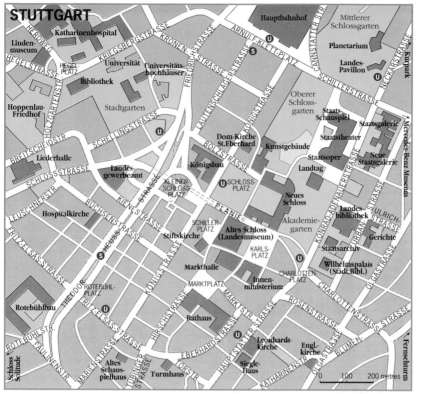

STUTTGART

(Map labels:) Katharinenhospital · Linden-museum · HERDWEG · HEGELSTRASSE · HEGEL-PLATZ · Universität · KRIEGSBERGSTRASSE · KRONENSTRASSE · FRIEDRICHSTRASSE · KAUTENSCHLAGERSTRASSE · ARNULF-KLETT-PLATZ · Hauptbahnhof · Mittlerer Schlossgarten · Planetarium · Landes-Pavillon · NECKARSTRASSE · Kurpark · Mercedes-Benz Museum · SCHILLERSTRASSE · Universitäts-hochhäuser · Bibliothek · Hoppenlau-Friedhof · Stadtgarten · HOLZGARTENSTR · BREITSCHEIDSTR · SCHELLINGSTRASSE · KÖNIGSTRASSE · Oberer Schloss-garten · Staats-Schauspiel · Staatsgalerie · Liederhalle · Landes-gewerbeamt · Dom-Kirche St.Eberhard · BOLZSTRASSE · Kunstgebäude · Staatstheater · Staatsgalerie · Neue Staatsgalerie · SCHLOSS-STRASSE · LEUTSCHNERSTR · BUCHSENSTRASSE · KIENESTRASSE · Königsbau · KLEINER-SCHLOSS-PLATZ · SCHLOSS-PLATZ · Staatsoper · Landtag · KONRAD-ADENAUER-STRASSE · FRITZ-ELSAS-STRASSE · HEUSTRASSE · PLANIE · Neues Schloss · Akademie-garten · Landes-bibliothek · ULRICH-STRASSE · URBANSTRASSE · Gerichte · Hospitalkirche · SCHILLER-PLATZ · Altes Schloss (Landesmuseum) · Stiftskirche · KÖNIGSTRASSE · KARLS-PLATZ · Staatsarchiv · OLGASTRASSE · Markthalle · Wilhelmspalais (Städt.Bibl.) · CHARLOTTEN-PLATZ · Rotebühlbau · Innen-ministerium · Innen-ministerium · CHARLOTTENSTRASSE · ROSENSTRASSE · Fernsehturm · ROTEBÜHLPLATZ · THEODOR-HEUSS-STRASSE · MARKTPLATZ · HIRSCHSTRASSE · MARKTSTR · Rathaus · HAUPTSTATTER STRASSE · ROSENSTRASSE · PAULINENSTR · MARIENSTRASSE · TÜBINGER STRASSE · Turmhaus · TORSTR · EBERHARDSTRASSE · Leonhards-Kirche · Engl.-kirche · BLUMENSTRASSE · Schloss Solitude · Altes Schaus-pielhaus · Siegle-Haus · KATHARINENSTR · OLGASTRASSE

0   100   200 metres

home of the Württemberg kings and now used for government purposes, the shop-lined neo-classical Königsbau, and the City Art Gallery. Linking through to the much more atmospheric Schillerplatz is the Altes Schloss, part medieval castle, part Renaissance palace, home of the Landesmuseum with its many memorabilia of the House of Württemberg as well as an excellent collection of Swabian religious sculpture. Beyond the expressway is one of Europe's great modern art galleries, James Stirling's Staatsgalerie (see page 202).

It is possible to walk from the city centre via parks and gardens to the far bank of the Neckar and Bad Cannstatt, Stuttgart's spa, with casino and Kurhaus.

A good 15km from the centre of Stuttgart is **Schloss Solitude**, a fine example of 18th-century rococo and a glimpse of life under the Württemberg rulers, who used it as a summer residence (open daily except Monday).

Several places of interest lie close to the Neckar and other rivers. To the north are **Ludwigsburg**, with Germany's largest baroque castle (guided tours daily), where mechanical figures act out fairy tales in the Märchengarten (Fairytale Garden); **Marbach**, where Friedrich Schiller was born in 1759 – his house (open daily) contains a few personal mementoes – and where today the impressive Schiller National Museum (open daily) attracts literary pilgrims; and **Besigheim**, retaining walls and towers. Felsengärten Hessigheim, a natural rock 'garden' towers over a bend in the Neckar.

Ludwigsburg's baroque castle

Stuttgart's Staatsgalerie

■ **The Staatsgalerie was founded by Wilhelm I of Württemberg in 1843. Its famous extension, inaugurated in March 1984, was designed by the British architect James Stirling. The modern building put Stuttgart on the map in the world of art and architecture. Its varied forms and bold use of different materials have made it one of the landmarks of Post-modernism – and it is surprisingly popular with the public. Some 25 per cent of the 70 million DM for its construction came from Lotto contributions collected since 1958......■**

Modern collection The art is worthy of the building, with works by Henri Matisse and Oskar Schlemmer, Joseph Beuys and Alberto Giacometti, Franz Marc and Giorgio de Chirico. Modern German art is particularly well represented. It also houses the largest Picasso collection in Germany.

The old gallery The mainstream collection of the Staatsgalerie provides an overview of the history of western European painting, with works from medieval times to the 19th century, from early altarpieces to French impressionists. There is a particularly fine collection of works from the local 15th-century Swabian school; other German works include Cranach's *Judith with the Head of Holofernes* and Hans Baldung Grien's *Man of Sorrows*. One of the most important works is the Herrenberg Altar, with vivid scenes of Christ's Passion painted by Jörg Ratgeb in 1518–19 for the Herrenberg collegiate church; it was brought to Stuttgart in 1892. Almost every 19th-century French painter is represented – including Manet, Monet and Cézanne. One of the best known works of German romantic painting, Caspar David Friedrich's *The Cross in the Woods*, is in the Staatsgalerie. If you favour romantic art, don't miss the eight scenes from *The Legend of Perseus* by English Pre-Raphaelite Edward Burne-Jones. The Dutch masters – Memling, Hals, Rubens and Rembrandt – are prominent too. Some of the best treasures are displayed in the basement – for security *and* to preserve the collection from possible environmental damage. The gallery is located at Konrad Adenauerstrasse 30–32, tel: 2125108. *Open*: Tuesday to Sunday 10.00–17.00hrs, Thursdays until 20.00hrs.

The Rathaus at Tübingen

After the establishment of the 'Cotta' publishing house – which published works by Goethe and Schiller – many distinguished writers and poets came to make their home in Tübingen. These included Friedrich Hölderlin, and the tower where he lived, insane, for 36 years, is on the river bank (it can be visited daily except Monday). The poets Eduard Mörike and Ludwig Uhland, as well as the philosophers Hegel and Schelling, also came to Tübingen.

▶ ▶ ▷ Tübingen

Situated on the tranquil upper reaches of the Neckar, Tübingen is one of Germany's oldest and most atmospheric university towns. Less plagued than Heidelberg by tourism, though quite its equal in charm, it has a castle, Hohentübingen, high above old colour-washed houses, their gables turned to the river.

The best view of the town is from the Eberhardsbrücke over the Neckar. The bridge gives access to a long island between two arms of the river. The Platanenallee promenade, so called because it is lined with plane trees, is a favourite place for an evening stroll.

Schloss Hohentübingen is of Renaissance date, built on the 11th-century foundations. Its entrance gateway bears the coat of arms of the House of Württemberg together with the Order of the Garter awarded to one of the dukes by Queen Elizabeth I of England.

The Marktplatz (market place), with its Neptune fountain, seems to be the hub of all the narrow winding streets and is still the focus of attention – particularly on market days (Monday, Wednesday and Friday). On one side of the square is the 15th-century (but much restored) Rathaus, and a short distance east (in Münzgasse) is the Protestant collegiate church of St Georg, which contains late Gothic features, including notably the rood screen, vaulting and tracery.

Founded on papal authority as a training centre for Protestant ministers in the Reformation, Tübingen University has become the focus for religious controversy with the removal of Hans Küng, an academic theologian, for criticising church dogma.

Excursion

Reutlingen, 10km east of Tübingen, retains town walls and numerous fine buildings, despite war damage. In particular see the Marienkirche, a strikingly unified Gothic church of the 13th and 14th centuries.

The Cistercian monastery at **Bebenhausen**, north of Tübingen, founded 1185, is encompassed by a double wall and centred on a late Gothic cloister (completed 1496). Guided tours are given daily.

Ulm Münster (right) boasts a set of 15th-century carved choirstalls (below)

The Fischerviertel (Fishermen's Quarter), among tributaries of the Danube, prompted writer Herman Hesse to describe Ulm as an 'extraordinary and beautiful city'. Here, in half-timbered houses, artisans once eked out a living.

▶ ▶ ▷   **Ulm**

Ulm's location at a significant crossing point of the Danube made it an important trading centre in the late Middle Ages. The city suffered severe damage in a bombing raid in 1944, which virtually destroyed the old centre, but much of the ancient fabric has now been restored. Ulm's most famous son was Albert Einstein, born here in 1879.

The best general view is from the Tahn Ufer on the far side of the Danube. Look out for the leaning gateway known as the Metzgerturm (butchers' tower). The Münster is one of the largest and most important religious buildings in Europe, and it was fortunately little damaged by the 1944 bombs. Construction began in 1377 and many important architects and artists made their mark on it before it was completed, with the tower and steeple, in 1890. The latter, the tallest in the world, soars 161m above the rest of the city. You can climb almost to the top (768 steps), for a small charge, and take in a view stretching from the Danube across the Black Forest to the Swiss Alps, if the weather is on your side. Above the doorway under the tower are carved details of the Book of Genesis, as well as figures of Mary and the Apostles. There is much to be seen in the massive interior, including a magnificent set of 15th-century carved choir stalls and a display of architectural plans by the various designers of the cathedral.

Try to preserve some energy for a visit to the huge Ulmer Museum – there are 50 exhibition rooms with a heavy accent on Gothic art in Upper Swabia, and works by 20th-century artists.

West of Ulm, the former abbey church at **Blaubeuren** (open daily; afternoons only in winter) is charmingly reflected in a deep blue pool. The building contains an exceptional 15th-century late Gothic altarpiece, the work of a group of local craftsmen.

▶ ▷ ▷ **Wertheim**

At the meeting point of the Main and Tauber rivers, Wertheim is a town of delightful half-timbered houses neatly erected along narrow streets amid a setting of wooded hills. The ruined Altes Schloss, towering over the town, was built by the Counts of Wertheim in the 12th century. There are wonderful views from here. A glass museum in Mühlenstrasse has collections of historic glass, while the 15th-century Kilianskapelle (St Kilian's chapel) is now a local museum; the basement here, of Gothic structure, served as an ossuary. In the Marktplatz you will see half-timbered houses and the Engelsbrunnen (Angels' Well), dating from 1574, named after the stone angels bearing the Wertheim coat of arms. From the left bank of the Tauber there is a stunning view of part of the town, with the Stadtkirche and the ruins of the Kurmainzisches Schloss.

▶ ▷ ▷ **Worms**

This cathedral city on the banks of the Rhine, one of the oldest in Germany, has a particularly eventful past. There was a Celtic settlement here, then a Roman garrison. According to the *Nibelungenlied* it was the seat of the Burgundian king. During medieval times over 100 imperial diets, or assemblies, were held in Worms, the most noted being the Reichstag of 1521 (Diet of Worms) which summoned Luther to stand before it. He refused to retract his doctrines and was banned from the Empire.

Besides industry, Worms has a flourishing wine trade. The famous Liebfraumilch comes from here, taking its name from the Liebfrauenkirche (Church of Our Lady) standing proudly in the midst of a vineyard to the north of the city. It contains a 15th-century Madonna and tabernacle.

One of the supreme examples of Romanesque architecture in Germany is the cathedral, the Kaiserdom, with two domes and four corner towers. Despite other parts of the city being badly damaged as a result of a succession of wars, the cathedral has been carefully maintained. St Martins Kirche, also Romanesque, has the same design as the cathedral.

The synagogue of Worms– the oldest in Germany – and the Jewish cemetery date back to the 11th century. There was a large Jewish community here up to the 1930s. The Alte Synagoge was rebuilt in 1961 and the cemetery contains over 1,000 gravestones and pillars carved in Hebrew, amazingly untouched by the Nazis. After Prague's, this is the second largest Jewish cemetery in Europe.

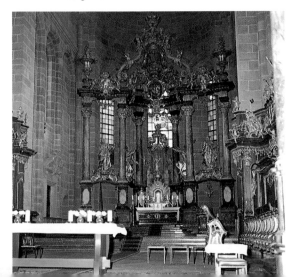

The altar in Worms cathedral

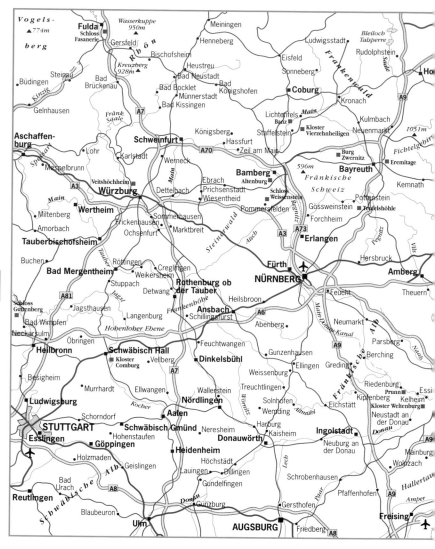

Stretching from Aschaffenburg in the northwest to Passau on the Austrian border far to the southeast, this region offers some of Germany's most fascinating historical cities including **Nürnberg, Regensburg** and **Würzburg**, and stretches of unspoiled countryside. The world-famous **Romantische Strasse** (Romantic Road) links medieval towns, while backwaters of the Bavarian Forest are explored by the **Bayerische Ostmarkstrasse**.

The region's cultural riches are unsurpassed; in the late Middle Ages and Early Renaissance, some of the most characteristically German contributions to the arts were made by painters (Altdorfer, Cranach and Dürer), or by master craftsmen (Veit Stoss and Tilman Riemenschneider). Their work can be see in museums such as the outstanding Germanisches Nationalmuseum at Nürnberg, or sometimes in its original setting – see

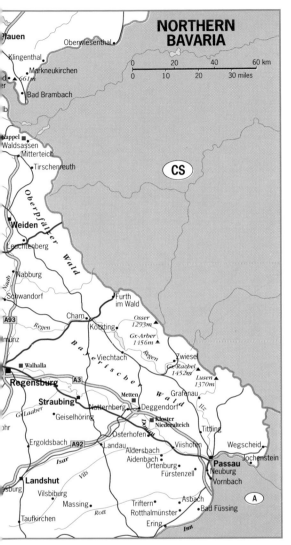

Riemenschneider's *Madonna in a Rose Garland* in the little church at Volkach. Architecture particularly worth noting includes the sumptuous 18th-century baroque and rococo edifices.

National Parks offer unparalleled opportunities for exploring, on foot, by bike or by canoe along the rivers. Rural scenery ranges from the romantic **Altmühl valley** to the mysterious depths of Europe's last remaining fragments of virgin forest in the **Bayerischer Wald**.

Enjoy the region for its food and drink. Hearty game dishes or spicy sausages from Nürnberg are complemented by famous beers (the world's oldest brewery is at **Freising**) or wines from Franconia, where Main valley vineyards rival those of Rhine and Mosel. This a favourite holiday area, with bargains to be had in remoter places along the border with Czechoslovakia.

The lower reaches of the Ahltmül have become part of the new Main-Danube Canal. Completed in 1992, this gigantic and bitterly controversial project connects the waterways of western and central Europe, enabling large vessels to ply between the Rhine and the Black Sea. Nowhere else has a river landscape been so utterly transformed nor so conscientiously restored, a process best seen at Essing, just downstream from Prunn. Here the idyllic riverside scene of village, barbican and ancient timber bridge seems untouched by by time.

▶ ▶ ▷ Altmühltal (Altmühl Valley)

This is one of Germany's most attractive river valleys, with unspoiled towns and villages, dramatic crags topped by castles and the nation's largest Naturpark Altmühltal (Nature Park). The river rises in the Frankenhöhe (Franconian Heights) near Rothenburg-ob-der-Tauber, crosses gently rolling countryside to the small spa town of Treuchtlingen, then twists deeply through the limestone of the Fränkische Alb (Franconian Jura), joining the Danube at Kelheim. The meadowlands, rock pinnacles and juniper-studded slopes are enjoyed by walkers and by cyclists on the riverside cycleway.

Downstream nestles Eichstätt, with cobbled streets and squares dominated by patrician houses and church towers. The cathedral's art treasures include the huge Pappenheim altar, an arresting late medieval depiction of the Crucifixion. There are fine views of the town from the hilltop Frauenberg pilgrimage chapel, or the chunky, chalk-white Willibaldsburg overlooking the river.

The most extraordinary castle is 11th-century Prunn, perched precariously over the river. At the end of the Altmühl valley is the pompous drum-like Befreiungshalle (Liberation Monument), built in 1842–63 by Ludwig I of Bavaria to commemorate the freeing of Germany from Napoleonic domination.

The 19th-century Befreiungshalle above Kelheim, commemorating the defeat of Napoleon

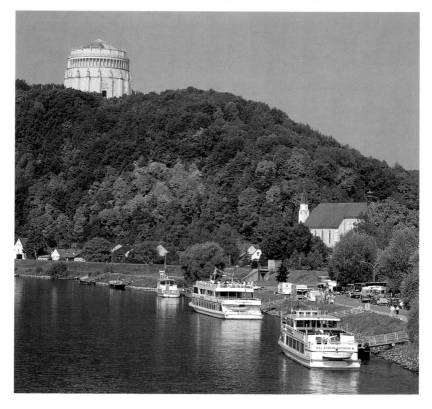

▶ ▷ ▷   Amber g

Untouched by wars and heavy industry, Amberg has within its medieval walls a variety of buildings from its prosperous past, including four fine gateways and the ancient bridge – the Stadtbrille (City Spectacles – check the reflection of its twin arches in the waters of the River Vils).

Dominating the market square is the gabled and arcaded Gothic Rathaus, one of the finest such structures in Germany. The churches include the stately St Martin's (1421), St George's, its interior baroquified in the late 17th century, and the Deutsche Schulkirche, a rococo gem. Stations of the Cross lead uphill to the late Renaissance pilgrimage church of Mariahilf, with its fine views over the town and the countryside of the Oberpfalz (Upper Palatinate).

Amberg holds its *Altstadtfest* in June and its *Bergfest* in July, though the products of its ten breweries can be sampled at any time!

▶ ▷ ▷   Ansbach

Administrative and cultural centre of Central Franconia, Ansbach is one of Germany's finest 'Residenz towns', its history and townscape fashioned by its role as the seat of its rulers, the Margraves of Brandenburg-Ansbach. Streets and squares feature many attractive buildings, from high-gabled medieval burghers' houses to the three-towered church of St Gumbertus, redesigned in the 18th century to become an ideal 'preaching church', dominated by the pulpit rather than the altar.

The Residenz itself is a splendid Renaissance structure, incorporating parts of the original medieval moated stronghold, and with a rococo interior containing the Bavarian state collection of Ansbach ceramics. Beyond is the palace's park, the Hofgarten, with stately avenues of lime trees, an impressive orangery and a memorial to the enigmatic foundling Kaspar Hauser, mysteriously murdered here in 1833 and the subject of fascinated speculation ever since.

▶ ▷ ▷   Aschaffenburg

The first Bavarian town for visitors coming from the Frankfurt direction, Aschaffenburg is dominated by the huge red sandstone Schloss standing four-square on a bluff overlooking the River Main. Known as the Johannisburg, it was erected at the start of the 17th century by the Bishop of Mainz, Aschaffenburg's overlord. The interior includes state apartments, fine paintings (including pictures by Cranach), and a range of glass and ceramics. Other master works including another Cranach and a Grünewald can be found in the town centre Stiftskirche, a church incorporating a variety of architectural styles from Romanesque onwards. Treasures of a different kind feature in the Automuseum with its 200-odd classic racing cars and collection of automobile art.

The town's two parks, Schöntal (in the centre) and Schönbusch (on the far bank of the Main) are excellent examples of German landscapers' attempts to imitate the 'English Style' in garden design.

Ansbach

Johannisburg, the 17th-century Schloss at Aschaffenburg

The position of Augsburg meant that it was strongly subject to the northward moving influences of the Italian Renaissance. Churches, patrician houses and public buildings were enthusiastically built or rebuilt, great artists including Holbein the Elder gave of their best and metalworkers created masterpieces in gold and silver, while Martin Luther's visits reflected the hold Protestantism had taken here.

Excursions

The Spessart East of Aschaffenburg the Main swings south then north again in a great bend forming the southern boundary of the Spessart, one of Germany's finest areas of unspoiled uplands. Here are some of the country's most extensive woodlands, magnificent stands of beech and oak stretching away to distant horizons – an awesome prospect even when viewed from the great scenic highway, the Frankfurt-Nuremberg Autobahn.

In the romantic setting of a deep forest valley lies **Schloss Mespelbrunn**, its picturesque silhouette reflected in the calm surface of its moat. Still inhabited, the castle's furnished interior is pleasingly evocative of the life of the provincial nobility.

The stretch of the Main upstream from Aschaffenburg forms part of the Franconian wine-growing area. It is a cheerful landscape of orchards, south-facing vineyards and jolly little towns and villages, among them half-timbered **Miltenberg** – 'the very essence of medieval Germany'.

▶ ▶ ▷ **Augsburg**

With a population of 250,000, Augsburg is Bavaria's third biggest city (after Munich and Nuremberg) as well as its oldest, founded in Roman times and named after Emperor Augustus. Commanding the Alpine trade routes linking Northern Europe to Italy, Augsburg enjoyed its heyday in the 15th and 16th centuries. Second only to London as a banking centre, it became the base of great financial and commercial dynasties such as the immensely rich Fuggers. Later names associated with Augsburg include Wolfgang Amadeus Mozart's father (who lived here in the 17th century, at no 14 Mittleren Gasse), Rudolf Diesel (who invented his engine at the MAN works), Willy Messerschmitt (famous for his fighter planes), and the playwright Bertolt Brecht (who was born here but who was no lover of the place).

What to see Augsburg has a big city centre, focussed on the Ludwigplatz with its imposing Renaissance Rathaus of 1620 and the landmark tower, the Perlachturm (good city views from the top). Some way north stands the Domkirche St Maria, originally

Romanesque but much altered and added to subsequently. It has splendid 11th-century bronze doors, stained glass which is among the country's oldest, and a Holbein altarpiece.

In order to celebrate its 1,600th birthday, Augsburg commissioned the construction of a number of fine fountains. The Augustusbrunnen (1594), with its figures of Emperor and river gods, stands in the Ludwigplatz, the Herkulesbrunnen (1596–1602) in the broad Maximilianstrasse to the south.

The Maximilianstrasse is a stately city artery, lined with a number of splendid residences, including the Fuggerhaus and the rococo Schaezlerpalais, which has art collections and a sumptuous Festsaal (banqueting hall).

At the end of the street is the tall tower of the church of St Ulric and St Afra.

Excursion

Just east of Augsburg is the small town of **Friedberg**, rebuilt after being burnt down in the Thirty Years' War. Its notable features include a castle, a pretty Rathaus, and above all Herrgottsruh, a pilgrimage church with an exuberant rococo interior.

The Rathaus and Perlachturm in the Ludwigplatz at Augsburg

Kissingen's saline waters and favourable climate (spring arrives here a good fortnight earlier than elsewhere) have attracted visitors since the 18th century, though the town's origins go back to the early Middle Ages and something of the atmosphere of an old Franconian town remains, especially around the Old Rathaus of 1577.
The town's heyday came in the 19th century, under the patronage of the Bavarian royal family. Poets, painters, and politicians (among them the Iron Chancellor, Bismarck, who visited no fewer than 15 times) flocked to take the waters. Russian and English guests were numerous, necessitating the building of both an Orthodox and an Anglican church.

▶ ▷ ▷   Bad Kissingen

Located among parks and gardens along the banks of the River Saale, this is Bavaria's most popular spa.
The spa buildings include an 1838 arcade and the monumental 1913 Regentenbau, a complex of halls and public rooms linked to the Wandelhalle a covered promenade. The Theatre, completed in 1904, has a fine *Jugendstil* interior. On the far bank of the Saale from the Wandelhalle is the immaculate Kurpark with buildings housing spa and casino.
Crowning a hilltop south of town are the ruins of Bodenlauben Castle, once the residence of the medieval poet and keen crusader Otto von der Bodenlauben; his statue forms part of the fountain on the Rathausplatz.

The Rhön Bad Kissingen is one of the main 'gateways' to this area of varied upland scenery which stretches northward to **Fulda**. Rising in places to over 900m, the rounded summits carry a covering of moorland and pasture rather than the more usual forest. This splendid walking country is also much favoured by gliding enthusiasts. The most extensive views, both involving a short hike of half an hour or so, are from the **Wasserkuppe** (950m) and from the **Kreuzberg** (928m).In the valleys are attractive little towns such as **Gersfeld**

Taking the air at Bad Kissingen

with its three castles, and **Bad Brückenau**, a spa with classical buildings inspired by the ubiquitous King Ludwig. **Bad Neustadt** has kept intact its ring of medieval fortifications; within the walls stands the former church of the Carmelites, dating from the 14th century but with an exceptionally fine baroque interior. On the far bank of the Saale are the spa facilities, including a Kurhotel comfortably installed within an 18th-century castle. **Münnerstadt** too has retained its walls, but its greatest treasure is the high altar by the great Riemenschneider in the parish church.
A favourite short excursion from Bad Kissingen is to **Bad Bocklet**, on the historic mailcoach which plies between the two spas, passing on the way the Renaissance castle at **Aschach**, its rooms filled with fine furniture and paintings as well as a collection of oriental art.

Deutscherordenschloss in Bad Mergentheim, residence of the Grand Master of the Order of Teutonic Knights from 1525 to 1809

The waters of the three springs of Bad Mergentheim are used in the treatment of digestive complaints. Though the waters were discovered at the beginning of the 19th century, the spa only really developed in the interwar period, and its trim architecture reflects the taste of the time.

▶ ▷ ▷ **Bad Mergentheim**

Pleasantly situated in the friendly valley of the River Tauber, this is an important stopping place along the Romantische Strasse, as well as a spa. In contrast to the newer spa town, the old town has a picturesque market place, churches, high-gabled Rathaus and ancient fountain. The most prominent structure is the ochre mid-16th century Deutschordenschloss (see also Ellingen). It is a fascinating assembly of high walls, gables, towers and turrets. Inside is a splendid Renaissance staircase. The baroque castle church has a light-filled interior with a magnificent ceiling painting; in the crypt are the tombs of long-dead Grand Masters.

Excursion

The parish church at **Stuppach**, 7km southwest, has a famous Madonna and Child by the great Grünewald, one of this tormented master's more spiritual paintings.

▶ ▶ ▶ **Bamberg**

Bamberg is perhaps the most perfect of all Germany's ancient cities, a wonderful synthesis of architecture of all periods in a harmonious setting of river vale and gentle hills.

Founded in 973, the city was made a bishopric by King Henry II and its division into two distinct districts is still apparent, the Bürgerstadt or merchants' town by the River Pegnitz, the Bischofsstadt or ecclesiastical quarter on the slopes above. Linking the two is the extraordinarily picturesque old town hall, an incongruous mixture of rustic half-timbering and rococo elegance perched on a tiny island in the Pegnitz. Downstream stretch the charming riverside dwellings of Bamberg's Little Venice, once the abode of fishermen.

Higher up is the Kaiserdom, the city's great cathedral, with its four tall towers finding their echo in those of St Michael's church crowning the hilltop in the middle distance. The cathedral is a triumph of the transitional period between late Romanesque and early Gothic. Its interior is enlivened by some of the most remarkable

The Alte Rathaus at Bamberg

sculpture in Germany. The Bamberger Reiter (Bamberg Knight) on his stone steed has come to represent the essence of medieval chivalry, while the tomb of Henry II and his Queen Kunigunde is one of the masterpieces of the great Tilman Riemenschneider (c1513). The royal pair appear again in the elaborately carved choirstalls, while the Marienaltar (1523) exemplifies the genius of the Nuremberg woodcarver, Veit Stoss.

The Domplatz (Cathedral Square) is overlooked on one side by the Neue Residenz with its splendid baroque interior, and on the other by the Alte Hofhaltung. Beyond the Renaissance gateway the undulating cobbled courtyard is enclosed by a delightfully irregular sequence of late Gothic galleried buildings beneath steep-pitched roofs pierced by dormer windows.

Bamberg offers much to the leisured explorer, including churches (from Gothic St Jakob to the rococo interior of St Gangolf), splendid town residences (the richly decorated Böttingerhaus or the riverside Concordiahaus) and museums (the Diocesan Museum off the cathedral cloister or the exemplary local history museum in the Alte Hofhaltung). A close-up of the city can be enjoyed from the Vierkirchenblick (Four Church View) to the south of the cathedral, a more distant prospect from the old Bishops' castle, the Altenburg, 3km southwest.

Excursions

Pommersfelden. 20km south, is Schloss Weissenstein, one of Germany's most grandiose baroque palaces, built (and, in part, designed) by Prince-Bishop Schönborn of Bamberg in 1711–18. The sumptuous interior with its great stairway is connected via a grotto room to the English-style park beyond.

The River Main joins the Pegnitz just downstream from Bamberg. Along its course lie a number of pretty little places, Zeil-am-Main, half-timbered Königsberg (north of the river), and Hassfurt, graced by a parish church (with a Riemenschneider carving) and the Ritterkapelle (Knights' Chapel), a minor masterpiece of late Gothic.

▶ ▶ ▶ Bayerischer Wald (Bavarian Forest)

Between the Danube and the Czech border stretch 6,000sq km of upland country, forming, together with the Sumava (Bohemian Forest) on the far side of the frontier, 'Europe's Green Roof'. Rising to 1,456m at the Grosser Arber, the area contains traces of primeval forest, ancient stands of spruce carefully preserved as part of Germany's first National Park. Woodland is continuous on the higher land, interspersed elsewhere with attractive farming countryside and meticulously modernised villages. Churches with onion domes pierce the skyline, little streams channel through steeply sloping meadows to tributaries of the Danube. Though there are no large towns, impeccably engineered roads stitch the whole area together, and the occasional two-coach train still trundles the single tracks of the surviving branch lines. With an abundance of accommodation, in hotels, pensions, private rooms and holiday flats, this is one of the areas favoured by Germans for their own holidays. Attractions are plentiful, from relics of the metal-working industries which flourished until recently to castle ruins perched on rocks, or little medieval towns. Many places have their 'Heimatmuseum', and there are curiosities like the snuff museum at Grafenau.

Klein Venedig, on the River Pegnitz, Bamberg

Long winters give good conditions for winter sports in the Bayerischer Wald. As well as some provision for downhill skiing, there are more than 2,000km of cross-country trails.

Drive **Passau to Cham**

Climbing from the Danube, the B85, known as the Bayerische Ostmarkstrasse, is a splendid scenic highway linking Passau on the Austrian border with Bayreuth. Near **Tittling**, look round the Museumsdorf Bayerischer Wald, where old buildings have been renovated.

Continue on the Ostmarkstrasse to Cham via Regen, located on the Schwarzer Regen, and Viechtach with a 17th-century Rathaus, or detour on the indirect route around the Grosser Arber.

Just north of **Neuschönau**, the Hans-Eisenmann-Haus, the visitor centre run by the Bavarian Forest National Park, has displays, leaflets (in English) and self-guided trails which tell you all about the origins of the great forest and its wildlife.

The road northwestwards to the Arber goes through country towns where the glass industry flourishes, though Spiegelau, Frauenau and Zwiesel are more like resorts than manufacturing centres.
Some glassworks can be visited, while Frauenau has an excellent

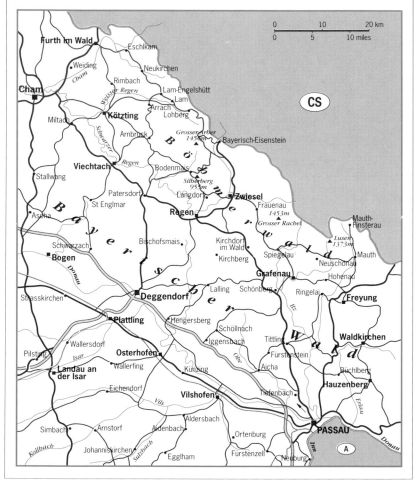

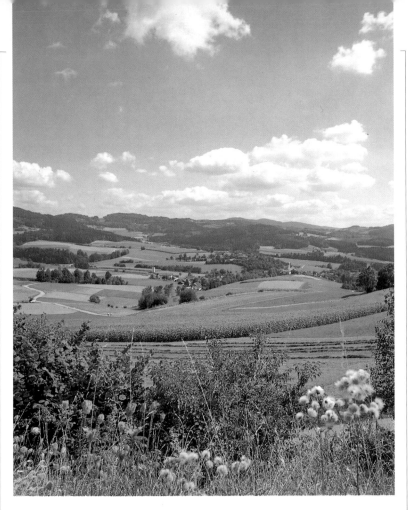

Open views across the Bayerischer Wald

Glasmuseum. **Bodenmais**, in the Bavarian Forest, deals in glass, but outside the town is the **Silberberg**, mined for its copper, tin and silver and now open to visitors (though no longer in production). To the north rises the Arber, with remnants of the inaccessible primeval forest. This is one of the most inhospitable areas in Germany. Frost occurs on 200 or more days a year and deep snow lies well into spring. Solitude can be enjoyed here, though not around the chalet on the banks of the **Arbersee**. An arduous ascent on foot (3 ½ hours there and back) will take you to the summit of the **Grosser Arber** (more easily reached by the skilift on the highway to **Lam**). This ridgetop road gives panoramic views of the mountains (notably from the Hindenburg viewpoint), before descending into gentler countryside around Lam.

The Ostmarkstrasse is rejoined at Cham, with its fine market place, either via Kötzting, rebuilt after a great fire in 1867, or Furth im Walde. Kötzting has a flamboyant Whit Monday procession (*Pfingstritt*) and Furth has the *Drachenstich*, a pageant in which an 18m animated dragon is spectacularly slain, with much jollity. Situated on the Regensburg-Plzeň (Pilsen) road, Furth is a frontier town; the Skodas of Czech shoppers can be seen parked among the local cars on its stately little market square.

NORTHERN BAVARIA

Wagner's real monument is the bulky Festspielhaus, on rising ground north of the city centre. Designed by Semper, but aesthetically no rival to the Markgräfliches Opernhaus, it provides the optimum setting for the master's works. At interval times during the Festival the attractive grounds fill with up to 1,800 people recovering from the operatic onslaught. Some admire the massive bust of Wagner by Arno Breker, one of the Third Reich's most successful sculptors, as well as representations of Cosima and of Liszt, who died during the 1886 Festival.

▶ ▶ ▷ **Bayreuth**

Founded as long ago as the 11th century, Bayreuth first came into its own in the 18th century under the rule of Margrave Friedrich and his energetic and talented spouse Wilhelmina, sister of Frederick the Great. A second flowering occurred in the late 19th century, when Richard Wagner made it the showcase for his innovative operas. The operatic tradition persists, attracting fans in their thousands to the Bayreuth Festival, held annually in July and August.

Traces of Bayreuth's medieval past can still be seen, for example in narrow alleyways and the typically Bavarian elongated market place, as well as the Gothic Stadtkirche (city church). The original residence of the Margraves, the Altes Schloss (Old Palace) goes back to the 14th century; its present appearance is due to 17th-century rebuilding.

The baroque age contributed most to Bayreuth's architectural character, again largely because of the energetic Wilhelmina. The Neues Schloss (New Palace, 1754) has light-hearted rococo interiors including grotto and garden rooms, and houses some of the town's museums. The grounds of the Hofgarten are an early example of romantic landscape design.

To the north is the 18th-century Markgräfliches Opernhaus. Undistinguished outside, its galleried interior shows the baroque style at its most theatrical.

Connected to the Hofgarten by a gateway, erected in 1874 to celebrate the composer's 61st birthday, is Wagner's Bayreuth residence, the classical Villa Wahnfried, now the National Wagner Museum. In the gardens stands the grave of the great man. His wife Cosima, daughter of Franz Liszt, is buried beside him, his faithful hound Russ a short distance away.

Marking the eastern extremity of the great limestone outcrop which begins far away in the Jura Mountains, Bayreuth is one of Germany's most romantically picturesque regions. The porous rock has been eroded to form some two dozen deep and narrow valleys, through which flow clear trout streams which once powered ancient mills. Medieval castles cap many crags; look for the one perched above the tiny town of Pottenstein. Nearby Tüchersfeld has an even more bizarre setting, with fairy-tale houses wedged among the rock pinnacles. Below ground, equally strange landscapes can be seen in the caves known as the Teufelshöhle, with weirdly shaped concretions and the bones of prehistoric animals.

Above and left: street scenes in Bayreuth

Excursions

The delectable grounds of the **Schloss Eremitage** (Hermitage Castle), 4 km northeast of Bayreuth, go back to the 17th century, when the Margraves would come here to escape court life in town. The original hermitage, the Altes Schloss, was built by the ruling Margrave in 1715.

The **Fichtelgebirge** (Fichtel Mountains), ancient granite-littered uplands, form a horseshoe-shaped massif enclosing eastward-facing lowlands, and are named after the extensive forests of *Fichte* (spruce) which clad their slopes. The area's abundant rainfall feeds rivers flowing to all points of the compass, the Eger east to the Elbe in Czechoslovakia, the Naab south to the Danube, the Weisser Main west to the Rhine.

The Ochsenkopf summit (1,024m) with its TV tower (chairlift from Bishofsgrün) gives majestic views. In contrast is the tranquil scene by the banks of the little Fichtelsee, set deep among the dark conifers, or the Luisenberg labyrinth, a chaos of granite blocks eroded into strange shapes and much admired by Goethe. Here is Germany's oldest open-air theatre, still the venue for summertime performances.

The towns in the sheltered lowland include the area's little capital, Wunsiedel with the Fichtelgebirge museum, and busy Marktredwitz, on the route leading to northwestern Czechoslovakia.

It was the indefatigable Wilhelmina who transformed the Scloss park into the delightful gardens that are there today, with hermit's retreats, lookouts, caves, pools and pavilions, artificial ruins, and the Neues Schloss, its semi-circular wings embracing an octagonal Temple of the Sun and a pool forming a fine setting for firework displays.

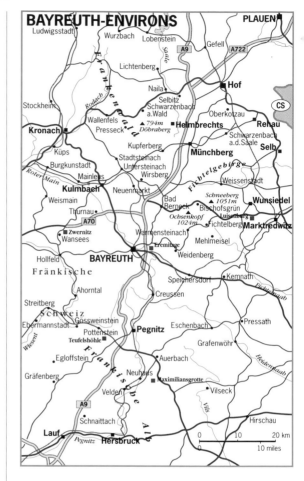

The picturesque potential of rocky outcrop and eerie forest was appreciated by Margravine Wilhelmina. Around the crag-top ruin of Zwernitz Castle she laid out a romantic landscape to tickle the refined sensibilities of her contemporaries and called it Sanspareil in the francophile fashion. Beyond Morgenländischer Bau (an oriental hermitage), winding paths lead past strange rock formations to fanciful features like the theatre conceived as a ruin and set in a grotto. The castle itself forms part of the artful composition; from its keep there is a wonderful panorama reaching far away to the Frankenwald and the Fichtelgebirge.

The **Frankenwald** (Franconian Forest) is Germany's smallest upland, with peaceful valleys, remote hamlets, deep forest, and wild areas of heath bog. The highest point is the Döbraberg (794m) with a tower giving panoramic views to the Fichtelgebirge to the south and the Thuringian heights to the north. North from Bayreuth is **Kulmbach**, with a famous brewery and overlooked by the Plassenburg, a splendid stronghold with a fine Renaissance courtyard. Once a prison, the castle now houses the Zinnfigurenmuseum, the national collection of 300,000 tin figurines. Kronach has beautifully preserved medieval half-timbered houses, including the birthplace of Cranach (1472–1553), painter of rugged landscapes and courtly nudes. Above the town rises its great fortress, the Rosenberg. With its triple ring of walls pierced by a single entrance above ground, this is Germany's most extensive medieval stronghold to remain intact. Its picture gallery includes works by Cranach.

One of the prettiest valleys in **Fränkische Schweiz** (Franconian Switzerland) is the River Wiesent, best seen from the viewpoints in the little market town and resort of Gössweinstein, also famous for its pilgrimage church.

▶ ▶ ▷ Coburg

During Germany's division, Coburg was very much on the edge of things, in a cul-de-sac ending at the East German border. Its name, linked to half the dynasties which once ruled Europe, never lost its fame and the place, busier now with the disappearance of the frontier, is still dominated by its two, very different, ducal castles. High above the town, and visible from far across Coburg's attractive rural surroundings, broods the majestic Veste (fortress), called 'the Crown of Franconia' because of its tower-studded outline. Founded in the 11th century and much rebuilt in Renaissance times by the vigorous Duke Johann Casimir, it ranks among the country's most splendid strongholds. Within its double ring of defensive walls are many treasures, including the 300,000-plus items of its print collection, paintings by German Masters (among them Cranach), arms and armour, furniture, and Johann Casimir's State Carriage of 1560. Martin Luther stayed here in 1530, his visit commemorated by the room named after him.

Linking Veste to town is the Hofgarten, its verdant slopes landscaped in the English manner and embracing a notable Natural History Museum. In the 16th century, the dukes moved down the hill into their new castle, the Ehrenburg. Remodelled externally to suit the 19th century taste for the Gothic, the palace retains much of its original interior, including its resplendent chapel and the Riesensaal (Giants' Room), so-called because of the 28 plaster heavies holding up the painted ceiling.

While the burghers built their fine half-timbered and high-gabled town houses, the Dukes gave the town a Renaissance touch. Johann Casimir was responsible for the academy known as the Casimirianum and for the Stadthaus facing the rococo Town Hall across the cobbled market square. The ducal imprint can be seen too in the Gothic Church of St Moritz, with its incredibly elaborate 13m (five storeys) memorial to Duke Johann Friedrich (d 1598) .

Veste Coburg – the Crown of Franconia

The Saxe-Coburgs
The influence of this aristocratic family was out of all proportion to its possessions or power. Comely rather than rich, its children were married off judiciously and, by the 19th century, were well established in many of the courts of Europe. Most famous of them was Albert – consort to the British Queen Victoria – born at nearby Rosenau Castle and brought up in the Ehrenburg. His statue stands in the market square. Coburg blood ran in Victoria's own veins; after Albert's death in 1861 she stayed here several times (her bedroom can be seen in the Ehrenburg). One of her grandsons, Carl Eduard, ruled the Duchy until its abolition in 1919. In the same year, Ferdinand von Coburg-Kohary, returned here after his abdication as Tsar of Bulgaria, devoting the rest of his life to ornithology. The birds he stuffed form the basis of the 8,000-strong collection in the town's Natural History Museum.

221

NORTHERN BAVARIA

▶ ▶ ▶ Dinkelsbühl

More compact than Rothenburg-ob-der-Tauber further up the Romantische Strasse (Romantic Road), Dinkelsbühl is one of Germany's most delightful medieval towns, perfectly preserved within its ring of walls, bastions and 16 towers.

The best approach is across the causeway leading to the late 14th-century gateway known as the Rothenburger Tor. From the gate the broad Martin Luther Strasse curves down to the market place with its splendid early Renaissance town houses, among them the Deutsches Haus, with seven projecting storeys reaching up into its high gable. The church of St George still has its Romanesque tower; it is one of the grandest hall-churches in southern Germany, with fan-vaulting spanning the lofty interior and good carving and statuary. Dinkelsbühl has many more delights; discover them on your own by wandering the narrow streets or take the guided tour (in German) on foot which starts at St George's. A walk around the ramparts at night is an atmospheric experience, especially in the company of the town's nightwatchman as he does his rounds.

Delightful Dinkelsbühl retains a medieval charm

Dinkelsbühl has escaped the ravages of wars, though there was a close shave in the course of the Thirty Years' War, when the fury of the besieging Swedes was mollified by an appeal made to their commander by the town's children. The event is marked by the Kinderzeche, a colourful ten-day carnival, held annually in July.

▶ ▷ ▷ Ellingen

Ellingen was for many years the headquarters of the Deutscher Orden (the Order of Teutonic Knights), a militant brotherhood of priests and soldiers, founded around 1190 during the First Crusade, but best remembered for their vigorous conversion to Christianity of the pagan population of the Baltic seaboard. Their sombre castle, built 1708–21, rears, cliff-like, over the town. Awkwardly approached from the side, it is enlivened by its main façade, a splendid staircase, rococo interiors and an elaborately decorated church. The corridors are hung with portraits of the Hochund Deutschmeister, the Order's leaders.

Ellingen was rebuilt following its destruction in the Thirty Years' War and is a little gem of baroque town planning, with a pretty Rathaus and several churches.

▶ ▷ ▷ Freising

Easily reached from the centre of Munich by S-Bahn suburban train, Freising is a city in its own right, the seat of a bishop as early as 739. The dominant feature of the town is the Domberg, a bluff of higher land looking out over the interminable flatlands stretching southwards to Munich. The chalk-white cathedral rises over a cluster of churches and other ecclesiastical buildings including the Prince-Bishop's Residenz, now a museum, and the Gothic Johannes-Kapelle, with its baroque interior. The cathedral interior exults in baroque splendour, but a more sombre era is evoked in the crypt, with its capitals and columns bearing strange figures of men and beasts.

▶ ▷ ▷ Ingolstadt

Strategically located on the upper reaches of the Danube, Ingolstadt is one of Bavaria's great cities, with a long history and a thriving present (oil refineries, Audi works). First mentioned in 806, Ingolstadt blossomed in the late Middle Ages. Come into town via the brick-built Kreuztor gateway of 1385. Beyond is the minster, dedicated to Our Lady, its high west gable flanked by asymmetrical towers. There are fine old houses, including the Ickstatt-Haus of 1740, a rococo confection in yellow with white stucco icing. From the same period is the interior of the church of Maria de Victoria, its painted ceiling a masterpiece of perspective effects.

Excursions

Weltenburg Abbey, (45km east via Neustadt), is sited on the Danube at the entrance to the Donaudurchbruch, a spectacular gorge cut by the river *en route* to its confluence with the Altmühl at Kelheim. A high point of German baroque, the abbey church's oval interior verges on high kitsch, with a tableau of St George smiting the dragon and cherubs flying around in chunky clouds. It certainly draws the crowds, whom you can join for beer (the abbey's own) and pretzels in the courtyard.

Ingolstad through the 14th-century Kreuztor gateway

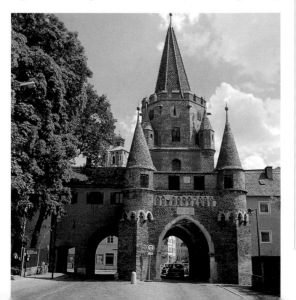

On a wooded bluff west of Friesing is Weihenstephan, famous for beer (the world's oldest brewery, founded 1040) and the prestigious Technical University of Munich.

Ingolstadt's importance as a fortress and garrison town was enhanced in the 19th century with the construction of massive fortifications. Most have been razed, but some severely classical gateways remain, including the Kavalier Heydeck. The Gothic Herzogschloss, a relic of earlier defences, is an appropriate setting for the Bavarian Military Museum.

Neuburg an der Donau is an old Residenz town 26km up the Danube from Ingolstadt. The place is dominated by the Renaissance palace built by Protestant Prince Ottheinrich, whose hope of making the town's Hofkirche a beacon of Protestantism in Catholic Bavaria was frustrated by the Counter-Reformation.

In 1475, at the peak of its prosperity and prestige, Landshut marked the wedding of its Duke George to a Polish princess with celebrations the lavishness of which became a byword all over Europe. These great days are recalled every three years by contemporary Germany's most extravagent pageant, the Landshuter Fürstenhochzeit, when revellers in period costume perform against the splendid stage set of Landshut's historic townscape.

Nördlingen's massive grey stone parish church of St George has a lofty white interior and an 89m tower nicknamed 'Daniel'. It is worth the climb for the view over the red roofs of the oval-shaped town. From here, an inner oval of streets can clearly be picked out, marking the course of an older ring of fortifications, long since demolished.

▶ ▶ ▷ **Landshut**

On the banks of the River Isar at the foot of Trausnitz Castle, Landshut has kept much of the appearance and atmosphere of the important provincial capital it once was. This old city is centred on two fine market streets lined with late medieval town houses, many with stepped gables and arcaded courtyards. The gently curving Altstadt dates to the founding of the city in 1204, and the Neustadt was laid out a century later.

The Altstadt is closed off by the church of St Martin, a bold Gothic brick building. Its slender tower rises to 133m, higher even than the castle behind it and the tallest structure of its kind in the world. Among the treasures of the light and airy interior is a huge Madonna and Child, carved in 1520 by a local man, Hans Leinberger.

In 1543, Duke Ludwig X moved from the castle into the Stadtresidenz, which has a splendidly decorated interior, part of which houses Landshut's museum. Not long afterwards, the Castle itself was refurbished for the lavish court life of Prince William of Bavaria. He kept the 13th-century chapel with its superb Romanesque statuary, adding a fine galleried courtyard in Renaissance style and had the famous Narrentreppe staircase painted with robust figures from the Italian comic theatre. The castle balcony gives a spectacular panorama over the town.

Excursion

A sixth of the world's hops are grown in the **Hallertau** area around Mainburg. This is pretty, up-and-down countryside, the hopfields alternating with other crops against dark woodlands. Pickers no longer camp in the fields to help with the harvest, but the season is still celebrated by the election of a Hop Queen in the village of Wolnzach.

Nürnberg's Schöner Brunnen fountain

225

▶ ▶ ▶ Nördlingen

Nördlingen's heyday came between the 14th and 16th centuries, when its great Whitsun Fair drew traders from all over Germany. Its subsequent stagnation may have been tough on the townsfolk, but helped preserve its townscape, much to the delight of today's many visitors for whom it is one of the principal stops along the Romantische Strasse. The town's ramparts, still intact after some 500 years, have 16 towers and five gateways, from which five main streets converge on the Marktplatz with its 13th- to 14th-century Rathaus.

Excursions

Two fine churches are within reach of Nördlingen. In spite of its baroque furnishings, the former abbey church at **Kaisheim** (6km northeast of Donauwörth) evokes the severe lives of its 14th-century Cistercian founders. **Neresheim** (19km southwest) has a fine abbey church too. The last work of Balthasar Neumann, it marked a fitting conclusion to the career of this foremost architect of the South German baroque. Under its three domes, the interior is unusually light and spacious, with fine ceiling paintings by the Tyrolean Martin Knoller.

▶ ▶ ▶ Nürnberg (Nuremberg)

Crowning the outcrop of warm red sandstone from which much of Nürnberg is built, the Burg or castle goes back to the city's founding years in the 11th century. Kings and emperors resided here for some 500 years, and the sprawling complex of buildings was added to, demolished, and rebuilt throughout this time. Thus the tall five-sided tower dates from c1040, the two-tier Imperial Chapel from the 12th century and the stables (now the youth hostel) from the late 15th century. From windows, towers and terraces there are fine views over

The daily Hauptmarkt, in Nürnberg, the site of Germany's biggest pre-Christmas market, the Christkindelsmarkt

Before the devastation wrought by the terrible air raids of 1945, Nürnberg was germany's greatest surviving medieval city. The destruction, though extensive, was not total, and sensitive rebuilding and restoration has respected the ancient street pattern, enabling the visitor to recapture the atmosphere of the city's heyday in the 15th and 16th centuries, when it was the principal focus of Germany's politics, culture, trade, science and technology.

In view of Nürnberg's longstanding role as the toy-manufacturing capital of Europe, it is fitting that the annual Toy Fair, the most important of its kind, is held here.

the city with its nearly complete ring of walls.

Directly below the castle are timber-framed and gabled houses crammed up against the ramparts. Albrecht Dürer lived in this quarter from 1509 until his death in 1528. The Dürer-Haus has good interiors and displays, though there are more copies than original works. In the Burgstrasse is the 16th-century Fenbohaus, now the city museum. Beyond it is the Rathausplatz with the Altes Rathaus and opposite it the twin towers of St Sebald's church, early Gothic, with outstanding artworks in the interior by Kraft (Christ Carrying the Cross), Vischer (Shrine of St Sebald) and Stoss (Passion and Crucifixion).

South is the Hauptmarkt – a daily market and site of the pre-Christmas Christkindelsmarkt. The Schöner Brunnen fountain competes with the gabled façade of the Gothic Frauenkirche (Church of Our Lady) and its 16th-century mechanical clock with automata that perform at noon.

Nürnberg's Altstadt is divided into roughly equal halves by the River Pegnitz. The combination of water, ancient buildings and bridges makes an atmospheric townscape. One arm of the river is bridged by the Heiliggeist-Spital, a hospital dating originally from the 14th century; downstream is the Weinstadl, a venerable wine-store which, together with an old water-tower, covered bridge and weeping willows makes the most idyllic scene.

Although the southern half of the Altstadt has a more modern air, it contains much of interest. The Gothic church of St Lawrence has a cathedral-like west front. Inside are splendid works; Stoss' multi-coloured carving of the Annunciation is suspended from the vaulting; the

tall tabernacle is carried by the sculpted figures of Adam Kraft and his apprentices. The Mauthalle of 1502 was built as a corn store; its six-storey roof is pierced by sinister hooded dormers, so characteristic of the city.

Nürnberg has an array of museums. Among the Verkehrsmuseum (Transport Museum) exhibits is the gleaming Adler, the locomotive which hauled the first ever German train along the line from Nürnberg to nearby Fürth. The Spielzeugmuseum holds the largest and most varied toy collection in the world. At the outstanding Germanisches Nationalmuseum, founded in the 19th century as part of the impulse towards German unity, exhaustion is only avoided by concentrating on a fraction of the exhibits. Don't miss the works of the great painters who spanned the transition from Middle Ages to Renaissance (Altdorfer, Cranach, Dürer) or the carvings and sculptures of their contemporaries including Kraft, Riemenschneider and Stoss.

▶ ▶ ▷ Passau

On its long and narrow tongue of land at the confluence of Danube, Inn and Ilz, Passau has one of the most spectacular settings of any German city. Wooded heights hem in the rivers and provide splendid sites for the pilgrimage church of Maria Hilf to the south and the Veste to the north, the great fortress built by the city's prince-bishops to keep unruly townsfolk under control.

Passau is still one of Germany's main gateways to Austria; white steamers sail from here to Vienna and beyond to Budapest and the Black Sea. Inland, the web of narrow streets leads eventually to the great cathedral with its trio of helmeted towers. Founded originally in the 8th century, it owes much of its present appearance to a thoroughgoing baroque rebuilding (c1680). Inside is the world's biggest church organ, installed in the 1920s and with a total of 17,330 pipes. Reconstruction spared the splendid Flamboyant Gothic east end of the cathedral, best viewed from the Residenzplatz, an irregular square flanked by fine Renaissance mansions.

The city's splendid roofscape is probably best appreciated from the lofty tower of the Veste. The Bishops began building the fortress in 1219 and then added to it over the centuries, eventually creating an extraordinary mixture of Gothic, Renaissance and baroque architecture. It now houses a medley of museums and galleries, and a folk museum.

To the west of Passau are delightful landscapes between the rivers Vils, Rott and Inn, dotted with baroque monasteries (Vornbach, Aldersbach and Fürstenzell, the last with a particularly splendid library), castles (Neuburg looming over the Inn, Ortenburg with one of the finest carved ceilings in Germany) and attractive small towns (Vilshofen, Aidenbach, and Rotthalmünster with a fine parish church and pilgrimage chapel).

Left: steins typical of Passau
Below: Passau, serene on the Danube

Regensburg's history goes back much further than the Middle Ages.
The Celts called it Radaspona, which survives in the city's French name of Ratisbonne. As Castra Regina, it guarded the frontier of the Roman Empire at the northernmost point of the Danube; the remains of the Roman Praetorian Gate still stand in the strangely-named street Unter den Schwibbögen.

Regensburg cathedral's rich sculptural decoration includes the famous *Angel of the Annunciation*, positively bursting with enthusiasm at the good news he has to tell, while another note is struck by the figures popularly known as the *Devil and his Grandma*, housed in niches in the main portal.

▶ ▶ ▶ Regensburg

The capital of eastern Bavaria, this historic cathedral city on the Danube was one of the largest in Germany to escape wartime destruction. Its narrow streets and intimate squares evoke its medieval heyday, when its merchants were among the most prosperous in Europe. Near the remains of the Roman Praetorian Gate rise the lace-like cathedral spires, added as late as 1869 to the great edifice begun in the 13th century. This is one of Germany's finest Gothic churches. The sequence of squares around the cathedral forms the kernel of the city, with ancient buildings crowding together. The cathedral's parish church, the Niedermünsterkirche, is a mid-12th century basilica built over the remains of three previous churches, the oldest of which goes back to the mysterious Merovingian Age (c700) and was erected on top of Roman remains. Across the Alter Kornmarkt is the ancient Liebfraukirche (Church of Our Lady). Its sumptuous interior is about as far as you could get from the remote world of primitive Christianity, having been remodelled in rococo style to suit 18th-century taste.

Whole days could be spent wandering Regensburg's labyrinth of streets and alleyways lined by venerable houses in a style as much Italian as German. Like their counterparts in San Gimignano, the city's leading families built towers in competition with each other; in the 13th century there were 60 such structures, of which 20 survive to give the city its unique skyline. Among them is the Baumburger Turm with its gallery and the Goldener Turm in the Wahlenstrasse, the city's oldest street.

The broad Danube makes a pleasing contrast to this medieval inner city, best appreciated from the upper arches of the Steinerne Brücke (Old Stone Bridge), built in the 12th century and for 800 years the only river crossing hereabouts. To the left of the towered gateway guarding the bridgehead is the immense roof of the 17th-century salt store, at its side Regensburg's oldest restaurant, the Historische Wurstküche.

Presiding over the far side of the city centre is the mostly 19th-century palace of the Princes of Thurn und Taxis. The palace incorporates the cloisters of the church of St Emmeran, famous for its tombs. Among them is that of poor Queen Emma, done to death in 876 and wearing an appropriately mournful expression.

The aristocratic air of an earlier era is captured in the Gothic Altes Rathaus, with splendid interiors redolent of the Imperial Diet which used to assemble here.

The Stadtmuseum (City Museum), in the buildings of an old monastery, displays a wonderful scale model of the city as it used to be and works of members of the Danube School, including Albrecht Altdorfer.

Excursions

Kallmünz, 27km northwest, is a self-conscious little place and a favourite subject for painters. The old stone bridge near the confluence of the contrastingly coloured waters of the rivers Vils and Naab is overlooked by the castle, ruined in the Thirty Years' War but still a wonderful lookout point.

Walhalla, a gleaming white copy of the Parthenon, sits incongruously in the utterly un-Grecian setting of

A view over the River Danube at Regensburg

wooded slopes running down to the Danube. Inspired
by Ludwig I of Bavaria and completed in 1841, it houses
busts of the great and good of Germanic history and
was intended to foster national unity. The climb up its
358 steps may encourage an appropriately reverential
mood; the splendid viewpoint over the Danube valley
and the ruins of Donaustauf Castle can be more easily
reached from the back.

The doorway of St Peter's Cathedral

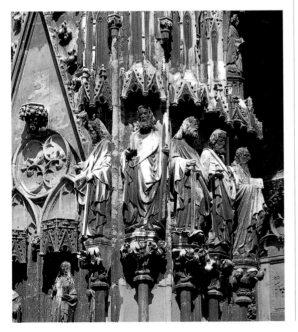

A far from mournful figure in
Regensburg's life is that of
Princess Gloria. Inheriting
the Thurn und Taxis fortune
(reputedly the biggest in
Germany) from her husband,
the late Prince, this trend-
setting doyenne of the
international jet-set features
regularly in the pages of
Germany's more salacious
mass-circulation magazines.

Albrecht Altdorfer raised
landscape painting to a high
pitch of emotional intensity –
and also found time to serve
his native Regensburg as
city architect.

NORTHERN BAVARIA

Both Nördlingen and the little Residenz town of Wallerstein lie in the vast fertile depression known as the Ries. Twenty km across, its origin was long a subject of controversy, but it is now known to have been created by the impact of a meteorite some 15 million years ago.

▶ ▶ ▶   **Romantische Strasse**

Of all the named tourist highways spanning the country, Germany's renowned Romantische Strasse is probably the most popular. Linking Würzburg in the wine-country of Franconia with the Alps at Füssen and some 350km long, it is less remarkable for the tranquil scenery it traverses than for the string of historic towns it passes through. Between them they encapsulate the essence of the country's past, from medieval *Gemütlichkeit* (Rothenburg-ob-der-Tauber, Dinkelsbühl, Nördlingen) via the mercantile magnificence of the early Renaissance (Augsburg) to the splendours of the baroque (Würzburg). The major destinations along the way are described under their own headings, but the following places should also be seen if at all possible.

The route strikes southwest from **Würzburg** (see page 235) to join the pretty valley of the Tauber at **Tauberbischofsheim,** an unspoiled medieval town with timber-framed buildings and a good local history museum in the old princely palace. Beyond **Bad Mergentheim** is **Weikersheim,** the ancestral home of the Hohenlohe family, with a splendid Knights Hall and a formal park. **Creglingen** and **Detwang** both have fine carved altarpieces by Tilman Riemenschneider, while **Feuchtwangen** boasts Romanesque cloisters which serve as an open air theatre in summer.

On the far side of the Ries, boldly standing out above the countryside, is **Harburg Castle,** no longer barring the way since the road tunnels straight through it.

On either side of Augsburg the road runs across the broad Bavarian plain. To the south of the city is the Lechfeld, today a NATO base and redolent of military memories. In 955 it was the site of one of the most decisive battles in European history, when Otto the Great finally put an end to the heathen Hungarians' incursions into western Europe and drove them back down the Danube. Beyond Landsberg lie the Alps, a spectacular barrier when seen from the town walls of Schöngau on a clear day. Easily reached from the Romantische Strasse as it nears its end at Füssen (page 245) are some of Bavaria's greatest architectural treasures, the glorious rococo church at Wies and the royal castles at Hohenschwangau and Neuschwanstein.

The River Main at Würzburg

▶▶▶ **Rothenburg-ob-der-Tauber**

Rothenburg is among Germany's best-preserved and most enchanting medieval towns. Once more important than Nürnberg, Rothenburg stagnated after the Thirty Years' War before being discovered by romantic artists and writers in the 19th century as the 'epitome of Germanic medievalism'.

Completely ringed by ramparts, the town overlooks the winding valley of the Tauber. A succession of charming pictures unfolds as you stroll the cobbled streets or pace the sentry-walk along the walls. A sea of red roofs rises above the half-timbered, high-gabled houses, no two quite alike, crowded together along the crooked streets. The highest roof is the Gothic St Jakobs-Kirche. Its cool interior holds a meticulously carved 1505 altarpiece by the great Riemenschneider. The focal point of the town is the Marktplatz, dominated by the Rathaus, half Gothic,

Rothenburg's perfect state of preservation is in part due to its having survived the Thirty Years War intact. The threat by General Tilly to raze the town was averted when Mayor Nusch proved himself able to drain a three-litre-plus measure of wine in one go. This feat – the so-called Meistertrunk – is commemorated by the mechanical figures on the clock attached to the Ratstrinkstube and, at less frequent intervals, by a colourful pageant.

half Renaissance, with a splendid Imperial Hall inside. Enjoy the view from the top of the 60m bell-tower.

Another excellent viewpoint is from the Burggarten, the little park on the promontory once occupied by the castle of the Hohenstaufens. Spanning the river below is the strange Doppelbrücke (Double Bridge), and not far away the even stranger Topplerschlösschen, a defensive tower on which an ordinary little house is perched.

Picturesque highlights of Rothenburg's townscape include the Plönlein, where changing street levels enhance the scene around the 1385 Siebersturm gateway; the patrician mansions along the Herrengasse; the Rodertor gateway flanked by twin little toll-houses, or the Gerlach Schmiede (Smithy) near by with its impossibly exaggerated gable.

Rothenburg-ob-der-Tauber retains its old world charm

▶ ▷ ▷ **Staffelstein**

Staffelstein, with its fine Rathaus, is one of a number of half-timbered small towns and villages on the fertile floor of the broad and tranquil valley of the Main, north of Bamberg. Just upstream is Lichtenfels, the country's basket-making centre. Attractive enough in themselves, these places are visited less for their own sake than for their proximity to two great works of baroque architecture facing each other across the tranquil vale.

Crowning the wooded height to the west is the massive monastery, **Kloster Banz**, founded by the Benedictines in 1069 and completely rebuilt in 1695–1768. The imposing domestic buildings (with collections which include a famous ichthyosaurus) are dominated by the twin spires of the great church, the work of Johann Dientzenhofer. The interior is outstanding, with splendid stuccos, colourful frescos and vigorous altarpieces. From the terrace are sweeping views across the valley towards the pilgrimage church of Vierzehnheiligen.

Vierzehnheiligen Pilgrimage Church is one of the key buildings of the 18th century in Germany. It is a place of pilgrimage, not only for the faithful but for anyone prepared to be persuaded that the German spirit is capable of the most sublime flights of fancy.

The Benedictine monastery of Kloster Banz, not far from Staffelstein

A stiff uphill walk from the large car park leads to a bevy of booths selling every conceivable kind of souvenir. The church's conventional exterior, in rough-looking ochre sandstone, is grand enough, with two tall towers, but gives little hint of the delights that lie beyond. Inside, the mood changes completely; all semblance of convention disappears in the abundant light that illuminates an extravagant interior in a froth of pink, gold and white decoration. The focal point is less the main altar at the east end than the central confection, 'half coral reef, half fairy sedan chair' (Nikolaus Pevsner), adorned with the figures of the 14 saints who gave the church its name. This ecstatic creation is the work of the great Balthasar Neumann. His patron was the ambitious prince bishop of Bamberg, Friedrich Carl von Schönborn.

▶ ▷ ▷   Straubing

Once one of Bavaria's most important cities, Straubing is still the centre for the rich arable region known as the Gäuboden and has kept much of the air of a prosperous provincial city of the late Middle Ages.

The Romans built a fort here to guard their Danube frontier; spectacular evidence of their presence is provided by the rich hoard of gold masks and other objects which is the pride of the town museum. The wealth of a later age is expressed in a heritage of fine buildings; this includes such churches as Romanesque St Peter's with its atmospheric walled graveyard, tall-towered Jakobskirche, and the little baroque jewel of the Ursuline church. Straubing's main landmark however is its 14th-century tower dividing the elongated market place into two parts; its corner turrets enabled an all-round watch to be kept for intruders or for the fires which could easily devastate the timber-built towns of the time.

Straubing's main festival, the biggest in Bavaria after Munich's Bierfest, is the annual Gäuboden Fair, held each August.

Excursions

Deggendorf, 34km southeast, resembles Straubing on a smaller scale, with a fine market place dominated by the town tower.

Near by are two splendid baroque monasteries, **Metten**, with a particularly fine library, and **Niederalteich**, the first foundation of its kind in Bavaria.

The rich agricultural land around Straubing was settled at an early date and is well endowed with old churches, including the picturesquely sited Romanesque church at **Rankam**. Of later date are the Benedictine buildings of the monastery at **Oberalteich**, completed in 1630, though the interior had to wait another 100 years before being decorated with its spectacular frescos.

Gently bustling Straubing

Straubing's most famous figure was Agnes Bernauer, a barber's daughter whose beauty so impressed Duke Ernst's son that he married her in spite of her humble origin. This so enraged the Duke that in 1435 he had Agnes tried on a trumped-up charge of witchcraft, then done to death by drowning in the Danube. The tragic tale is re-enacted in the courtyard of the ducal castle every four years.

233

▶ ▶ ▷   Waldsassen

In the Middle Ages, many monasteries were established in the densely wooded uplands along the ancient border between Bavaria and Bohemia. Monks toiled to convert the forest to farmland and bring Christianity to the few inhabitants. Waldsassen (1133) is one of the greatest of these centres of medieval civilisation. It stood for centuries on its own until the little town to which it gave its name began to develop in the early 17th century.

The monastery buildings date from 1681–1704. The long, narrow church is one of the masterpieces of the great Bavarian baroque architect, Georg Dientzenhofer, who worked with a cosmopolitan team including the Italian Carleone, who embellished the interior with 200 stucco angels. Attracting special reverence is a battered figure of Christ, found hanging on the border barrier with Czechoslovakia in 1951 at the height of the Cold War.

In the monastery itself is the library. Karl Stopl, the master-carver responsible for this extraordinary interior, took as his theme everything that goes into the production of a book; the sequence of 10 figures supporting the upper level includes the humble rag-collector (gathering raw materials for paper), the author, critic (his bound hands symbolising his unproductive vocation) and the reader (a portrait of the artist himself).

Excursion

The gentle hills and vales of Waldsassen have always attracted admirers, including Goethe. Tirscheneuth, to the south, is the area's market centre. The Renaissance Rathaus survived a great fire in 1814. All around are pools and ponds, breeding carp and trout.

On a hill to the northwest of Waldsassen stands one of the most unusual buildings in Bavaria, the pilgrimage church of Kappel. Commissioned by the Abbot of Waldsassen, Dientzenhofer designed a church to honour the Holy Trinity, linking together three rounded apses, each topped with a bulbous tower. Seen across the fields, the church's exotic outline is more reminiscent of Holy Russia than Catholic Bavaria.

Waldsassen dates largely from the early 17th century

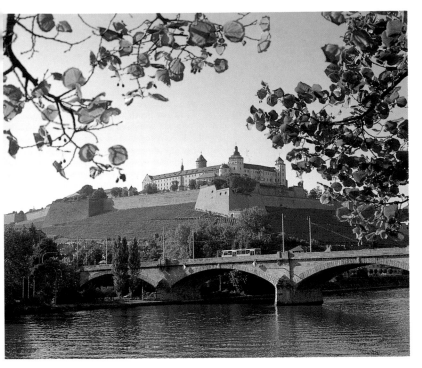

▶ ▶ ▶ Würzburg

This university city, the ancient seat of powerful prince-bishops, is sited among vineyards on the steep banks of the River Main.

Celtic tribesmen first fortified the strategic height occupied by the massive Marienberg fortress, but Würzburg's history really begins with the martyrdom here in 689 of an Irish missionary, St Kilian. His gravestone is in the cathedral named after him, in the centre of the old city on the far bank of the river.

Kilian's mission was to convert the locals to Christianity; Würzburg is notable for its many churches. One of the oldest is the round, thick-walled Marienkirche in the fortress courtyard. The Marienberg itself was rebuilt and extended over the years to become a most formidable stronghold. Occupied for nearly 500 years by the prince-bishops, it now houses the splendid collections of the regional museum (Mainfränkisches Museum); its greatest treasures are the tenderly-sculpted sandstone figures of Adam and Eve, by the great Tilman Riemenschneider (1460–1531), who was both artist and mayor.

By the 18th century, the Marienberg had become too cramped for the bishops' life-style and they moved to purpose-built quarters on the far side of the city. Their new address, the Würzburg Residenz, designed by Balthasar Neumann, is the greatest baroque building of its kind in Germany, dominating the vast cobbled square linking it to the town. Its interior spaces are staggering, both in sheer size and lavishness of decoration. They include the grand staircase, covered by the largest

The Marienberg fortress overlooks the river at Würzburg

ceiling painting in the world (by the Venetian Tiepolo), the oval Kaisersaal (with *trompe l'oeil* painting, also by Tiepolo) and the sumptuous Gartensaal, the great ground floor room linking the palace to the gardens beyond. These form a perfect example of rococo garden art and make an ideal background for the summer Mozart Festival. Neumann's palace chapel, the gorgeous Hofkirche, is a favourite place for weddings.

Würzburg suffered almost as grievously as Dresden in World War II, when an air raid left most of the city centre in ruins. Bravely rebuilt, it is a cheerful and lively place, with plenty of wine taverns and a buzz of student life. Its restored churches include the splendidly severe Romanesque Cathedral, with the gravestones of the prince-bishops, among them two wonderful examples by Riemenschneider.

Opposite the Cathedral is the Neumünster, built over St Kilian's grave and given a fine baroque façade in the early 18th century. It also has a garden with the grave of Germany's medieval troubadour, Walter von der Vogelweide. In the market place stands the Gothic Marienkapelle, with Neumann's tombstone at its portal. Near by is the fine rococo façade of the Haus zum Falken, meticulously restored after the bombing. Spared destruction were the two great charitable institutions founded to house the city's senior citizens, the Bürgerspital of 1319 and the Johannesspital of 1576. Both derive part of their income from their vineyards; their produce is dispensed in their atmospheric wine-taverns.

Würzburg's only church to survive the war unscathed was the Kappelle pilgrimage chapel. Owing its good fortune to its isolated position above the wooded ravine separating it from the Marienberg, it is yet another dazzling display of baroque virtuosity by Neumann.

Excursions

On either side of Würzburg, the deep valley of the Main forms one of Germany's most distinctive wine-growing areas. Its excellent wines are relatively dry and come in stumpy flasks quite different from the elegant bottles of Rhine and Mosel.

Upstream from the city, one delightful little place succeeds another: **Sommerhausen,** favoured by artists, half-timbered **Ochsenfurt** ('Oxford') within its ramparts, **Frickenhausen,** accessible only through one of its four gateways, **Marktbreit, Sulzfeld**... Walled **Volkach** has many picturesque houses, a 16th-century Rathaus and a local museum in the baroque Schelfenhaus. Crowning the hilly vineyards outside the town is Maria im Weinberg (Our Lady of the Vineyard), the Late Gothic pilgrimage church housing one of Riemenschneider's most delicate works, *Madonna in a Rose Garland.*

The summer palace of the prince-bishops of Würzburg, **Veitschöchheim** (7km northwest), has an exquisite rococo garden, a delight of hedged enclosures, playful statuary and the Grosser See, an artificial lake with an even more artificial Mount Parnassus rising from it.

This jewel of landscape architecture was rescued from neglect by the indefatigable King Ludwig I of Bavaria, who restored it to its former glory.

236

The splendid Würzburg Residenz

Wagner

■ **Revolutionary, exile, focus of scandal, writer and composer, Richard Wagner's life at times matched the more dramatic passages of his titanic operas. Certainly, in works such as *Tristan und Isolde*, the themes of his own eventful life found most eloquent musical expression.....■**

In 1834, at the age of 21, Wagner was appointed director of the Magdeburg opera. Here he wrote his first operas, and married a singer, Minna Plater, with whom he lived for 25 years in a largely unhappy marriage. To escape his private life he composed increasingly, including *Rienzi* (1840) and *Der fliegende Holländer* (*The Flying Dutchman*, 1842). In the latter, the romantic idea of redemption through love – a theme recurring in Wagner's operas but absent from his marriage – is first expressed. Mixed receptions of his next, less conventional, works, including *Tannhäuser*, reinforced his belief in his own ability; this period of musical innovation even saw him as a political revolutionary, manning barricades at Dresden.

With the help of his friend Liszt, *Lohengrin* (1850) was triumphantly performed in Weimar – despite Wagner's enforced exile in Zürich due to the failure of the Dresden uprising. In Zürich he began a passionate affair with the wife of a Swiss benefactor and conceived the idea for *Tristan und Isolde*, while also working on the summit of his artistic achievement, *Der Ring des Nibelungen*, a cycle of four epic operas based on German mythology.

New rules Wagner abandoned the traditional 'rules' of recitative and aria for a continuous musical dialogue, and used the *leitmotiv*, a representation of symbols and characters in musical terms, to perfection.

Scandal erupted again when Cosima, Liszt's daughter and the wife of composer Hans von Bülow, bore Wagner a child. She later obtained a divorce and, after Minna's death in 1866, married Wagner in 1870.

In his later years, Wagner turned his attention to the foundation of the ideal opera house; in 1876 the Bayreuth Festspielhaus was opened with a complete performance of the *Ring* cycle. (The opera house is now the venue for the annual Bayreuth Festival.) After a full life, which among other things saw him writing on a variety of subjects, including vegetarianism and hygiene, Wagner died in 1883. He is buried at Wahnfried, his Bayreuth villa.

237

Above: Spy's impression of Wagner, from Vanity Fair, 1877
Top: Richard and Cosima Wagner

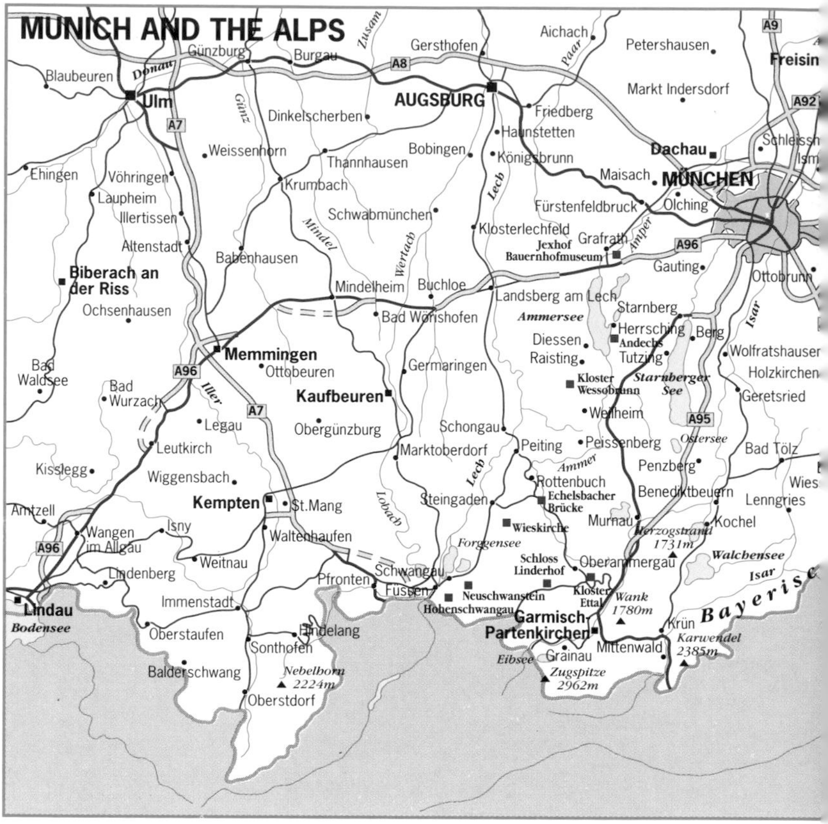

The panorama from Munich's Olympic tower makes this region appear remarkably compact. The easy-going, cosmopolitan Bavarian capital lies on a fertile plain that extends southwards towards the snowy peaks of the Alps, Germany's highest and most dramatic mountains. In between are neat, clustered villages, pine forests, sparkling lakes and gently rolling pastures. It is a rewarding area for exploration, with a host of entertainment and cultural offerings in Munich itself, magnificent scenic variety and (particularly away from the Alps) a number of historic small towns. All over the area are examples of Bavarian baroque churches and castles, many of them spectacular compositions with ornate stucco and frescoed ceilings.

While the German Alps comprise only a thin strip (the bulk of the great range lies in Italy, Austria, Switzerland and France), the mountains form a backdrop that is the key to much of the charm of the low-lying hinterland. The scenery immediately around Munich is rather flat, but further south are several lakes, popular for walks, boat trips and sailing. The Alps themselves can be enjoyed by driving along the **Deutsche Alpenstrasse** (German Alpine Road), a scenic theme road threading its way from **Lindau** to **Berchtesgaden** and passing close to the four remarkable 19th-century castles of Ludwig II, Bavaria's mad king, whose extravagant fantasies now provide

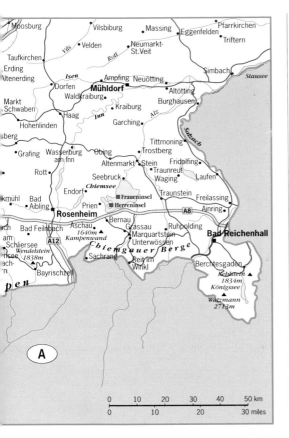

Moosburg · Vilsbiburg · Massing · Pfarrkirchen
Velden Neumarkt- · Eggenfelden · Triftern
Taufkirchen St.Veit
Erding
Altenerding Isen · Ampfing Neuötting · Simbach · Stausee
· Dorfen Mühldorf · Altötting
Markt Waldkraiburg · Burghausen
Schwaben · Kraiburg
Hohenlinden Haag Inn Garching Alz
sberg
· Grafing Wasserburg · Öbing Tittmoning Sulzach
am Inn · Trostberg
Altenmarkt · Stein Fridolfing
Seebruck · Traunreut
Rott · Waging Laufen
Endorf Chiemsee · Traunstein Freilassing
kmühl Bad · Prien ■ Fraueninsel
· Aibling Rosenheim ■ Herreninsel
Bernau Ainring
A8
ch Bad Feilnbach Aschau · Grassau Ruhpolding
am 1640m Marquartstein Bad Reichenhall
Schliersee A12 Kampenwand Unterwössen
see Wendelstein Chiemgauer Berge Berchtesgaden
ach- 1838m · Sachrang Reit im Kehlstein
n Winkl 1834m
Bayrischzell Königssee
p e n Watzmann
2713m

A

0   10   20   30   40   50 km
0   10   20   30 miles

MUNICH AND THE ALPS

239

Bavaria with its top tourist attractions. Tourism is big business, with numerous resorts geared to winter sports, and medical and non-medical 'cures'. For most of the year, many Alpine summits can be reached by cable-cars and chair-lifts; at the top there's often a strategically sited restaurant. Walking is by no means confined to arduous mountain ascents; easy paths, meticulously signposted, give gentle strolls through woods, along gorges, around lakes and up to viewpoints. The mountain resort towns are not especially interesting.

Southern Bavaria – with the notable exception of liberal Munich – is staunchly conservative, both politically and in outlook. You will see men wearing Bavarian hats and *Lederhosen* (leather trousers), and women with *dirndl* (embroidered) dresses; festivals are celebrated with great gusto, particularly May Day, when huge maypoles are erected and decorated. The tradition of painting murals (and the name in old-fashioned Gothic lettering) on house exteriors is widespread. Food is hearty and traditional – quantities of pork, dumplings, potatoes and sauerkraut are *de rigueur* in country areas. The region is strongly Catholic: *Grüss Gott* (God's greeting) is the standard greeting (never *Guten Tag*), and churches have a prosperous look. Much of the region is accessible within a day trip from Munich, but beware of crowds and traffic jams at peak times in the main sights and resorts.

Wessobrunn Abbey, west of the Ammersee, is famous for the Wessobrunner Gebet (Wessobrunn prayer), a poetic fragment of nine lines which dates from the last 30 years of the 8th century. Although written in a Bavarian dialect, the Wessobrunn Prayer is often considered the oldest known text written in the German language.

Ammersee: popular with weekenders

▶ ▷ ▷   **Ammersee and Andechs**

Ammersee, a 35km lake situated west of Munich, is a popular weekend retreat with small, quiet resorts, reedy shores and pleasant, low-rise hills. Boat trips and yacht hire are on offer, and swimming is quite feasible in the warmer months. The west side is more built up, but Herrsching, on the east shore, is the main resort and a starting point for gentle lakeside walks.

The pilgrimage church of the Benedictine monastery of Andechs, close to Herrsching, is one of the rococo masterpieces of Bavaria, with frescos and stucco by J B Zimmermann. Carl Orff (1895–1982), composer best known for *Carmina Burana*, is buried here. The tower offers a good view of the lake. Next door, the monastery Bräustüberl (beer-hall) does a roaring trade in the excellent beer produced by the monks and dispensed straight from the barrel. The monastery shop sells a Klosterlikör, and its own bottled beer.

Höher Peissenberg, southwest of the lake and accessible by road from the village of Höhenpeissenberg, has been a place of pilgrimage since the 16th century, when peasants erected a chapel on this lofty site, with its magnificent panorama of the German Alps (on a clear day you can even discern the restaurant on top of the Zugspitze). The church has been expanded and given the ubiquitous rococo treatment; note the elaborate parquetry on the organ loft. Railings on the roof of the adjacent house mark the site of the world's first weather station, set up in 1781. Observations were made first by Augustinian monks and then by priests and teachers; in 1937 an official weather station was set up here.

The huge satellite dishes at **Raisting**, just south of the Ammersee, dominating the area, constitute the world's largest telecommunications centre. A free-entry visitor centre (open Monday to Friday, 08.00–12.00, 12.45–17.00 hrs; weekends 12.00–16.00hrs) is located within the huge white sphere.

▶ ▶ ▶ Berchtesgadener Land

Jutting into Austria, Germany's southeastern corner offers glorious Alpine scenery; **Salzburg** is within close reach just across the border. The vicinity of **Schonau** and **Berchtesgaden** is recommended as a base for exploration.

Berchtesgaden itself is a comfortable medium-sized resort with an active centre; turn-of-the-century villas full of character perch on the hillside. The menacing form of the Watzmann (2,713m) looms high to the south; not surprisingly the mountain inspired many artists and is the subject of local legends. The town is a place for bad-weather diversions. Particularly enjoyable are the still-functioning Salt Mines (open Easter and May to October, 8.30–17.00hrs; rest of year daily except Sunday, 12.30–15.30hrs), where visitors don miners' clothes, travel on mine wagons, slide down a slope (heavy-duty trousers are issued for the purpose) and raft across a subterranean lake; miner guides explain the salt-extraction process. In the town centre are the Heimatmuseum (open Monday to Friday, 09.00–12.00, 14.00–17.00hrs, Saturday 09.00–13.00hrs), with a display of local woodcrafts, and the Residenz (open daily except Saturday, 10.00–13.00, 14.00–17.00hrs; last admission one hour before closing), formerly an Augustinian priory, then from 1810 a Wittelsbach palace and now a museum housing a collection of weapons and paintings.

For details of guided walks (May to October) visit the National Park offices in Berchtesgaden (tel 08652-64343) or Königsee (tel 08652–62222).

As with much of Bavaria, the area has many baroque

Tables with a view at a Berchtesgaden mountain-top café

Many Bavarian doorways bear the chalked legend C+M+B (plus the year date) over them, an age-old device to bring blessing on the building; the initials stand for Caspar, Melchior and Balthasar, the three magi or wise men, known in medieval legends as the three kings of Cologne.

BERCHTESGADENER LAND

Left: Berchtesgaden, an active holiday resort set on the hillside, and an ideal base for exploration of the Berchtesgadener Land mountains

churches. The most photographed are probably **Ramsau** and the idyllically-sited **Maria Gern**.

The road up to the 1,820m summit of the **Kehlstein**, southeast of town, takes a zigzag course with views all the way. The road is closed to motor vehicles but a bus operates from Obersalzberg-Hintereck to a point near the top. From here, between May and mid-October, a lift built into the mountain ascends to the Kehlsteinhaus (Eagle's Nest), the remnant of Hitler's mountain retreat, now a restaurant. Connecting buses leave from Berchtesgaden post office. Below the summit are the remains of the **Berghof** where Hitler hosted foreign dignitaries, including Neville Chamberlain.

Often likened to a Norwegian fjord, the much-visited **Königsee** stretches over 8km below the mighty slopes of the Watzmann, its depths plummeting over 190m. At the lake's northern end, from the village of Königsee (a tourist trap of kitschy souvenir shops, fortunately invisible from the lake itself) boat trips are available over the length of the water, with breathtaking vistas all the way. The round trip takes an hour and three quarters and operates all year, weather allowing. Attractions near the far end include short walks to the chapels of St Johann and St Paul, and a more ambitious ascent to an ice 'chapel', which even the summer heat fails to melt (allow an hour each way). A pleasant 75-minute circular walk, the Malerwinkel Rundweg, starts to the left of the main boat pier (at the lake's north end), taking an easily managed gravel track up into the trees. The crowds disappear and you are soon rewarded with views over the Königsee.

Also from Königsee you can take the cable lift up the **Jenner** (1874m), where the mountain-top restaurant gives views of the lake on one side and of nearby Austria on the other.

The Almbachklamm, a gloomy chasm of dramatic rock overhangs and swirling waterfalls can be explored between May and October by a gently rising path (admission payable), which can be followed for an hour and a half to the Theresienklause Dam; the best of the gorge is seen at the beginning. The car park is signposted from highway 305, northeast of Berchtesgaden at the 5.5km post.

Reichenhall Bad is a spa reputed to have the most powerful saline springs in Europe; look for the Quellenbau (guided tours daily, April to October; Tuesday and Thursday only, rest of year), a curious saltworks built by Ludwig I in grandiose medieval style in 1834. If driving here from Berchtesgaden, you are recommended to take highway 305 westwards for the splendid scenery of the Schwarzbach Pass.

Walk The Hintersee

This small lake nestles beneath the wooded lower slopes of the Schottmalhorn (2,045m) and the Hochkalter (2,607m). The walk round takes about 45 minutes, with an optional climb of the Wartstein (15 minutes).

Start at the Seeklause car park at the 25km post on the Ramsau–Weissbach road, west of Berchtesgaden. Turn left out of the car park, along the road, which soon crosses a stream; immediately turn right on broad path with wooden railings. Ignore turns to the right, and walk through the **Zauberwald** (magic wood). After following the shore, reach a T-junction and turn left, signposted Fussweg am See (path around the lake). After 30m, detour right to the **Wartstein** (signposted), keeping right at subsequent junctions until the summit, with its fine view and tiny cave shrine. Return the same way to the bottom, turn right and continue the signposted Fussweg am See, which passes in front of the hotels and branches off left. The final section leads left along the footpath by the road.

Walk The Wimbachtal

The **Wimbachklamm**, west of Berchtesgaden on highway 305 at the 19km post, is a pretty gorge and a starting-point for walks along the Wimbachtal: from the car park, take the rising road (closed to motor traffic) called Wimbachweg; after the road becomes unsurfaced, fork left into the gorge. Two-and-a-half hours' gentle ascent leads you to the Wimbachgrieshütte, sited in a majestic post-glacial valley below the Watzmann and the Hochkalter. There is a handily placed restaurant (Wimbach Schloss) midway. Return the same way.

▶ ▶ ▷ Chiemsee

Bavaria's largest lake looks best from the northern side, particularly from the little resort of Gstadt; the Alpine foothills form part of a distinguished backdrop. It makes a good base for walks, with easy ones in the vicinity of the lake itself and more energetic rambles in the hills to the south. Boating is the other main attraction, with yachts for hire in many of the resorts, and a passenger boat service making stops around the lake. Try to see both of the principal islands. On **Herreninsel**, the larger, stands the unfinished palace of Ludwig II. The king decided to make a replica of Versailles, but only built the central portion before funds ran out. What exists is impressive, with a hall of mirrors and formal French gardens. This would have been the largest of Ludwig's castles. **Fraueninsel** (women's island) was so called because of its Benedictine nunnery; there was once a monastery on the Herreninsel. From Prien, on the west side of the lake, a steam train pulls 19th-century wooden carriages 2km to the pier for boats to the islands.

Fraueninsel, in Chiemsee

Local tourist offices stock booklets detailing the annual classical music festival held in several venues in the area between May and July.

To the south lie the Alpine foothills, a fine area for medium to energetic walks without the daunting scale of the Alps proper. The **Kampenwand** (1,664m) is a popular objective and has cable lifts to get you up to the high ground. **Reit im Winkl** is an Alpine resort of considerable charm.

▶ ▶ ▷ Dachau

A few places in the world cause a frisson because of their very names. Dachau town, now a much-expanded commuterdom for Munich, cannot forget the traumas of its notorious past as the site of the Third Reich's first concentration camp, established in 1933 in a former munitions factory. The camp has become a memorial museum (open daily except Monday, 10.00–17.00hrs; free).

Although not an extermination camp, torture, disease and death were commonplace. The barrack quarters have gone, but accurate reconstructions have been made giving an idea of the cramped conditions prisoners had to endure. Around the perimeter fence, watchtowers still stand. The Jourhaus (camp guard house), formerly the camp entrance, still displays the chillingly inappropriate legend *Arbeit macht frei* (work makes freedom). The gas chambers, disguised as shower rooms, were never used for extermination, but hanging by the stake, a common punishment, was carried out within them; adjacent are the cremation ovens, which kept burning day and night. A museum now occupies one side of the site, with a disturbing account of the camp and a half-hour film (in English at 11.30 and 15.30hrs).

As an antidote to the bleakness of the visit to the camp, walk into **Dachau town**, perched above the River Amper. Despite its proximity to Munich, its centre has an unspoilt small-town atmosphere, with a pretty Hofgarten (castle garden), a nicely laid out local museum and a Gemäldegalerie (picture gallery) of works by a colony of artists who were attracted to the area because of the unique light of the Dachauer Moos, an area of heathland. Both the museum and gallery are open Wednesday and Friday 10.00–16.00, Thursday 14.00–18.00, Saturday 11.00–17.00 and Sunday 13.00-17.00hrs.

Dachau is easily visited from Munich; take the S-Bahn 2 (direction Petershausen) to Dachau, from where, outside the station, bus 722 takes you to the KZ Gedenkstätte (concentration camp memorial).

▶ ▶ ▶ Füssen, Neuschwanstein and Höhenschwangau

Füssen abuts the Forggensee, a popular sailing area, and has its back to the Alps. Among several scenes of picturesque charm is the cobbled main street, the Reichenstrasse, with a trio of the town's most distinguished buildings at its far end – church, abbey and Höhenschloss. Close by, an archway gives on to a riverside park by the Lech. The Benedictine abbey of St Mang now operates as a local museum (open April to October, Tuesday to Sunday, 11.00–16.00hrs; November to March, Tuesday to Saturday, 14.00–16.00hrs), with a violin-maker's workshop among the display items; above all it is an enjoyable place to wander around, with a host of well preserved baroque rooms, including a delicious oval library. Within the Höhenschloss (open Monday to Saturday 10.00–12.00, 14.00–16.00, Sunday 10.00–12.00hrs; December to March Thursday 14.00–16.00hrs only) is an exhibition of medieval religious art from the Allgäu and Swabia.

Königschlösser (Royal Castles) Despite monstrous tourist crowds for most of the year, the spectacular castles of Ludwig II – Linderhof (see page 261), Herrenchiemsee (see page 244), Höhenschwangau and Neuschwanstein – seldom disappoint. Fair-weather timing assists an appreciation of the mountain setting. There is quite a lot of walking involved, particularly a steep haul up from the car parks by Höhenschwangau to Neuschwanstein; you may prefer to make use of the horse and carriage service. Make Höhenschwangau the first visit to avoid a sense of anticlimax (see also **Walk** on page 248).

Dachau: grim snapshots

- Over 206,000 prisoners were registered between 1933 and 1945; numerous other internees were never registered. Jews, religious and political dissenters and other undesirables were brought here.

- 31,591 died in the camp; thousands more were executed.

- In addition to camp work, many prisoners were victims of human experimentation, which included infection with malaria and high-pressure experiments.

- Punishment, including hanging from the stake and lashing, was dispensed for the most trivial offence, such as not making beds correctly.

- SS men during 1940–1 executed many Jews by removing the prisoners' caps and hurling them into the neutral zone, ordering the Jews to retrieve them; when they did they were shot 'for trying to escape'.

- Roll-call often lasted hours when not all the prisoners could be found. They would stand absolutely still, even in freezing conditions, as the slightest movement would be severely punished. Many of the sick simply collapsed on the spot.

Linderhof, one of Ludwig II's spectacular castles

Höhenschwangau is the older of the two castles, built in the 12th century, but destroyed by Napoleon and restored by Crown Prince Maximilian (later Maximilian II) in the 1830s. Ludwig spent his early years here. The décor is troubadour style, with wall-paintings of Bavarian knights and folk heroes; Ludwig's bedroom is decorated with stars that were illuminated in the evening.

Neuschwanstein stands high and mighty, bristling with turrets and mock-medievalism, its interior styles ranging from Byzantine through Romanesque to Gothic. This fairy-tale fantasy come true was built between 1869 and 1886 for Ludwig II; the king spent less than six months here before being certified insane and drowning mysteriously in the Starnberger See. Only about a third of the building was actually completed; the unfinished character is manifest everywhere – the second floor is a mere shell, doorways lead to nothing but suicidal drops, and steps in the throne-room lead to a throneless stage. The 15 rooms you do see on the tour show astonishing craftsmanship and richness of detail which extend to the lamp fittings and elaborate central heating system. Woodcarving in Ludwig's bedroom took 14 carpenters four and a half years to complete. Wagner's operas feature everywhere, in the form of murals and even a mini-grotto recalling the Venusberg in *Tannhäuser*.

The best view of the castle is from the nearby **Marienbrücke** (Mary's Bridge), which spans a deep gorge. On the path between here and the castle is a splendid vista of Höhenschwangau and the Alpsee. (Both castles: open daily April to October 08.30–17.30, November to March 10.00–16.00hrs.)

A recommended extra to the visit is the cable-car ascent of the **Tegelberg** (1,720m), signposted between Höhenschwangau and Schwangau. It operates all year (until 17.00hrs in summer and 16.30hrs in winter) and has a summit restaurant.

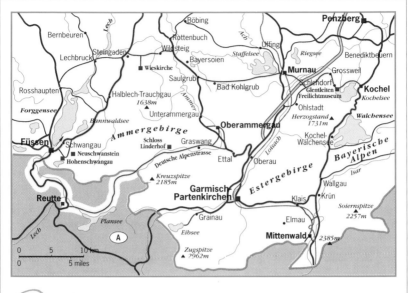

Drive The Deutsche Alpenstrasse

A tour around and into the heart of the German Alps, using the Alpine Road for much of the way.

From the attractive town of Füssen, the road heads northeast past the turning for Höhenschwangau and Neuschwanstein castles – the famous castles of Ludwig II – and skirts the Bannwaldsee before reaching Steingaden. Head east.

Detour south at the signpost for the sumptuous baroque **Wieskirche**. Between the lakes, the **Staffelsee** and **Kochelsee**, is the turning for the

Glentleiten Freilichtmuseum (open-air museum), with its collection of reconstructed rural buildings.

From Kochel, the road climbs into the Alps, passing the prettily set Walchensee, best seen by taking the cable-car up the Wendelstein. Detour to the village of **Mittenwald** before continuing to **Ettal Abbey**, and past **Linderhof**, a Ludwig II castle.

Cross the Austrian border to reach Reutte and continue on to Füssen.

Walchensee

Walk Höhenschwangau and Neuschwanstein

A good way of seeing both castles and the Marienbrücke, and avoiding the crowds. Allow 1 hour for walking and at least 2 for sightseeing.

Park at either of the first two car parks (on the left of the road) for the castles. Cross the road and take the steps to the left of the information centre to Höhenschwangau. After seeing the castle, retrace your steps for a few metres then, just after the end of the castle building, keep right at a fork, to drop down to hotels and restaurants. Cross the road and take steps to the left of the Schloss Hotel, up to reach the road. Cross over and take the stony path opposite, which ascends steadily. At the top, there is a surfaced track near a wooden shelter; detour right and immediately left to the Marienbrücke; return to the shelter and turn right to Neuschwanstein (don't miss the viewpoint over Höhenschwangau which shortly appears on the left). After leaving the castle, follow the main driveway down, forking right after 500m down steps (signposted Cafe Kainz) to reach the main car parks.

Schwangau, the village close to Höhenschwangau, is famed for its Colomansfest, on 13 October, when the thanksgiving for horses and cattle takes place. With a grand procession of horse-drawn carriages, the festival marks the return of the cattle from the summer pastures and the work-horses from the forests.

Höhenschwangau, set among the mountain crags

*Left: Garmisch
Partenkirchen
Below: winter sports
have become a
major business*

▶ ▶ ▶ Garmisch Partenkirchen and surroundings

Garmisch Partenkirchen is really two towns, joined together but different in character; Garmisch has village origins, and retains some old-world rusticity in Frühlingstrasse (in the northern outskirts) and surroundings, with quaint whitewashed, gabled houses and the village fountain; Partenkirchen has been a town for much longer, and has lively, narrow main streets. Both have expanded for tourism, above all for the winter sports industry, together to become the largest German Alpine resort. As the site of the 1936 winter Olympics and the 1978 downhill skiing world championships, the town is endowed with an Olympic ice stadium and ski-jump. It is not a place to get away from the crowds, but nearby villages make good bases.

The towering **Zugspitze** (2,962m), Germany's highest mountain, dominates the area and can be reached effortlessly by rack railway from Garmisch; clear-weather views justify the substantial fee, and there is a

Zugspitze, towering over Garmisch Partenkirchen

Near the peaceful village of Grainau, west of Garmisch, the tiny Badersee is sited secretively among the trees. For a few marks you can hire a boat and view an endearingly ludicrous statue of Nixe, a nymph, placed at the bottom of the lake by Ludwig II.

restaurant at the top. A quicker but less exciting way up is by cable-car from the **Eibsee**, itself a lovely lake encircled by a 7km footpath. Other mountains where you can ascend by chair lift from town and walk down gently graded paths include the **Wank** (1,780m) and the **Eckbauer** (1,237m); both have summit restaurants.

Whatever the weather, be sure to visit the famous **Partnachklamm**. From the Olympic ski stadium, walk or take a horse and carriage along a traffic-free road 2km to the entrance to the gorge. The path along it is one of the wonders of the Alps, snaking near the bottom of the immensely deep chasm past spraying water and remarkable rock formations. A cable-car runs from the gorge entrance to the Hotel Graseck; from the hotel, follow the track up the valley, enter the gorge at its far end, and walk back down. Less crowded owing to its relative inaccessibility is the **Höllentalklamm**, sandwiched between the bases of the Alpspitze and Waxenstein; allow at least two hours each way; start from Hammersbach, southwest of Garmisch.

Walk Eckbauer and the Partnachklamm

A route taking the chairlift up the Eckbauer, a superlative viewing platform, with close-ups of the Alpspitze. The Gasthof on the summit serves excellent fresh buttermilk. An easy ascent zigzags into a valley of Alpine meadows before the finale along the Partnachklamm, a magnificent gorge.

Take the Eckbauerbahn (chair-lift) from the ski-stadium in Garmisch. At the top, walk past the Berg Gasthof Eckbauer and follow signs for the *Partnachklamm, down through woods, later forking right to reach a track near the Graseck Hotel. Turn left (a detour is possible soon after this, to Hohe Brücke, a high bridge over the gorge; return to the main route) to reach the top entrance to the gorge, which you follow downstream; if this is closed, follow the track the other way, past the Graseck Hotel, to the bottom entrance. From the bottom entrance, either walk along the traffic-free road or take a horse and carriage.*

▶ ▷ ▷ Kaufbeuren

The unspoilt town centre, with its twisting, cobbled streets, merits exploration; the tourist information office (in the Rathaus) publishes a walk about town, in English. A walk along the town walls to Kaufbeuren's northwest corner leads past the Fünfknopfturm (five-spired tower) to the 15th-century church of St Blasien; with its greatly treasured high altar by the master Bavarian woodcarver Jörg Lederer (1518), with golden-robed figures of the Virgin and Child, St John the Baptist and St Anne. The Heimatsmuseum in Kaisergässchen (open daily except Monday and first Tuesday in month, 09.00–12.00, 14.00–17.00hrs; Saturday 09.00-12.00hrs) features an impressive collection of crucifixes. In Ludwigstrasse, the Puppentheater (open Thursday to Saturday 10.00–12.00, 14.30–17.00, Sunday 10.00–12.00hrs) displays puppets from Europe and the Far East.

The town's big event is in July, when the Tänzelfest takes place. This medieval-style pageant is played out by 1,600 children and is accompanied by processions and re-enactments of scenes from the town's history.

▶ ▷ ▷ Kempten

A busy commercial centre rather than a tourist destination, Kempten has some good museums (all open Tuesday to Sunday, 10.00–16.00hrs; closed at Christmas). These are the Alpenländische Galerie (Alpine arts), Alpinmuseum (people and mountains of the Alps), the Museum für Kunst und Kulturgeschichte (closed until end of 1993; applied art), the Allgäuer Heimatmuseum (regional museum for the Allgäu), and the Römisches Museum (Roman Museum). East of the town centre, across the River Iller, the Archäologischer Park (open Tuesday to Sunday, 10.00-17.00, November to April 10.00-16.30hrs; closed January and February; guided tours on Sunday at 11.00hrs) occupies the site of the Roman town of Cambodunum. The complex includes a partial reconstruction of a Roman-Celtic temple and archaeological finds from the vicinity.

▶ ▶ ▷ Landsberg-am-Lech

On the Romantische Strasse (Romantic Road, page 230) and quickly reached by public transport from Munich, the hillside town of Landsberg has retained an authentic old-world atmosphere without losing its workaday spirit. The signposted Stadtrundgang (circular town walk) takes in the best of Landsberg, weaving down crooked alleys and beneath arches, and climbing on to the largely intact town ramparts with its series of gateways and views of red roofs huddled by the River Lech. Since the route is complicated, collect a free town map showing the walk from the tourist office; this is situated in the Rathaus (town hall), whose rich stucco exterior by Dominikus Zimmermann graces the Hauptplatz. Zimmermann was also responsible for the Johanniskirche, in the design for which he used the plans for the more famous Wieskirche (page 265). Of the town's towers and gateways, the Bayertor is the most renowned and is one of the largest Gothic fortifications in southern

Chosen by Henry the Lion as a castle site in the 12th century, Landsberg became a regional centre in the Middle Ages and gained prosperity particularly as a trading town for salt mined in southeast Bavaria and sold to Swabian merchants. In this century, Adolf Hitler was imprisoned here following his unsuccessful *Putsch* of 1923, and wrote *Mein Kampf* while incarcerated.

251

Kaufbeuren

Germany. The Neues Stadtmuseum (open Tuesday to Sunday, 14.00–17.00hrs) has a fair miscellany, including medieval religious art. In Hintere Salzgasse, between the Rathaus and the river, is the more modest Puppenstuben Museum (open same hours) which displays a fun collection of antique toys.

▶ ▶ ▷ Mittenwald

In a beautiful Alpine setting close to the Austrian border, the village has expanded as a tourist resort but retains much charm, with a photogenic array of painted houses and numerous corners of old-world rusticity, with whitewashed walls, wooden balconies and green or brown shutters. Outside the church stands a statue of violin-maker Matthias Klotz; the craft continues to be carried out here by Anton Maller, who can be seen working behind his shop window. The Geigenbau Museum close by (open 10.00–11.45, 14.00–16.45hrs; mornings only at weekends and feast days) commemorates this local industry.

Excursions

Cable-car and chair lift excursions include the **Karwendel** (2,384m) by Mittenwald and, further north, the **Herzogstand** (1,731m), majestically placed above the attractive **Walchensee**.

Monument to a music-maker: the statue of violin-maker Matthias Klotz, in Mittenwald

Matthias Klotz (1653–1743) brought the violin-making tradition to Mittenwald. He is thought to have been a pupil of the great Amati of Cremona. This industry may have saved Mittenwald from economic oblivion after Venetian merchants, who had brought prosperity to the village, returned to Italy. Mittenwald violins are highly regarded by musicians and fetch good prices. Today's souvenir spin-offs include miniature violins and liqueurs sold in violin-shaped bottles.

▶ ▶ ▶   München (Munich)

Germany's third largest city contrasts sharply with the cosy conformism of much of the rest of southern Bavaria. With its exuberant atmosphere and vitality it is one of the great cultural centres of Europe. Despite wartime devastation the city has a seductive flavour – blue-and-cream trams, tree-lined boulevards, fountains, parks, pavement cafés, beer-halls and beer-gardens. Its array of museums is unrivalled in the country.

Central Munich is easy to see on foot. East of the main railway station, from **Karlstor**, one of the surviving city gateways, runs the principal pedestrianised street, busy with shoppers, buskers and tourists. At its eastern end, **Marienplatz** is at the heart of Munich, and is dominated by the somewhat sinister looking Gothic Neues Rathaus, its exterior jollified by the famous carillon, where mechanical musicians, jousting knights and dancing coopers perform at 11.00hrs and at other times posted below the clock. Close by are the **Frauenkirche** (closed until 1994), the symbol of Munich, with huge twin onion-domed towers that dominate views from all around, and the Renaissance church of **St Michael**, with Wittelsbach tombs in the crypt. Immediately south of the Marienplatz, the **Viktualienmarkt** is a cheerful food market, excellent for regional cheeses and prepared hams in particular; high quality is matched by high prices.

A short distance southwest are two of the finest churches, the **Damenstiftskirche**, high baroque and thick incense, and the astonishing **Asamkirche**, the ultimate statement in rococo, with no square centimetre unadorned in its dark, compact interior.

In the north-central area lie some of Munich's most impressive streetscapes; **Max-Joseph Platz**, presided

The Gothic Neues Rathaus

MUNICH AND THE ALPS

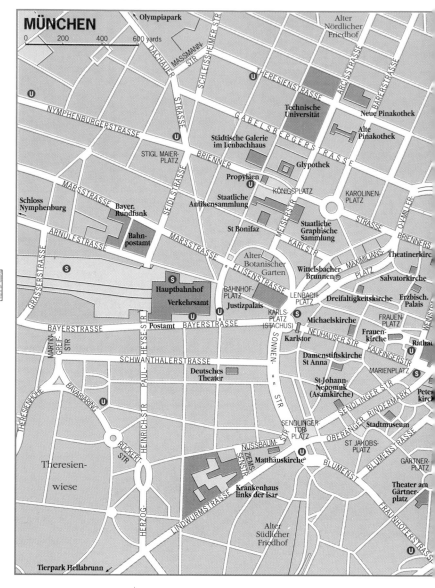

over by the massive Corinthian columns of the National-theater and the southern end of the huge Residenz which marks the western end of **Maximilianstrasse**. This is a tree-lined thoroughfare known for its high-class boutiques and galleries and punctuated at its far end by the towering Maximilaneum (1874), the Bavarian Parliament and Senate. **Odeonsplatz**, full of students on bicycles, has a reconstructed look, but the regularity of the composition is very pleasing. Adjacent is the massive dome of the baroque Theatinerkirche (1677), with a bright yellow façade which contrasts with a cool, intricate grey-stone interior. Across the road, the Hofgarten offers a peaceful retreat from the city bustle.

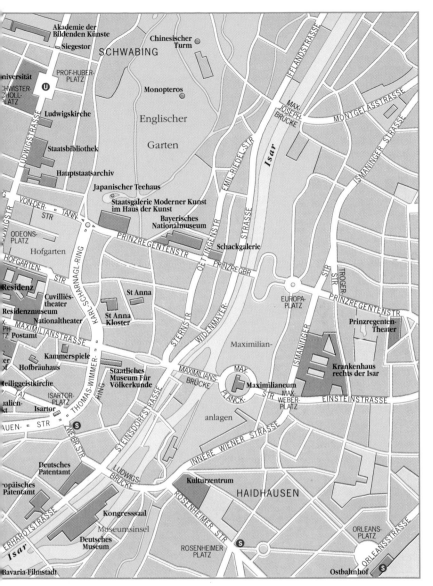

Akademie der Bildenden Künste
Siegestor
Chinesischer Turm
SCHWABING
Universität
PROF.-HUBER-PLATZ
GESCHWISTER-SCHOLL-PLATZ
Ludwigkirche
Monopteros
Englischer Garten
Staatsbibliothek
Hauptstaatsarchiv
Japanischer Teehaus
Staatsgalerie Moderner Kunst im Haus der Kunst
Bayerisches Nationalmuseum
Schackgalerie
VON-DER-TANN-STR
ODEONS-PLATZ
Hofgarten
HOFGARTEN-STR
Residenz
Cuvilliés-theater
Residenzmuseum
Nationaltheater
Postamt
MAXIMILIANSTRASSE
St Anna
St Anna Kloster
PRINZREGENTENSTR
OETTINGENSTR
PRINZREGBR
PRINZREGEN
EUROPA-PLATZ
Prinzregenten-Theater
Kammerspiele
Hofbräuhaus
Heiliggeistkirche
Isartor
ISARTOR-PLATZ
Staatliches Museum Für Völkerkunde
STERNSTR
WIDENMAYERSTR
MAXIMILIANS BRÜCKE
MAX PLANCK
Maximilian-
Maximilianeum
MAX-WEBER-PLATZ
EINSTEINSTRASSE
Krankenhaus rechts der Isar
Deutsches Patentamt
Europäisches Patentamt
STEINSDORFSTRASSE
INNERE WIENER STRASSE
LUDWIGS-BRÜCKE
Kulturzentrum
HAIDHAUSEN
ROSENHEIMER STR
Kongresssaal
Museumsinsel
Deutsches Museum
ROSENHEIMER PLATZ
ORLEANS-PLATZ
ORLEANSSTRASSE
Isar
Bavaria-Filmstadt
Ostbahnhof

Isar
IFFLANDSTRASSE
MAX-JOSEPH-BRÜCKE
MONTGELASSTRASSE
ISMANINGER STRASSE
EMIL-RIEDEL-STR
STRASSE
TROGER
ISMANINGER STR
KARL-SCHARNAGL-RING
THOMAS-WIMMER-RING
KLENZESTR
ERHARDTSTRASSE
LUDWIGSTRASSE

255

The Odeonsplatz looks northwards to the Siegestor, a triumphal gateway close to the university; beyond it lies Leopoldstrasse, the main axis of the district of **Schwabing**, which offers numerous bars, pavement cafés, theatres, cabarets and other entertainment venues. Around Münchener Freiheit, just east of Leopoldstrasse, is good territory for browsing in secondhand shops.

Northwest of the centre are **Ottostrasse**, packed with pricey antique shops, and the main **museum quarter**.

The **Englischer Garten** (English Garden) extends along the banks of the River Isar for some 7km and is one of the largest city parks in the world. The 'garden'

Quick History

- The city's name means 'monks', a reminder of a monastic settlement established here in the ninth century. The Münchener Kindl (little monk) is the city emblem even today.

- Munich became the ducal residence of the Wittelsbachs in 1255, and the Bavarian capital in 1503. During the Thirty Years' War the city was a stronghold of German Catholicism.

- The city was enriched by the Wittelsbachs in the 18th century, when churches and two palaces were built. In the 19th century, Ludwig I endowed the city with its university and its great collections of art and antiquities.

- In 1920 Adolf Hitler launched his National Socialist Party's programme at a crowded meeting at the Hofbräuhaus.

- Post-war years have brought great prosperity. BMW are among many companies to have their headquarters here.

resembles parkland landscaped in the English manner, with informal areas of grass and mature woodlands, and is the haunt of strollers, cyclists, joggers, sunbathers, picnickers and the occasional nudist. The Chinesischer Turm (Chinese Tower), with its beer-garden, is a popular rendezvous. Boat hire is available on the lake, the Kleinhesseloher See.

Less countrified in character, but equally popular, is the **Olympia Park**, north of the centre, the site of the ill-fated 1972 Olympic Games, when Israeli athletes were taken hostage and died in a tragic shoot-out. Today people come for walking, jogging and boating, and for the range of sports facilities which include the Olympic swimming pool. You can walk into the strange tent-like structure of the Olympic stadium. On clear days thousands take the lift up to the top of the Olympic Tower for a panorama of Munich and the Alps. The tower is open daily until midnight.

City tours in English Panorama Tours (tel: (089) 1204–248) run bus tours around the city; **Radius Touristik** (tel: (089) 596113) offer personal guided tours by tram, bicycle and on foot.

Museums and galleries A 20DM ticket covers entry for all state-run museums in Munich.

Alte Pinakothek and Neue Pinakothek *Barer Strasse 27 and 29* Together these form one of the world's great art galleries. The Alte Pinakothek contains paintings up to the 18th century, and is famed for works by Dürer (*Self Portrait*, *The Four Apostles*, *The Baumgärtner Altar* etc), and for its Spanish, Dutch and Italian collections. Across the street, the Neue Pinakothek, reopened in 1981 after wartime destruction, exhibits late 18th- and 19th-century art, from Turner and Gainsborough to the French and German impressionists.

Open: daily except Mondays, 09.15–16.30hrs, plus Tuesdays and Thursdays 19.00–21.00hrs).

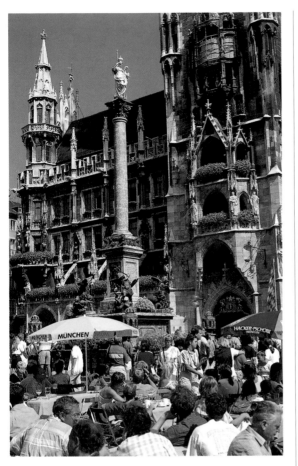

Munich's public transport system works admirably well, but can confuse the newcomer. You can buy tickets individually or in blue strips (which works out cheaper); if choosing the latter, you need to use one ticket for short journeys (five bus or tram stops, or three train or subway stops) or two tickets for longer journeys. You are allowed to transfer on to different modes of transport as long as you don't double back on your direction of travel; short journeys must be completed within one hour, long journeys within two hours. If you are doing a lot of travelling or are in a group, buy a *Tageskarte* (day pass). As soon as you are about to use whichever ticket you have opted for, validate it in one of the automatic stamping machines. Day passes must be validated for the first time you travel only. Travellers without validated tickets may be fined on the spot.

Munich's Marienplatz

Antikensammlungen *Königsplatz 1* Adjacent to the Glyptothek (see page 258), the state collection of classical art owes its origins to the collecting endeavours of Ludwig I and boasts some superb Etruscan gold jewellery and a renowned set of Greek decorated vases.
Open: daily except Monday, 10.00–16.30hrs; Wednesday 12.00–20.30hrs.
Bavaria Film Studio *Bavariafilmplatz* Guided tours of the largest movie studios in Europe.
Open: March to October, daily, 9.00–16.00hrs.
Bayerisches Nationalmuseum *Prinzregentenstrasse 3* Three floors of Bavarian arts and crafts. Highlights include wooden sculptures by Tilman Riemenschneider and a wonderful collection (the world's largest) of nativity tableaux.
Open: daily except Monday, 09.30–17.00hrs.
Deutsches Museum *Museumsinsel 1* Rated the world's foremost museum of science and technology, this has something for everyone, from do-it-yourself chemistry experiments and complicated models of hydraulics and bridges to areas of more mainstream appeal, such as

MUNICH AND THE ALPS

Munich is well endowed with theatres and concert halls. The Münchener Kammerspiel is one of the most famous theatrical companies; the Cuvilliés-Theater makes an evening out just for the architecture. The Nationaltheater in Max-Joseph Platz is a venue for opera and ballet. Munich has a number of resident orchestras, including the Bayerisches Rundfunk Sinfonie Orchester and the Münchener Philharmonie. For details of events contact the tourist offices in the railway station or near the Rathaus.

historic cars, locomotives, musical instruments, space travel and aircraft. Open: daily, 09.00–17.00hrs.

Glyptothek *Königsplatz 3* Greek and Roman statuary, nearly all collected by Ludwig I; housed in an aptly classical building designed by Leo von Klenze.
Open: daily except Monday 10.00–16.30hrs; Thursday 12.00–20.30hrs.

Lenbachhaus *Luisenstrasse 33* Of interest for the Italianate villa, complete with 19th-century furnishings, and for the Kandinsky collection of works by the Blauer Reiter group of expressionist painters. Free entry.
Open: daily except Monday, 10.00–18.00hrs.

Nymphenburg In the western suburbs stands this great summer residence of the Wittelsbachs, the former rulers of Bavaria. Although built and added to over many centuries, the palace has a strikingly unified symmetry. The best-known feature of its splendid baroque interior is the Schönheitsgallerie, 36 beauties of the day painted 1827–50 for the pleasure of Ludwig I. Adjacent to the house is the Marstallmuseum, with a grand array of

royal carriages and sleighs, and a room of Nymphenburg porcelain.

Behind the palace lies perhaps the chief glory, a park of canals, a lake and a series of whimsical hunting lodges and pavilions. Of these, the Amalienburg steals the show, a neat essay in rococo, with a hall of shimmering mirrors: from the centre you see yourself reflected in all ten of these. The Magdelenklause was built as a mock-hermitage, complete with a bizarre grotto chamber.

Next door, the attractive Botanical Garden has an alpinum, rhododendrons and glasshouses.
Open: daily except Monday, 09.00–12.30 and 13.30–17.00hrs; 10.00–12.30 and 13.30–16.00hrs October to March. Botanical Garden daily, 09.00hrs to dusk; glasshouses closed 11.45–13.00hrs.

Residenzmuseum *Max-Joseph Platz 3* The vast baroque palace of the Wittelsbachs, painstakingly restored after extensive wartime damage; different parts of the building are open in the morning and evening, since there is far too much to see at once. In addition to the state rooms, do not miss the magnificent vaulted Antiquarium (begun 1568) housing statues collected

from the classical world, a dazzling treasury of pristine jewel-encrusted riches dating from the 11th century onwards, and the enchanting Cuvilliés-Theater (separate admission), a rococo creation by François de Cuvillies, still used for performances. Within the same complex, but requiring separate admission, are museums of coins and Egyptian art.

Open: daily except Monday, 10.00–16.30hrs; Cuvillies-Theater open Monday to Saturday, 14.00–17.00hrs, Sunday and Feast Days, 10.00–17.00hrs.

Spielzeug Museum *Marienplatz* In the tower of the old town hall is this nostalgic treasure-house of retired dolls, vintage model cars and pre-war teddies.

Open: Monday to Saturday, 10.00–17.30hrs, Sunday, 10.00–18.00hrs.

Staatsgalerie Moderner Kunst *Prinzregentenstrasse 1* Gallery of 20th-century art and sculpture, particularly strong on German modern art.

Open: daily except Monday, 09.15–16.30hrs, plus Thursday 19.00–21.00hrs.

Stadtmuseum *Jakobsplatz* In a former arsenal, this is more than just the city local history museum, with floors devoted to brewing, the early days of photography, a film museum, a worldwide collection of musical instruments, and a splendidly entertaining puppet and fairground museum.

Open: daily except Monday, 10.00–17.00hrs; Wednesday 10.00–20.30hrs.

ZAM *Westenriedstrasse 26* Seven quaintly unrelated museums in one: pedal cars, memorabilia relating to the Empress Elisabeth of Austria, bourdalous (fancy china containers), corkscrews, padlocks, chamber pots and even Easter bunnies.

Open: daily, 10.00–18.00hrs.

Munich is a major beer producer, and its citizens drink to that during the Oktoberfest, which features bands, sideshows and the famous beer halls (below)

Munich is one of Europe's foremost beer-producing cities, famous the world over for its annual Oktoberfest (last Saturday in September to first Saturday in October) on the Theresienwiese fairground on the west side of the city. The Oktoberfest is a binge of unashamed beer-guzzling, with barbecues, processions and general merrymaking thrown in. Equally famous are the beer-halls: huge, high-ceilinged affairs with noisy Bavarian brass band music. The Hofbräuhaus, northeast of Marienplatz, is the most touristy; the Mathüser Stadt, in Bayer Strasse near the station, is the largest, while the Forschungsbrauerei serves some of the most obscure beer varieties.

259

MUNICH AND THE ALPS

The passion play at Oberammergau

The passion play was first performed in 1633 after villagers had been spared the ravages of the plague; the play now takes place every ten years, the next occasion being in 2000. Some one hundred day-long performances are given to aggregate audiences of over 500,000 by a cast of 1,700. Men grow long hair and beards for the event. Competition among the locals for the major parts is keen; traditionally Mary is always played by a virgin. The 1674 text mentions use of trumpets but the music has been lost; the music now used is by Rochus Dedler (1779–1822). The text itself, rewritten in 1750 and 1850, has created controversy for its alleged anti-Semitic message.

 Oberammergau and area

Known the world over for its passion play, Oberammergau is physically dominated by a rock pinnacle known as the Ettaler Mandl. The village has a number of painted houses and a pretty baroque church but gets completely overridden with visitors at peak times. Its main streets cater to the mass tourist trade, notably with its plethora of shops selling locally produced wood-carvings (mostly of religious themes). The Heimatsmuseum has a display of antique wooden artefacts.

In the Passiontheater (open daily, 09.30–12.00, 13.30–16.30hrs) you can see the monumental-style stage set used for the passion play and look backstage, set out as an exhibition of costumes, props and models of former sets.

Ettal, the next village to the south, has two claims to fame. One is Ettaler, a sweet herbal liqueur originally made by monks. The other is the great Benedictine abbey church, with an unusual 12-sided nave beneath a huge dome, modelled on the Church of the Holy Sepulchre in Jerusalem; although a 14th-century foundation, the church interior is high baroque, with a painted ceiling by Johann-Jakob Zeiller.

Westwards from Ettal, the valley drive towards Reutte in Austria is a fine one, passing the peaceful village of

Painted buildings at Oberammergau, internationally known for its passion play

Ludwig II

■ **Born in 1845 in Nymphenburg Castle, near Munich, Ludwig II was a member of the Wittelsbach dynasty, and became king of Bavaria at the age of 18. Within two years of his accession to the throne he became involved in a war with Prince Otto von Bismarck of Prussia; Bavaria was defeated, and the Prussians took over the Bavarian army.....■**

In 1870 Bavaria was, under Bismarck's influence, drawn into the war between Prussia and France that was to be the catalyst in the formation of the German Empire, of which Bavaria was a part. Bismarck now had Ludwig truly under his thumb, and ordered the Bavarian king to send a letter naming William I of Prussia as the Emperor of Germany. Disillusioned, Ludwig lost all interest in politics and became increasingly eccentric. He built a trio of castles – Linderhof, Neuschwanstein and Herrenchiemsee – at stupendous expense. A stage-set designer drew the first sketches for Neuschwanstein, the most theatrical of the three; Ludwig watched the progress of building through his telescope at Höhenschwangau. Linderhof, the only one of Ludwig's royal castles to be completed, was the king's favourite. Louis XIV became Ludwig's inspiration: his dream was of absolute rule. He gave financial aid to Richard Wagner, whose operas fired his imagination. But the funds ran out; his extravagance, homosexuality and near or actual insanity worried the Bavarian government, who colluded with Luitpold (his uncle and successor) to depose him. Ludwig was certified insane in his bedroom at Neuschwanstein and, a few days later, on 13 June 1886 he and his physician were found drowned in the Starnberger See. It has never been ascertained whether this was an accident or an assassination.

Graswang and the entrance to **Schloss Linderhof** (open daily except Christmas and New Year, 9.00–17.30hrs; closes 16.00hrs October to March; guided tours in English), completed in 1878 for Ludwig II and modelled on the Petit Trianon at Versailles. Its interior, though nothing as spectacularly bizarre as Neuschwanstein (page 246) has characteristically lavish adornments, full of mirrors, painted ceilings and gilded cherubs, in a mixture of Renaissance and baroque styles. The grounds have some wonderfully offbeat features, including a grand cascade, a water jet which shoots higher than the Schloss itself, a grotto modelled on the Venusberg of Wagner's opera *Tannhäuser,* and a Moorish Kiosk resplendent with a 'peacock throne'.

Locally produced wood-carvings are sold in several Oberammergau shops

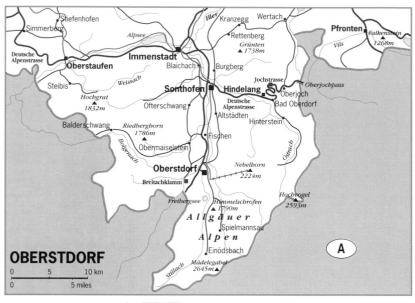

OBERSTDORF

A view of the Oberstdorf valley

▶ ▶ ▷ Oberstdorf and area

Oberstdorf is a busy valley resort, excellently placed for exploring the Allgäuer Alps; it flourishes as a winter sports (top-class skiing and skating facilities), climbing and hiking centre. More peaceful bases include **Fischen**, on the valley floor but bypassed by the road, remote **Balderschwang,** high up a lonely side valley, **Oberstaufen**, large and well-kempt, **Altestädten**, with its characteristic wooden Allgäuer houses, and **Hindelang**, nestling in green countryside.

From Oberstdorf, horse-drawn carriages leave every day to the **Stillachtal**, the southernmost valley in Germany, with Einödsbach as its southernmost village. The road is closed to motor traffic and affords magnificent mountain views. Southwest of Oberstdorf, the **Kleines Walsertal**, an enclave of Austria, can only be reached from Germany and has typical wooden farms and modest family hotels within a dramatic Alpine setting. The walk along the **Brietachklamm**, west of Oberstdorf, squeezes through a magnificent gorge and beneath unlikely-looking overhangs (closed during the spring thaw). Cable cars from the east side of town whisk you up to the **Nebelhorn** upper station, for a chair lift to the summit (2,224m), which is graced with a summit restaurant and breathtaking panorama extending westwards to the Bernese Oberland in Switzerland.

▶ ▶ ▷ Ottobeuren

The mighty Benedictine abbey church of Ottobeuren dwarfs the adjacent small town. Founded in 764, the abbey prospered under the patronage of Charlemagne and the complex was rebuilt in the 18th century by Johann-Michael Fischer. It is Germany's largest baroque church, and the proportions are quite cathedral-like, with a nave 90m long and transept 60m across. Its

Ottobeuren's abbey church

interior is wonderfully light, and adorned with frescoes by Amigoni, J B Zimmermann and J J Zeiller and stucco work by J M Feuchtmayr. The Trinity organ, built by K J Riepp, is one of the most splendid in Europe.

▶ ▷ ▷ Starnberger See

The largest lake close to Munich is served by a suburban railway service which makes it a good out-of-town base for the Bavarian capital. It is well suited for yachting (boat hire available), strolls and relaxation; the scenery is undramatic but pleasant. A boat sails around the lakes; stops include the Votive Chapel at Berg, in memory of Ludwig II who drowned here in 1886 and whose body was recovered at Possenhofen, the lake's main bathing beach. The best views are had from the Bismarckturm (Bismarck Tower) south of Berg, and Ilkahöhe, a modest hill southwest of Tutzing, the main resort.

Just to the south lies the peaceful and unspoilt **Ostersee**, part of a complex of over 20 small lakes, with reedy shores and wooded isles. The 8km Rundweg Ostersee, a circular path, gives an easy two-hour walk; the car park is between Seeshaupt and Penzburg.

At **Kochel**, the Franz Marc Museum exhibits a collection of work of the great 20th-century Bavarian artist (open Tuesday to Sunday, 14.00–18.00hrs).

Northwest of Ottobeuren, Memmingen has an attractive town centre of arcaded buildings and patrician houses, with the irregular Marktplatz dominated by the Gothic tower of the Nikolaikirche (fine murals and stalls within). Parishaus, a pink and white building north of the Rathaus, houses the tourist office, which issues a leaflet detailing a walk around town. The Hermansbau (1766) is the town's finest house, and now contains the local museum (open daily except Saturday and Monday, 10.00–12.00, 14.00–16.00hrs), worth a look for its oak staircase and stucco ceilings; exhibits include porcelain, dolls' houses, clocks, medieval religious art and an 1825 model of Memmingen.

Walk The Heini-Klopfer Ski-Jump and the Freibergsee

A varied walk (1–2 hours) that begins with a gentle riverside path; either ascend on foot or take the ski-lift up; the routes rejoin at the Eibersee, a small lake encompassed by wooded slopes, before the final descent.

Start at the car park northeast of the Freibergsee, in the Stillachtal. From the west side of Oberstdorf, drive along the road southwards, signposted Fellhornbarn and Schiflugschanze; the car park is seen in the trees after 4km, on the right.
Walk to the back of the car park and

cross the footbridge; turn left, and follow the river 1.5km to reach the ski-jump. Either take the ski-lift to the top, and turn right at the path above the lift or carry forward (now on a traffic-free road, which rises; at the top, fork right and follow signs to Freibergsee, past Gasthof Schwand, then forking right just before ski jump). At next major fork (1km), bear right downhill, initially along power lines, then right again (signposted Parkplatz) to a river where you go right to cross the footbridge into the car park.

Schliersee

Wangen im Allgäu:
the Rathaus

▶ ▷ ▷   Tegernsee and Schliersee

Two lakes in beautiful settings. The **Tegernsee**, encompassed by wooded hills, can be enjoyed from a one-and-three-quarter-hour boat trip and from the 1,722m summit of **Wallberg**, reached by cable car from just above the south end of the lake. The shores are considerably built up with weekend villas and a string of smart but unremarkable resorts. The **Schliersee** feels more in the mountains. The town of Schliersee itself has boat hire, a swimming pool and a surfing school. Higher up is the smaller **Spitzingsee**, finely set and well developed with winter sports facilities; lake swimming is best at the southern end. In summer it is excellent for walking: the hills have Alpine character without being as daunting as the larger scale mountains further south; cable cars and chair lifts ascending Taubenstein (1,693m) and Stümpfling (1,506m) operate most of the year and offer a good basis for high-level walks.

▶ ▷ ▷   Wangen im Allgäu

An appealing Swabian town with a wealth of painted houses. Its old town is a simple crossroads, centred on the Marktplatz and entered by two frescoed gateways, the Frauentor (Ravensburg Gate) of 1608, the symbol of Wangen, and the St Martin Tor (Lindau Gate), with its pyramidal roof and intriguing array of gargoyles. A local museum within a half-timbered building devotes itself to cheese-making and folk art in the Allgäu.

The rolling hills around Wangen make good walking and cycling country, with quiet roads, forests and sleepy villages. **Isny**, to the east, is another unspoilt old town, with 13th-century ramparts and a pretty corner by the church of St Jakob and St Georg and 17th-century monastery buildings (now a hospital). A signposted Stadtrundweg (town walk) takes in the best of it.

▶ ▷ ▷ **Wasserburg am Inn**

Wasserburg occupies a naturally fortified site all but surrounded by a tight meander of the turbulent River Inn, itself lined with white cliffs. During the Middle Ages this was one of the most prosperous towns in Bavaria, when it became a river port for Munich on a salt trading route and was allowed to levy tax on salt which passed through town. Wasserburg's fortunes slumped after 1504 when the salt road moved course, and later suffered ravages of war and plague. Its heyday gone, Wasserburg nevertheless retains a legacy of old merchants' houses and characterful winding streets. Opposite the Rathaus, the façade of the Kernhaus displays outstanding 18th-century stucco work by J B Zimmermann. Behind the Rathaus, the local museum (open Tuesday to Sunday) has items relating to the town's past, and a collection of carriages. The main town gateway dates from 1374 and displays wall paintings of two warriors bearing the banners of Wasserburg and Bavaria; within it, the Erstes Imaginäres Museum (open Tuesday to Sunday) houses a collection of old masters with a difference: all of them are fakes. Through the gateway, carry on over the Inn bridge, turn left into Kellerstrasse for a path up to a fine viewpoint over the town.

265

Wasserburg am Inn

▶ ▶ ▷ **Wieskirche**

Located amid quiet, green meadows, the famous Wieskirche stands almost by itself. It was built as a pilgrimage church to house a figure of the Scourging of Christ, which had allegedly shed miraculous tears. The architect, Dominikus Zimmermann, gave it a wonderfully light, frothy interior, with an outstanding frescoed dome depicting the Gate to Paradise. His composition was a personal masterpiece (so much so that he spent the rest of his life in a house close by) and is one of the great rococo buildings of Europe.

Arriving
A valid passport is required to enter Germany but EC nationals and visitors from Australia, New Zealand, Canada and the USA on a tourist/business visit of up to three months do not need a visa (provided they do not intend to take up employment in Germany).
British citizens can use a UK Visitors' Passport, which is valid for one year. As Germany has been unified a relatively short time, it is advisable to check entry regulations with your appropriate German Embassy before departure (addresses under **Embassies**).

By air The main international airports are Frankfurt, Düsseldorf, Cologne, Munich and Berlin. Internal air services connect these and other airports within Germany. The Lufthansa Airport Express Train also links certain airports and major city centres (see **Public transport**). There is a regular airport bus transfer, which runs between Berlin's Tegel and Schönefeld airports.
All German airports connect efficiently with the local urban transport network. In some cases there is a connecting coach service; other airports tie in with the metro system.

By boat To Germany:
Scandinavian Seaways (tel: 0255 241234) operates the only direct sailing to Germany. It sails out of Harwich, Essex, to Hamburg (from mid-March to end December). The crossing takes 20-plus hours.
To Holland: Crossing to Holland from the UK means a shorter sea journey and unless you specifically want to visit the north of Germany, it is an alternative jumping off point. Sealink (tel: 0233 647047) operates from Harwich to the Hook of Holland – a crossing which takes roughly seven hours.
Olau Lines (tel: 0795 666666) runs one daily and one overnight ferry from Sheerness, Kent, to Vlissingen. From Vlissingen, the A58 then the A67 lead to the German border, where the signs for Essen, Duisberg

and Düsseldorf begin to appear.
To Belgium: Another option is to arrive at a Belgian port. P&O European Ferries (tel: 081 575 8555) sail from Dover to Ostend, crossing time around 4 hours. P&O also operate from Felixstowe to Zeebrugge, with five-and-three-quarter-hour day-sailings.
North Sea Ferries (tel: 0482 77177) also sail from Hull to Zeebrugge; low season bargain prices are offered for the fourteen-and-a-half-hour crossing.
To France: It could be that if you're heading for central and southern Germany a quick sea crossing to Dunkerque , Boulogne or Calais works out best for you. Work out the savings in time and petrol; ask a travel agent for advice and your motoring organisation for a route map.
Driving times from Channel ports to German destinations vary from three hours to Cologne, to 12 hours down to Munich.
Ferry companies which serve these ports from the UK include Sealink, P&O and Sally Line (tel: 071 409 2240)
All ferry companies offer special deals of one sort or another, for instance concessions for family groups, senior citizens, special sailings and so on. It's advisable to ask what kind of offers are available before booking.

By coach Eurolines (tel: 071 730 0202) have frequent coach departures from London Victoria to Frankfurt, Hamburg, Munich, Berlin, Leipzig, Dresen and many more destinations Sample travel times are fourteen-and-a-half hours to Cologne, 23 to Berlin, and 25 to Dresden. Special children's fares operate on all routes.
For travellers going to Germany from parts of the UK outside London, Translines coaches (tel: 071 730 0202) depart from major UK cities (Reading, Manchester, Cardiff Edinburgh, etc.). At one time their destinations used to be British Army of the Rhine bases, though some of them now stop in the local town centre, as well.

TRAVEL FACTS

By rail British Rail (tel: 071 834 2345) operates eight services a day from London Victoria, with a Channel crossing at Dover either by ferry (which takes four hours) or jetfoil (1 hour 40 mins). There are also two services a day departing from Liverpool Street, with a Harwich–Hook of Holland crossing (taking 7+ hours).

Depending on how you cross the Channel and what time train you catch in London, travel times vary. Travel for the under-26-year-olds is slightly cheaper, while the Rail Europe Senior Card knocks one third off prices. To qualify for this you need to be a UK resident and to hold a BR Senior Citizens' Rail Card – after which a supplement is paid to obtain the European version.

The InterRail Pass is worth considering if you plan to travel around inside Germany. It is valid for one month and good for all European railways it also cuts the cost of travel on British trains and on some channel ferries. Visit a British Rail Travel Centre for full details.

Camping

Germany abounds in campsites – there are about 2,600 sprinkled liberally around the country. including the former East Germany. The standard is high: even the most basic have toilet and washing facilities plus on-site shop. Top class campsites feature swimming pools, supermarkets, discos and all the trimmings.

Campsites are located by a blue sign carrying the international camping symbol: a black tent on a white background, Most are open from Easter to October, with around 400 staying open all year. June to September is the busiest season and as reservations are usually made on site, you must get there early to avoid disappointment, especially in popular places; better still, book in advance.

A list of campsites can be obtained free from the German National Tourist Office (address under Tourist Offices). The German Camping Club (DCC) publishes a complete guide, available from 28 Mandlestrasse,

D–8000 Munich 40, while the German motoring organisation ADAC also produces a guide to over 1,000 sites (address 8, AM Westpark, D–8000 Munich 40).

If you prefer to pitch your tent outside official campsites, you must first ask the permission of the landowner or local police.

Most of the major car rental firms will also rent out a camper van.

Children

If you're in need of a baby-sitter, enquire first at your hotel reception – they may well offer this service. Tourist offices in most towns and cities keep updated lists of recommended baby-sitters and details of local crèche facilities. In Munich, there is a tourist office-approved baby-sitting service, whose sitters speak English (tel: 089 229 291 or 089 394 507 for details).

Under-fours travel free on public transport and children aged four to 11 go half price. Reduced rates are usually offered in hotels and guest houses for children, and it is the norm for attractions such as museums and historic buildings to offer discounts for younger visitors. Germanic theme parks tend to take the form of fairy-tale tableaux lands, such as the Märchenwald, with its adventure playground, at Wolfratshausen near Bad Tolz in the Bavarian Alps, the Märchenparadies near Heidelberg (with miniature and funicular railways) and the Taunus Wonderland at Wiesbaden.

Attractions at Phantasialand at Brühl (halfway between Bonn and Cologne) include re-creations of the Wild West, ancient China and pre-war Berlin, a massive roller coaster and overhead monorail. Zoos and puppet theatre are popular features throughout the country.

Climate

Generally speaking the weather in Germany is rather similar to that in Britain: changeable, neither extremely hot nor cold, and sprinkled with rain.

The climate does not get dramatically warmer the further south you go. Berlin has an average

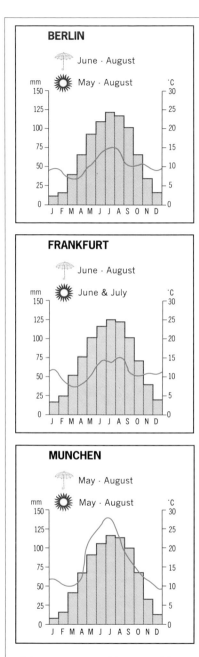

BERLIN

☂ June · August

☀ May · August

FRANKFURT

☂ June · August

☀ June & July

MUNCHEN

☂ May · August

☀ May · August

July temperature of between 15° and 24°C, more southerly Munich of between 13° and 24°C. This city also has an above average summer rainfall, However, Hamburg in the north is consistently several degrees cooler than, for instance, Frankfurt in the centre. Berlin used to be famous for its bracing air – the Berliner Luft – while South Bavaria has its Föhn. This mountain wind can spring up at any season, causing a sudden change in temperature as it brings very warm conditions and a cloudless sky.

Summers are usually pleasantly hot and dry throughout the country. Towards the Alps they get shorter, starting around May, and ending in warm autumns. May or October are good times to visit Germany; the popular haunts can get crowded in the peak tourist months of June to September. Later, snows start around November, and winter can be very cold: the January temperature in Berlin and Munich, for example, can hit a minimum of -5°C.

Crime

Violent crime is less common in Germany than in many other countries though since unification crime figures have risen dramatically. Trouble spots, as in any other nation, are large cities such as Hamburg, Frankfurt, Lübeck and Berlin, where the usual car theft and house robberies are a hazard of urban life. As a tourist, it makes sense to avoid attracting unwanted attention by flaunting expensive jewellery and camera equipment and it is irresponsible to leave baggage unattended, valuables on show in your car or your vehicle unlocked. Wear a shoulder bag on the side away from the street, or use a money belt for cash and travellers' cheques. It is a good idea to have photocopies of important documents, including passport, driving licence and travellers' cheques, and to keep them in a safe, separate place from the originals. If you are unlucky enough to fall foul of thieves, register the theft straightaway with the police (Polizei). This is necessary if you wish to claim on your travel insurance. In an emergency, the number to ring is 110. When arriving at the police station, make sure you have some form of identification (one instance where your photocopies could come in useful).

CONVERSION CHARTS

FROM	TO	MULTIPLY BY
Inches	Centimetres	2.54
Centimetres	Inches	0.3937
Feet	Metres	0.3048
Metres	Feet	3.2810
Yards	Metres	0.9144
Metres	Yards	1.0940
Miles	Kilometres	1.6090
Kilometres	Miles	0.6214
Acres	Hectares	0.4047
Hectares	Acres	2.4710
Gallons	Litres	4.5460
Litres	Gallons	0.2200
Ounces	Grams	28.35
Grams	Ounces	0.0353
Pounds	Grams	453.6
Grams	Pounds	0.0022
Pounds	Kilograms	0.4536
Kilograms	Pounds	2.205
Tons	Tonnes	1.0160
Tonnes	Tons	0.9842

MEN'S SUITS

UK	36	38	40	42	44	46	48
Rest of Europe	46	48	50	52	54	56	58
US	36	38	40	42	44	46	48

DRESS SIZES

UK	8	10	12	14	16	18
France	36	38	40	42	44	46
Italy	38	40	42	44	46	48
Rest of Europe	34	36	38	40	42	44
US	6	8	10	12	14	16

MEN'S SHIRTS

UK	14	14.5	15	15.5	16	16.5 17
Rest of Europe	36	37	38	39/40	41	42 43
US	14	14.5	15	15.5	16	16.5 17

MEN'S SHOES

UK	7	7.5	8.5	9.5	10.5	11
Rest of Europe	41	42	43	44	45	46
US	8	8.5	9.5	10.5	11.5	12

WOMEN'S SHOES

UK	4.5	5	5.5	6	6.5	7
Rest of Europe	38	38	39	39	40	41
US	6	6.5	7	7.5	8	8.5

Do not inadvertently commit a crime yourself by, for instance, crossing the road before the green light for pedestrians shows. This may be acceptable behaviour at home, but is illegal in Germany. Far more serious is being caught in possession of drugs, of any sort – imprisonment or deportation is the penalty.

Customs

There are no restrictions on the import or export of German Marks (DM) or any other foreign currency. Your private car is exempt from duty (subject to re-exportation) as is a standard tank of fuel and 10 litres in spare cans.

Duty free allowances for taking goods into Germany are as follows (imports from EC countries in brackets): 200 (300) cigarettes; or 50 (75) cigars, or 250 (400) g of tobacco. 4 (1.5) litres of alcohol over 22% proof; or 2 (3) litres below 22% or 2 (1) litres of sparkling wine and 2 (5) litres of other wines. If the goods are bought in duty free shops, the lower limit applies. Alcohol and tobacco are only duty free for people over 17.

Disabled visitors

The German government agency involved in assisting disabled people has details of hotels with special facilities to meet their requirements. Write to Help for the Handicapped (Hilfe für Behinderte), Kirchfeldstrasse 1 4000–Düsseldorf. The wheelchair symbol (a wheelchair set in a box) indicates access for disabled tourists. Airports and rest stops on the autobahns are all equipped with toilet facilities, and at major railway stations staff are specially briefed to help passengers in wheelchairs, etc.

Access guides produced in Germany by social services departments or groups of residents list hotels, restaurants, buses, etc accessible to disabled visitors. RADAR (25 Mortimer Street, London W1N 8AB, tel: 071 637 5400) can give callers an idea which towns offer the best facilities. RADAR has also published its own guide to holidays and travel worldwide which lists useful contact organisations,

Driving

The condition of autobahns, major and minor roads is excellent in the former West Germany; in what was East Germany, there is still some way to go to bring roads up to a similar standard. The autobahns are toll-free.

Foreign motorists may drive a vehicle for up to one year in Germany with a national or international driving licence. Holders of Australian and US licences must carry an official translation. (Contact your Embassy or GNTO.) Third party insurance is compulsory. Check with your insurers and they will issue a Green Card to show that they have extended your cover to allow driving abroad.

If you come from outside the EC you do not need an international car registration document, though you should always have your ordinary registration documents with you. Germans drive on the right side of the road; traffic coming from the right normally has right of way. Children under 12 are not allowed to travel in a front seat unless they are using special seats or safety belts suitable for children or unless the rear seats are occupied by other children. It is compulsory for driver and passengers to wear seat belts if they are fitted.

Drivers go very fast on autobahns. There is no official speed limit in the former West Germany, though the recommended maximum of 100–130 kph there is now legally enforceable in the former East. There is a countrywide official limit on country roads of 80–100 kph and in built-up areas of 50 kph.

On-the-spot fines are levied for speeding, and other road offences such as using abusive language, making derogatory signs and running out of petrol on the motorway! Drinking and driving rules also vary: in the former East, the rule is absolutely nil alcohol when driving. In the West, a little is allowed. The level of alcohol in the bloodstream must be under 80mg/100ml.

In the case of a breakdown, contact the ADAC (Allgemeiner Deutscher Automobil Club). On autobahns

Mozart's house, Augsburg

emergency orange telephones are sited at regular intervals (follow the yellow marker arrows). Ask for 'Strassenwachthilfe'. On minor roads, dial 110. The ADAC do not charge you for their labour, but only for materials (unless it's a serious problem, so check that your insurance covers this). In the former East the Auto Club Europa (ACE, Märkisches Ufer, O–1026 Berlin) also provides emergency assistance. Filling stations are regularly sited along autobahns and in urban areas off the main roads. Lead free – Bleifrei – is available everywhere though less common in the former East. Petrol prices vary, tending to be higher on autobahns, cheaper at self-service – SB-Tanken – stations.

Car rentals: Pre-booking a rented car from home can save time and using a major company means you can pick up at one place and drop off at another for no extra charge. Most airports, railways stations and larger towns have booking offices if you prefer to arrange car rental (*Autovermietung*) in Germany. International firms include Hertz, Avis and Budget. Ask at the local tourist office for German companies. The minimum age at which you can rent a car is 21 and you need to have held a full driving licence for 1 year.

Electricity
The current in Germany is 220 volts, 50 cycles. Sockets are the two-pin type.

Embassies/Consulates*
Within Germany:
Australian: Godesberger Allee 105–107 5300 Bonn 2; tel: 0228 81030.*
Canadian: Friedrich Wilhelmstr. 18, 5300 Bonn 1; tel: 0228 231061*
Eire: Godesberger Allee 19, 5300 Bonn 2; tel: 0228 376937
New Zealand: Bunderskanzlerplatz 2 – 18, 5300 Bonn 1; tel: 0228 228070
UK: Unter den Linden 32-4, Berlin; tel: 9220 2431
US: Neustädtische Kirchstrasse 4–5, D–1080, Berlin; tel: 9220 2741.
At home:
Australia: German Embassy, 119 Empire Circuit, Yarralumla AC, Canberra, 2600; tel: 701911
Canada: PO Box 379, Postal Station A, Ottowa, Ontario KYN8VA; tel: 613 232 1101
Eire: 31 Trimelston Ave, Booterstown, Blackrock, Co Dublin; tel: 316.93011
New Zealand: 90-92 Hobson St, Wellington; tel: 736036
UK: 23 Belgrave Square, London SW1X 8PZ; tel: 071 235 .5033.
USA: 4645 Reservoir Road NW, Washington DC 20007 – 1998; tel: 202 298 8140

Emergency telephone numbers
Police: 110
Fire Department: 112
DZT (Deutsche Zentrale für Tourismus – German National Tourist Board), Frankfurt (tel: 069 75720)

Etiquette
In Germany, never, *but never*, call anyone by their first name unless you are invited to do so. Germans tend to be formal in business and in their private lives, too, though the younger generation takes a more relaxed attitude to this rule. Always use either Herr or Frau; it is considered an insult to address a woman as Fräulein, until you know for sure that she is a Miss rather than a Mrs. You should also say, 'Guten Morgen, meine Dame,' as opposed to 'meine Frau'. When speaking to a professional person, eg a doctor, address him/her as Herr or Frau Doktor.
The distinction between 'Sie' and 'Du' – both meaning you – is comparable to the difference between the French 'vous' and 'tu' . You must wait to be told to use the familiar 'Du', though it's always safe to use it with children and animals. Germans shake hands whenever they meet, even if it's only a casual encounter between neighbours on the stairs. Expect to offer to kiss a woman on both cheeks when greetings are conducted. Another German custom is to bring a gift when invited to someone's home. The safest and most welcome item to take is a bunch of flowers. As you will pick up pretty quickly if asked to a meal, Germans hold the fork in their left hand and the knife in their right.

Health
Currently, no immunisations are required for entry into Germany. Health care is privatised, all Germans belonging to a health insurance scheme. EC citizens are entitled to free medical treatment in Germany, on production of Form E111. Get hold of one in advance of your holiday, from post offices.
In addition you should take out travel insurance to cover expenses connected with illness – such as a special flight home or longer hotel stay – that are not covered by E111. And to be able to make a claim, remember to keep receipts of all medical treatment, prescriptions and other expenses to give your insurers

once home. The number for emergency/weekend doctors and dentists can be found in local telephone directories for German cities. If you want to ensure an English-speaking medico, contact the local consulate, which should hold details.

Doctors' consulting hours are usually 07.00–20.00hrs in hospital outpatients' departments; doctors' surgeries about 10.00–noon, 16.00–18.00hrs (times vary); closed Wed pm. (Hospital outpatients' provide an emergency service outside these hours, too.)

Dispensing chemists are open during normal shop hours; in larger towns they display a list of late night and Sunday opening pharmacies (see Pharmacies).

Hitch-hiking

Hitch-hiking is not illegal, except on the autobahns and their feeder roads, although it is not encouraged. Since German unification and the increase in crime, motorists have generally become more suspicious of picking people up. Every major city has a Mitfahrerzentrale, which are useful alternatives. Drivers inform this office when and where they are travelling and those wanting a lift – and willing to share the cost of petrol – pay a fee to the office to get the driver's name and telephone number. This is by far the cheapest way of travelling around the country by car, but again, not without hazards.

Lone travellers should always be aware of the inherent dangers of taking lifts with strangers. Some cities have women-only Frauenmitfahrerzentrale.

Insurance

Make sure you take out travel insurance. It should cover you for accident or illness in the areas of motoring and health, and also for the loss or theft of valuables while on holiday.

This insurance is best taken out at home before departure. Speak to your insurers, travel agent or motoring organisation, when planning your trip.

Laundry

Most towns of any size in former West Germany have a launderette –'Waschsalon' – with prices from DM5 for a wash (usually including soap). Camp sites have their own washing facilities.

Language

Like all widely spoken languages, German has various dialects. In the north you will hear *Plattdeutsch* (Low German), which covers a number of dialects descended from Old Saxon – one of the main early forms of German – and spoken roughly north of a line from Aachen in the west, through Köln and Kassel to Wittenburg and Frankfurt-an-der-Oder in the east. To the south of this line the dialects spoken are forms of *Hochdeutsch* (High German), descended from Old High German, the other ancestor of the modern language. However, there is a standard official German language, known as *Schriftdeutsch* (written German). This was the creation of Martin Luther, who evolved a compromise language from the current dialects for his translation of the Bible. When spoken, the standard language is inevitably affected by local dialect. This spoken version, called *Umgangssprache* (colloquial speech), is universally understood.

Pronunciation guide
Vowels
a (short) as in hut eg Hand (hand)
a (long) as in father eg sagen (say)
e (short) as in bet eg Wetter (weather)
e (long) as in day eg geben (give)
i as in fit eg bitte (please)
o (short) as in lost eg voll (full)
o (long) as in coach eg Mond (moon)
u as in boot eg gut (good)
ä (short) as in wet eg Äpfel (apples)
ä (long) as in wait eg spät (late)
ö as in fur eg schön (beautiful)
ü as in blue eg über (over)
ai as in spy eg the River Main
ei eg eins (one)
au as in how eg Maus (mouse)
ie as in tree eg Lied (song)
eu as in boy eg treu (true)
äu eg Fräulein (Miss)

Consonants

Most are pronounced as written. The following are exceptions.

ch is either a throaty sound as in Scottish loch eg Nacht (night), or an unvoiced sh sound eg nicht (not)
j is as y in yacht eg ja (yes)
r is rolled
s is as z in zip eg sein (his)
sch is as sh in shut eg scheinen (to seem)
sp/st are pronounced shp/sht eg sprechen (speak), Stadt (town)
v is as f in fit eg Vater (father)
w is as v in very eg Wand (wall)
z is as ts in bits eg Zeit (time)

Words and phrases
Days of the week
Sunday	Sonntag
Monday	Montag
Tuesday	Dienstag
Wednesday	Mittwoch
Thursday	Donnerstag
Friday	Freitag
Saturday	Samstag
	or Sonnabend

Months of the year
Januar	Juli
Februar	August
März	September
April	Oktober
Mai	November
Juni	Dezember

Basics
yes/no	ja/nein
please	bitte
thank you	danke (can also mean 'no thank you')
hello	Guten Tag; Grüss Gott (in the south)
goodbye	Auf Wiedersehen
Do you speak English?	Sprechen Sie Englisch?
I don't understand	Ich verstehe nicht
Help!	Zu Hilfe!

Questions
Where is/are	Wo ist/sind
the bank?	die Bank?
the station?	der Bahnhof?
the airport?	der Flughafen?
the bus-stop?	die Bushaltestelle?
the police station?	das Polizeirevier?

the nearest toilets?	die nächsten Toiletten?
right	rechts
left	links
straight ahead	geradeaus
How much is..	Wieviel kostet
the fare?	der Fahrpreis?
the entrance fee?	der Eintritt?
When...	Wann...
does the museum open?	wird das Museum geöffnet?
does the train leave?	fährt der Zug ab
at 10 o'clock	um zehn Uhr
at half past 10	um halb elf

Staying and eating
I'd like...	ich hätte gern
a single room	ein Einzelzimmer
a double room	ein Doppelzimmer
with bath	mit Bad
open	Geöffnet
closed	Geschlossen
Waiter!	Herr Ober!
May I see the menu, please?	Die Speisekarte bitte
breakfast	das Frühstück
lunch	das Mittagessen
dinner	das Abendessen
bread	das Brot
butter	die Butter
egg	das Ei
cheese	der Käse
vegetables	das Gemüse
fruit	das Obst
coffee	der Kaffee
tea	der Tee
beer	das Bier
wine	der Wein

Numbers
0	null	17	siebzehn
1	eins	18	achtzehn
2	zwei	19	neunzehn
3	drei	20	zwanzig
4	vier	21	einundzwanzig
5	fünf	30	dreissig
6	sechs	32	zweiunddreissig
7	sieben	40	vierzig
8	acht	50	fünfzig
9	neun	60	sechzig
10	zehn	70	siebzig
11	elf	80	achtzig
12	zwölf	90	neunzig
13	dreizehn	100	hundert
14	vierzehn	101	hunderteins
15	fünfzehn	500	fünfhundert
16	sechzehn	1,000	tausend

Lost property

All bus and railway stations have lost property offices; look for their numbers in the telephone directory or enquire at the station for the Fundbüro.

It is very important to read carefully the instructions for loss issued with your travellers' cheques. Make a separate note of the serial numbers of all cheques (or take photocopies) and of the telephone number to call in case of emergencies. Major issuing companies will have refund facilities available. Contact their nearest office or, failing that, the nearest bank.

Register loss of cheques to the police immediately, and if you are stranded without money, contact the local consulate.

Follow similar procedure for the loss or theft of Eurocheques and cheque cards. Lost passports should be reported to the police station at the earliest opportunity and again, contact your consulate if you need emergency travel papers.

Maps

Road atlases: The RV Auto At!as is an easy to handle spiral-bound atlas comprising detailed maps of West Germany (scale 1:200,000) plus additional coverage of the former East (scale 1:800,000) for route planning. It also includes an index to the West section and town plans for 40 major cities.

If you take the short ferry crossing the Automobile Association's 1:1,000,000 double-sided map of the whole of Germany could be useful as it extends to Channel ports from Dieppe.

Hallwag's 1:850,000 map of the unified Germany includes plans showing approach and through roads in all big cities and a 'distoguide' giving distances between major cities.

Hostelling: The Youth Hostels Map of Germany (Mairs) shows the location of hostels on the map plus a full list with addresses and phone numbers for the former West Germany (East Berlin only is covered in the East).

Walking: Special tourist maps of West Germany – 'Sonderkarte – showing footpaths and cycling routes in popular destinations are compiled by the German Topographic Society. A full list can be obtained from Stanford's, 12 Longacre, London WC2E 9LP (tel: 071 836 1321).

For the former East Germany, Kompas Wanderkart serve a similar purpose. They are to order only from Stanford's; allow five weeks for delivery.

Media

The German daily newspaper widely regarded as the most serious and influential is the *Frankfurter Allgemeine Zeitung*, to be compared with the *Times* of London and the *New York Times*. Each major city has more than one daily, most of them appearing in the mornings, added to which local magazines will give you a run-down on what's on where.

In Berlin, for instance, the two best magazines for this type of information are *tip* and *zitty*. The *Bild*, owned by the Springer group, is the mass circulation popular daily of the type which the Germans refer to as the 'Boulevard' press.

The Australian-born press baron Rupert Murdoch has a stake in *Super!* which he introduced to East Berlin soon after the Wall fell, while the late Robert Maxwell invested heavily in *Berliner Zeitung*, also aimed at capturing readers in the east.

Most television sets can get CNN, Super or Sky, besides the wide variety of German channels. The two popular nationwide TV broadcasting stations are ARD and ZDF. Visitors to Berlin can still listen to the BBC World Service on FM, under an agreement dating back to when the three Western allies – Britain, France and the US – still had control over West Berlin.

Money matters

In July 1990 the German Mark – Deutschemark, or DM – became the official currency of the united Germany. 1 DM equals 100 Pfennig (pf). Coins are: 1, 2, 5, 10 and 50 Pfennig; 1, 2, 5 and 10

Deutschemarks. Notes come in denominations of 10, 20, 50, 100, 200, 500 and 1,000 DM.

There are money exchanges – Wechselstuben – at airports, border crossings and major rail stations, that generally stay open 06.00–22.00hrs daily. Branches of the Deutsches Verkehrs-Kredit Bank, situated in railway stations, usually also stay open until 18.00hrs.

Otherwise, normal banking hours are Monday to Friday, 08.30 or 09.00 to 12.30 or 13.00hrs, then 14.30–16.00hrs (17.30hrs on Thursdays). Banks are closed on Saturday and Sunday.

You can also change money at post offices, which are open Monday to Saturday, 08.00–18.00. (Saturdays until midday). This applies to larger branches in main towns only.

Travellers' cheques can be cashed in banks, currency exchanges and post offices; but used directly in only smarter shops in main cities. Eurocheques, backed by the appropriate card, can be cashed in banks and exchanges and also used in some shops and restaurants, but always take the precaution of checking first, because, unlike most of Europe and the States, credit cards are not widely used in Germany. It's always worth taking one, but never depend on being able to use it.

National holidays
1 Jan: New Year's Day
6 Jan: Epiphany (only in Baden-Württemberg and Bavaria)
Good Friday
Easter Sunday/Easter Monday
1 May: Labour Day
Ascension Day (in May, changes annually)
Whit Sunday and Whit Monday
18 June: Corpus Christi (honoured only in certain areas)
15 August: Maria Himmelfahrt (Assumption of the Blessed Virgin Mary, only in Bavaria and Saarland)
3 October: Day of German Unity
1 November: All Saints' Day (honoured only in certain areas)
Day of Prayer and Repentance (in November, changes annually)
25/26 December: Christmas

Opening hours
Shop opening hours are normally 09.00–18.30hrs, Monday to Friday, though some remain open until 20.30hrs on Thursday. (In addition, some close at midday for a couple of hours.) On Saturday, they shut up shop at 14.00hrs, except for the first Saturday of each month, when they're allowed to stay open until 16.00hrs. Only flower shops and bakers can open on Sundays (between 11.00 and 15.00hrs). Railways stations come to the rescue: shops in their vicinity are usually open late and at weekends. Time your arrival carefully at restaurants off the beaten track; they often serve meals only between 13.00 and 14.00hrs, then again from 17.00–20.00hrs.

Business people are usually at their desks no later than 09.00hrs and Government offices close punctually at 16.00, or 14.00hrs on Fridays. For doctors' hours, see above under **Health.**

Evening entertainments – theatre, concerts, and so on – usually start at 20.00hrs, normally lasting two hours.

Organised tours
Deutsches Touring runs a variety of coach tours, such as the Romantic Road trip from Würzburg (at the top of the road) to Füssen (where it ends), or vice versa. A variety of packages lasting from two to seven days is on offer; details from the company at Am Romerhof 17, 6000-Frankfurt am Main 90.

See the German countryside afloat, on a river trip. The Köln–Düsseldorfer (KD) Line offers trips on the Rhine, Mosel and Elbe. Trips range from five hours to five days and concessions for children and senior citizens are a regular feature. KD Lines is at Frankenwerf 15, 5000-Köln 1 (tel: 0221 208 80). Their UK representative is KD German Rhine Line, 28 South Street, Epsom, Surrey KT18 7PF (tel: 0372 742033).

Weisse Flotte boat company makes tourist trips on the Havel, Elbe, Oder and Saale rivers, and the Baltic Sea. Contact them at Terrassenufer 1–2, O–8010 Dresden.

Hiking is very popular and the

Jugendherbergswerk (German Youth Hostel Federation) publishes a list of guided walks, from two-day trips to cross-country treks. Contact them at Hauptverband, Bismarckstrasse 8, D–4930 Detmold.

In addition, local tourist offices will be happy to suggest local tour opportunities.

Pharmacies

German chemists or their assistants are usually able to speak some English. If you are taking a course of drugs and need to have a prescription filled while staying in Germany, get your doctor at home to write out a prescription using the generic rather than brand name. It's a good idea to have a letter from him or her to the effect that you need the drug for health purposes. Check before leaving home that what you are taking with you is not illegal in Germany.

In larger towns, pharmacies – Apotheken – display late-night or 24 hour rota lists. Alternatively, ask at your hotel reception or local police station where to find one open. Apotheken trade in pharmaceuticals only – make-up, hair bands and toothbrushes must be purchased at a Drogerie.

Police

German police – Polizei – are well-mannered and expect members of the public to be equally correct. When speaking to a police officer, for instance, you would be expected to use the formal 'Sie' for you, rather than 'Du'.

Post offices

The main post office – Hauptpostamt – in any large town is usually located near the railway station. Mail posted in the former West Germany reaches the UK within a few days; from the former East, it may take a little longer. Stamps for letters to EC countries cost from 70pf to DM1, post cards around 60pf.

To send a letter Poste Restante mark it Postlagernde Briefe/Sendungen and Bitte Halten. As it will be filed alphabetically, according to surname, write that first on the address. Mail is kept, free of charge, for two weeks. When collecting it, take along some ID.

Telegrams can be sent from post offices, or by telephone (see **Telephones**).

Public transport

Domestic air services between cities are frequent, fast but an expensive way to travel. Within Germany, check with Lufthansa at Frankfurt airport (tel: 069 690 71222) for best ticket options. The other German airline, LTU, also offers intercity services, as does British Airways.

The Air Travel Advisory Bureau, 41–45 Goswell Road, London EC5 7DN (tel: 071 636 5000) can advise on agents who specialise in discount flights.

If you arrive at one airport and want to transfer to another, check the Lufthansa Airport Express Trains, linking Düsseldorf, Köln, Bonn and Frankfurt.

German trains come in a variety of types, but all on time. The Deutsches Bundesbahn (DB) of the former West and the Deutsches Reichsbahn (DR) of the East are not yet fully integrated and trains tend to be slower – but cheaper – on the latter.

S-bahn trains are commuter-types; the D and E trains are somewhat faster; FD trains really pick up speed, while the new InterRegio or IR trains, which link sizable towns, are fast and comfortable. Intercity trains are superquick as are their border-crossing counterparts the Eurocity or EC trains. InterCity Express or ICE trains linking Munich and Hamburg don't quite break the sound barrier but go very fast indeed.

German Rail passes cover unlimited travel for 5, 10 or 15 days countrywide.

If you are under 26 you are eligible for an InterRail Pass from British Rail. This gives one month's unlimited travel in up to 24 countries, including Germany. (It also entitles you to pay half fare on tickets in this country and for some cross-channel ferries.) Ring 071 834 2345 for further details or enquire at a main railway station or British Rail International accreditied travel agents.

There are numerous passes and permutations on offer for every age group of travellers, from pre-teens to over-60s. Contact your GNTO to obtain details of deals; in the UK enquire at German Rail Sales, c/o DER Travel Service, 18 Conduit Street, London W1 (tel: 071 499 0577) or German Railways (tel: 071 233 6588).

Coaches link rural areas which railways cannot reach. Many are owned by the DB and are timed and routed to complement the train service.

Buses German towns operate their own local buses and one ticket will often be transferable between these and other forms of city transport, such as the S-bahn, the Strassenbahn (trams) and the U-bahn (underground).

On entering the bus, train or tram, passengers insert their tickets into a machine which validates them for that trip. Inspectors make frequent rounds to check that tickets are valid – and they are tough on fare dodgers.

Taxis can be hailed in the street or hired from ranks at railway stations, hotels and so on. They carry an illuminated roof sign. Fares are made up of a basic charge plus payment per kilometre travelled. This varies from place to place, as do surcharges for luggage, though this is usually in the region of 50pf per item.

Senior citizens

Certain discounts on public transport systems for senior citizens are available, but since these benefits are regularly updated, it's best to get the latest information from the Deutsches Zentrum für Altersfragen, M. von Richthofenstr 1, 1000 Berlin 42.

KD Lines offer half price boat fares one day a week; check with the company (address under **Organised tours**). German railways – DB – sell Senior Pass cards which allow for half-price travel for part or whole of the week (ask your GNTO for details).

Student and youth travel

There are over 600 youth hostels in Germany which accept members of all associations affiliated with the International Youth Hostel Federation, based at 9 Guessens Road, Welwyn Garden City Herts, AL8 6QW (tel: 0707 332487), Residents of the UK can obtain membership of the Youth Hostel Association from their office at 14 Southampton Street, London WC2 (tel: 071 836 1036).

Deutsches Jugendherbergswerk Hauptverband (the German youth hostel association) publishes a complete list of hostels; it is on sale (DM6.50) at tourist offices and hostels themselves. It's wise, particularly in the high season, to pre-book accommodation in hostels; officially, there's a three-day limit to your stay, though if the hostel is not full you may be able to remain longer. It is worth noting that in Bavaria priority is given to under-27s. The DJH is at Bismarckstrasse 8, Post-fach 1455, D–4930 Detmold, Germany (tel: 5231 740139 151).

You can book hostels in the former East Germany via Jugendtourist GmbH, Alexanderplatz 5, 1026–Berlin and Jugendherbergsverband Postfach 105, 1080-Berlin. If you are under 23, or a student under 27, enquire about the Tramper Monats Ticket, entitling holders to one month's unlimited travel on the DB system (except the ICE) and DB buses. Prices start around DM290 (300 + ICE). Ask at railway stations for details (taking along some ID to prove your age).

Telephones

Making a telephone call in Germany is fraught with pitfalls for the tourist unaccustomed to the idiosyncrasies of the system. Much of the trouble stems from having two systems, in fact, as eastern and western networks have not yet been fully integrated.

Public call boxes in the former West take 10pf, DM1 and DM10 coins. About half take phone cards – Kartentelefone – which you buy at the post or tourist office, price DM12 or DM50. Local calls cost 30pf for five minutes. You can make international calls except from booths marked 'National', and to call the former East Germany you must use the international code, which is 0037 (then delete the initial 0 from the city code).

In the former East, look out for the bright yellow phone booths; these allow you to dial direct to West Germany. However, this is not entirely straightforward, as the code number of the place you are trying to reach varies depending on where you are calling from!

Another point of difference is that reverse charge calls are possible in the East but not in the West. Alternatively, go to a post office, where the connection is made for you and you pay after the call. Directory enquiries is on 1188 or, for Europe, 0118. The operator is on 010 (for Germany) and 0010 (for abroad). Call rates are lower after 20.00hrs and at weekends. To dial Britain the code is 0044; Eire, 00353; USA and Canada, 001; Australia 0061; New Zealand 0064.

Time

German time is one hour ahead of Greenwich Mean Time (two hours in the summer). It is six hours ahead of Toronto and New York time, nine hours behind Eastern Australian time and 11 hours behind New Zealand.

Tourist offices

Staff are normally very helpful and will provide, often free, maps and literature on attractions in the area, plus a list of local hotels. Sometimes they may be willing to book you a room for a small fee.

The head office of the German National Tourist organisation, the Deutsche Zentrale für Tourismus, is Beethovenstrasse 69, D–6000-Frankfurt am Main (tel: 069 75 72 0). In the UK the GNTO is at 65 Curzon Street, London W1Y 7PE (tel: 071 495 3990). In the USA the GNTO is at 747 Third Avenue, 33rd Floor, New York, NY 10017 (tel: 212 308 330). Canada has the Office National Allemand du Tourisme, at 175 Bloor Street, East, North Tower, 6th Floor, Toronto, Ontario. M4W 3R8 (tel: 416 968 986). In Australia, the GNTO is at

Lufthansa House, 12th Floor, 143 Macquerie Street, Sydney, 2000 (tel: 02 3 67 38 90/02.2 21 10 08). In Eire the GNTO has no office; enquiries are dealt with by the London office. For New Zealand, the nearest office is in Australia.

Tourist offices in major German cities include: Deutscher Fremdenverkehrsverband, Niebuhrstrasse 16b, 5300 Bonn 1 (tel: 0228 21 40 71 72); Martin-Lutherstrasse105 W–1000 Berlin 62 (tel: 030 21234) and Informationzentrum, Am Fernsehturm, 1020 Berlin (tel: 030 212 4675); Dr Rudolf-Friedsrichs-Ufer 2, 8060 Dresden; for Baden-Württemberg area the address is Esslingerstrasse 8, W–7000 Stuttgart 10 (tel. 0711 247364); for Bavaria, it is Postfach 221352, W–8000 München 22, (tel: 089 212397-0); and for Hamburg, the office is at Burchardstrasse 14, W–2000 Hamburg 1 (tel: 040 300510).

Walking and hiking

There are more than 132,000km of walks in Germany. Detailed information can be obtained from the Verband Deutscher Gebirgs- und Wanderverein, Reichsstrasse 4, D–6600 Saarbrücken 3. The Deutsches Alpenverein, Praterinsel 5, D–8000 Munich 2, can advise on hiking in the Alps and runs mountaineering courses: contact the Verband Deutscher Ski-und Bergführer, Lindenstr. 16, D–8980 Oberstdorf, which also runs courses.

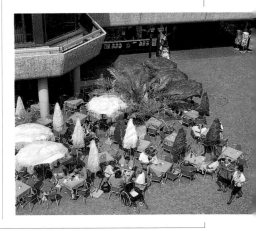

DIRECTORY

Accommodation

The following recommended hotels have been divided into three price categories:

budget: you are likely to find a double bedroom for between DM80 and DM225, including breakfast for two.

moderate: you are likely to find a double bedroom for between DM225 and DM375, inclusing breakfast for two.

expensive: you are likely to pay over DM375 for a double room, including breakfast for two.

BERLIN

Expensive

Bristol Kempinski
Kurfürstendamm 27, D-1000 Berlin 15 (tel: 88 43 40). Regards itself as the only place of its class in West Berlin. Highly traditional, rather staid furnishings. Restaurants with elaborate and ambitious and, of course, very expensive menu.

Hotel Schweizerhog
Budapesterstrasse 21-31, 1000 Berlin 30 (tel: 269 60). Hard to fault. Pleasant staff; comfortable and relaxing public areas, and sensible planned bedrooms. Part of the Inter-Continental group; its sister hotel is just over the road. Pleasant glimpses of Tiergarten foliage from many of the bedrooms. Informal bistro and more formal restaurant serving good food with Swiss specialities.

Hotel Seehof Berlin
Lietzensee Ufer 11, 1000 Berlin 19 (Charlottenburg; tel: 3 20 02 0). The main attraction of this hotel is its location, overlooking one of Berlin's many glacial lakes, the Lietzensee. Some way out of the centre, in a quiet residential side-street just off Kantstrasse, and about 10 or 15 minutes' lakeside walk from the Charlottenburg palace and its associated museums. No immediately convenient U-Bahn, but there is a bus stop less than half a minute from the main entrance. Ask for lake view – though roadside rooms are not noisy. Heated indoor pool. Large airy restaurant (Au Lac) with worthwhile menu.

Moderate

Alsterhof Ringhotel
Augsburgerstrasse 5, D-1000 Berlin 30 (tel: 2 19 96 0). Set behind Berlin's big department store, KaDeWe. Considerable style inside, despite ugly exterior. Well-equipped and practical bedrooms, useful location. Stylish restaurant, festooned with agreeable modern prints and flower paintings. Conservatory annexe.

Hecker's Hotel
Grolmanstrasse 35, 1000 Berlin 12 (tel: 88 90 0). Just off Ku'damm in a quiet side-street close to Uhlandstrasse U-Bahn: very convenient for exploring Berlin. Friendly, rustic restaurant in style of Westphalian inn. Bright, spacious bedrooms, good range of facilities, giving good value for such a central location.

Hotel Am Zoo
Kurfürstendamm 25, 1000 Berlin 15 (tel: 884 37 0). Excellent central location, just opposite Meinekestrasse. Modern, streamlined – no superfluous frills. Surprisingly peaceful; most rooms face a well-kept inner courtyard garden. Breakfast is 'obligatory'.

Hotel Residenz Berlin
Meinekestrasse 9, 1000 Berlin 15 (tel: 88 28 91). Elegant building of considerable architectural interest, with captivating Jugendstil decoration. Ancient and rather terrifying lift travels up to bedrooms on the upper floors. High-ceilinged rooms give a sense of Berlin's pre-war beauty. Facilities include multi-channel TV, minibar. Thoroughly interesting and individual. French cuisine in restaurant (Grand Cru).

Budget

Hotel Meineke
Meinekestrasse 10, 1000 Berlin 15 (tel: 88 28 11). Distinguished building, encrusted with balconies, escutcheons and fancy gables. Entrance hall has barrel-vaulted ceiling and tapestries of hunting scenes on the walls. Light, clean breakfast room. Large, plain bedrooms. Good value. Limited parking space; public garage across the road.

Hotel-Pension Dittberner
Wielandstrasse 26, 1000 Berlin 15 (tel: 881 64 85). Charming and idiosyncratic. Frau Lange's *pension* is something of a cult among worldly bargain-hunting travellers. Classy art gallery on the ground floor. The rooms may not be faultless, the facilities may be rudimentary, but for these prices there is nowhere better in Berlin. A recent facelift has added to the general spotlessness.

Hotel-Pension Jewel
Meinekestrasse 26, 1000 Berlin 15 (tel: 8 82 71 41). Those prepared to brave an entryphone system and a 'traditional' lift will find young, friendly staff and clean (if rather dark and cramped) rooms. Popular with younger travellers.

Hotel-Pension Modena
Wielandstrasse 26, 1000 Berlin 15 (tel: 8 81 52 94). Directly below the Dittberner, on the second floor, and, in its way, just as recommendable for its good housekeeping. Pleasant and welcoming owners. Clean rooms.

Hotel West-Pension
Kurfürstendamm 48–9, 1000 Berlin 15 (tel: 881 80 57 58). Right on the Ku'damm; front rooms could be noisy.

NORTHWEST GERMANY

Expensive

Atlantic Hotel An der Alster 72, 2000 Hamburg (tel: 040 2880). Elegant and famous turn-of-century hotel near lake. Swimming pool.

Inter-Continental Friedrichswall 11, 3000 Hannover (tel: 0511 36770). Well-located in the centre of town, modern.

Vier Jahreszeiten Neuer Jungfernstieg 9, 4000 Hamburg (tel: 040 34940). Ultra-luxury and well-run hotel located by the Binnenalster. Excellent Service.

Moderate

Benen-Diken-Hof Süderstrasse, 2280 Sylt Ost (tel: 04651 31035). In the Ultra-pretty village of Keitum, this attractive bed and breakfast is part of the Romantik group. Swimming pool.

Bergström Hotel Bei der Lüner Mühle, 2120 Lüneburg (tel: 04131 3080). Comfortable, well situated at the water's edge in the Wasserviertel.

Europäischer Hof Kirchenallee 45, 4000 Hamburg (tel: 040 248248). Modern, elegant, near station. Swimming pool.

Fürstenhof Celle Hannoverschestrasse 55, 3100 Celle (tel: 05141 2010). Elegant former palace in centre, with good service. Swimming pool.

Welfenhof 3300 Braunschweig, (tel: 0531 48170). Part of the well-run Swiss-owned Mövenpick chain; very central. Swimming pool.

Parkhotel Steimkerberg Unter den Eichen 55, 3180 Wolfsburg (tel: 05361 5050). Quiet, surrounded by a delightful park. Well furnished bedrooms.

Rungholt Kurhausstrasse 35, 2285 Kampen (tel: 04651 4480). Located in one of the most idyllic spots on the island of Sylt, with uninterrupted views of the dunes.

Stadt Hamburg Strandstr 2, 2280 Westerland (tel: 04651 8580). On the island of Sylt. Tastefully furnished, antique-Biedermeier-style furniture.

Budget

Friesenhof Hauptstr 16, 2283 Wenningstedt (tel: 04651 41031). Former Friesen guest house turned into a modest modern hotel, located on the island of Sylt.

Kaiserhof Kronsforder Allee 11-13, 2400 Lübeck (tel: 0451 791011). Bed and breakfast hotel in tastefully renovated town houses, town's oldest hotel. Swimming pool.

Waldersee Walderseestr 39, 3000 Hannover – List (tel: 0511 698063). North-east of centre, in List, opposite park. Bed and breakfast hotel. Swimming pool.

Am Wasserturm Blasberg 13, 2390 Flensburg (tel: 0461 36071). Quiet, at edge of Volkspark. Simple and tasteful in style. Swimming pool.

RHINELAND

Expensive

Breidenbacher Hof Heinrich-Heine-Alle 36, 4000 Düsseldorf (tel: 0211 13030). Luxury, with a bar where all the 'in' people meet.

Bristol Prinz-Albertstrasse 1, 5300 Bonn (tel: 0228 2 6980). Luxury hotel, located near station. Swimming pool.

Escelsior Hotel Ernst Trankgasse 1–5, 5000 Köln (tel: 0221 2701). Famous personalities usually stay here, good reputation for excellent service and comfort. Very expensive.

Hotel im Wasserturm Kaygasse 2, 5000 Köln (tel: 0221 20080). Declared a city memorial, in a former watertower. Spacious and comfortable, renovated at the end of 1989. Roof terrace with views.

DIRECTORY

Moderate

Diehls Hotel Am Pfafendorfer Tor 10, 5400 Koblenz (tel: 0261 72010). A pleasant hotel on the banks of the Rhine, by the Ehrenbreitstein citadel. Swimming pool.

Esplanade Fürstenplatz 17, 4000 Düsseldorf (tel: 0211 375010). Modern, comfortable bedrooms with cable TV. English-style restaurant.

Favorite Parkhotel Karl Weiserstr 1, 6500 Mainz (tel: 06131 82091). Set in an attractive location, surrounded by trees at the edge of the city's Stadtpark. Comfortable, well-kept and clean.

Hanseat Belsenstrasse 6, 4000 Düsseldorf, 11 Oberkassel (tel: 0211 575069). Smart bed and breakfast town house hotel over the Rhine from the centre; rooms are simple and tasteful.

Savoy Oststr 128, 4000 Düsseldorf (tel: 0211 360336). Subdued and elegant, known for its excellent restaurant. Swimming pool.

Uebachs Leopoldstrasse 3–5, 4000 Düsseldorf (tel: 0211 360566). Understated atmosphere, quiet, top quality.

Budget

Brenner Rizzastr 20–22, 5400 Koblenz (tel: 0261 32060). Small central bed and breakfast hotel with friendly and efficient service. Garden.

Haus Eggert Zur Haskenau 81, 4400 Münster (tel: 0251 32083). A former country farmhouse near Münster – Handorf. Now part of the Ring Hotel group.

Eurener Hof Eurener Strasse 171, 5500 Trier – Euren (tel: 0651 88077). Rustic-style décor; rooms are well furnished. Swimming pool.

Petrisberg Sickingenstrasse 11–13, 5500 Trier (tel: 0651 41181). Modern bed and breakfast hotel in wonderful position on vine-clad hill above town (20 minute walk).

Schlosshotel Kommende

Ramersdorf Oberkasselerstrasse 10, Romersdorf, 5300 Bonn 3 (tel: 0228 440734). Elegant small hotel in grounds of castle. Italian restaurant.

Schloss Wilkinghege Steinfurterstrasse 374, 4400 Münster (tel: 0251 2130). 16th-century building in quiet rural situation, with atmospheric restaurant.

CENTRAL GERMANY

Expensive

Arabella Grand Hotel Konrad-Adenauerstrasse 7, 6000 Frankfurt/Main (tel: 069 29810). Very modern, luxury hotel. Swimming pool.

Frankfurt Intercontinental Hahnstrasse 9, 6000 Frankfurt/Main (tel: 069 26050). First class international hotel near river. Swimming pool.

Nassauer Hof Kaiser Friedrichplatz 3, 6200 Wiesbaden (tel: 0611 1330). Opposite the Kurhaus, theatre and casino lies this ultra-elegant luxury hotel. Ample facilities, including swimming pool.

Hessischer Hof Friedrich Ebert Anlage 40, 6000 Frankfurt/Main (tel: 069 75400). Elegant town house, furnished with antiques, to the west of the centre.

Moderate,

Aukamm Hotel Aukamm–Allee 31, 6200 Wiesbaden (tel: 0611 1729777). Quiet, near the Kurhaus, comfortable and cosy.

Schwarzer Bock Kranplatz 12, 6200 Wiesbaden (tel: 0611 1550). Traditional old hotel (dating from 18th century) with high standards of service.

Swimming pool.

Zum Löwen Markstrasse 30, 3408 Duderstadt (tel: 05527 3072). Built in the 16th century and thoroughly renovated in 1988 with all modern facilities. Good cooking.

Budget

Domus Erzbergerstrasse 1–5, 3500 Kassel (tel: 0561 72960). Elegant and charming, in Jugendstil.

Hardtwald Hotel Philosophenweg 31, 6380 Bad Homburg (tel: 06172 121310). Modern, in a quiet area. Attractive terrace.

Parkhotel Ropeter Kasseler Landstr 45, 3400 Göttingen (tel: 0551 9020). Extremely quiet, despite its proximity to the autobahn and main roads that lead to the city. Swimming pool.

Schlosshotel Wilhelmsthal at the Schloss Wilmhelmsthal, 3527 Calden (tel: 05674 848). Rococo castle with fine terrace, 14km from Kassel.

Westend Westendstrasse 15, 6000 Frankfurt/Main (tel: 069 746702). Old-fashioned bed and breakfast in residential area, with atmosphere, a private house. Garden.

EASTERN GERMANY

Expensive

Bellevue Köpckestr 15, 0–8010 Dresden (tel: 003751 56620). Expensive by Western standards, with good service and plenty of facilities, including swimming pool.

Merkur Gerbestrasse, 0–7010 Leipzig (tel: 0037 417990). Very large; modern.

Moderate

Leipzig Astoria, Am Hauptbahnhof 2, 0–7010 Leipzig (tel: 0037 41 72220). Large; by the station.

Chemnitz Chemnitzer Hof, Theaterplatz 4, 0–9010 Chemnitz (tel: 0037 716840). Large and renovated; special rooms for non-smokers.

Weimar Elephant, Am Markt 19, 0–5300 Weimar (tel: 0037621 2173).

Established in the 17th century, one of Germany's most famous hotels, with a guest list to prove it. Large bedrooms; high prices.

Erfurter Hof Am Bahnhofsplatz 1, 0–5000 Erfurt (tel: 003761 51151). New station; despite its delapidated appearance, the interior is modern and fairly comfortable.

Dorint Hotel Kreuzeck Am Kreuzeck, 3380 Goslar (tel: 05325 741). Located in one of the most attractive and well known spots in the Upper Harz – at the spa of Hahnenblee, 15km from Goslar. Swimming pool.

Dresdner Hof An der Frauenkirche 5, 0–8010 Dresden (tel: 003751 48410). Central. One of Dresden's well-known and over-priced hotels built when the Communists were still in power. Swimming pool.

Hahnenkleer Hof Parkstr 24a, 3380 Goslar, (tel: 05325 2011/12). Modern, in the spa of Hahnonblcc, with beer garden and swimming pool.

Newa Prager Strasse, 0–8012 Dresden (tel: 0037 51 4967112). Large hotel near station.

Budget

Halle Stadt Halle, Ernst-Thälmann Platz 17, 0–4002 Halle (tel: 0037 46 38041). Simple and modern.

Zum Löwen Rudolf Breitscheidstr, 0–7010 Leipzig (tel: 0037 41 72 2220). Simple, modern, near centre.

THE SOUTHWEST

Expensive

Brenner's Park-Hotel Schillerstr 6, 7570 Baden–Baden (tel: 07221 90000). One of the most luxurious hotels in the country (host to Queen Victoria among others). Plenty of facilities, including swimming pool.

Der Europäische Hof Hotel Europa, Friedrich Ebert Anlage 1, 6900 Heidelberg (tel: 06221 5150). Traditional, family owned, quiet inner courtyard, good cuisine at the 'Kurfürstenstube'.

Hirschgasse Hirschgasse 3, 6900 Heidelberg (tel: 06221 4032160). A historic inn dating from 1472, with beautifully and individually decorated bedrooms. Excellent restaurant.

Am Schlossgarten Schillerstrasse 23, 7000 Stuttgart (tel: 0711 20260). A luxury hotel with good location, facing the Palace gardens.

Steigenberger Badischer Hof Lange Strasse 47, 7570 Baden–Baden (tel: 07221 22827). Comfortable well furnished rooms. Swimming pools and elegant restaurant.

Steigenberger Hotel Graf Zeppelin Arnulf Klett Platz 7, 7000 Stuttgart (tel: 0711 299881). Luxury hotel, opposite the station, but relatively quiet. Swimming pool.

Moderate

Alt Heidelberg Rohrbacherstr 29, 6900 Heidelberg (tel: 06221 9150). Near the old town, with excellent restaurant.

Bayerischer Hof Am Bodensee, 8990 Lindau (tel: 08382 5055). On the island, near the port. Swimming pool.

Hohenlohe Weilertor 14, Schwäbisch Hall (tel: 0791 75870). Most of the rooms have large balconies. The hotel is neatly tucked away behind trees and lies directly on a small lake. Swimming pool.

Krone Uhlandstr 1, 7400 Tübingen, (tel: 07071 35011). Solid hotel with formal or rustic-style bedrooms.

Maritim Parkhotel Friedrichsplatz 2, 6800 Mannheim (tel: 0621 45071). *Jugendstil*, elegant, with

formal atmosphere and good service. Swimming pool.

Öschberghof Golfplatz 1, 7710 Donaueschingen (tel: 0771 840). On an 18-hole golf course, used more by companies arranging seminars than ordinary tourists. Swimming pool.

Romantik Hotel Der Kleine Prinz Lichtentaler Strasse 36, 7570 Baden–Baden (tel: 07221 3464). Small, elegant and stylish hotel in a pedestrian zone.

Steigenberger Inselhotel Auf der Insel 1, 7750 Konstanz (tel: 07531 25011). Formerly a monastery, now turned into a luxury lakeside hotel.

Zum Ritter St Georg Haupstr 178, 6900 Heidelberg (tel: 06221 24272). Renaissance exterior dating back to 1592, one of the comfortable Romantik group hotels.

Zum Roten Bären Oberlinden 12, 7800 Freiburg (tel: 0761 36913). One of the country's famous old inns. The cellar dates back to 1120, thoroughly modernised. Good cooking.

Budget

Bad Hotel Otto Neidhart Allee 5, 7264 Teinach–Zavelstein (tel: 07053 290). A former royal residence turned into a luxury hotel, with a corridor linking the hotel directly to the spa facilities including swimming pool.

Hohenried Zeppelinstr 5, 7290 Freudenstadt (tel: 07441 2414/16). Most rooms have private balconies, in peaceful hotel just outside this large Black Forest resort. Swimming pool.

Das Pelikan Türlensteg 9, Schwäbisch Gmünd (tel: 07171 3590). In the middle of the old town this is an old building which has recently been renovated.

Am Schelztor Schelztorstrasse 5, 7300 Esslingen (tel: 0711 351 2441). Comfortable, central – opened in 1986.

Schloss Döttingen Hubertusstr 2, 7176 Braunsbach (tel: 07906

DIRECTORY

1010). 16km from Schwäbisch Hall. Former hunting lodge turned into a simple but comfortable hotel. Swimming pool.

Schwarzwaldhotel Birkenhof Wildbaderstr 95, 7290 Freudenstadt (tel: 07441 4074). Newly decorated; two restaurants; swimming pool and a squash court for fitness fanatics.

Schwarzwaldhof Hohenriderstrasse 74, 7290 Freudenstadt (tel: 07441 7421). Rustic hotel in a peaceful setting near a 9-hole golf course. Swimming pool.

Victoria Eisenbahnstr 54, 7800 Freiburg (tel: 0761 33211). Small and friendly hotel, with a restaurant that serves a range of vegetarian dishes.

Weber Hotel Frankenthalerstr 85, 6800 Mannheim – 31-Sandhofen (tel: 0621 77010). Styled like an old farmhouse, but with all possible modern comforts on offer.

NORTHERN BAVARIA

Moderate
Aschaffenburger Hof Frohsinnstrasse 11, 8750 Aschaffenburg (tel: 06021 21441). Centrally located, quiet, with good range of modern facilities.

Central Kulmbacherstr 4, 8670 Hof (tel: 09281 815233). Modern, rustic style interior; frequently used for conferences and meetings.

Bären Hofbronnengasse 9, 8803 Rothenburg-ob-der-Tauber (tel: 09861 6031). Quietly situated, recently well refurbished. Good cooking.

Walfisch Am Pleidenturm 5, 8700 Würzburg (tel: 0931 50055). A family run inn with views and good home-cooking.

Steigenberger Hotel Am Kurwald 2, 8399 Bad Griesbach (tel: 08532 1001). A large and spacious spa hotel with all the appropriate facilities. Swimming pool.

Budget
Bavaria Feldkirchenerstrasse 67, 8070 Ingolstadt (tel: 0841 305417). Tasteful though small hotel, offering good value for money. Swimming pool.

Bayerischer Hof Bahnhofstr 14, 8580 Bayreuth (tel: 0921 88588). Modernised hotel near station, with fine swimming pool and a restaurant terrace.

Bischofshof am Dom Krautesmarkt 3, 8400 Regensburg (tel: 0941 59086). Old inn with beer garden and offering very good food.

Deutsches Haus Weinmarkt 3, 8804 Dinkelsbühl (tel: 09851 2346). Quaint, old-fashioned timbered house, with antique furnishings. Good restaurant.

Weinhaus Steichele Knorrstrasse 2, 8500 Nürnberg (tel: 0911 204378). Central, old fashioned family-run wine tavern, with good cooking.

Wilder Mann Am Rathausplatz, 8390 Passau (tel: 0851 35071). Fine old mansion with renowned restaurant.

Zirbelstube Friedrich-Overbeckstrasse 1, 8500 Nürnberg–Worzeldorf (tel: 0911 88155). Small and pretty, in canal setting to the south of town. Highly regarded restaurant-with-rooms.

MUNICH AND THE ALPS

Expensive
Vier Jahreszeiten Maximilianstrasse 17, 8000 München (tel: 089 230390). Luxury hotel with all the expected facilities, including a rooftop swimming pool and highly rated restaurants.

Bayerischer Hof Promenadeplatz 2–6, 8000 München (tel: 089 21200). Plenty of facilities, including a variety of restaurants and swimming pool. Elegant Palais Montgelas annexe.

Moderate
Splendid Maximilianstrasse 54, 8000 München (tel: 089 296606). Centrally situated bed and breakfast hotel, with elegant, traditional décor.

Staudacherhof Höllentalstr 48, 8100 Garmisch Partenkirchen (tel: 08821 55155). Large chalet bed and breakfast hotel, with excellent views. Swimming pools.

Budget
Alpenhotel Kronprinz Am Brandholz, 8240 Berchtesgaden (tel: 08652 61061). Spacious bedrooms and elegantly furnished dining areas.

An der Oper Falkenturmstrasse 10, 8000 München (tel: 089 2900270). Simple, good value bed and breakfast hotel near the Opera.

Biederstein Keferstrasse 18, 8000 München (tel: 089 395072). Simple modern bed and breakfast, in a residential area near Schwabing.

Englischer Garten Liebergesellstrasse 8, 8000 München (tel: 089 392034). At the edge of the Englischer Garten, in Schwabing, a simple bed and breakfast guesthouse in converted water mill.

Garmisch Hof Bahnhofstrasse 53. 8100 Garmisch Partenkirchen (tel: 08821 51091). Stylish chalet in centre, with fine garden and views.

Geiger Alpenkette, Stanggass, 8240 Berchtesgaden (tel: 08652 5055). Ideal setting, some distance away from the resort centre. Swimming pools

Gasthof Zur Rose Dedlerstrasse 9, 8103 Oberammergau (tel: 08 822 4706). Traditional little inn, simple and friendly, with good food.

Turmwirt Ettalerstrasse 2, 8103 Oberammergau (tel: 08822 3091). Popular old hotel which hosts jolly folk evenings.

Index

INDEX